Radical Sovereignty

Radical Sovereignty

DEBATING RACE, NATION, AND EMPIRE
IN INTERWAR LATIN AMERICA

Tony Wood

UNIVERSITY OF CALIFORNIA PRESS

University of California Press
Oakland, California

Library of Congress Control Number: 2025948068

ISBN 978-0-520-39124-6 (cloth : alk. paper)
ISBN 978-0-520-39126-0 (pbk. : alk. paper)
ISBN 978-0-520-39127-7 (ebook)

Manufactured in the United States of America

GPSR Authorized Representative: Easy Access System Europe,
Mustamäe tee 50, 10621 Tallinn, Estonia, gpsr.requests@easproject.com

34   33   32   31   30   29   28   27   26   25
10   9   8   7   6   5   4   3   2   1

CONTENTS

FIGURES

ABBREVIATIONS

ABB	African Blood Brotherhood
ANERC	Asociación de Nuevos Emigrados Revolucionarios Cubanos (Association of New Revolutionary Cuban Emigres)
APRA	Alianza Popular Revolucionaria Americana (American Popular Revolutionary Alliance)
BOC	Bloque Obrero y Campesino (Workers' and Peasants' Bloc)
CNOC	Confederación Nacional Obrera de Cuba (National Workers' Confederation of Cuba)
CROM	Confederación Regional Obrera Mexicana (Mexican Regional Workers' Confederation)
CSLA	Confederación Sindical Latino Americana (Latin American Trade Union Confederation)
CSUM	Confederación Sindical Unitaria de México (Unitary Trade Union Confederation of Mexico)
DAI	Departamento de Asuntos Indígenas (Department of Indigenous Affairs)
DOI	Defensa Obrera Internacional (International Workers' Defense)
ENA	Escuela Nacional de Antropología (National School of Anthropology)

III	Instituto Indigenista Interamericano (Interamerican Indigenista Institute)
INI	Instituto Nacional Indigenista (National Indigenista Institute)
IPN	Instituto Politécnico Nacional (National Polytechnic Institute)
IPS	Investigaciones Políticas y Sociales (Political and Social Investigations [unit of Mexican security service])
KIM	Kommunisticheskii Internatsional Molodezhi (Communist Youth International)
KMT	Kuomintang (Chinese Nationalist Party)
KUTV	Kommunisticheskii Universitet Trudiashchikhsia Vostoka (Communist University for the Toilers of the East)
LADLA	Liga Antimperialista de las Américas (Anti-Imperialist League of the Americas)
LCAEV	Liga de Comunidades Agrarias del Estado de Veracruz (League of Agrarian Communities of the State of Veracruz)
LJC	Liga de Juventudes Comunistas (Communist Youth League)
LNC	Liga Nacional Campesina (National Peasant League)
MLSh	Mezhdunarodnaia Leninskaia Shkola (International Lenin School)
PAP	Partido Aprista Peruano (Peruvian Aprista Party)
PBL	Partido Bolchevique Leninista (Bolshevik Leninist Party)
PCC	Partido Comunista de Cuba (Cuban Communist Party)
PCM	Partido Comunista de México (Mexican Communist Party)
PIC	Partido Independiente de Color (Independent Party of Color)

PLM	Partido Liberal Mexicano (Mexican Liberal Party)
PNL	Partido Nacionalista Libertador del Perú (Nationalist Liberation Party of Peru)
PRV	Partido Revolucionario Venezolano (Venezuelan Revolutionary Party)
SEP	Secretaría de Educación Pública (Secretariat of Public Education)
SRI	Socorro Rojo Internacional (International Red Aid)
UCSAYA	Unión Centro Sud Americana y de las Antillas (Central South American and Antillean Union)
UNAM	Universidad Nacional Autónoma de México (National Autonomous University of Mexico)
UNIA	Universal Negro Improvement Association
UPH	Union Patriotique d'Haiti (Haitian Patriotic Union)

Introduction

IN THE 1920S AND 1930S, Latin American radicals sought to reimagine the tangled relationships between race, nation, class, and sovereignty. In Mexico City in the 1920s, a cluster of anti-imperialist Peruvian exiles proposed a pan-continental, "Indoamerican" federation stretching from the Rio Grande to Patagonia. At the turn of the 1930s, several Latin American Communist parties—inspired by the Communist International's approach to race and the "national question"—began calling for Indigenous groups and people of African descent to be granted the right to "national" self-determination; that is, to establish separate, sovereign states if they so desired. Neither of these boundary-breaking proposals came to fruition, yet I argue that the debates from which they emerged played an underappreciated role in shaping the trajectory of the Latin American radical left in the interwar period, and that they generated a rich repertoire of ideas that continue to resurface in the present.

Radical Sovereignty reconstructs a string of transnational debates that unfolded across locations as far-flung as Mexico City, Havana, Moscow, Brussels, and Buenos Aires. They involved a globe-trotting cast of characters, from Mexican peasant leader Úrsulo Galván to the Vietnamese revolutionary Ho Chi Minh; from Peruvian political activists such as Víctor Raúl Haya de la Torre and the poet Magda Portal to the US Communist Harry Haywood; and from the Cuban trade unionist Sandalio Junco to the Soviet diplomat Aleksandra Kollontai.

The debates at the heart of this book brought together individuals and organizations that had been powerfully shaped by the dual impact of the Mexican and Russian Revolutions. In Mexico, what had begun in 1910 as an uprising against the authoritarian rule of Porfirio Díaz quickly turned into

1

an all-encompassing social revolution. The demise of Mexico's ancien régime sent shock waves across Latin America: While elites trembled, frustrated middle classes, hard-pressed peasants, and urban workers alike drew inspiration from the Revolution's electrifying example. The Bolshevik Revolution of 1917 had a similar effect on a global scale, as the overthrow of tsarism sparked hopes among the oppressed in much of Europe and the colonized world.

This book focuses on a heterogeneous segment of the Latin American left for whom these epoch-making events opened up new political horizons. This includes not only Communists and socialists, but also peasant radicals and progressive anti-imperialists. Together, these groups laid crucial groundwork for rethinking how the left should approach the issues of race, nation, and empire. In the course of their discussions, they developed innovative analyses of contemporary imperialism, of revolutionary strategy, and of the nature of racial domination. In the process, they called into question not only the external borders of existing nation-states, but also internal divisions between social classes, ethnic groups, and categories of citizen. Underpinning their debates was a shared investment in the more fundamental question of sovereignty: how to define it and defend it, but also how to expand its meanings and extend its reach.

DEFINITIONS

I use the term *radical left* to describe several different political tendencies, and it is worth spelling out my criteria. In Latin America, the origins of the organized left lie in socialist and anarchist groups formed in the late nineteenth century.[1] In the 1910s and 1920s, these groups were joined by formations aligned with Communism, inspired by the global wave of enthusiasm that had greeted the Russian Revolution. The establishment of the world's first workers' state made the Union of Soviet Socialist Republics (USSR) a new lodestar for many radicals across Latin America, generating a qualitatively new set of transnational solidarities and connections.

Since these connections are central to my argument, much of this book focuses on Latin America's Communist movement. This means not only the national parties affiliated with the Communist International (Comintern), founded in Moscow in 1919, but also several other entities that were Communist aligned, including trade unions and nominally freestanding organizations such as the Anti-Imperialist League of the Americas, discussed in chapter 2. Often more loosely organized than political parties, in several cases these groups had a broader social basis than the local Communist Party, drawing in middle-class sympathizers and attracting the participation of prominent public figures.

However, non-Communist organizations also play critical roles in this story. They include groups such as the Alianza Popular Revolucionaria Americana (APRA; American Popular Revolutionary Alliance), formed in the mid-1920s by Peruvian exiles scattered between Europe and Mexico. Though it initially had few adherents, APRA had a disproportionate presence in Latin American political and intellectual debates of the time. I also include Mexico's peasant leagues, which emerged out of the agrarian ferment of the Mexican Revolution and could mobilize large numbers of people, exerting a powerful influence on Mexico's national scene for much of the 1920s. Part I describes an anti-imperialist convergence that brought together the Communists, APRA, and the peasant leagues; the focus of parts II and III is more squarely on the Communist movement, but even here there was considerable overlap and interchange with other political tendencies. Limiting my attention to the Communist movement alone, then, would artificially isolate the political discussions I am trying to reconstruct from the context that formed them.

One important left-wing tradition I will largely not be addressing, however, is anarchism. While anarchists were integral to the early emergence of Latin America's left, in the 1920s their influence waned as the fortunes of other ideologies and modes of political organization—whether Communist, socialist, or populist—improved. Anarchism remained a significant current within the labor movement, but in many cases Communism absorbed a sizeable proportion of its personnel and energies.[2] Most importantly, due to their rejection on principle of the pursuit of state power, anarchists were not centrally involved in the debates at the center of my study.

In seeking a single term to capture the variety of groups and tendencies I address, I have settled on *radical left* for two reasons. First, it is more capacious than *Communist left* and does greater justice to the broader discussions that are my subject. Second, it aims to avoid any conflation of these specific groups with "the left" tout court. Many other kinds of popular politics were present in this period, whether formally organized or identified with the "left" or not, and my focus in this book is on a specific subset of them.

The problem that preoccupied the disparate groups I have termed the radical left was that of how to make the revolution in Latin America. For many of these radicals, the goal was an immediate overthrow of existing regimes and landed oligarchies. Some anti-imperialists and progressive nationalists sought to emulate postrevolutionary Mexico, while for others the precise form and nature of what would come after the revolution could be worked out later. For the Communists, the ultimate aim was the creation of a worldwide workers' and peasants' state modeled on the Soviet system. Yet the time frame envisaged and the strategic means for attaining that goal were subject to recurrent revision, in large part due to shifts in policy by the Comintern.[3]

These shifts not only impacted Latin America's Communist parties; they also had repercussions for other segments of the left, which often went from being allies to rivals as a result. It is therefore worth giving a brief sketch and periodization of these strategic swings. At its foundation in 1919, the Comintern's goal was the immediate global spread of revolution, but from 1923 to 1928, in the face of setbacks in Europe and amid a growing recognition of the revolutionary potential of Asia, the organization adopted a strategy it termed the "United Front." Communists would form alliances with workers in other parties and movements in order to build broader coalitions that would only later—the timing was generally left unspecified—move toward the seizure of power. In Latin America, this meant a convergence with progressive nationalists against imperialism, a development typified by the Anti-Imperialist League of the Americas, discussed in chapter 2.

At this stage, Communist strategy globally was premised on the assumption that much of the world had first to experience a bourgeois revolution before it could then proceed to a proletarian one. In 1928, however, the Comintern swung to a very different approach, in the belief that capitalism's terminal crisis was approaching and that a direct leap to socialist revolution was possible. The organization adopted a new strategy, termed *class against class*, that called for Communist parties and their affiliates to abandon previous alliances and begin to challenge for power. Dubbed the "Third Period," this phase of the Comintern's existence coincided with the onset of the Great Depression and a repressive uptick in much of the world; in Latin America, Communist parties were often forced underground, and in places where they did rise up, they were brutally crushed.[4] In 1935, having registered that successful seizures of power were not imminent anywhere, the Comintern changed its strategy once again, calling for the formation of a "Popular Front" with social-democrats and progressive nationalists to counter the threat of fascism. This phase lasted until 1939, when Stalin's pact with Nazi Germany forced Communist parties worldwide into painful ideological contortions. Wartime alliances brought a brief return to anti-fascist unity before the Comintern's final dissolution, as a concession to the USSR's allies, in 1943.[5]

The debates at the center of this book were profoundly affected by these strategic twists. With each change in the Comintern line, Communist parties reframed their policies in an attempt to adapt. As a result, the character of rifts and polemics with their rivals shifted, and divergences on one question were often accelerated by newly emerging differences on another. Yet at the same time, the unfolding of Latin American discussions did not merely reflect Comintern dictates; the process of adaptation always responded to national contexts and concerns, creating space for contention and ambiguity. The debates on self-determination are a key example of this, since they unfolded in the midst of the Comintern's most sectarian phase. While much of the existing scholarship on this period sees the late 1920s and early 1930s as one of growing ideological conformism, my findings show that in these same years Latin American Communists engaged in substantive and far-reaching discussions on the key questions of race, nation, and empire.

INTERVENTIONS

In reconstructing these debates, *Radical Sovereignty* goes against a widespread assumption that Latin America's left was, as one scholar put it, "historically and notably silent on questions of ethnicity and race" until the end of the twentieth century.[6] Recent scholarship has presented a more complex picture, pointing to more dynamic and productive interactions—as well as tensions and clashes—between left-wing movements and Black and Indigenous groups.[7] In exploring these themes I extend a growing body of work that moves away from the previously dominant focus on hub-and-spokes relations between Moscow and the many national parties of which the Comintern was composed.[8] Several scholars have made use of the post-Soviet opening of the Comintern's archives to enrich our understanding of the global Communist movement, including a significant focus on its transnational dimensions.[9] By highlighting Latin America's role in these networks, I build on the work of Latin American historians such as Daniel Kersffeld and the late Ricardo Melgar Bao, as well as on that of Russian specialists of Latin American Communism such as Víctor and Lazar Jeifets.[10]

Radical Sovereignty connects these fresh perspectives on the history of the left to three further fields of scholarship. First, I link discussions of interwar Latin America to the growing literature on transnational radical networks. Several studies have explored the impact of cross-border links on radical politics in other parts of the globe in the late nineteenth and early twentieth centuries.[11] Others have noted the role played by the radical left in broader social movements, including those against racism and colonialism, and have highlighted the importance of specific cities as hubs for radical organizing and as spaces of transnational encounter.[12] While much of this scholarship has focused on links between imperial metropoles and their "peripheries," recent contributions have addressed Mexico City's role as both a gathering point for radicals and site of novel political imaginaries.[13] I build on these efforts by linking the story of encounters in Mexico to a wider series of transnational debates. By putting sources from Mexico and Cuba in dialogue with material from the Russian archives, moreover, I offer an alternative mapping of radical thought, in which influences flowed back and forth between Latin America, the USSR, and the colonial world.

A second area of scholarship I seek to extend is the dynamic literature on race and nation in twentieth-century Latin America. Here, too, transnational approaches have made signal contributions.[14] For understandable reasons, many English-language studies have centered on the outsized influence of the United States and its structures of racial domination. Yet as I demonstrate, conceptions of race in Latin America were also bound up with global influences and ideological currents. The radical debates around race provide a powerful example of this. Communist calls for self-determination for oppressed "national minorities" are often viewed as dogmatic attempts to apply Soviet thinking to the rest of the world. My findings show, however, that the idea emerged out of a confluence of radical Pan-Africanism with anti-colonialism and Bolshevik nationalities policy. This transnational convergence was partly what prompted Cuban Communists to take up the banner of anti-racism in the 1930s and to join the successful campaign to include an antidiscrimination clause in the Cuban Constitution of 1940. I also show that in Mexico, Communist debates on self-determination left their imprint on government policies and knowledge-production around the "Indigenous question" in the 1930s and beyond.

My study also brings together research on the Indigenous question with scholarship on the struggle for Black rights in Latin America. Much of the previous literature has tended to focus on one or the other. To some extent this reflects a broader assumption that the two groups have occupied different positions within Latin America's racialized social landscapes.[15] But as the following chapters make clear, in the 1920s and 1930s what were called the "Indian" and "Negro" questions were regularly discussed in tandem, within a transnational dialogue that embraced a variety of political and intellectual tendencies, from Communism to Peruvian *indigenismo*, and from Marcus Garvey's Black nationalism to African and Asian anti-colonialism.

Finally, *Radical Sovereignty* engages a third field of scholarship on nationalism, decolonization, and self-determination. Having achieved statehood in the early nineteenth century, mainland Latin American countries have tended not to feature in studies of decolonization or in discussions of the spread of the doctrine of self-determination, both seen as largely twentieth-century phenomena.[16] Indeed, where Latin America is mentioned it is as a precursor, its independence retrospectively defined as part of a "first decolonization" that took place in the Age of Revolutions. Yet key components of the region's radical left were integrally involved in contention over the nation-state in the interwar period, and their discussions were driven by the same questions that fired the imaginations of anti-colonial activists in Africa and the Caribbean in these same years.[17] The debates I reconstruct in chapter 5 were animated by the problem of how to overcome the legacies of colonialism and achieve lasting freedom for Black and Indigenous peoples; the Cuban Communist Party's endorsement of Black self-determination, discussed in chapter 8, emerged out of an encounter between global Communism, anti-colonialism, and Black internationalism that places it squarely within the same global anti-colonial conjuncture.

Adom Getachew has argued that in the interwar era, Black anti-colonial thinkers on both sides of the Atlantic made innovative attempts to imagine a postimperial order that would transcend the boundaries of nation-states.[18] I argue that the radical debates at the center of my study constituted another powerful attempt to rethink the question of sovereignty, and that they offer a new perspective on the passage between the end of the First World War and the 1960s moment of decolonization. Far from disappearing from view in that interval, the concept of self-determination went on a series of transnational journeys that included Latin America; as it did so, it raised profound questions within the Latin American radical left about the relationships between race, nation, class, and sovereignty.

CHAPTER OUTLINE

Part I focuses on Mexico City in the mid-1920s as a gathering point for Latin American anti-imperialists and on the innovative political thinking they developed there. In chapter 1 I evoke the distinctive brand of internationalism that emerged from the convergence of Communists, peasant movements, and radical exiles from Latin America and beyond. Chapter 2 explores the common anti-imperial agenda these currents developed. While it drew on a long anti-imperialist tradition, it was also distinctively shaped by transnational connections with the Comintern and with anti-colonial movements from across the world. This iteration of Latin American anti-imperialism was especially novel in its adoption of a global, systemic perspective, making parallels between Latin America's situation and those of colonized peoples elsewhere in the world and linking both to the depredations of capitalism.

By the end of the 1920s, however, this broad anti-imperial unity had run aground. The explanations commonly offered focus on the Comintern's markedly sectarian turn with the adoption of the "class against class" strategy after 1928. In chapter 3 I argue for an alternative interpretation, in which competing transnational perspectives on key issues of the day—Nicaragua and Haiti, the role of the middle class, the nature of the revolutionary state, China—presented divergent political and strategic choices. How the different tendencies within Mexico City's radical left responded to these issues depended on differences in their relation to the Mexican state. Where APRA held up the postrevolutionary regime as a model for Latin America, the Communists adopted an oppositional stance, to which the state responded with repression. This brought the curtain down on Mexico's role as a transnational hub, scattering most of the key figures in the preceding chapters into new exiles.

In part II the scene shifts to a range of sites—Moscow, Buenos Aires, the Caribbean, Peru—to follow the further development of these divergences. If in Mexico City the contention had centered on revolutionary strategy and relations to the Mexican state, the turn of the 1930s brought forth still more profound differences over the nation-state itself: whether to bolster it in the name of anti-imperialism, as APRA argued, or dismantle and remake it in the name of racial equality, as the Communists came to believe. Chapters 4 and 5 retrace debates within the Communist movement on Black and Indigenous self-determination. The main locations for these discussions were

Moscow and Buenos Aires, but the personnel involved were drawn from across Latin America, the United States, the USSR, and the colonial world. The debates in Moscow were conducted in several languages, as were most Comintern proceedings at that time, though French and English continued to serve as the main lingua francas; in Buenos Aires, Spanish was for the first time the dominant language at a Comintern gathering.

At its Sixth Congress in Moscow in 1928, the Comintern endorsed the right to territorial self-determination of Black and Indigenous peoples in the Americas, an idea that was then taken up—after heated debates—by Communist parties in the United States and in Latin America. Chapter 4 reconstructs the emergence of this policy through a confluence of Bolshevik thinking about national minorities with rising anti-colonial sentiment and a radical Black internationalism influenced by Pan-Africanism. I devote special attention to the pivotal role played by Harry Haywood, a Black US Communist who was in Moscow in the second half of the 1920s and was centrally involved in Comintern discussions of race. It was amid debates over applying the self-determination policy to the Black population of the US South that Latin American Communists raised the idea of extending the same right to Indigenous people.

Chapter 5 tracks the contention over race, nation, and self-determination that unfolded within Latin America's Communist movement either side of 1930. The Comintern's adoption of the self-determination policy challenged the Latin American left to dismantle existing nation-states in order to address centuries-old legacies of discrimination and marginalization. Yet when Latin American Communists gathered by the Río de la Plata in mid-1929, many of them opposed the idea, objecting to the emphasis it gave to racial identities over class. While some scholars have previously addressed these disagreements, I offer a fuller and more detailed account, focusing on contributions by Sandalio Junco and the Peruvian Marxist José Carlos Mariátegui.[19] The latter's ideas on race have largely been considered in isolation from their original context; I resituate them within the debates of the time and explore the dynamic exchange of ideas they prompted. The archival record reveals some surprisingly nuanced attempts on the part of Latin American Communists and Comintern envoys to grapple with the "problem of race," as well as some all too familiar blind spots about the realities of racism and discrimination in the region.

Chapter 6 turns to APRA and its evolution from pan-regional anti-imperialist movement to Peruvian political party. I retrace this shift by focusing on Magda Portal, who in 1929 gave the fullest account to date of APRA's critique of imperialism and its embrace of the Mexican Revolution as a model. Portal saw APRA's goal as a continent-wide project of radical social transformation. Yet from 1930 onward, APRA increasingly gravitated toward a nationally bounded view, and despite its attempt to fuse nationalism and anti-imperialism, it gradually tilted toward the first of these terms, in the process coming to define itself in direct opposition to the Communist movement.

Part III follows the impact of Latin American Communists' advocacy of Black and Indigenous self-determination in Cuba and Mexico. I chose these two countries because, first, there was no single place where the same agenda was put forward for both Black and Indigenous peoples; and second, although Communist parties in Chile, Ecuador, and Bolivia also adopted the self-determination policy, Cuba and Mexico offered a suggestive set of contrasts, both in terms of initial responses to the policy and with regard to its effects over the long run.[20]

In 1932 Cuba's Communist Party began to describe Cubans of African descent as an oppressed "national" minority and to support their right to territorial self-determination in Oriente, the island's easternmost province. Three years later the party dropped the policy, instead enthusiastically adopting Cuban nationalist symbols and slogans. Yet as I argue in chapter 7, the party's advocacy of Black self-determination left a lasting imprint on the country's political landscape: It served as the focal point for the Communists' take-up of racial equality. As one of the most consistent champions of this principle on the island, the party recruited many Cubans of African descent over the course of the 1930s, which transformed its composition and social basis for decades to come. Cuba's Communist Party was also influential in carrying forward the campaign to include an antidiscrimination provision in the 1940 Constitution. In that sense, while often dismissed as a passing delusion, Black self-determination had lasting political and institutional effects.

In Mexico, while the Communist Party did briefly take up self-determination for the Indigenous, the policy had its greatest impact outside the party's ranks. As I show in chapter 8, the strongest advocates for self-determination were prominent leftist intellectuals and state functionaries, many of whom were actively involved in government policies regarding the Indigenous in the 1930s and had a shaping influence on the emerging discipline of anthropology. Through figures such as the labor leader Vicente Lombardo

Toledano, who travelled to the USSR in the 1930s and publicly endorsed Soviet nationalities policy, a Marxist-influenced current took shape that emphasized the country's plural identity, seeking to allow room for the autonomous development of its myriad cultures.

Finally, in the epilogue I explore the afterlives of the debates reconstructed in the preceding chapters. In Mexico, ideas put forward in the 1930s resurfaced in subsequent years in the form of calls for Indigenous "autonomy." Elsewhere in Latin America, the end of the twentieth century brought a resurgence of Indigenous mobilizations that raised similar demands for *autodeterminación*, while Black movements across the region continued to struggle against the consequences of racism. I conclude by noting the wider resonances of the interwar debates for contemporary Latin America, where Black and Indigenous movements alike are still pressing for more egalitarian configurations of the nation-state.

SOURCES AND METHODS

The source base for this book reflects the transnational nature of the discussions at its core. I draw on materials from sixteen archives and repositories across seven sites, written in multiple languages. These range from Comintern documents housed in Moscow—those relevant to my purposes were written variously in French, German, Russian, and Spanish—to Mexican and Cuban newspapers, magazines, posters, flyers, and photographs. I have also drawn on private correspondence, memoirs, and transcripts of oral interviews with participants in these events. Throughout, my goal was to combine analysis of the political and intellectual history contained in documents produced by parties, governments, and organizations with a sense of the lived experience of these transnational encounters.

This, then, is a work of political and intellectual history; but since people are the agents of politics and the carriers of ideas, I have tried to produce what might be called "embodied political and intellectual history." To that end, I have retraced the backgrounds, political trajectories, and geographical movements of several key figures. A few of them are relatively well known: Julio Antonio Mella, Víctor Raúl Haya de la Torre, and Magda Portal, for example, have all been the subjects of multiple biographies, and Harry Haywood wrote a substantial autobiography. But I also focus on less prominent people, piecing together their itineraries through the fragmentary traces they left. In several cases, it was precisely the transnational nature of my approach that enabled me to gain a clearer picture of their lives. Comintern documents provided key details on Úrsulo Galván's and Sandalio Junco's stays in the USSR that have largely eluded scholars working solely from Mexican and Cuban sources; Mexican newspaper articles on the Indigenous question from the 1930s shed light on Cuban Communist Jorge Vivó's journey to the Caucasus a few years earlier.

The personal stories that anchor my analysis are in many ways what the editors of the *American Historical Review*, introducing a set of articles under the rubric "transnational lives," described as "microhistories stretched across a transnational canvas."[21] Yet at the same time, border-spanning experiences such as those I describe helped to give that transnational canvas its texture and dimensions. My aim has been to do justice to the multiple scales on which the actors in my study simultaneously lived, worked, and thought.[22] This methodological wager is integrally linked with the book's arguments: While much transnational scholarship has drawn attention to the movement of ideas, people, and things across national borders, in the debates I reconstruct in my central chapters the nation-state itself became a vital political problem with which these itinerant actors were concerned.

A NOTE ON TERMINOLOGY

Anyone working on race and ethnicity in Latin America faces a similar linguistic dilemma. The terms used in my sources reflect the racialized categories of their time, and to use them unquestioningly in the present is to risk reifying those categories and the power relations they supported. Conversely, however, to apply contemporary designations to historical actors is to project back in time ways of thinking that would have been foreign to the people involved (e.g., the prefix Afro-, which many Cubans of African descent in the 1930s rejected, but which has increasingly entered circulation in recent decades). To this temporal dilemma we should add the problems of translation: The racial categorizations that have historically applied in Cuba or Mexico are, of course, not the same as those prevalent in the United States, making the same words carry very different meanings.[23]

With these concerns in mind, in the following chapters I have used the terms *Black* or *Indigenous* when referring to people of African or Indigenous descent more broadly, while at the same time noting where the words used in the sources differ meaningfully from contemporary usage—for example, where *indígena* appears instead of the more common *indio*. I have also retained lowercase forms when quoting directly from sources, since capitalization implies precisely the kinds of coherent Black or Indigenous identity and political agency that were the subjects of contention in this period. Finally, there is an additional set of complications worth noting. In Cuba, people of African descent were (and are) identified using the categories *negro/a*, *mulato/a*, and *mestizo/a*. Yet distinctions readily apparent to Cubans were not always so to outsiders, who very likely placed into the category of *negro* people who would not have applied that term to themselves nor have been described as such by other Cubans. The terms *mulato* and *mestizo* rarely appear in Comintern materials relating to Cuba, which strongly points to such a process of silent recategorization. Among other things, this prompted me to treat with extra caution all estimates made of the number of "Black" people in the Partido Comunista de Cuba (PCC; Cuban Communist Party), since it was not clear who was doing the categorizing and on what basis. As well as noting these issues here, I have discussed them in the relevant chapters, as recurrent reminders of the constructed nature of the racialized landscapes through which these historical actors moved.

PART ONE

_____

Mexico City (1923–1929)

ONE

"Our Internationalism"

AT ZAPATA'S TOMB

On April 10, 1924, a large crowd marched through the streets of Cuautla in the state of Morelos. They were on their way to the town's cemetery to honor the memory of Emiliano Zapata, the Mexican peasant leader and revolutionary who had been murdered five years earlier. They had come from across Mexico to pay their respects, filling the streets with flowers and flags.[1] Many had arrived by train from the capital, only fifty miles to the north but a day's journey away on tracks that wound slowly through the mountains. The travelers packed the carriages "to the roofs," in the words of one eyewitness.[2] At Cuautla station they were joined by throngs of armed peasants, many of them waving the red and black banners of Mexico's *agraristas*, an anarchist-inspired peasant movement pushing for land redistribution. But this was hardly an event for the radical fringe: The Mexican Congress sent a sizeable delegation, and the man who gave the main speech was Secretary of the Interior Plutarco Elías Calles, who would be elected president of Mexico that July.

The ceremony at Zapata's tomb itself was brief, as delegations from across the country laid enough wreaths to form "a real mountain." Afterward came the speeches and the food. Calles vowed to continue Zapata's revolutionary legacy—a pledge that the crowd greeted with a storm of applause.[3] There were also speeches in Nahuatl, the Indigenous language most commonly spoken in Morelos, as well as one by veteran *agrarista* Antonio Díaz Soto y Gama, who compared Mexico to Bolshevik Russia and announced that Latin America's proletariat was waiting for Mexico to redeem it. This was greeted by "cheers for Russia and proletarian América."[4]

The gathering in Cuautla captures the heady mix of revolutionary rhetoric, peasant mobilization, and radical internationalism that was in the air in 1920s Mexico. The country was just emerging from a decade of turmoil. The military phase of the Mexican Revolution was over, and the victorious factions were turning their attention to the task of reconstructing a shattered country.[5] In 1917, delegates from contending armies had hammered out a new constitution that codified a range of social and labor rights, nationalized land and natural resources, and laid the basis for a far-reaching agrarian reform. But the Constitution's paper promises had yet to turn into tangible gains for the broad mass of the population. The class contention that the revolution had unleashed was far from settled. Indeed, for more than a decade Mexico would continue to be traversed by socioeconomic battles between peasants and landowners, workers and bosses, religious and political dissidents and the state.

At the same time, the new regime was attempting to take its place on the international stage. Although Mexico sent envoys to the Versailles negotiations in 1919, it was barred from membership in the League of Nations and found itself excluded from efforts to construct a new global order from the ashes of the First World War.[6] An outsider in interstate relations, it became a beacon for progressives and radicals across Latin America. Most of the region was still dominated by authoritarian figures allied with landowners and foreign commercial interests. Revolutionary Mexico seemed to offer a living model for how to challenge their power, a blueprint unfolding before the eyes of the world.

But as the cheers for Bolshevik Russia in Cuautla testify, Mexico was not the only model on offer. On the other side of the globe, the Russian Revolution had spread panic among Europe's anciens régimes and had struck a chord within much of the European working class; it also raised the hopes of millions living under colonial rule. Within weeks of seizing power, in December 1917 the Bolsheviks issued an "Appeal to the Toiling Masses of the World," which summoned "workers of all lands to fight for a general armistice, for universal peace without annexations and indemnities, based on self-determination of nations."[7] The message resonated widely, its anticolonial thrust adding to the Russian Revolution's mystique.

In March 1919, the Bolsheviks created an organism dedicated to advancing the revolution on a global scale: the Communist International or Comintern. Also known as the Third International, it was designed to supersede the Second International, which had been formed by social-democratic parties in the late nineteenth century but had disintegrated amid the mutual slaughter of the First World War. Although most of the delegates at the Comintern's founding congress represented European countries, its reach soon extended much further, into South and East Asia, the Middle East, Africa, and the Americas. Communist parties mushroomed in the 1920s, and the Comintern became the umbrella organization for a movement that spanned the globe, making Moscow the self-proclaimed headquarters of world revolution.

Even as Moscow became a kind of Red Mecca, Mexico emerged as a crucial bridgehead for the Comintern's activities in the Americas. Within a few months of its founding, the Comintern dispatched an envoy to Mexico City, and it sent three additional delegates two years later.[8] At the same time, Mexico and Soviet Russia developed closer ties at the interstate level: In 1924 Mexico became one of the first countries to establish full diplomatic relations with the Bolshevik regime. A sense of kinship, as states born out of parallel revolutions and as fellow pariahs in the international order, for a time brought Mexico and Soviet Russia together—though as we will see, tensions between the two would multiply as the 1920s wore on.

The story told here takes 1920s Mexico as its point of departure because that time and place offer a remarkable window on debates that shaped the Latin American left in the interwar period and beyond. In this moment of radical possibility, progressives and radical leftists tackled key questions: the form revolution should take in Latin America, the role of Indigenous peoples and how best to combat racism, the nature of imperialism, and the character of the revolutionary state. In the process, they developed creative but often divergent approaches and strategies. There was much they could agree on, including a broad consensus around the need to oppose US economic dominance over the Americas. But there were also stark disagreements—between Communists and other anti-imperialist movements, between peasant radicals and the Comintern, and within the Communist movement itself—that proved enduring. The coalescence of an anti-imperialist consensus is the subject of the next chapter, while I address the mounting tensions between different portions of the radical left in chapter 3.

All of these debates were animated by different forms of internationalism—or better, by different ideas about how local and national contexts were connected to the wider world. For some of the actors in this story, their encounters with Mexico gave concrete form to ideas they held to be universal; for others, transnational connections shifted their understanding of their own context; and for others still, the national and international realms remained distinct, if not in tension with one another. This chapter explores what the local and the international meant for different parts of the radical left in the fevered wake of the Mexican and Russian Revolutions. Although the connections forged at this time took a variety of forms, they were driven by similarly urgent and interconnected questions. What lessons should Latin Americans take from the Mexican and Russian Revolutions, and how directly should they seek to emulate their examples? What kinds of political project became thinkable in the light of these twin upheavals? This chapter looks at several of the political currents that converged in Mexico and highlights what each contributed to the radical internationalist mix. First, however, it may be helpful to situate the 1920s radical ferment relative to previous instances.

RADICAL CROSSROADS

The 1920s were not the first period in which Mexico was the scene of radical transnational organizing. Mexico City had a long history as a cosmopolitan hub, as the largest city in Spain's American empire and a vital node linking Atlantic and Caribbean trade routes to East Asia. In the mid-nineteenth century it had been host to Cuban pro-independence rebels, including José Martí.[9] In the closing years of that century, anarchist currents took root in Mexico in large part thanks to the efforts of European immigrants.[10] In the 1900s and 1910s, in the lead-up to the Revolution and in its turbulent midst, activists in the United States and Mexico created a cross-border network around the anarchist Partido Liberal Mexicano (PLM; Mexican Liberal Party), with close links to the Industrial Workers of the World (IWW).[11] For the PLM and its leader, Ricardo Flores Magón, the liberation of Mexican peasants was only one stage in an international struggle pitting workers against their exploiters.

Mexico had also been a refuge for radicals during the First World War, notably including Indian anti-colonial activist M. N. Roy and thousands of "slackers" who had fled the United States to avoid conscription.[12] Over the following decade it became a magnet for activists, thinkers, writers, and artists from across Latin America and beyond. An array of exiles—Cubans, Peruvians, Venezuelans, Colombians—were able to operate in relative freedom there. Radicals from farther afield also settled in the Mexican capital in these years, including US leftists such as the Communist writer Bertram Wolfe, the poet Langston Hughes, and the photographer Tina Modotti.

The man recording the scenes at Cuautla evoked earlier was another of the cluster of Latin Americans who set themselves up in Mexico City in the 1920s. Víctor Raúl Haya de la Torre had been expelled from Peru in 1923 for organizing student protests against the government of Augusto Leguía. His experiences during two stays in Mexico in the 1920s left a strong imprint on his thinking: Together with several other fellow exiles from Peru, Haya would found the pan–Latin American anti-imperialist APRA movement, which took Mexico's revolution as the model for a sweeping transformation of the continent.

By the 1920s, then, Mexico had long been a crossroads for many different kinds of radical politics. What was distinctive about the latest iteration of transnational radicalism? I argue, first, that the combination of the Mexican and Russian Revolutions generated a newly global sense of interconnection. Mexican revolutionaries mingled with exiled Latin American anti-imperialists; peasant activists from Veracruz and Michoacán rubbed shoulders with Japanese, Swiss, and Polish Comintern envoys; and Indian anti-colonialists met with Communists from the United States, among many others. Second, I argue that Mexico was more than a passive stage where these people converged; it both transformed them and was transformed by them in turn. For Mexico, these transnational encounters were an integral part of the 1920s political and cultural ferment, while for the outsiders, their time in Mexico was often a watershed in the development of their thinking. In what follows I explore these mutual transformations by focusing on three radical currents: the peasant leagues, the exiled anti-imperialists of the APRA movement, and the Partido Comunista de México (PCM; Mexican Communist Party).

FROM TLACOTEPEC TO MOSCOW

Armed *campesinos* had been the engine of insurgency during the Mexican Revolution. Their pressure ensured that agrarian reform was enshrined in the 1917 Constitution, in particular in Article 27, which nationalized land and laid the legal basis for its redistribution. Thereafter, postrevolutionary governments had to pay homage to the Revolution's agrarian roots, even if their willingness to actually redistribute land wavered. In the meantime, the broad current known as *agrarismo* took new forms with the founding of peasant leagues in many parts of Mexico. By the mid-1920s, the peasant *ligas* had around two hundred thousand members across nine states, making them a significant force in national politics. This upswell of energy is why historian Leticia Reina dubbed the 1920s the period of "galloping agrarianism."[13]

The largest and most prominent of the *ligas* was the Liga de Comunidades Agrarias del Estado de Veracruz (LCAEV; League of Agrarian Communities of the State of Veracruz), which was founded in March 1923 and within a couple of years had around thirty thousand members.[14] Its leader was Úrsulo Galván, whose trajectory gives us some insight into the radical peasant politics of the 1920s. Born in 1893 into a landless peasant family in rural Tlacotepec, he moved to the city of Veracruz in his teens and became a carpenter, before fighting in the Revolution and working in the oil fields of Tampico.[15] In the early 1920s, Galván was among those who helped form peasant cooperatives in the countryside in his home state, and in 1922 he took an active part in a citywide tenants' strike in Veracruz.[16]

Galván's experiences are a good example of the inherent ambiguity of the category of *campesino*. Though peasant cultivators and industrial laborers are often treated as distinct social groups, there was considerable overlap between them. "Peasants" and "workers" were in many cases the same people, shuttling back and forth depending on economic or personal circumstances. They themselves tended to identify as *campesinos*, yet they saw no contradiction between asserting that status and simultaneously claiming the label of "proletarian." In the 1920s, hundreds of people who straddled these categories gravitated toward the PCM.

By the time Galván established the Veracruz League in 1923, he was also a leading member of the PCM. In April 1923 he was elected to its national executive committee and placed in charge of its agrarian policy.[17] That summer, Galván received an invitation to attend the founding congress of the Comintern's new "Peasant International", the Krestintern, which was initially designed to capitalize on a wave of rural unrest in Eastern Europe but soon took on a more global character.[18] In making the trip, Galván became the first of a string of Mexican peasant delegates to travel to the USSR. Their experiences not only gave their attraction to the Soviet model a more concrete basis; they also brought them into contact with peasants from other parts of the world, whose analyses of colonial domination clearly resonated with their own view of Mexico's situation.

Galván arrived in the Soviet capital on October 6, 1923. Like many other visitors to Moscow, he attended a gala event at the Bolshoi Theatre, where he heard what he called the "strange, semi-savage songs" of Siberia's native peoples, comparing them to those "common among our own indigenous people."[19] He also met leading Bolsheviks and was struck by the modesty of their appearance, describing Nikolai Bukharin as "poorly shaven, wearing a vulgar leather jacket."[20] When the Krestintern Congress opened on October 10, there were delegates of more than forty nationalities in attendance, both from within the former tsarist empire and beyond.[21] Galván was among the eleven people elected to the congress presidium, alongside representatives from several European countries, Russia, Japan, the United States, and Indochina. The delegate from the latter is listed as Nguyen Ai Quoc, who would later become better known under another of his noms de guerre, Ho Chi Minh.[22]

Galván and Ho both addressed the congress on October 11. When Ho took the podium he asserted that, while the assembled European and American delegates were exploited within their own countries, those in colonies such as Algeria or Indochina were "doubly exploited": "We are exploited as proletarians, and we are exploited as conquered races."[23] Galván, meanwhile, highlighted the energizing effect that Bolshevism had had, remarking that "in the six years since the Russian Revolution took place, the movement not only in Mexico but also in other countries of South America has received a great boost."[24] Both Ho and Galván linked the struggle in their countries to those taking place in Europe. But for the moment, neither seemed to draw a direct connection between Asia and the Americas, between Mexico and Indochina. One reason for this may have been that Galván and Ho were intently focused on the Soviet model of revolution and on the question of whether their countries could replicate it. Then there is the fact that delegates from outside Europe already had their work cut out convincing the Comintern to broaden its gaze.[25] Ironically, given the Comintern's internationalist mission, in the early 1920s there was also a dearth of linguistic expertise, which made communication difficult: There were so few Spanish speakers on staff that no transcript of Galván's remarks exists, only a German-language précis. This would rapidly change in the second half of the 1920s, as a whole Spanish-language bureaucracy developed in Moscow—a shift encouraged by the growth of contacts such as those made by Galván.

The links Galván forged with the Krestintern were fundamental to the Veracruz League's version of internationalism—which in turn was integral to its view of the "peasant question" as a whole. In October 1924 the League published a pamphlet laying out the organization's history and principles. Though titled *El agrarismo en México* (Agrarianism in Mexico), more than a quarter of its pages were devoted to translations of Krestintern theses and resolutions. Implicit parallels between Mexico and revolutionary Russia also loomed large: Images of Red Army soldiers were scattered throughout the text. One is a large formal group portrait; another depicts a small group sitting in their barracks listening to their commissar, overlooked by a portrait of Lenin.[26] Here the Russian Revolution figured not as a remote foreign development but as a vivid example of successful armed revolt in a predominantly agrarian society—the outcomes of which the League's leader had seen for himself only a few months previously.[27]

This imagined kinship with the USSR was only one aspect of the Veracruz League's global outlook. From early on, the League made plain its rejection of a nationally bounded view of the agrarian question: One section of the October 1924 pamphlet is titled "The Peasant Problem Is Not Only a National Problem." It explained that "the Peasant Question is only an aspect of the great social problem (we will not tire of repeating it), of the problem of the proletarian class in all countries." This border-spanning class identity made clear that any solution could not stop at national frontiers: "The peasants of Mexico will not resolve our problem totally and to our satisfaction if it remains unsolved in the other countries."[28]

Two months later, this internationalist perspective became the framing premise of the Veracruz League's drive to create a national-level peasant organization in Mexico. At its Second Congress in Jalapa in December 1924, the League announced that it would take on the task of bringing together peasant organizations across Mexico where these already existed, and would set them up in states where they did not.[29] Yet from the outset, this was part of a strategy that looked beyond Mexico's frontiers. On the following day, the same congress passed a resolution insisting that the national body it planned to form would be "incomplete" if it remained "a solely and exclusively national organization." "For it to realize its destiny," the Veracruz League asserted, "it is not enough to make it only national, but rather [it must be] International."[30] For the League, internationalism and the national arena were not in contradiction or counterposed to one another, but rather connected and complementary frameworks of action.

Behind this dual strategy lay an awareness that the source of many of their problems lay just across Mexico's northern border. Latin American countries were effectively US colonies, the December 1924 resolution argued, and even the strongest among them would be unable to face up to the United States alone. "Our Internationalism," the resolution stated, "is not the child of a crazed enthusiasm for empty phrases . . . but of the need to take preventive measures, to bolster ourselves against the enemy . . . THE IMPERIALISM OF NORTH AMERICA."[31] This was why, it explained, the Veracruz League had decided formally to align itself with the Comintern. Through an alliance that extended far beyond the regional level, the League aimed to link Latin America's *campesinos* to workers and peasants across the globe.

INDOAMERICAN VISIONS

Imperialism would also become the central category in Haya de la Torre's politics, which were decisively reshaped by his experiences of exile, in particular by postrevolutionary Mexico. Expelled from Peru in October 1923 for his activism as head of the country's student federation, he passed through Panama and Cuba before arriving in Mexico the following month.[32] Even this brief journey had an immediate impact on Haya's understanding of Latin America's place in the world. As he put it at the end of 1923, he only became fully aware of "the painful reality of imperialism's advance . . . in all its threatening magnitude when I arrived in Panama, Cuba, and Mexico."[33] For Haya, Panama and Cuba were nominally sovereign republics but remained effectively under Washington's control. Mexico, by contrast, provided a model of a revolutionary state that was seeking to forge a path out of that subordination. As a student leader and editor of the magazine *Claridad* in Lima, Haya had been a strong supporter of the new postrevolutionary regime.[34] But more than that, his time in Mexico supplied him with a way of thinking about what Latin America had in common vis-à-vis its powerful northern neighbor.

Before arriving in Mexico City, Haya had forged links with the Mexican student federation and, through *Claridad*, was also well connected to literary circles; the Chilean poet Gabriela Mistral initially put him up in the Mexico City suburb of San Ángel.[35] It was through these contacts that Haya got a job working as personal secretary to José Vasconcelos, the Mexican education minister. As head of the newly created Secretaría de Educación Pública (SEP; Secretariat of Public Education), Vasconcelos played a leading role in the cultural politics of the postrevolutionary regime, inaugurating "missions" that sought to expand rural education and fostering the period's best-known visual legacy: It was his sponsorship that kick-started Mexican muralism.

Vasconcelos's most notorious contribution, however, lay in his ideas about race.[36] At a moment when eugenics was in the ascendant, European and North American race thinking vaunted the superiority of white people while stressing the desirability of racial "purity." In Latin America, eugenics took a different form, recognizing the highly mixed character of the region's societies and emphasizing instead the possibility of "improving" them through "constructive miscegenation."[37] In 1925 Vasconcelos produced one of the most influential statements of this line of thinking, couching it in highly mystical language. *La raza cósmica* (The cosmic race) described Latin America's mixing of Indigenous, European, and African cultures and phenotypes as a positive good and argued that it would produce a higher synthesis—a *mestizo* "cosmic race"—in which the best characteristics of each would be combined. Yet even as he celebrated *mestizaje* or racial mixing, Vasconcelos still attributed specific traits to distinct racial groups, and there was a clear hierarchy among those traits, with Europeans supposedly accounting for the most "civilized" components in the mixture. In effect, Vasconcelos turned European or North American race thinking inside-out while preserving its racialized premises.

Vasconcelos's ideas were highly influential at the time, circulating widely in Latin American intellectual circles. *La raza cósmica* appeared the year after Haya worked for Vasconcelos, and it seems plausible that the two men discussed its key concepts in the run-up to its publication. These concepts clearly left their mark on Haya; it was while working for Vasconcelos that he began to refer to "Indoamérica."[38] The term was designed to reaffirm the Indigenous heritage of Latin America, in contradistinction to the "Anglo-Saxons" farther north—a dichotomy Vasconcelos expounded on in *La raza cósmica*. This emphasis on Latin America's Indigenous identity would become central to the political lexicon of the movement Haya cofounded in the mid-1920s. It was also during his stay in Mexico—and in particular after his trip to Cuautla—that the category of the "Indian" began to appear more often in his writings.[39]

It may seem strange that Haya, coming from a country with a large Indigenous population, had to travel thousands of miles from Lima to Mexico before he began to pay more attention to the Indigenous. Growing up in an educated middle-class family in the northern city of Trujillo, he would certainly have been familiar with the Peruvian anarchist Manuel González Prada's 1904 text "Nuestros indios" (Our Indians), and with attempts to remedy their plight such as the Pro-Indigenous Association, founded in Lima in 1909. He would also have followed news of the Rumi Maki (Stone Hand in Quechua) uprising, a largely Indigenous peasant movement that shook Peru's southern highlands in 1915–16. But in his writings Haya, like many others, still tended to depict Peru's Indigenous peoples as long-suffering victims. In Mexico, by contrast, he saw Indigenous people playing an active role in the transformations he was witnessing—not as passive symbols of oppression, but as armed political actors.

For Haya—and for other Peruvians, as we will see—the encounter with Mexico's Indigenous was transformative. He was certainly impressed by the combination of militancy and good manners among the Mexican peasants he met in Cuautla, many of whom would have been Indigenous: They were "armed to the teeth," Haya observed, but "polite, cordial, and calm." They also expressed their own freewheeling internationalism; when he told them there was no *agrarista* movement in Peru, one of them immediately replied, "We have to go there."[40]

Latin America's Indigenous identity was clearly central to Haya's concept of *Indoamérica*—both a heritage and a present-day demographic reality that distinguished it from North America. But while Vasconcelos's views had a cultural and ethnoracial basis, Haya would differ from his patron and employer in taking a more materialist approach. Here another crucial influence on Haya's thinking was his encounter with Mexican Communism. It was in Mexico that Haya first crossed paths with an organized Communist Party, through friendships he established with muralist Diego Rivera, Communist leaders Rafael Carrillo and Manuel Díaz Ramírez, and exiled radicals such as the American Bertram Wolfe and the German Alfons Goldschmidt.[41] An article Haya wrote in December 1923 laid out a clearly Marxist-influenced view of Latin America's position in the world economy, mapping class categories onto the hemisphere's geography: "Our América," he wrote, "contains a great feudal sediment, and its economic primitivism, its nascent industrial progress, characterize it more as a large proletarian region, economically colonial."[42] From this it followed, according to Haya, that the battle between Anglo- and Latin America was of a fundamentally economic nature.

But Haya gave this materialist view a new twist, arguing that the unity required in the face of US imperialism was a fusion of nation-states: "The union or confederation of our América is a revolutionary imperative of the purest economic character." A few lines later he went further than confederation, arguing that it was the task of the younger generation to carry out "the labor of destroying borders, of curing our peoples of hostile patriotism."[43] This pan-regional, integrationist perspective clearly harked back to the idea of a single great Latin American state propounded by Simón Bolívar in the 1820s. Bolívar's original vision had run aground on the divergent interests of the newly independent states that emerged from Spain's empire, but it had remained on the horizon for many Latin Americans as a tantalizing dream of future unity. Haya, like other anti-imperialists of his generation, sought to revive that dream in the twentieth century, this time with a much stronger emphasis on economic considerations. In this revised form, it would become central to the ideology of Haya's APRA movement.

APRA TAKES SHAPE

The event later claimed as APRA's moment of origin took place on May 7, 1924, in Mexico City. According to the movement's own mythologized accounts, at a gathering of the Mexican student federation in the Simón Bolívar Amphitheater of the National Preparatory School, Haya presented his hosts with the flag of his new organization: a gold circle enclosing a map of Latin America, on a rich red background.[44] Today, there is even a commemorative plaque outside the venue, unveiled in 1987 by the then Peruvian president and APRA leader Alan García.

The placement of APRA's mythological origins in Mexico contains an element of truth, yet the actual story of its birth is rather different. While the germ of a continent-spanning movement emerged through Haya's encounter with postrevolutionary Mexico, as a political organization it would only gradually take shape over the next two years, mainly through Haya's contacts with other Peruvian exiles in Europe. Its program and even its name were not finalized until 1926.[45] Why, then, the claim that it emerged fully formed in Mexico in 1924? A major part of the reason may have been that placing APRA's origins in Mexico, rather than Europe, underlined its Latin American character: An emphasis on ideas and solutions native to the region—as distinct from "imported" doctrines such as Communism—would become a central part of APRA's discourse. A Mexican origin story also linked APRA directly to the revolution it sought to emulate on a hemispheric scale.

But there was another motivation behind the ex post facto rewriting of APRA's origins. As we will see, APRA and the Communists would become bitter rivals within the space of a few years. However, in 1924 Haya was still strongly influenced by Communism, and connections to the USSR had a far greater influence on his thinking than is commonly acknowledged—making APRA itself a neglected example of the dual impact of the Mexican and Russian Revolutions.[46] It was in his exchanges with the Comintern that Haya first articulated the basic platform of what would later become APRA; in the wake of this, in Europe, he and other Latin American exiles formed the movement itself.

Ironically, the strength of Haya's connections with Communism was evident at the event later claimed as marking APRA's birth. The red banner unfurled on May 7 was designed by Diego Rivera for the Mexican student movement, and at the time, Haya praised it as an emblem of "pulsating aspirations for justice" among the "Indoamerican youth," describing it as the flag of "Our Generation": "a Communist flag."[47] The event itself was a send-off before his departure on a trip organized with the help of his friends in the PCM, Manuel Díaz Ramírez and Rafael Carrillo.[48] He was heading to Moscow.

Haya spent nearly four months in Russia, from July to October 1924.[49] He attended and spoke at Comintern gatherings, including meetings of its Executive Committee; like Galván the year before, he also addressed a meeting of the Krestintern, alongside Ho Chi Minh.[50] The writings Haya produced during this time idiosyncratically combine pan–Latin Americanism and materialism. Shortly after arriving in Moscow, for example, he wrote a primer for Comintern delegates on Latin America that took a Vasconcelian approach, referring to a "racial hostility of all the Indo-Hispanic peoples towards the [Anglo-]Saxons."[51] But Haya also gave great importance to economic factors, highlighting the increasing grip of US capitalism on the region. Ranged against it was "a strong mass movement, whose affirmative tendency is to unite the twenty dispersed states into a Latin American federation that will form a united front against the imperialist danger."[52] The idea of a pan-regional federation, as noted previously, can be traced to Bolívar. But by 1924 there was also another, more concrete model on offer, and Haya was standing in it: the Soviet Union, formed in 1922 out of the former components of the Romanov empire.

Haya clearly took inspiration from the Soviet Union when devising the movement that would become APRA. In January 1925 he wrote to the Swiss Comintern official Edgar Woog (who used the alias "Stirner") seeking support for a new political project.[53] He planned "to form a great party on the basis of workers and peasants in Peru," which would be designed to seize power there "within two months." As if this accelerated timetable were not ambitious enough, Haya's movement would also "try to be international within Latin America," aiming to secure "the unity of the people of the Continent against Yankee imperialism." Haya went on to make clear what the model for this organization was: "Both the maximum and minimum program of the Party will be that of the Communist Parties, but it will not use the word to avoid calling down upon itself [echarse encima] the world offensive against communism."[54]

As originally conceived, the proto-APRA would have been pan-continental in scope and Communist in all but name. Haya may, of course, have been framing his project in terms designed to appeal to Moscow. But the program he laid out in the rest of his letter to Stirner is consistent with the main points of the agenda APRA later developed. These included nationalization of land and industry; a "continental campaign" of anti-imperialism; and pan-Latin American unity, framed as unfolding in two stages—"federalization first, then centralization."[55] (This two-stage process, incidentally, directly echoed Lenin's views: A federal state was a necessary step on the road to the ultimate goal of a centralized super-state.) Haya's embryonic program also included several radical measures that did not subsequently reappear: nationalization of Church lands; what he called "communization of land," driven by "indigenous agitation on the basis of the Incaic tradition"; the establishment of cooperatives on the Soviet model; and the dissolution of the Peruvian military and the "creation of a new army under [instruction from] a Russian military mission."[56]

At the same time, Haya insisted that the new political organization be adapted to Latin American conditions. Only the most hard-headed of people, he wrote, could think that "a revolution in the Americas could be made with literature from Europe." What was needed was "a mass party that would base itself on national conditions."[57] There is a tension, to say the least, between Haya's desire to model his movement on the Bolsheviks and his insistence that European models were inadequate to the Latin American context. The same unsteady mix of emulation of and distance from Communism would run through the APRA movement even as it took shape, with the Soviet Union now featuring alongside anti-colonial struggles.

The name "APRA" itself first appeared in 1926. That April, in a letter to his fellow Peruvian, Esteban Pavletich, Haya wrote that he was "battling to organize the A.P.R.A." As in his correspondence with Stirner, he again depicted it as a substantively Communist undertaking: "The point is to give our movement a really communist, Marxist, Leninist character, WITHOUT SAYING SO, WITHOUT CALLING OURSELVES COMMUNISTS OR LENINISTS but rather *acting* as such."[58] The Soviet influence was also apparent when it came to organizational form: Haya envisaged APRA functioning much like the Comintern, as a single international body with "national sections." In the same letter he affirmed, *"Our APRA will be a great red army or it will be nothing."*[59]

But even as Haya was drawing on the Soviet precedent, he insisted that APRA should be "typically Latin American, like the Chinese movement, like the Moorish movement if you will."[60] The referent in the latter case was the rebellion then under way in Spanish Morocco under the leadership of Abd el-Krim. Haya had expressed his solidarity with the rebels in a 1925 article, describing the combined assault by Spanish and French colonial armies as "the murder of a people."[61] The "Chinese movement" he had in mind, meanwhile, was the Kuomintang (KMT; Chinese Nationalist Party). At the time, the Kuomintang was still seen as an ally by the Communist movement. As part of its United Front strategy, from 1923 to 1928 the Comintern instructed Communists worldwide to form anti-imperialist alliances with nationalist forces; in China, it pressured the fledgling Communist Party to embed itself within the Kuomintang. For Haya, this strategy offered a model for APRA's relations with Latin American Communist parties, and he frequently referred to his movement as "a Latin American Kuomintang"—though as we will see, the implications of making that parallel shifted dramatically within a few short years.[62]

Fittingly for a movement with such a transnational frame of reference, APRA came together through transnational networks. It first took shape in 1926 among Peruvian exiles in Paris, with further cells developing soon afterward in Buenos Aires and Mexico, joined by the end of the decade by APRA committees in Chile, Bolivia, Costa Rica, El Salvador, and New York City.[63] Its program was first publicly articulated by Haya in London, in a December 1926 article titled "What Is the APRA?"[64] More than anything else, it was this article, in which Haya was described as the "Leader of the 'United Front' Latin America Anti-Imperialist Party," that secured his status as the movement's founder. APRA's program consisted of five points: (1) "action of the countries of Latin America against Yankee Imperialism"; (2) "the political unity of Latin America"; (3) "the nationalization of land

and industry"; (4) "the internationalization of the Panama Canal," presumably meaning the transfer of the Canal Zone from US imperial sovereignty to shared interstate governance; and (5) "the solidarity of all the oppressed peoples and classes of the world."[65]

For Haya, all of these points were interconnected, as part of a single anti-imperialist agenda. The struggle against US domination required a direct confrontation with Latin America's ruling classes; in order to overcome the division imposed on Latin America's masses by these elites, "the overthrow of the governing classes is indispensable, political power must be captured by the workers, and Latin America must be united in a Federation of States."[66] Haya's dream of pan–Latin American unity, then, involved more than an alliance: He envisioned the creation of a federated super-state spanning the whole region. The parallel with the Soviet Union is again obvious. The demand for the internationalization of the Panama Canal, meanwhile, had been raised by anti-imperialists elsewhere in the region; the canal was a crucial chokepoint for regional trade. Its inclusion in Haya's five-point program underscored his increasing interest in the economic, rather than "racial," dimensions of US hemispheric dominance.

In affirming APRA's solidarity with oppressed peoples—the fifth point of the program—Haya consciously placed his movement within a global anti-imperial framework. Yet even as he expressed these affinities, he felt the need to assert APRA's freestanding nature, describing it as "an autonomous movement, completely Latin American, without foreign interventions or influences."[67] The distinction between the Latin American and the "foreign" was telling: It presumed exactly the pan-regional unity Haya's movement was designed to produce. It was also ironic: APRA was a movement of exiles, forged by people who had left their own countries for Europe or for other parts of Latin America. Haya remained in Europe for another several months, but it was among Peruvians in Latin America that APRA emerged most fully. One of its main hubs was Mexico City, where APRA's exiled Peruvians debated and at times joined forces with the peasant leagues and the Communists.

LOS BOLCHEVIQUES

The PCM was also a transnational enterprise from the outset. Emerging out of Mexico's Socialist Party, it was founded in November 1919 with the active involvement of Indian nationalist M. N. Roy, who had arrived in the

Mexican capital in 1917, and Comintern envoy Mikhail Borodin, who spent three months in Mexico in late 1919.[68] Like other Communist organizations set up around the world at this time, the PCM was nominally a section of the Comintern and saw itself as part of a single worldwide political formation. Though initially small and riven by infighting, the PCM was a vital conduit for ideas and influences, bringing radicals in Mexico into contact with a globe-spanning network of Communists, anti-imperialists, and anti-colonial activists.

For the first few years of its existence, the PCM's membership was limited to urban laborers and artisans in the capital, railroad workers, and oil workers in Tampico, with scattered members in the countryside in Veracruz and Michoacán.[69] But that picture began to change in the mid-1920s, thanks in large measure to the close relationship it developed with the peasant leagues, which made the PCM one of the few Latin American Communist parties with a significant base among the peasantry. Externally, in its early years the PCM operated under the influence of the US Communist Party, which adopted something of a tutelary stance toward its Mexican peer.[70] US cadres were closely involved in PCM discussions, including expatriates based in Mexico such as Bertram Wolfe. A Brooklyn-born socialist, Wolfe had moved to Mexico in 1922 and immediately joined the PCM. He was a key point of contact between the Mexican and US Communist Parties, and between the PCM and the Comintern. In the summer of 1924 Wolfe even attended the Comintern's Fifth Congress in Moscow as one of the PCM's official delegates.

By the mid-1920s, however, the PCM was forging closer ties with the Comintern and leveraged those connections to assert its autonomy. A turning point came in October 1924 with the arrival of the Soviet Union's first official ambassador to Mexico, Stanislav Pestkovsky, who now offered Mexico's Communists a direct line to Moscow. US journalist Carleton Beals described Pestkovsky as "a big, booming man with gnarled tobacco teeth showing through a dark beard" and as "brusque, tactless but jovial."[71] Pestkovsky had a distinguished revolutionary pedigree: A member of the Bolshevik Party since 1904, he had been a deputy in the Petrograd Soviet in 1917 and had led the seizure of the city's telegraph office during the October Revolution.[72] In a moment laden with symbolism, he presented his diplomatic credentials to President Álvaro Obregón on the anniversary of that revolution. The same evening, he spoke at a PCM gathering at the Colegio San Ildefonso, where he recounted the Bolsheviks' triumph against a

FIGURE 1. Stanislav Pestkovsky speaking at a PCM event in the Anfiteatro Simón Bolívar, Mexico City, 1924–25. From Fototeca Nacional, INAH, Mexico.

backdrop of murals recently completed by Diego Rivera and José Clemente Orozco.[73]

Pestkovsky would spend two years in Mexico, combining his role as Soviet ambassador with an active presence in the Communist movement (see figure 1). At the Soviet mission on the Calle Río Rhin in what is now the Colonia Cuauhtémoc, he hosted parties to mark the death of Lenin, May Day, and the anniversary of the Russian Revolution. Mexican officials were invited to these gatherings, as well as to screenings of films such as Sergei Eisenstein's *Battleship Potemkin* (1925). At the same time, Pestkovsky worked closely with the PCM and contributed some of the embassy's modest resources to the party's newspaper, *El Machete*.[74]

El Machete was itself another significant factor in the PCM's improving fortunes, mainly because it gave the party a cultural prominence that was out of proportion to its size. The paper's founders included the painters Diego Rivera, Xavier Guerrero, and David Alfaro Siqueiros, and the poet Graciela Amador. It was Amador who came up with the name and wrote a poem explaining the paper's aims: "The Machete can be used to cut cane / to open up paths through dark forests / to decapitate snakes, cut out the chaff / and to bring down arrogance of the impious rich."[75]

Founded in 1924 by an independent radical artists' union, *El Machete* wasn't originally a party organ. But given its editors' clear Communist sympathies, it was no surprise when it became the PCM's official paper a year later. From the outset, it made effective use of graphic elements, breaking up columns of tight print with bold woodcuts and line drawings, often the work of Guerrero or Siqueiros. The paper also frequently included *corridos*, popular songs, with political lyrics. One featured the ghost of Emiliano Zapata, returning to ask what had become of the Mexican Revolution since his death. ("Has everyone caved in? / So quickly forgotten / Their sacred promises / For the good of the poor?")[76]

Beyond its coverage of Mexico, *El Machete* was resolutely internationalist. As one might expect of a Communist outlet, it gave particular attention to Soviet Russia. The front page of its first issue acclaimed the Bolshevik Revolution as a model for Mexico, and thereafter it devoted regular space to life in the new workers' state. But its horizons were not limited to the USSR. Its first issue carried items on Peru and on Mahatma Gandhi and "passive resistance" in India, and subsequent numbers featured a regular "international section" which, among other things, reported on the rise of fascism in Italy; lynchings in the United States; labor struggles in Cuba; and anti-imperialist movements in Morocco, China, and the Philippines.[77] This already strongly internationalist outlook was given a further boost from 1925 onward by the arrival in Mexico of radical exiles from elsewhere in Latin America.

"A UNIVERSITY OF PEOPLES"

On the corner of Calle Bolívar and Calle República de Uruguay in Mexico City's historic center stands a two-story colonial mansion, its lower floor vivid pink, while its upper story has rickety ironwork balconies and peeling white paint. In 1799 the young Simón Bolívar stayed in the house during his brief visit to Mexico, which is why decades later, his legendary status as founding father of Spanish American independence secured, the street was named after him. In the second half of the 1920s, a cluster of Latin American exiles all shared lodgings in this building. They reveled in its connection to the Liberator, seeing him as a precursor to their own aspirations for pan-continental unity. On the first floor were the Venezuelans Gustavo and Eduardo Machado and Salvador de la Plaza, who had fled the dictatorial rule of Juan Vicente Gómez, and the Peruvian Jacobo Hurwitz, who escaped the worsening political climate under Augusto Leguía. Two more Venezuelans, Carlos Aponte and Bartolomé Ferrer, lived on the second floor, as did the house's best-known resident at the time, the Cuban Julio Antonio Mella.[78]

By the time Mella arrived in Mexico in February 1926 he was already a bright star in the Latin American radical firmament.[79] Born Nicanor McPartland in Havana in 1903 to a Dominican father and an Irish mother, he enrolled at the University of Havana in 1921 and rose rapidly to the leadership of a vibrant student movement. But Mella's influence extended far beyond student circles. In March 1923 he joined the Agrupación Comunista in Havana.[80] This was the core of what became the PCC, founded in August 1925, with Mella's name heading the list of those elected to the new Central Committee.[81] In the meantime, he had also founded the Cuban section of the Anti-Imperialist League of the Americas, a Communist-led organization headquartered in Mexico that is the subject of the next chapter. The League's Cuban section organized demonstrations calling for the return of the US naval base in Guantánamo Bay to Cuban sovereignty, for pan–Latin American solidarity, for the internationalization of the Panama Canal—a year before Haya laid out APRA's five-point program—and for Puerto Rican and Filipino independence.[82]

What linked all of these sites, of course, was the power of the United States. Having acquired Puerto Rico and the Philippines in the Spanish-American War of 1898, the United States helped Panamanian separatists gain independence from Colombia in 1903 and then seized control of the Panama Canal Zone the following year. Opposition to Washington's sway was formative for Mella and other Cubans of his generation. But it was the core of a broader set of solidarities. In October 1923 Mella's student federation passed a resolution condemning the abuses suffered by the peoples of the Caribbean, Central America, the Philippines, Ireland, Egypt, India, and Morocco.[83] Two years later, Mella and his comrades in the Anti-Imperialist League cultivated the support of the local Chinese community, in particular the Havana chapter of the KMT.[84] For Mella, this kind of solidarity was about much more than rhetorical gestures; it went to the heart of his entire worldview. As he put it in 1925, "No revolutionary in the current moment can fail to be internationalist. He would cease to be a revolutionary."[85]

Mella's increasing prominence drew the attention of the Cuban government. In September 1925 he was arrested along with several other leftists and convicted of "acts of terrorism."[86] In December he went on hunger strike, prompting a wave of solidarity. Demonstrations in support of Mella took place across Cuba and in Mexico City; the Mexican Senate even sent a cable to President Gerardo Machado demanding Mella's release.[87] The outcry eventually compelled the Cuban government to free him. But Mella's position was tenuous—and not only because he had incurred Machado's wrath. The PCC was also displeased; it had not been consulted about his hunger strike and had ordered him to desist, to no avail. In January 1926 the Central Committee charged Mella with "indiscipline" and expelled him from the party. Passing through Havana a few months later, Pestkovsky called the decision "political suicide" and pushed the party leadership to reverse it.[88] But by that time Mella had left; using false papers, he got on a banana boat to Honduras, and from there he made his way through Guatemala to Mexico.[89]

On arriving in the Mexican capital in February 1926, Mella immediately became a key player in radical left circles. He joined the PCM and began writing prolifically for *El Machete*. He was also at the center of a network of Cuban exiles, founding a political organization dedicated to the overthrow of Machado named the Asociación de Nuevos Emigrados Revolucionarios Cubanos (ANERC; Association of New Revolutionary Cuban Emigres). Along with the other residents of the house on Calle Bolívar, Mella was also deeply involved in the anti-imperialist organizing discussed in the next chapter.

Technically, Mella was still a student; he had enrolled to study law at the Universidad Nacional Autónoma de México (UNAM; National Autonomous University of Mexico). But it was Mexico's radical ferment that he really wanted to explore, writing to comrades in Havana, "In this atmosphere of revolutionary agitation and experience, unique in the Americas, it is as if I am in a university of peoples." In the same message, Mella connected the revolutionary curriculum he was pursuing in Mexico to battles being waged in the colonial world. "Look at how our brothers in Asia and Africa are rushing to obtain their liberation," he wrote, adding, "Listen to the heart of América and you will hear how it beats faster out of joy at [their] actions."[90] For Mella, internationalism was a form of solidarity that collapsed geopolitics and physiology, joining the quickening pulses of Latin American youth to growing anti-colonial agitation and giving political questions a bodily immediacy.

The different political currents described previously—peasant radicals, Communists, the anti-imperialists of APRA—all converged at the founding congress of the Liga Nacional Campesina (LNC; National Peasant League), held in Mexico City from November 15 to November 20, 1926. Úrsulo Galván of the Veracruz League was one of the main organizers of the congress, which brought together delegates from sixteen of Mexico's states. Also in attendance were Communists such as Mella, Carrillo, Rivera, de la Plaza, Gustavo Machado, and Xavier Guerrero, as well as *apristas* such as Pavletich. Mexican official circles were also represented, with envoys from the Secretariats of Agriculture and the Interior, and one from the Secretariat of Public Education, Miguel Othón de Mendizábal.[91] The gathering had a strong internationalist cast, too; there were speakers from Peru, Colombia, Ecuador, and the Netherlands.[92]

This diverse cast of characters no doubt contributed to the global perspective of the congress. But the proceedings also testified to the strength of *campesino* internationalism within Mexico. Delegates from Michoacán and Mexico State noted the effects of US and European imperialism on the rest of the world, and there were motions calling for solidarity with the peoples of the Americas and the USSR. The congress also voted to send a delegate— Mella himself—to the Anti-Imperialist Congress to be held in Brussels in February 1927.[93] The motto originally proposed for the LNC by the Durango peasant leader José Guadalupe Rodríguez Favela was "*Campesinos* of the World, Unite!"—deliberately echoing the slogan launched almost eighty years earlier by Karl Marx and Friedrich Engels in the *Communist Manifesto*. But in the end Galván, freshly elected the LNC's president, proposed a more hemispherically oriented alternative: "*Campesinos* of the Americas, Unite!"[94]

Hemispheric unity and opposition to imperialism were central to the new national peasant league's conception of its role. There was also a clear enthusiasm for border-spanning initiatives. When PCM member Rafael Ramos Pedrueza expressed the hope that the peasant union "not only be one of Mexico or of the American Continent, but rather INTERNATIONAL," he was "deliriously applauded by the assembly."[95] At times this internationalism was accompanied by an anti-nationalism, with many delegates hostile to what they saw as manifestations of patriotism. When the *agrarista* Antonio Díaz Soto y Gama played down the value of the Soviet example to Mexico, arguing that "Zapata, through his work, is greater than Lenin himself," he was immediately countered by Ramos Pedrueza, Pavletich, and the Colombian-born *agrarista* Julio Cuadros Caldas.[96] All three compared Mexico's as yet timid agrarian reforms unfavorably with the Soviet regime's success in abolishing the old landowning regime. Cuadros Caldas also noted that Soto y Gama had famously spoken out against the national flag at the Aguascalientes Convention of 1914, in the heat of the Mexican Revolution; he added that "the proletarian world does not recognize borders in its struggle for liberation." Ramos Pedrueza for his part insisted that "at present there are only two flags: that of the stars and stripes which symbolizes exploitation, pillage and oppression; and the red one, symbol of liberty, justice and human fraternity."[97] The congress concluded with a militant expression of class-based internationalism: Delegates sang the "Internationale," which the proceedings described as "the sublime anthem of our class war, which carries within its verses the entire revolutionary dynamic that has shaken the Proletarian World."[98]

In many of the instances discussed in this chapter, internationalism took the form of conceptual connections or expressions of solidarity—seeing similarities in the condition of colonized peoples, making parallels between the Mexican and Russian Revolutions, and seeking allies among the Latin American peasantry. But at times it seemed that transnational connections were expected to provide concrete, practical assistance. In June 1928 a Mexican peasant awaiting execution in Texcoco, fifteen miles northeast of Mexico City, sent a handwritten letter to the Krestintern asking for help. A native of San Mateo Chipiltepec in Mexico State and a member of the peasant league there, Jesús Rojano had been convicted of murdering one of his landlord's hired enforcers. His pleas that he had acted in self-defense fell on deaf ears. Now what would happen to his three children, whose mother had died six years previously? "Which is why I beg of you, esteemed and fine *compañeros*: you who are the model for the entire suffering world, if you can do something for this comrade even though he is far away from you . . . I will thank you."[99]

I have been unable to find out what happened to Jesús Rojano, and to how many other entities he sent similar letters. But the fact that he would turn, in his hour of need, to an organization halfway around the world points to the strength and persistence of Mexico's *campesino* internationalism. In

Rojano's case it was, to be sure, an internationalism born of dire necessity. But a kindred urgency seems to underpin the many varieties of internationalism discussed in this chapter. All were rooted in a shared conviction that the national and international realms were permeable; all shared the hope that faraway agencies might help reshape local fates, and that actions taken here and now might play their part in making the wider world anew.

TWO

Against Empire

LIBERATION'S MARCH

An Indigenous man is breaking free of the chains that bind him.[1] He is wearing a worker's overalls and boots and is striding across a map of Central and South America. Above him, where the United States should be, there is cluster of skyscrapers, from whose serried ranks come yet more chains that stretch southward across Mexico and Cuba to entrap Central and South America too. This image by Xavier Guerrero, a Mexican Communist artist of Indigenous descent, adorns the cover of the first issue of *El Libertador*, published in Mexico City in March 1925 (figure 2).[2] The magazine was the organ of the Liga Antimperialista de las Américas (LADLA; Anti-Imperialist League of the Americas), a movement that would serve as one of the main focal points of anti-imperialist activism in Latin America for the next four years.[3]

Although the process of liberation has begun for the man in Guerrero's drawing, there is clearly a much larger task still in store—and it is one that must be conceived on a planetary scale. The image neatly encapsulates LADLA's distinctive anti-imperialist politics, which produced a remarkable convergence between a diverse range of groups, from Communists to the peasant leagues to Haitian exiles fighting the US occupation of their country. Its ideological range was matched by its sociological and geographical breadth: Headquartered in Mexico City, LADLA came to have branches across much of Latin America and drew support from very different social strata. Perhaps most strikingly, LADLA's anti-imperialism was rooted in a newly global sensibility: It consistently connected Latin America's problems

EL LIBERTADOR

ORGANO DE LA LIGA ANTI-IMPERIALISTA PANAMERICANA

DIBUJO INDIO

TOMO I.   MARZO DE 1925.   NUM. 1.

10   CENTAVOS   ORO   AMERICANO

FIGURE 2. Cover of *El Libertador*, no. 1, March 1925. Courtesy of New York Public Library.

to anti-colonial struggles elsewhere, framing the region's fate in relation to an increasingly interconnected world.

This chapter examines the coalescence of this new anti-imperialism in Mexico in the 1920s, focusing on LADLA and its organ, *El Libertador*. As we have seen in chapter 1, Mexico City at this time was home to a remarkable ferment, in which Mexican peasant activists met with Comintern envoys, and the exiled Peruvians who founded the APRA shared lodgings with Cuban and Venezuelan Communists. Through the PCM's links with the Soviet Union, this diverse set of actors came into contact with anti-colonial activists from China, Southeast Asia, India, and Africa. These encounters nourished a radical internationalism that only heightened the Latin Americans' awareness of the global context in which their local and national struggles were embedded.

By the 1920s, anti-imperialism was not, to be sure, a novelty in Latin America. Ever since independence, the region had proved all too vulnerable to breaches of sovereignty by the US and European colonial powers. The very concept of "Latin" America was forged in the mid-nineteenth century in pan-regional opposition to the looming "Anglo-Saxon" power to the north.[4] Mexico itself had lost a vast swathe of territory to the United States in 1848 and suffered further incursions during the armed phase of its Revolution, prompting anti-imperialist sentiment—directed in particular at US corporations and landowners—to spike to new levels.[5]

But the 1920s iteration of Latin American anti-imperialism broke new ground in its global and systemic understanding of imperialism. Within this broader framework, imperialism was seen as operating simultaneously along a number of axes: political, military, economic, and cultural. While this signaled a need for more complex and subtle analyses, it also meant that there were multiple forms of oppression against which Latin Americans could stand in solidarity. At the same time, the global sensibility underpinning this anti-imperial politics made clear that its project had to look far beyond the confines of any given nation-state. Imperialism's long reach demanded a response on a commensurate scale. For all of the players concerned, the radical internationalism that informed their thinking was also a vital tool for redressing the imbalances of world power.

In what follows, I situate LADLA against the backdrop of anti-imperialist activism in interwar Latin America, recounting LADLA's origins and placing *El Libertador* within Mexico City's radical publishing ecosystem. I then reconstruct LADLA's understanding of imperialism, which linked Latin

America's current subordination both to the colonial oppressions of the past and to the modern-day mechanisms of finance capitalism. After highlighting *El Libertador*'s coverage of struggles elsewhere in the world, I analyze its ambiguous approach to the question of race. Finally, I examine Mexican solidarity efforts with Nicaragua, then under US occupation. These initiatives were a striking success for Mexico City's anti-imperialist milieu, highlighting the broad reach of anti-imperial sentiment.

In its attempt to foster a radical internationalism from below, LADLA was in some respects a forerunner of the transnational solidarities that developed in the era of decolonization, and in particular in the wake of the 1959 Cuban Revolution.[6] Yet I argue here that what was most innovative about LADLA was its attempt to engage with the structural conditions of its own time and to reinvent the left's understanding of Latin America's place in the world in newly global and systemic terms. Its efforts, which grew out of the radical internationalisms described in chapter 1, also laid crucial groundwork for the debates that would grip the radical left in subsequent years, and which form the subject of future chapters.

RADICAL HUBS

Mexico City was not the only place in Latin America that witnessed an upsurge of anti-imperialist activism in the 1920s. A rich variety of organizations and publications emerged in several cities across the region. As well as looking to the Mexican and Russian Revolutions, many of them took inspiration from Argentina's university reform movement of 1918. In Lima, student radicals including Haya de la Torre founded the Universidades Populares González Prada in 1921, aiming to forge links between manual and intellectual laborers. In Havana, the Universidad Popular José Martí, founded in 1923, similarly brought together student federations and the capital's workers. In Buenos Aires, anti-imperialist writers José Ingenieros and Alfredo Palacios founded the Unión Latinoamericana in 1925 to coordinate likeminded intellectuals across the region.[7] In each of these places, a vibrant publishing scene accompanied and amplified these efforts: Lima had the Popular Universities' bulletin and *Claridad*, later joined by the newspaper *Labor* and the seminal journal *Amauta*, both edited by José Carlos Mariátegui; Havana had the student magazine *Juventud* and the anti-imperialist *América Libre*, as well as outlets linked to the labor movement; Buenos

Aires had a plethora of radical newspapers as well as Ingenieros's magazine *Renovación*.

But Mexico City was distinct from the region's other radical hubs in one crucial respect. It was the only place in Latin America where the anti-imperialism of the left found sympathy and even support from within the government. Many of those who had made the Mexican Revolution were deeply committed to anti-imperialist ideas—indeed, they saw the new revolutionary state as a tool for realizing that vision. There was a considerable overlap between Mexican officialdom and the radical anti-imperialist milieu: Secretary of Agriculture Ramón de Negri attended and spoke at anti-imperialist events, state governors such as Adalberto Tejeda of Veracruz subsidized radical publications and conferences, and Mexican diplomats and migration officials smoothed the way for radical exiles to enter the country. For an important section of Mexican state officials, anti-imperialism was congruent with their own agenda.

This created an unusually favorable climate for anti-imperialist politics. As we have seen in chapter 1, Mexico City became a gathering point for exiles from across Latin America, as well as for the Comintern and for anticolonial activists from Asia. M. N. Roy is by far the best known of the latter, but other Indian nationalists such as Heramba Lal Gupta and Pandurang Khankhoje also settled in Mexico in the 1920s and were closely connected with its anti-imperialist milieu.[8] (An agronomist, Khankhoje worked at the new National School of Agriculture in Chapingo, where Diego Rivera painted some of his most celebrated murals in 1926, one of which appears on the cover of this book; a new type of maize Khankhoje developed features in Rivera's work.)

Within the fertile soil of 1920s Mexico, a variety of organizations took up the banner of anti-imperialism. The most prominent were the PCM, the peasant leagues, and APRA, alongside a smaller pan-Latin Americanist outfit called the Unión Centro Sud Americana y de las Antillas (UCSAYA; Central South American and Antillean Union), set up in Mexico in 1927 by the Venezuelan Carlos León and the Argentine Alejandro Maudet.[9] Also present were Haitian exiles such as the brothers Charles and Pierre Moravia Morpeau and Joseph Jolibois (fils) of the Union Patriotique d'Haiti (UPH; Haitian Patriotic Union), who tried to rally opposition to the US occupation of their country.[10] But the key organization was the one in which all of these groups at different times converged and collaborated: LADLA.

Founded in late 1924, LADLA was initially based at Calle Bolívar 55 in Mexico City's historic center—next door to the house shared by Julio Antonio Mella and other radical exiles—before moving two blocks east, to Calle República de El Salvador 94, in 1928. Although it was created at the instigation of the Communists, LADLA drew in people from across the anti-imperial milieu and had a cross-class social profile, attracting workers, peasants, middle-class professionals, and members of the bourgeoisie alike. It also had a disproportionately strong cultural presence thanks to the involvement of artists such as Xavier Guerrero, Diego Rivera, and David Alfaro Siqueiros. A final notable feature of LADLA was its thoroughgoing transnationalism: Its organizational mechanisms and political agenda leapfrogged national frontiers, as did many of its key personnel. Starting in 1925, LADLA sections were set up in one country after another, from Argentina to Puerto Rico.

LADLA's origins reflect this deeply transnational character. The idea that Communists should seek to form a cross-class anti-imperialist movement was integral to the Comintern's global strategy in the early 1920s, as it sought to undermine the grip of the Great Powers on their colonies and open the way for the worldwide spread of revolution. This would require some compromises, however. In June 1920 the Comintern's Second Congress adopted its "Theses on National and Colonial Questions," which insisted that "all Communist parties must assist the bourgeois-democratic liberation movement in [colonial] countries."[11] This approach, known as the United Front strategy, was first put into action in China, where in 1923 the Chinese Communist Party embedded itself within the much larger nationalist KMT. Keen to see this model replicated elsewhere, for several years the Comintern instructed its affiliates to make anti-imperialist alliances with forces that would in other circumstances be deemed class adversaries.

Although Latin American countries were formally independent, the Comintern viewed them as part of the "semi-colonial" world.[12] Like China, they too were subject to the economic and military dominance of outside powers. Mexico's Communists certainly saw the parallel: In October 1924, *El Machete* ran an article on China subtitled "The[ir] Situation Is Notably Similar to Ours."[13] This same article also contained the first reference made in Latin America to "anti-imperialist leagues," referring to their formation in China thanks to growing resentment of outside interference in Chinese affairs.

But while Comintern strategy and China's newly formed leagues were part of LADLA's formative matrix, the immediate spur for founding an equivalent organization in Mexico was much closer to hand. It lay in Communist attempts to counter the influence of the Pan-American Federation of Labor. This had been founded in 1918 under the auspices of the American Federation of Labor (AFL) and the Confederación Regional Obrera Mexicana (CROM; Mexican Regional Workers' Confederation), both of which the Communists saw as collaborationist. The Pan-American Federation was due to hold its congress in Mexico City in December 1924, which the PCM saw as an attempt by the US labor establishment to extend its influence over Latin America. In the run-up to the December congress, *El Machete* published several articles criticizing AFL leader Samuel Gompers for helping to tamp down labor unrest in the United States and for backing US military interventions across Latin America.[14]

It was in this context that LADLA made its first appearance. Just days after the Pan-American Federation of Labor congress opened, *El Machete* published two manifestos signed by the "Pan-American Anti-Imperialist League" (as we will see, the organization's name would soon change).[15] The first manifesto is addressed to Chilean and Peruvian workers, urging them to set aside their differences over the disputed territories of Tacna and Arica in the name of anti-imperial solidarity. The second is addressed to delegates at the Pan-American Federation congress, urging them not to reelect Gompers as the federation's head. (Gompers was reelected but died only a few days later; thereafter the influence of the Pan-American Federation of Labor declined.)

In early 1925 the new anti-imperialist organization acquired a secretariat. Its original composition reflected LADLA's transnational blend of influences: It included Rafael Carrillo, general secretary of the PCM; the US Communists Bertram and Ella Wolfe; and Pestkovsky, the Soviet ambassador.[16] While the PCM provided a lot of LADLA's key personnel, the US Communist Party furnished basic financial resources, and the Comintern mainly supplied ideological guidance. In its early stages, this triangle of PCM, Comintern, and US Communist Party produced some awkward tensions, which surfaced in debates over LADLA's name and base of operations. At the PCM congress in April 1925, Mexican party members objected to the term "Pan-American," which they would have associated with US government-led regional initiatives. The US Communist Party delegates in attendance conceded that the label might give rise to "possible misinterpretations."[17] Four months after making its debut, the Pan-American Anti-Imperialist League acquired a less compromised name with the same hemispheric sweep: the Anti-Imperialist League of the Americas.

But while the question of LADLA's name was quickly settled, there were still arguments over financial resources and where the organization would formally be based. The Mexicans insisted that it should be headquartered in Mexico City, but US Communist Party delegate Charles Phillips—then operating under the pseudonym "Manuel Gómez"—rejected the idea, preferring the US party's stronghold of Chicago. In mid-1926 the Comintern intervened, tilting the scales toward the Mexicans. Edgar Woog, aka "Stirner," had been closely involved with the PCM during two spells as Comintern envoy in Mexico in 1919–20 and 1921–22. Now working in the Comintern apparatus in Moscow, he resolved the dispute over LADLA's headquarters once and for all. On principle, he wrote, "the center for Latin America should always be ... in that Latin American country which is, for the moment, the center of resistance to American imperialism in Latin America."[18] This was a strong endorsement of Mexico's postrevolutionary status as a hub for radical organizing. By early 1926 LADLA's Mexican Secretariat had indeed become the center of an anti-imperialist network that stretched to Argentina, Brazil, Colombia, Cuba, Ecuador, Puerto Rico, and Venezuela. By November of that year, LADLA also had a presence in the Dominican Republic, El Salvador, Honduras, Peru, and Uruguay.[19]

In arguing for Mexico City as the preferred base for LADLA, Stirner made a distinction between the goals of anti-imperialist organizing in the United States and in Latin America. In the latter, the aim was "to organize a movement against imperialism of the United States and ... rally all elements," drawing on different social classes. In the United States itself, however, the focus was more specifically on the working class: "We aim to awaken the workers to the menace of imperialism." He summed up the difference in a striking contrast: "Our work in Latin America centers around nationalism; our work in the United States around internationalism."[20] Stirner's analysis echoed the Comintern's strategy of supporting nationalist forces in the colonial and "semicolonial" world. But his identification of Latin American anti-imperialist organizing with "nationalism" tout court underplayed the many kinds of internationalism that went into it.

LADLA's own composition and activities were examples of the rich interactions between national and international frames.

Each of the political currents within LADLA contributed something valuable and different. The Communists provided LADLA's core staff and publicized its events to the PCM's base. Although the party only had a few hundred members at this point, it had a strong presence among artisans and manual workers in the capital and other industrial centers, as well as among railway workers. Communism also linked LADLA to the Latin American exile milieu, which included many of the organizers most closely involved in the league: The Cuban Julio Antonio Mella and the Venezuelans Salvador de la Plaza and Gustavo Machado all joined the PCM upon arriving in Mexico while still maintaining ties with organizations back home. Their displacement was, in a sense, one of the means through which LADLA extended its geographical reach. Just as Mella had cofounded a Cuban exile organization, the ANERC, de la Plaza and Machado similarly established the Partido Revolucionario Venezolano (PRV; Venezuelan Revolutionary Party) in the Mexican capital; both organizations worked closely with LADLA.

The same exile milieu supplied many of LADLA's non-Communist personnel. The Peruvian APRA members Jacobo Hurwitz, Esteban Pavletich, and Nicolás Terreros, all of whom arrived in Mexico in 1926, each collaborated with LADLA in different ways: Pavletich and Terreros wrote for its magazine, *El Libertador*, while Hurwitz was an integral member of the editorial team and later joined LADLA's secretariat. Whereas the Communist Party supplied LADLA with a connection to parts of the working class, APRA was a bridge to middle-class anti-imperialist sentiment. Haya de la Torre developed close relationships with Mexican government officials and, through sympathetic journalists such as the Honduran Rafael Heliodoro Valle, with major newspapers such as *Excélsior*. These connections gave APRA a public platform out of proportion to its actual size, enabling Haya and other *apristas* to convey their anti-imperialist message to an audience beyond the left. LADLA benefited from this extended reach, gaining regular coverage of its events and solidarity campaigns.

Other figures from Mexico City's exile milieu joined forces with LADLA. Members of the Central American outfit UCSAYA, the Haitians of the Union Patriotique, and the Spanish anticlerical activist Belén de Sárraga, for example, all spoke at LADLA events, each advancing their causes under the common umbrella of anti-imperialism.[21] Non-Communist labor unions and student federations also affiliated with LADLA, helping it broaden its sociological scope.

But the most numerically significant political current within LADLA was the peasant leagues. By the mid-1920s, as we have seen, they had some two hundred thousand members across several states, and the leagues' territorial spread helped LADLA establish chapters in many parts of Mexico, from Sonora, Chihuahua, Nuevo León, and Tamaulipas in the north to Michoacán, Chiapas, and Oaxaca in the south.[22] The symbolic importance of the peasant component to LADLA is underlined by the fact that Veracruz peasant leader Úrsulo Galván was listed as the first editor of LADLA's magazine, *El Libertador*.

ANTI-IMPERIAL BULLETINS

More than a platform for expressing LADLA's views, *El Libertador* was a vital organizing tool in its own right. Given the movement's social breadth and ideological heterogeneity, the magazine was the place where LADLA could most regularly and clearly articulate its shared ideas, and where it could announce and report back on its events and campaigns. A closer look at the magazine therefore allows us to map out LADLA's thinking and capture what was distinctive about its version of anti-imperialism.

In January 1925, Bertram Wolfe wrote to the US Communist Party from Mexico City announcing plans to launch an "anti-imperialist bulletin for the Latin-American countries." It would be, Wolfe said, "a bulletin of complete Marxist orientation but we shall ask the collaboration of leading left liberals and socialists." The aim was "to give the bulletin a wider circulation and to use it in the building of a mass movement against imperialism."[23] When *El Libertador*'s first issue appeared in March 1925, Wolfe was not publicly named on the masthead: Galván was credited as the editor and muralist Xavier Guerrero as administrator. Wolfe had good reason to tread carefully: under Article 33 of the Mexican Constitution, foreigners could be expelled for intervening in Mexican politics, and that June, Wolfe and his wife were indeed deported to the United States.[24] But over the next few years, *El Libertador* met the goals Wolfe had set. By 1928 it had a print run of five thousand copies, and each issue, usually no more than sixteen pages in length, conveyed a strongly Marxist analysis of imperialism while drawing in a range of non-Communist collaborators.[25]

A country-by-country list of contributors included in the June 1927 issue reads like a global anti-imperialist *Who's Who*.[26] It includes José Carlos Mariátegui in Peru; the Argentine socialist Alfredo Palacios; Cuban leftists such as the poet Rubén Martínez Villena and the historian Emilio Roig de Leuchsenring; Puerto Rican nationalist leader Pedro Albizu Campos; Brazilian Communist Octávio Brandão; from the United States, writers such as Upton Sinclair, Carleton Beals, Scott Nearing and Samuel Inman; and from Europe, writer Henry Barbusse, philosopher Bertrand Russell, and Soviet Commissar of Enlightenment Anatoly Lunacharsky. Among the Mexican authors there were the diplomat Jesús Silva Herzog and the former education minister José Vasconcelos, as well as the muralist José Clemente Orozco. Many of those listed under their countries of origin were actually based in Mexico City at the time, including the Venezuelans de la Plaza and Gustavo Machado, and the Peruvians Pavletich, Hurwitz, and Terreros.

From the outset, *El Libertador* positioned itself as part of a broader anti-imperialist ferment. Its opening editorial noted that it was "not the first magazine against North American imperialism," listing a string of Latin American writers who had already taken up the cause. What they had sown was "now beginning to sprout, and its fruit is: 'organization.'" In pursuit of that goal, *El Libertador* announced that "it will not close its columns to any genuinely anti-imperialist tendency nor open them to any contrary tendency." The magazine was also avowedly global, promising to cover anti-imperialist developments in Russia, China, Persia, Morocco, Egypt, and India, as well as in Latin America and the United States.[27]

LADLA's magazine was part of a whole ecosystem of radical publishing in Mexico at the time. Many of the currents that converged in LADLA had their own outlets: The Veracruz Peasant League had a newspaper, *La Voz del Campesino* (The voice of the peasant), and in 1928 APRA's Mexico City cell—founded by Pavletich, Hurwitz, and Terreros shortly after their arrival in 1926—launched a magazine titled *Indoamérica*. The Venezuelans had their own organ, *Libertad*, as did the exiled Cubans of ANERC, titled *Cuba Libre*. Mainstream Mexican newspapers such as *Excélsior*, *El Demócrata*, and later *El Nacional* offered space to views from the anti-imperialist left and regularly covered LADLA demonstrations. Haitian activist Joseph Jolibois may have been exaggerating slightly when he wrote to a friend in Port-au-Prince in 1928 that "each one of our articles is communicated to about fifty newspapers in [the] Mexican Republic." But his sense of connection to a broader community is evident: "You have no idea of the struggle here," he wrote, adding, "The work is colossal."[28]

The network of radical publications extended far beyond Mexico, connecting LADLA with other anti-imperial hubs across the Americas. In 1926, *El Libertador* ran a list of magazines and journals with which it exchanged copies; they ranged from Communist newspapers and literary magazines in Buenos Aires to *The Nation* in New York, and from Lima's anarchist paper *La Protesta* to the organ of Havana's KMT chapter, *Man Sen Yat Po* (People's voice daily).[29] This continent-spanning network acted as a relay system for anti-imperialist content. *El Libertador's* first issue announced a version of what would today be called "copyleft": Any of the magazine's contents could be freely reproduced without permission, as long as the original source was credited.[30] Expressing the sentiment behind such practices, in 1926 Haya wrote to a fellow Peruvian exile that "it doesn't matter if you repeat yourself," adding that "on the contrary, you must repeat yourself a great deal.... But you have to write."[31] Within Latin America's broader anti-imperial ecosystem, repetition was cross-fertilization, as what would otherwise be rival tendencies shared space, personnel, and ideas to boost their collective chances.

DEFINING THE DANGER

"A danger threatens Latin America," warned *El Libertador's* opening editorial. From north to south, it said, the United States "slowly and silently continues on its way to Tierra del Fuego, buying and nullifying, fomenting and destroying; doing as it pleases across two entire continents."[32] For the region's radicals, there was no question that the power of the United States represented the greatest threat to their countries' well-being. Latin Americans had long been painfully aware of Washington's reach, from the abuses of filibusters such as William Walker, who in 1856 invaded Nicaragua and briefly made himself the country's president, to the enshrining of the Platt Amendment in Cuba's 1901 Constitution, giving the United States an open-ended right to intervene in the island's affairs. US dominance was therefore central both to Latin Americans' understanding of what imperialism was and to their visions of resistance to it.

The idea that the region should unite in the face of the challenge from the North had been a recurrent dream, from Simón Bolívar's proposals for a pan-regional confederation onward. Mexico City's anti-imperial milieu of the 1920s certainly saw themselves as part of this broader tradition: *El Libertador* was named after Bolívar and headquartered on the street that bore his name. In April 1926 the magazine reinforced the connection by issuing a call for a "Bolivarian Congress" of Latin American anti-imperialists, to be held in Panama on the hundredth anniversary of a gathering at which Bolívar had hoped in vain to forge pan-regional unity.[33] But LADLA and its allies added two novel elements to their definition of imperialism: They extended their geographical horizons to encompass European empires in Africa and Asia, and they developed a materialist analysis of US power as part of a global capitalist system.

It's not difficult to see why US interference in Latin American affairs would loom especially large in the 1920s. *El Libertador*'s opening editorial listed a string of places that the United States had militarily occupied or intervened in since the turn of the century—"Cuba, Panama, Haiti, Santo Domingo, Nicaragua, Veracruz"—describing them as "successive steps in the agony of a continent." It was Nicaragua, as we shall see, that consumed the lion's share of LADLA's attention and solidarity. But *El Libertador* also condemned the US occupation of Haiti, underway since 1915, denouncing the occupying authorities' closure of schools and muzzling of the press and assailing US violations of Haitian sovereignty.[34] And as noted earlier, Joseph Jolibois of the UPH spoke at several LADLA events.[35]

But Washington exerted its sway in many other forms besides the use of military force. As *El Libertador*'s opening editorial noted, "Uncle Sam supports autocracies," enabling the kinds of repression meted out by Gerardo Machado in Cuba and Juan Vicente Gómez in Venezuela. The magazine carried several items denouncing Gómez's rule and characterized Peruvian strongman Augusto Leguía as an "instrument of imperialism."[36] Machado was a special target for Mexico City's anti-imperialists, mainly thanks to the presence of so many radical Cuban exiles—Mella foremost among them. It was Mella's prolific writings that contributed most centrally to the image of Machado as a "tropical Mussolini."[37] The October 1926 issue of *El Libertador* ran an itemized list Mella had drawn up of Machado's many abuses of power, from the undemocratic manner of his ascent to his suppression of the labor movement.[38]

For radical anti-imperialists, Latin America's tyrants were only the local representatives of a much larger set of forces. As Mella explained in June 1925, the likes of Machado and Gómez were not simply allies of Washington but also "henchmen" of United Fruit and other US companies, and their grip on power was motivated by the need to keep profits flowing into those companies' coffers. In Cuba itself, he asked, "Haven't the magnates of Washington and Wall Street always imposed on us the president that suited their interests?" Hadn't these same distant forces blocked progressive change by insisting that "they would not recognize any revolutionary government. . . until it paid homage to the lords of sugar and petroleum?"[39]

For Mella, it was the financial power of the dollar that made US imperialism distinct from its historical predecessors. "Yankee dominance in the Americas is not like the old Roman dominance through military conquest," he argued; nor was it like British imperialism, which he defined as "imperial commercial dominance disguised as Home Rule." US power instead took the form of "absolute economic domination with political guarantees when they are necessary"—meaning treaty obligations such as the Platt Amendment.[40] The tight political constraints that US dominance imposed on Cuba were central to Mella's description of his countrymen as "a people that has never been free." But other Latin American countries faced similar barriers. An item in *El Libertador*'s first issue described Mexico as all but a US colony, detailing the scale of US investments across its economy and observing that even after the Revolution, "Mexican politics depends on the interests of Yankee capitalists."[41] A short notice in the same issue asserted that "the first duty of a Latin American government seems to be that of satisfying North American bankers. Its last duty is . . . the same."[42]

Mexico City's anti-imperialists were expressing a familiar idea here, articulated many times in Latin America and beyond: Political independence needed to be accompanied by economic sovereignty to have any real purchase. What was new was the link they made between this recurring concept and a systemic critique of capitalism. It was not simply that Latin American states had fallen short of attaining full sovereignty due to interference from their stronger neighbor to the north; it was the mechanism of capitalist exploitation that tied their countries into this subordinate relation to the United States. In other words, US hemispheric dominance was inseparable from the global dominance of capitalism. Mella expressed this entwinement when he argued that most of Latin America was not free because "it belongs to the only State, the only Power, that absorbs all the others: the United States of Wall Street."[43]

Other contributions to *El Libertador* underscored the reach of US finance: Translations of texts by US leftists Scott Nearing and Samuel Inman analyzed Wall Street's dominance of the Caribbean and examined the role of the dollar in cementing US influence over the region.[44] This same financial power oppressed US workers, too, which was why Mella elsewhere urged that "we must form one single army of all those exploited by Wall Street."[45] *El Libertador*'s opening editorial similarly emphasized that ordinary people in Latin America and the United States were up against "a monster with two heads"—one named "Imperialism," sowing devastation in Latin America, and the other named "Capitalism," besetting workers and small farmers in the United States.[46]

To be sure, Wall Street was not the only financial center to exert its influence over Latin America. Several contributions to *El Libertador* took up the role of British banks in the region, for example detailing the investments of London's financial houses in Argentina and Chile.[47] Yet British capital was losing ground to US interests everywhere, and in the wake of the First World War, the United States was taking over as the world's dominant power. An "Anti-Imperialist Balance Sheet" published in *El Libertador*'s January 1926 issue included a diagram of the new global hierarchy: a pyramid with the United States on top and states such as the United Kingdom, France, and Japan below it as "second-class powers," followed by "semi-colonial countries" and regions such as Latin America, China, and Persia, with colonized countries at the bottom.[48]

Within this new world order, the tasks of resistance to US power and opposition to global capitalism were more closely aligned than ever. According to Mella, the outlines of a future world empire were already taking shape through intergovernmental summits and the financial sway of Wall Street. The ideal of Latin American unity once expounded by Bolívar was no longer an abstract, literary fantasy: "The unity of the Americas has already been realized by U.S. imperialism." What was needed was a counterproject of true unity, forged from below "by the revolutionary forces that are enemies of international capitalism: workers, peasants, the indigenous, students and vanguard intellectuals."[49]

Mella's list of potential revolutionary forces showcased the convergence of different radical traditions. It brought together the proletarians of Marxist doctrine with the peasant and Indigenous masses so recently mobilized, for example, during the Mexican Revolution, while maintaining a key role for students and intellectuals, categories that included many of Mella's comrades in Havana and Mexico City. The hemispheric unity he advocated was only one component, however, of a global contest that pitted "capitalism the exploiter with multiple masks" against "the exploited people who have begun different struggles with different nuances." In colonial countries these took the form of rebellions against the metropolitan power, while in the metropoles the oppressed faced off against their own capitalists. Latin Americans, according to Mella, had to do battle both with local tyrants and with "the common metropole which is politically located in Washington."[50]

This sense of a single but differentiated struggle was crucial to LADLA's anti-imperialism. While opposition to US dominance in Latin America was the guiding theme of its activism, LADLA saw that dominance as a regional manifestation of a single, global system. As an item in the October 1925 issue noted, "Of the 111,500,000 square miles that constitute the surface of the globe, 75,000,000 are colonies, protectorates, occupied regions or 'spheres of influence.' Of the 1,750,000 inhabitants of the world, 1,250,000 live in colonial and semi-colonial countries."[51] This view of imperial domination as a shared global condition was the foundation for the connections LADLA constantly drew between Latin America's situation and struggles unfolding elsewhere.

GLOBAL HORIZONS

The scope of *El Libertador*'s coverage reflects this global framing. Though Latin America was the main topic of most of the items it ran, its horizons stretched from the Americas to Africa to East Asia. It devoted attention to the Filipino struggle for independence from US rule, lamenting the fact that Latin America and the Philippines were linked not only by a shared Spanish colonial heritage but by a common subjugation in the present.[52] With regard to North Africa, *El Libertador* foregrounded the rebellion in the Rif, featuring a portrait of its leader Abd el-Krim on the cover of the October 1925 issue and running articles by Haya de la Torre and Carrillo condemning the combined Spanish–French counterinsurgency operations.[53] It also covered anti-imperialist activism in the metropoles, reprinting a 1925 resolution by British trade unionists condemning the Labour government's imperialist policies in India, Egypt, South Africa, and elsewhere.[54]

Within *El Libertador*'s global frame, one recurrent focus of attention was China. In a dozen issues between July 1925 and August 1927, the magazine devoted six articles to the country, as well as making repeated references to it in items on other topics.[55] In the mid-1920s, Communists across the world were deeply invested in China's fate, in part thanks to the Comintern's endorsement of the KMT as a standard-bearer for colonial liberation. As Mella put it in a 1926 article, "For all colonial and semi-colonial peoples the Chinese Revolution is an example and a hope."[56] We have seen in the previous chapter how Haya de la Torre often compared his APRA movement to the Chinese Nationalists, even labeling it a "Latin American Kuomintang."[57] Indeed, while Communists often held up the USSR as a model for revolutionary transformation, both they and other Latin American radicals saw China as more directly sharing many of their region's structural characteristics: In both cases, a largely rural population was simultaneously facing off against imperial powers and local elites.

The connections Mexico City's anti-imperialists made between Latin America's struggles and those elsewhere were more than conceptual. An opportunity to give practical substance to their global framing came with the Congress against Colonial Oppression and Imperialism, held in Brussels in February 1927.[58] The gathering had been organized by the League Against Colonial Oppression, formed in late 1926 at the instigation of the Comintern and led from Berlin by Willi Münzenberg.[59] Some of the anti-imperialists who had been attracted to LADLA were also involved in the organizing committee for this league, including the Mexican ambassador to Germany, Ramón de Negri.[60] In Mexico City, *El Libertador* and *El Machete* published advance notices about the Congress, less to promote attendance—it would have been prohibitively expensive for their readers to make the journey to Europe—than to highlight the significance of a meeting that promised to connect disparate realms of anti-colonial struggle.[61]

In Brussels, European delegates dominated numerically for obvious reasons: There were twenty-three French delegates and close to twenty delegates each from Germany and England, plus eight from Holland.[62] But China and India were strongly represented, with seventeen and thirteen delegates respectively. The KMT and its branches outside China accounted for most of the Chinese delegation, while India's delegation was led by Indian National Congress envoy Jawaharlal Nehru, later the first prime minister of independent India. There were handfuls of delegates each from the United States, the Dutch East Indies, Korea, Vietnam, South Africa, and Italy, and one or two each from a scattering of countries in North and West Africa and the Middle East.

Within this global array of delegates, Latin America as a region was among the most strongly represented, with nineteen delegates. This included five representing Mexican organizations, five doing the same for Puerto

Rico, and others representing Colombia, Cuba, Peru, Central America, and Venezuela.[63] Strikingly, many of these delegates were based in Mexico City, once again underlining its status as an anti-imperial hub. Alongside Mella as LADLA delegate were representatives of Mexico's National Peasant League, the CROM, and the Mexican student federation. More surprisingly, Mexican delegates also represented organizations with which they seemingly had little connection: Former Secretary of Education José Vasconcelos represented the Puerto Rican Nationalist Party, and revolutionary general Juan Andreu Almazán signed the Congress's resolutions on behalf of the Haitian League of the Rights of Man and of the Citizen.[64] These men likely assumed these roles because of the logistical and financial difficulties delegates from Puerto Rico and Haiti would have faced in getting to Brussels. But these apparent incongruities also reflect Mexico's role on the international stage: As prominent figures from a revolutionary state, Vasconcelos and Almazán felt they could claim to stand for the broader cause of Latin American anti-imperialism.

In June 1927, *El Libertador* devoted almost an entire issue to resolutions from the Brussels Congress. The manifesto adopted there denounced the "exploitation, forced labor, undisguised slavery, annihilation of cultures, of civilizations" that had accompanied—indeed enabled—the rise of first the European imperial powers and then the United States.[65] It linked that process to the expansion of capitalism, a "system, cruel and barbaric, which has now reached its highest degree of perfection." This latest stage involved a hierarchy of domination that took various forms: "from simple *de facto* control to veiled forms of dependence, from the most absolute and most basic slavery to . . . traditional forms of medieval feudalism and personal subjection."[66] The Congress's conception of imperialism as a global, ramified system closely matched LADLA's view. Crucially, the idea that imperialism affected both formally colonized countries and de jure sovereign states—independent but still subject to "veiled forms of dependence"—was what enabled the Brussels Congress and LADLA to link Latin America's anti-imperialist impulses to struggles elsewhere. The Congress's resolution on Latin America referred to "an awakening of national revolutionary consciousness" in the Americas and observed that "all the other peoples who struggle against imperialism: China, India, Egypt, are struggling against our common enemy."[67]

El Libertador's coverage of the Brussels Congress also sheds light on LADLA's complex and largely unarticulated relationship to the question of race. One of the few items it ran that was framed in explicitly racial terms was a translation of the Brussels Congress's "Resolution on the Black Question," which appeared in its June 1927 issue.[68] This was a landmark document, highlighting the depth of racialized oppression in Africa and beyond and making several concrete demands of European colonial powers: African control of African land and administration, a free press, the right to assembly, abolition of military service.[69] But it also called for "the emancipation of the black peoples of the world." This broader agenda involved not only the elimination of social, economic, and political restrictions and the establishment of racial equality; the resolution also called for "full and absolute independence" for Latin American countries with substantial Black populations: Haiti, Cuba, the Dominican Republic, and Puerto Rico.[70] The implication here was that, for these countries as for colonized territories in Africa, the realization of sovereignty would in itself constitute a step toward Black liberation. This was an important precursor to the ideas about self-determination that the Communist movement would begin to adopt only a year later (I discuss these in subsequent chapters).

Yet even as the Brussels resolution put forward this expansive global program of liberation, it added a startling caveat when it came to Latin America. With the exceptions of Cuba and Panama, where US occupations had "transplanted the barbaric customs" of the occupiers, it argued that "in Latin America . . . blacks do not suffer under the yoke of any special oppression."[71] Denials of this kind would recur frequently in Latin American discussions about race, even cropping up in the Communist debates I address in chapter 5.

A different ambiguity in LADLA's approach to race surfaced in its handling of Indigenous peoples. On the one hand, LADLA seemed to reject the very concept of race as a pseudoscientific distraction. An item in *El Libertador*'s first issue, titled "Enough of 'Races,'" dismissed the idea of superior and inferior races as an invention of so-called men of "science" and argued forcefully against any racialized conception of Latin America's struggle against imperialism.[72] A second article by the same pseudonymous author observed that, despite the scientific pretenses of those using racial categories, basic information on the Indigenous was lacking: "Data: there are none. No statistics either."[73] The author argued that racialized pseudo-science should not blind the left to its real adversaries, who should be identified in class terms: The enemy was not "the Anglo-Saxon race" but "the North American banker."[74]

On the other hand, the items *El Libertador* ran about Indigenous peoples consistently identified them as a coherent racial category, contradicting the earlier dismissal of race. The same author who had written "Enough of 'Races'" simultaneously argued that "the Indian" should form the basis of the anti-imperialist movement in Latin America as a whole, viewing the Indigenous as a collective subject that could be roused to action in the same way as colonized peoples elsewhere.[75] According to that author, the way to secure the support of the Indigenous was to organize them in agrarian leagues; he clearly had the example of Mexico's peasant *ligas* in mind. The author also stressed the need to "re-establish their culture" by educating them in their own languages—a demand that, as we will see in subsequent chapters, ran directly counter to the strongly assimilationist policies of the Mexican government of the time.

The idea that the Indigenous as such could be crucial political actors would be most forcefully articulated two years later by José Carlos Mariátegui (see chapter 5). But even then, this stance remained highly contested within the Communist movement. For APRA, too, the exact role of the Indigenous remained fuzzy at best; despite APRA's vaunting of the "Indo-American" label, the Indigenous component of their agenda was largely an abstract proposition, geared more toward asserting a shared non-European identity than to opening the way for Indigenous political action. For Haya de la Torre, the fate of the Indigenous was only one aspect of the broader anti-imperial struggle. In a May 1927 letter to the literary Grupo Resurgimiento in Cuzco, Haya argued that the oppression of the Indigenous had a systemic character, and that therefore "the indigenous problem cannot be separated from imperialism." For that reason, as he saw it, the Indigenous question was "eminently international."[76]

Framing the Indigenous question in transnational rather than national terms was a highly characteristic move for Mexico City's anti-imperialist milieu. Yet while this may have enabled activists and thinkers to make connections between local and global struggles more readily, it came at the cost of conceptual clarity about the categories that were being distantly conjoined. As we will see in chapter 3, once they started to look more closely at these ambiguities, stark differences of opinion began to emerge. But in the meantime, there were still powerful points of convergence, and none more so than Nicaragua.

"HANDS OFF!"

The Nicaragua solidarity campaign was the major success story of anti-imperialist organizing in late 1920s Mexico. US troops had occupied the country from 1912 to 1925, returning a year later to shield local elites from a rebellion led by Augusto Sandino. The six-year pacification campaign that followed became what an embedded *New York Times* correspondent called a "practical laboratory" for the development of aerial warfare, as US Marines burned villages and crops and dive-bombed civilian populations.[77] This brutal campaign met with broad condemnation across Latin America and from across a large part of the political spectrum.[78] In Mexico, pro-Sandino sentiment was strong, and the Calles government's covert support for the rebels added further strains to already tense diplomatic relations with the United States.[79]

For Mexico City's anti-imperialists, Nicaragua became the object of a broad and urgent consensus. Opposition to the US occupation brought a range of organizations together around a clear and morally compelling agenda, providing an immediate focus for solidarity efforts. *El Machete* carried running commentary on events in Nicaragua, publishing dispatches from the front lines and splashing Sandino's military successes across its front page.[80] It even printed a *corrido* in honor of the Nicaraguan resistance: "This is the story of Nicaragua / the weak and unhappy nation / where the Yankees with their squadrons / have brought crime and dishonor."[81]

El Libertador covered Nicaragua from early on, condemning the US occupation as it ended in 1925.[82] After US troops were redeployed against Sandino in 1926, the volume of coverage increased, and as the second occupation ground on and resistance to it stubbornly continued, Nicaragua came to dominate the magazine as a whole, accounting for a sizeable share of each issue. From 1928 onward, in the space of only eight issues *El Libertador* published more than twenty items about the country. These ranged in length and genre, from reportage to documents to appeals for funds. To cite just a few examples, the magazine translated Carleton Beals's profile of Sandino and ran dispatches from the front lines—LADLA members Gustavo Machado and Esteban Pavletich both traveled to Nicaragua to join

Sandino's forces for a time—as well as publishing Sandino's correspondence with Henri Barbusse.[83]

Alongside this extensive coverage, LADLA organized a string of Nicaragua solidarity events. This included an "anti-imperialist week" in Mexico City at the end of June 1925 that culminated in a mass meeting on July 4.[84] That gathering was addressed by speakers including the PCM's David Alfaro Siqueiros, who denounced "imperialist attacks" on Haiti, Nicaragua, China, and Russia—again linking Latin American struggles to a global agenda. In 1926, LADLA organized two "Grand Anti-Imperialist Rallies" in Mexico City in June and December, at both of which Nicaragua featured prominently.[85] A poster for the December event listed an organizing committee that, besides LADLA, included the National Peasant League, the local KMT branch, and trade unions of railroad workers, carpenters, textile workers, and students.[86]

The pace of solidarity efforts picked up dramatically after January 1928, with the formation of the Comité Manos Fuera de Nicaragua (Hands Off Nicaragua Committee), known as Mafuenic.[87] A crucial figure in pulling Mafuenic together was the Swiss Communist Fritz Sulzbachner, commonly known as Federico Bach.[88] He arrived in Mexico in the summer of 1927 as an envoy from the League Against Imperialism, the name assumed by Münzenberg's League Against Colonial Oppression immediately after the Brussels Congress. Bach joined LADLA's Continental Organizing Committee and immediately took a very active part in setting its priorities. On January 10, 1928, he wrote to Münzenberg announcing Mafuenic's foundation earlier that week.[89] As Bach described it, the organization had a dual aim: to gather funds to pay for medical and other supplies for Sandino's army and to raise awareness of the resistance through public meetings and propaganda work.

LADLA hosted Mafuenic at its new headquarters at Calle República de El Salvador 94 (figure 3). While Bach may have helped catalyze Mafuenic's formation, the day-to-day work of running the organization fell to its general secretary, the Peruvian *aprista* Jacobo Hurwitz. His fellow *aprista* Nicolás Terreros was also centrally involved, speaking at several Mafuenic events. Communists such as Mella, Diego Rivera, and Gustavo Machado were on the organizing committee, and members of the peasant leagues, including Úrsulo Galván, also played a prominent part.

Mafuenic quickly gained visibility, partly because it could draw on the personnel and networks not only of the PCM and the peasant leagues, but also of other organizations linked to LADLA, from unions to anticlerical

FIGURE 3. Hands Off Nicaragua Committee, Mexico City. Photograph by Tina Modotti, 1928. From Library of Congress.

groups and Socorro Rojo Internacional (SRI; International Red Aid), the Mexican branch of the Comintern's organization for assisting political prisoners. There were also representatives of exile groups such the Haitian Patriotic Union and UCSAYA. Members of each of these organizations took part in Mafuenic meetings or spoke at its rallies, as well as raising the issue of Nicaragua within their own settings, creating a feedback loop that heightened awareness among the rank and file.

Perhaps most crucially, the Mexican public was from the outset receptive to Mafuenic's message. Pro-Sandino sentiment was widespread, extending far beyond the radical left to encompass the mainstream press and officials in the Calles government. Mexican newspapers regularly covered Sandino's military successes and Nicaragua solidarity meetings in Mexico itself.[90] On January 8, 1928, *Excélsior* referred to a "continental clamor" to end the killing in Nicaragua, and it kept returning to the theme in the run-up to the Pan-American Conference, an intergovernmental meeting held in Havana from January 16 to February 20, 1928. Its editorials hoped that Latin

FIGURE 4. Flyer for Mafuenic, 1928. From National Archives and Record Administration, RG 59, 810.43 Anti-Imperialistic [sic] League.

American governments would take a stand on Nicaragua at the summit, as well as pressing for a broader commitment to nonintervention; but both aspirations were dashed.[91]

Mafuenic was strikingly successful in focusing pro-Sandino sentiment on both a national and a local scale. By early February, only weeks after the organization was created in Mexico City, there was a branch in Jalisco; others soon followed in Monterrey, Puebla, Veracruz, Tampico, Ciudad Victoria, Pachuca, Durango, and Oaxaca.[92] On February 11 and 12, the fledgling organization announced two "Mafuenic days" for the collection of funds; a flyer advertising the action featured a plane dropping bombs out of a crimson sky onto rolling Nicaraguan hills and exhorted readers to remember the "massacres of Chinandega, Ocotal and Chipote" (see figure 4), in which US Marines had attacked Sandino's forces by air and on the ground.[93] An event held at the Teatro Virginia Fábregas in the capital on April 4, 1928—only two months after Mafuenic was launched—drew five thousand people.[94]

Several more events were held in Mexico City, under the watchful eyes of both the Mexican government and US diplomats. The US consul general dispatched a detailed report to the State Department in Washington about a gathering on July 4 at the Salón Alhambra, for which flyers were "quite profusely distributed throughout the city." Chaired by Diego Rivera, the meeting was attended by around 150 to 200 people, "the great majority being of the 'peon' class with a scattering of 'red' intellectuals."[95] Speakers included Mella, Hurwitz, the Bolivian leftist Tristan Maroff, and an unnamed Haitian activist (probably Jolibois). The Mexican feminist performer Concha Michel also sang three revolutionary *corridos*, one of which was the song dedicated to Nicaragua mentioned earlier.[96] At another meeting on July 9, the head of the local Mafuenic committee in the working-class Mexico City neighborhood of Colonia Peralvillo read out a poem about the deployment of US troops in Veracruz in 1914—a reminder that Mexico itself had recently experienced occupation by US forces, testifying to the strong affective basis to feelings of solidarity with Nicaragua.[97]

Outside Mexico City, the peasant leagues provided the organizational infrastructure for Mafuenic as they had done for LADLA, setting up events and hosting speakers. In Veracruz state, such events were held not only in the eponymous city and the state capital, Jalapa, but also in the countryside. Villa Cardel, for example, held a meeting on July 9, 1928, that was addressed by Sandino's brother Sócrates, Diego Rivera, and Gustavo Machado, who had just returned from Nicaragua.[98] Sócrates Sandino and Machado went on to address crowds in the capital and in Guadalajara, where they were the guests of honor at a bullfight on September 4, 1928.[99]

But the most spectacular moment of publicity for Mafuenic came in the Mexican Congress on November 26, 1928, when Hernán Laborde, then serving as a congressional deputy for the Unified Railway Workers Party, made a speech denouncing US imperialism. A PCM member, Laborde was also involved in LADLA and was a contributor to *El Libertador*.[100] While he was speaking, he proceeded to unfurl an American flag reportedly seized from US Marines by Sandino's forces at El Zapote on May 14, which Sandino had sent to Mafuenic as a token of appreciation for its support.[101] Laborde's gesture prompted outrage in the congressional chamber, and several deputies tried to wrest the flag from him.[102] It was an unmistakably physical demonstration of transnational politics in action: A battle prize taken during Nicaragua's struggle for sovereignty was paraded in the Mexican Congress by a Communist to highlight the common hemispheric struggle against US imperialism.

The formation and early success of Mafuenic marked a high point for Mexico City's anti-imperialist milieu. The organization's geographical spread across Mexico and its effective use of popular cultural forms testified to the anti-imperialist left's sociological reach at this time. It demonstrated a capacity to expand the Mexican public's awareness of Nicaragua, giving a specific focus to wider anti-imperialist sentiment and channeling both sympathy and funds toward Sandino's cause.[103]

"OUR JUBILANT TRANSOCEANIC MESSAGES"

This chapter has focused on LADLA as the leading exponent of a distinctive anti-imperialist politics that developed in 1920s Mexico. The agenda it put forward was novel in seeking to understand Latin America's problems through a transnational frame and in tying the region's attempts to withstand the combined pressures of Washington's guns and Wall Street's dollars to anti-colonial struggles elsewhere. This systemic view linked imperialism to capitalism as intertwined forms of domination, subjecting populations across the globe to varying forms of oppression and exploitation.

LADLA's anti-imperialism was animated by a constellation of ideas that owed much to the quickened tempo of global politics in the years after the First World War, as well as to the intellectual and artistic ferment unleashed by the Mexican Revolution. A poem written in Mexico in 1927–28 by Esteban Pavletich conveys some of its potency: its messianic fervency, its global geographical sweep, its modernist motifs. Opening with an evocation of links between US capitalism and Latin American dictators—"skyscrapers / standard oils / machados gómez leguías"—it then surveys the landscapes of the continent, hearing the "unknown cry of América" in the "pampas of vagabond silences," and finding in the Andes "stone motors / for autochthonous / rebellions." The rivers of the region, meanwhile, would serve as "travelers' paths / for our jubilant transoceanic messages." The poem's final lines weave together global and local anti-imperial causes, binding Andean geography and the concept of a unified mestizo region labeled "Indoamérica" to a wider struggle spanning from Central America to East Asia:

in Indian souls
titikakas
on which to splash down the hopes disentangled
in the violent forests of the KUO MIN TANG
men of indoamérica
nicaragua will be our last sadness.[104]

Pavletich's lyricism offers a tantalizing prefiguration of later Latin American solidarities with what became known as the Third World. Indeed, although we should be careful not to draw too direct a line between the 1920s and the moment of decolonization, there are connections between LADLA's activities and, for example, those of postrevolutionary Cuba: Raúl Roa, Cuban foreign minister from 1959 to 1976, was in his youth a member of the Havana chapter of LADLA.[105]

But more importantly, in its own time the anti-imperial coalescence of the 1920s was a highly significant episode in Latin American politics, developing a powerful analysis of contemporary capitalism and imperialism and making crucial connections between the region's struggles and those elsewhere. Nourished by a footloose radical internationalism, it opened up new ways of thinking about Latin America's place in the world even as it placed questions of revolutionary strategy firmly on the agenda.

Yet there were sobering limits to what LADLA's radical transnationalism was able to achieve. As the next chapter shows, the unity on which its successes were built proved fragile. The organization was highly vulnerable to the sectarian divisions between Communists and other leftists that began to multiply in 1928. Even as it was making headway with its Nicaragua solidarity efforts, ideological and strategic disagreements within Mexico City's anti-imperialist milieu began to multiply. At the same time, mounting repression by the Mexican state worked to isolate the PCM and LADLA still further from potential allies. The anti-imperial coalescence I have described would not have been possible without the favorable climate Mexican national politics provided at the time. Its participants would soon discover how swiftly and dramatically the political winds could change.

THREE

Anti-Imperial Rifts

CONTINENTAL CITIZENS

In December 1927, the Mexican Senate unanimously approved a resolution on "continental citizenship." It was brought to the floor by Higinio Álvarez, a senator from Colima, who asserted the need to consolidate the "current of Latin American confraternity which has made itself felt in the last few years." To that end, he proposed that each Latin American state amend its constitution in order to "grant the status of citizen, with the rights and obligations accorded to nationals, to all Latin American citizens." By dissolving the boundaries between citizenship regimes, this would ensure that the rest of the world saw Latin America "as if it were a single powerful Nation."[1]

Álvarez's proposal testified to the appeal of continent-spanning visions in the 1920s. It was widely applauded both within Mexico and beyond, receiving favorable press coverage in Peru and Cuba; even LADLA sent the Senate a congratulatory telegram.[2] The idea of "continental citizenship" drew upon internationalist currents within the Mexican revolutionary tradition, as well as on the progressive legal thinking that had found expression in the Constitution of 1917, billed as the world's first social-democratic charter.[3] It also took up once more the Bolivarian dream of a single, pan–Latin American state, which had found modern-day proponents in the APRA movement. Haya was in Mexico at the time of the Senate debates, giving well-publicized lectures on his conception of "Indoamerica" and on the need for pan–Latin American economic and political unity.[4] The Senate's Commission on Constitutional Affairs even cited Haya in its endorsement of Álvarez's proposal, which mapped closely onto APRA's program. The proposal would finally, the commission argued, "resolve the problem of the single *patria*, of the *patria* founded on the continuity, unity, and solidarity of the Hispano-American republics."[5]

Yet this euphoria was short lived. The proposal was swiftly rejected by Panama, and no other Latin American country took it up, killing off whatever momentum the project had. Still more dramatic shifts were to come in Mexico. Starting in 1929, many of the foreigners who had found safe haven there—including the Latin American political exiles featured in previous chapters—were detained and then deported. Within the space of little more than a year, the Mexican government went from considering legislation that would treat all Latin Americans as conationals to regarding many of them as "pernicious foreigners," in the wording used by Mexican officialdom. The vision of a continental citizenship that would abolish frontiers had flipped into its opposite: a national realm tightly guarded against possible subversion by outsiders, who could be cast out at the whim of the authorities. What had previously been a remarkably hospitable environment for radical activism suddenly became altogether less welcoming.

The main reasons for this abrupt reversal lie in the political turbulence Mexico experienced in the late 1920s. The postrevolutionary regime, already combating the Catholic insurgency of the Cristeros from 1926 to 1929, faced revolts by discontented factions of the army in 1927 and again in 1929. It was also plunged into a succession crisis by the assassination of president-elect Álvaro Obregón in July 1928. Though carried out by a Catholic extremist, the killing prompted a government crackdown on the Mexican left and on radical exiles that continued through 1929.

This sea change in Mexico's internal political climate coincided, moreover, with the Comintern's adoption of a new strategic orientation. In 1928 the organization entered what it termed its "Third Period," which would last until 1935. Believing the terminal crisis of capitalism to be imminent, the Comintern instructed its affiliates around the world to abandon any attempts at cross-class alliances and focus on organizing the working class for a direct seizure of power. In Latin America, this new strategy of "class against class" put an end to collaborations between Communist parties and progressive nationalists, torpedoing the basis on which initiatives such as LADLA had been built.[6] Communist parties also adopted a more directly hostile stance toward the region's governments. In Mexico, this meant that what had previously been an ambiguous relationship between the state and the Communist Party turned into one of outright confrontation. In 1929 the government banned the PCM, forcing it underground; by early 1930, rising tensions between Mexico and the USSR had led to a break in diplomatic ties.[7]

These upheavals deepened a series of fractures that were already developing within Mexico City's anti-imperialist milieu. Disagreements that had first arisen in 1927 began to multiply from 1928 onward, as *apristas* and Communists aired their differences in increasingly antagonistic exchanges, most famously encapsulated in Mella's polemical critiques of Haya.[8] The sources of discord included burning political issues of the day—notably Nicaragua—as well as theoretical and strategic questions. Class alliances were one of the crucial themes: Should workers and peasants join with the local bourgeoisie against external domination, as APRA urged, or seek to forge their own path, as the Communists now insisted? Behind this lay another substantive divergence, pitting APRA's pan-continental vision against the class-based internationalism of the Communists. Where APRA's program involved winning power at the national level and then federating the region's nation-states, the Communists wanted to smash all of those states through mass insurrection and remake them from below.

The red thread connecting these points of contention was the question of how to relate to Latin America's existing nation-states. Should they be consolidated in the face of US imperialism, or be dismantled and remade in the name of a higher unity? The convergence of Communists, *campesinos*, and *apristas* described in preceding chapters was founded on a shared belief that opposition to US and European domination had to exceed the boundaries of nation-states. Yet this anti-imperial consensus ultimately ran aground on differences between how the political currents within it related to one particular nation-state: postrevolutionary Mexico.

These differences became decisive once Mexico's political environment began to change, and the conditions that had made the transnational coalescence of the 1920s possible gave way to forces that helped pull it apart. The diverse currents within the anti-imperial milieu took distinct stances with regard to the Mexican state, ranging from close ideological alignment to cautious coexistence to mutual hostility. For its part the Mexican state displayed a range of attitudes to the anti-imperialist currents. Parts of it actively encouraged and supported anti-imperialist efforts, as we have seen in chapter 2. But other parts of it were less well disposed to leftist politics, treating the Communists in particular with persistent suspicion, which ultimately escalated into repression.

This chapter traces the disintegration of Mexico City's anti-imperialist milieu over the course of 1927–29. I begin by identifying the early signs of divergence and describe the contrasting relationships the *apristas*, Communists, and peasant leagues had with the Mexican state. I then chart the widening of fractures between these three political currents and the disparate effects on each of the crackdown unleashed by the Mexican government in 1928–29. Finally, I analyze the breakdown of the anti-imperialist milieu and the death or dispersal of many of its key participants. If the mid-1920s had brought a remarkable convergence between different political strands, by the end of the decade they were all set on separate and incompatible paths. More than simply marking the end of a striking political moment, the dissolution of the anti-imperial milieu laid the basis for divisions that would prove an enduring feature of Latin America's political landscape, defining the stances movements would take and the choices militants would make for decades afterward.

FAULT LINES

Some of the main fault lines along which the anti-imperial consensus would crack were apparent even during the period of greatest unity. The first signs of trouble came in February 1927. At the Brussels Congress against Colonial Oppression and Imperialism, seven delegates refused to sign the main resolution on the Americas. Led by Haya, this group produced a postscript that referred to "certain reservations about the conception of imperialism in Latin America and about the organization of the united front," stating that it would formulate them "at the appropriate time."[9] The reasons for the postscript remain unclear. According to the account Haya published several years later, the nub of the issue in Brussels was cross-class alliances. Curiously, he claimed that he spoke out against aligning with the bourgeoisie—the opposite of APRA's avowed strategy of building a "united anti-imperialist front of manual and intellectual workers."[10] Other participants in the Brussels Congress, including Mella and the Peruvian leftist Eudocio Ravines, claimed Haya's goal was simply to draw attention to APRA.[11] Haya certainly hoped to claim leadership of Latin America's anti-imperialist forces, and he may have wanted to create some distance between APRA and LADLA. Personal ambitions and rivalries also clearly played a role, and they fed into the bitter polemics that later developed between Haya and Mella.

But beyond the motivations of individuals, two intertwined issues emerged here that would repeatedly resurface over the next two years. One was whether political strategies devised in Europe were applicable to Latin America. Mella and the Communists argued that they were, while APRA insisted on the need for Latin American solutions. The second was what kind of transnational organization was considered legitimate: one linked to the global agenda of the Comintern or one wedded to a project for regional unity?

Haya broached both these issues just before the Brussels Congress in a letter to the Cuban newspaper *Mañana*. The struggle against imperialism in Latin America, he argued, was necessarily international, and for that reason his APRA movement would be organized internationally, the better to "carry out what should be América's second war for independence."[12] The quest for independence involved finding Latin American solutions to the region's problems: "We should do something for ourselves, shake off Europe's tutelage a little." This did not mean ignoring the rest of the world, since there were worthy models to be found elsewhere. Haya returned once more to the Chinese example. "We want a revolutionary organism with roots in the consciousness of the masses like the Chinese Kuo Min Tang," he argued.[13]

In the mid-1920s, as we have seen, solidarity with China was a point on which Mexico City's anti-imperialists all agreed. Yet soon China was to become a source of bitter division. In early April 1927, *El Machete* celebrated the KMT's capture of Shanghai, emblazoning its front page with an image of a Chinese worker breaking free of his shackles over the headline "The Awakening of the Orient."[14] But within days the alliance between the KMT and Chinese Communists was shattered: On April 12, Nationalist troops massacred several thousand Communists in Shanghai.[15] After purging Communists from its ranks, the KMT unleashed a "White Terror" that would claim up to a million lives.[16] The remnants of the Chinese Communist Party went underground, many fleeing to rural areas, where they spent the next decade rethinking the party's whole approach to revolution.

These events had tremendous implications for the world Communist movement. Having pushed China's Communists to align themselves with Chiang Kai-shek, the Comintern belatedly rushed to rethink its policy. The slaughter in Shanghai destroyed the idea that Communists should join forces with nationalists anywhere else. Indeed, the Chinese debacle contributed to the vehemence with which the Comintern turned to its new strategy of "class against class" starting in 1928. In Mexico, coverage of the

KMT in *El Machete* and *El Libertador* swung 180 degrees, from admiration to condemnation.[17] This was only the first of several dizzying ideological turnarounds.

For APRA, the events in China had a different meaning. Haya had first described his movement as a "Latin American Kuomintang" in 1926, when the KMT was still aligned with the Comintern. But he continued to use the label after 1927. For example, in an article published in the Cuban *aprista* journal *Atuei* in early 1928, he again held up "young China" as an example for Latin America, arguing that "the only anti-imperialist party similar to the Kuomintang is APRA."[18] Originally, the KMT–APRA parallel implied a cross-class anti-imperial convergence that would include the Communists. But now it began to connote something very different: a national liberation program explicitly set against that of the Communists. The implications of Haya's stance took time to play out, but the transnational parallels would have been readily apparent, sending tremors of disquiet through Mexico City's anti-imperialist milieu.

INDOAMERICANISM AND THE STATE

The most crucial factor in understanding how and why rifts opened up between Mexico City's anti-imperialists is the varying relationship they each had to the Mexican state. Previous chapters have evoked the favorable climate postrevolutionary Mexico provided for radical exiles. The reach of anti-imperialist ideas was greatly extended by the sympathetic attitude of parts of the Mexican state. To some extent this reflected the foreign policy stance of the Obregón and Calles administrations, which between them had established full diplomatic relations with the Soviet Union, had supported Sandino's rebellion in Nicaragua, and had thus far stood firm in negotiations with US oil companies.[19] There was also, as noted in chapter 2, a significant overlap in personnel between radical anti-imperialist circles and Mexican officialdom.

Yet the Mexican state's sympathies were not evenly distributed. The clearest beneficiaries were the *apristas*, who found refuge and employment in Mexico City. Haya had spent several months working for José Vasconcelos in 1923–24. His fellow APRA members Jacobo Hurwitz, Esteban Pavletich, and Nicolás Terreros all arrived in Mexico in 1926. More Peruvian exiles came in 1927, including the poet Magda Portal.[20] The Peruvian lawyer and economist Carlos Manuel Cox also arrived that September, his way smoothed by Mexican officials.[21]

More than just providing a home for APRA's exiles, Mexico gave them a platform. When Haya returned to the country in November 1927, the Mexican education ministry gave him a salary and covered his expenses.[22] The SEP also arranged for Haya to give a series of public lectures at the National Preparatory School in December 1927, which were extensively promoted in the Mexican press, especially in *Excélsior*.[23] It was in these lectures that Haya first fully articulated his analysis of Latin American history, at the same time that he set out a distinctive view of the state.[24] It is worth lingering on these arguments, since they had immediate political consequences.

Haya opened by paradoxically asserting that "Latin America does not, unfortunately, have a name"—meaning that it "lacked a unanimous expression that would embrace all the nations situated south of the Río Bravo."[25] He listed various terms that had been applied to those countries, tying each to a particular historical period: "Hispanoamericanism equals Colonial Era; Latinamericanism equals Independence and Republic; Panamericanism equals Imperialism, and Indoamericanism equals unification and freedom." Where *Hispanoamericanism* implied a subordinate attachment to Spain, *Latinamericanism* denoted the thwarted pan-continental aspirations of the time of Bolívar, and *Panamericanism* the subjugation of the region to US power. The final equation, by contrast, evoked not a historical stage but a desired condition or, indeed, a destiny—and for Haya, APRA was to be its bearer.

Haya went on to analyze Latin American history through a series of dialectical categories drawn from Hegel. Precolonial societies were the thesis, he asserted, the Spanish Conquest was the antithesis, and colonialism was the synthesis. Despite achieving independence, the republics of Spanish America had not escaped this underlying reality: According to Haya, their social structures still had a "feudal" character. As a result, there had been no "logical and normal" evolution toward capitalism. Instead, there was "a superposition of various social stages," ranging from "primitive societies" to "landowners with the mentality of the fifteenth century" to "the great capitals, industrial centers . . . which think in the modern way."[26] As we will see in chapter 5, similar ideas about the parallel presence of disparate historical realities were articulated at this time by Haya's fellow Peruvian, José Carlos Mariátegui, with whose writings Haya would surely have been familiar.[27]

The strategic significance of this reading of Latin American history became clear in two conclusions Haya drew from it. One was that the region's problems were "unique," and that what was therefore needed was to "discover the reality of América, not to invent it." The failed importation of European models, Haya argued, "gives us the great historical lesson of searching for ourselves."[28] The second was that the state in Latin America reflected the region's layering of historical epochs. Marx and Engels had famously described the modern state as "but a committee for managing the common affairs of the whole bourgeoisie."[29] In Latin America, by contrast, Haya argued that it represented an "indefinite and fluctuating social reality." According to Haya, rather than being the organ of a single class, the state swung between serving "the latifundist class" and "the semi-industrializing caste of agents of imperialism."[30] Rather than being in essence a hostile entity, then, in Haya's conception the state was a tool that could be wielded by different groups—and could therefore be put to anti-imperialist uses if placed in the right hands.

Both of these arguments shaped APRA's response to the divisions of the next two years. Haya had previously insisted on the inadequacy of European models to Latin America; here he laid out a historically grounded reason for this. At the same time, he argued for a tactically flexible attitude toward the state. In APRA's case, this was dictated by more than the practical needs of exiles: They saw the new postrevolutionary regime as the best example to date of a Latin American state apparatus being used to advance an anti-imperialist agenda. In an April 1927 letter to Solomon Lozovsky, head of the Comintern's trade union organization, whom he had befriended during his visit to the USSR in 1924, Haya summed up his attitude to the Calles government: "Of course, that government is not a socialist one but it is the best political power we have to resist imperialism."[31] For Haya, then, countering US hemispheric dominance required a rapprochement with forces beyond the left, including state-level authorities. His assessment of the Calles administration was shared by many others at the time, including the radical peasant leagues.

BETWEEN THE PALACIO NACIONAL
AND THE KREMLIN

The peasant leagues' relationship to the Mexican state in the mid-1920s was shaped by two impulses. One was a desire to maintain the momentum of the land redistribution unleashed by the Mexican Revolution. This meant cultivating good relations with local and national government officials. At the same time, the leagues were committed to a transnational, revolutionary framing of the peasant question, and maintained ties to the Krestintern, the Comintern's peasant organization. Up until 1928, these two impulses remained compatible, but thereafter tensions between them began to increase.

Throughout the 1920s, Mexico's governments continued to seek the support of radical *campesinos*. Local and national officials established semipatronal ties with the peasant leagues; Veracruz governor Adalberto Tejeda, for example, strongly backed the Veracruz League and even helped fund Úrsulo Galván's 1923 trip to Moscow.[32] Conversely, the leagues repeatedly came to the government's aid in moments of crisis. In 1923 the Veracruz League joined forces with the Obregón government to put down a rebellion led by former president Adolfo de la Huerta. Detachments of armed *campesinos* were even officially incorporated into the 86th Battalion of the Mexican Army, in which Galván served as lieutenant colonel.[33]

The Veracruz League's readiness to assist the Obregón government is not difficult to understand. In the League's view, the Mexican state was the peasantry's first line of defense against a counterrevolution that might reverse the gains of the previous decade. The same logic runs through the National Peasant League's responses to events in the late 1920s. Under Calles, land redistribution slowed down, and landlords began to reassert their power in the countryside, often through the use of paramilitary "white guards" (*guardias blancas*). *El Machete* frequently reported on killings of local *campesino* leaders, which often happened in areas where the leagues were strongest, such as Veracruz and Michoacán.[34] Primo Tapia, the head of the Michoacán League, was assassinated in April 1926.[35]

In this troubled context, the peasant leagues sought to remain on good terms with the Mexican state. In May 1927 they had again rallied to the government's side amid another rebellion, this time led by generals Arnulfo Gómez and Francisco Serrano, who sought to block Obregón's return to the presidency. The radical *campesinos* once more decided to align themselves with Obregón. As the National Peasant League put it in a September 1927 letter to the Krestintern in Moscow, peasants and workers "see in General Obregón the guarantee of their revolutionary conquests."[36] Reasoning along the same lines as Haya, the National Peasant League argued that even though Obregón might not represent "the advanced tendency of the Mexican Revolution, at least he embodies the defensive and contentious force in face of the restorationist attempts of the forces of reaction, supported by Yankee capital."[37]

At the same time, however, the peasant leagues continued to frame the peasant question as one that transcended national borders, and they maintained their connections with the Krestintern in Moscow. It was partly thanks to Krestintern support that the Veracruz League was able to continue publishing its newspaper, *La Voz del Campesino*, and in August 1926 the Krestintern contributed 2,000 roubles (around US$1,000 at the time) for the organization of the National League's founding congress.[38] The following year, the National League sent four delegates to Moscow for celebrations of the tenth anniversary of the October Revolution, including Durango peasant leader José Guadalupe Rodríguez Favela.[39] At a Krestintern meeting in mid-November 1927, at which he shared a stage with African National Congress delegate Josiah Gumede, Rodríguez Favela insisted that the problems Mexican peasants faced spanned national frontiers, arguing that "the whole world suffers from imperialism."[40]

For Mexico's radical peasants, the national and international arenas were still complementary. Cultivating good relations with the Mexican state was a means of safeguarding the gains made during the Revolution; ties to the Comintern gave them access to transnational networks for the broader struggle against imperialism. Yet the conviction that these two arenas were compatible would come under increasing strain in 1928–29, in large part because of mounting tensions between the Communist movement and the Mexican government.

CALLE MESONES VS. CALLE RÍO RHIN

The PCM's relationship with the Mexican state in the 1920s was highly contradictory. Barry Carr aptly describes it as "confusing—subject to sudden enthusiasms followed by equally abrupt disenchantment."[41] This was partly due to the ambiguities of the postrevolutionary regime, which vaunted its radical roots while making many compromises with the wealthy and powerful. Unable to resolve its stance toward this chameleonic entity, the PCM "oscillated violently between two extreme positions": on the one hand, "uncritical acceptance of the anti-capitalist potential of the Mexican Revolution," and on the other, "blunt, undifferentiated condemnation."[42]

Yet there was a further reason for the PCM's disorientation, and it stemmed from the transnational nature of the Communist movement itself. As the local section of a worldwide movement headquartered in Moscow, the party was embedded within an extensive network of contacts and solidarities. But for the same reason, it was subject to outside pressures. The Comintern handed down global policy directives that the PCM leadership at Calle Mesones was supposed to apply. But there was often a mismatch between the interests of Mexican Communists and the needs of Soviet foreign policy—a gap that widened at the end of 1920s, as the governments of Mexico and the USSR grew increasingly estranged.

When Mexico and the Soviet Union first established diplomatic ties in 1924, there was a sense of kinship between the two countries. On presenting his credentials in the Kremlin, Mexican ambassador Basilio Vadillo observed that "in recent years, for equivalent reasons . . . our peoples have entered into new forms of national life," seeking among other things to "reestablish the dignity of the proletariat."[43] Yet while Mexican officials initially framed their relations with the USSR in these fraternal terms, the first Soviet envoy to Mexico had a different understanding of the situation. From his arrival in October 1924 until his departure two years later, Stanislav Pestkovsky played two roles in parallel: that of Soviet ambassador and that of Communist militant. Alongside his activities at the Soviet legation on the Calle Río Rhin, he attended and spoke at PCM rallies and LADLA meetings. Pestkovsky's dual role landed his mission in trouble—and it would obstruct the work of his successors, too.

From the outset, the mere presence of a Soviet mission drew the ire of Mexican conservatives and, crucially, of Washington. The US ambassador to Mexico, James Sheffield, had arrived the same month as Pestkovsky, and was so irritated by the warm reception the latter received that he considered boycotting Calles's inauguration a month later.[44] Statements made by the Soviet government around this time further inflamed the situation. In May 1925, Soviet Foreign Minister Georgii Chicherin described Mexico as "a very convenient base for further extension of our ties in America"—confirming the anti-Communist view that Pestkovsky was using Mexico as a beachhead for continental subversion.[45] Tensions between the National Palace and the Calle Río Rhin continued until Moscow recalled Pestkovsky in October 1926.

His successor was the prominent Bolshevik feminist Aleksandra Kollontai.[46] Before her departure, she was personally instructed by Stalin to separate Soviet diplomatic activities from those of the Communist movement.[47] This was easier said than done, given her celebrity; the US authorities denied her a transit visa, and on arriving in Veracruz in December 1926 she was greeted at the dock by a large crowd waving red flags. "This is absolutely impermissible," she told Lev Khaikis, the embassy secretary, adding, "I am an official person." Both privately and publicly, Kollontai tried to create a distance between the embassy and revolutionary agitation, clashing with her staff over their "excessively tight relations with the local communists." Days after presenting her credentials to Calles, Kollontai argued with Khaikis about the inappropriateness of having a banner that read "Workers of the World Unite!" hanging over a sofa in the embassy. ("We're extraterritorial," Khaikis replied nonchalantly.)[48]

On December 21, Kollontai wrote in her diary, "I feel all the time that volcanoes are bubbling and boiling beneath us."[49] She meant it literally, but a seismic metaphor would not have been misplaced: Her entire six-month tenure in Mexico was disrupted by personal problems and political intrigue. Her diaries convey a sense of exhaustion, as well as unease at being so far from Moscow when decisive political battles were unfolding within the Bolshevik Party.[50] Yet she felt compelled to stay at her post, partly for gendered reasons: As one of only a few prominent female diplomats, she felt she had to prove that a woman could fill that role just as well as a man, if not better.[51] She was scarcely helped by a lack of resources. The Soviet embassy apparently did not have its own car and chauffeur, so when she left official dinners, she pretended she wanted to go for a stroll and then went around the corner and got a cab.[52]

Despite her more professional approach, the problems besetting Kollontai in Mexico were essentially the same as those Pestkovsky had faced: the inescapably ideological character of the Soviet presence, which made it impossible for the USSR's representatives to separate themselves from the Communist movement. US officials energetically fanned anti-Communist sentiment. In January 1927, US Secretary of State Frank Kellogg presented a report to the Senate Foreign Relations Committee that painted Mexico as a key base for Bolshevik activity against the United States.[53] Kollontai denied that the USSR had any such agenda, telling Mexican Foreign Secretary Aarón Sáenz, "We will not and do not intend to interfere with Calles's policy because he is struggling for Mexico's independence."[54] Amid heightened tensions with Washington over the fate of US-owned oil concessions, radicals within the Mexican government sought out Soviet support. On

January 28, Interior Minister Tejeda, formerly governor of Veracruz, asked Kollontai what the Soviet government would do if the United States declared war on Mexico. To her evasive offer of "moral solidarity," he apparently replied: "Give us two shipfuls of weapons and two of bread, that's real."[55] But Kollontai was keen to keep a low profile and tried to focus on Mexican–Soviet trade ties.

In March 1927, however, a crisis erupted that put an end to her mission. The Soviet railway workers' federation had decided some months earlier to send 50,000 roubles—some US$25,000 at the time—to support an ongoing strike by Mexican railway workers.[56] When the money arrived, the Calles government was furious. The ensuing weeks brought a barrage of hostility in the press. "Not a day goes by without poison in the newspaper," Kollontai wrote.[57] By early April, her superiors in Moscow had decided to replace her that summer.

Ironically, the very factors that undermined Kollontai's work only confirmed her analysis of Mexico's importance for the anti-imperialist cause. On May 30, days before she left the country, Kollontai and Khaikis jointly drafted a report for the Comintern that identified Mexico as "the spearhead of the struggle against U.S. imperialism," pointing to its role as a center of solidarity for movements in Nicaragua, Venezuela, Cuba, and other countries.[58] Yet they also noted the "dualism" of the Calles government, arguing that in Mexico, "the bourgeois revolution is incomplete," with the country still subject to "the influence of feudal holdovers." Given the small size and weakness of the PCM, they continued, the Comintern had to recognize "the impossibility for the present moment of carrying out a revolutionary movement in Mexico under an openly communist flag."[59] For that reason, they recommended a "'Sinification' of our policy in Mexico"—that is, applying the same approach as in China and subsuming local Communist forces into a broader anti-imperialist alliance. Coming barely a month after the massacre of Communists in Shanghai, the China parallel is surprising to say the least. As well as confirming how deep the attachment to the Comintern's previous China strategy was, Kollontai's and Khaikis's analysis notably echoes Haya's assessment of the Mexican state. Yet as we will see, this view would soon be criticized from the left in Mexico, and it was immediately contested in Moscow.

By this time, there was a growing consensus in the Comintern apparatus that the Mexican and Bolshevik Revolutions had not been so similar after all. Tensions between the Soviet and Mexican governments had undermined the previously fraternal atmosphere, and the Comintern was now questioning Calles's progressive reputation. In late December 1927, a "Mexican Commission" created by the Comintern's Latin Secretariat held a two-day meeting at which Stirner defended the PCM's decision to back Obregón in the battle to succeed Calles.[60] Using a logic similar to the National Peasant League's, he argued that supporting Obregón was the best means of defending the gains of the Revolution. But other Comintern functionaries were not convinced: Boris Vasiliev, deputy head of the Comintern's Department of Organization, accused the PCM of wanting to "form a defensive wall around the Calles government."[61] Why should Communists shield what was in essence a bourgeois regime?

The arguments aired at the Mexican Commission signaled a growing distance between the Comintern's priorities and those of the PCM. The PCM had tried to strike a balance in its attitude toward the Mexican government, on the one hand recognizing its progressive features—including its support for anti-imperialist causes such as Nicaragua—while on the other criticizing the slow pace of agrarian reform, for example. But as the rift between the Mexican and Soviet governments widened, the party found itself in an increasingly difficult position. Before long it would be flung into open conflict with the Mexican state, at a moment when political differences between Communists and *apristas* were gathering pace.

PLANS AND ARMIES

In January 1928, Haya announced in the Mexican press that he planned to run for the Peruvian presidency.[62] A few days later, APRA's Mexico City cell drafted a manifesto laying out an altogether different plan for taking power in their home country. It announced the formation of the Partido Nacionalista Libertador del Perú (PNL; Nationalist Liberation Party of Peru), a "politico-military organism" that aimed to topple the Leguía government and implement APRA's program within Peru: nationalization of land and industry, redistribution of land to peasant producers, and secularized education.[63] The manifesto did not go into detail on the exact means through which this would be achieved, but it was consistent with the strategy Haya had laid out in his 1925 letter to Stirner, discussed in chapter 1: a radical insurrectionary movement that would couch its demands in Latin American rather than Communist terms. The PNL's emblem was to be the APRA flag, while its slogan would be the battle cry of Mexican revolutionaries such as Ricardo Flores Magón and Emiliano Zapata: "¡*Tierra y Libertad!*"

The "Plan de México" and Haya's presidential bid proved hugely divisive, both in Peru and among Mexico City's exiles. In Lima, Mariátegui had been close with the *apristas* and regularly published their work in his journal, *Amauta*. He now broke with Haya, and partly in response to Haya's move accelerated his efforts to form the Peruvian Socialist Party, founded in September 1928.[64] Mariátegui viewed Haya's plan as irresponsible adventurism, its methods akin to those of nineteenth-century strongmen. As he put it a year later in a letter to Pavletich, "Haya has placed himself on the terrain of an opportunist and petty bourgeois personal *caudillaje*," concluding that "there can be no doubt about his turn to the right."[65]

In Mexico City, Haya's plans alienated many of his fellow *apristas*. First Nicolás Terreros and then Jacobo Hurwitz broke with APRA. Both were closely involved in LADLA, and they now gravitated toward Communist circles. In the June 1928 issue of *El Libertador*, Hurwitz laid out the reasons for his departure from APRA.[66] He denounced Haya and APRA for "abandoning . . . the international anti-imperialist movement." By advancing its own separate plan for taking power in Peru, APRA was misdirecting the movement's energies, narrowing its scope from a continental struggle to a single country. The final paragraphs of the article are headed with three damning words designed to sum up Hurwitz's criticisms of the organization: "*El APRA nacionalista.*"

It wasn't just Haya's schemes for power in Peru that caused tensions. At the same time that he announced he would run for the Peruvian presidency, Haya declared himself willing to help oversee elections due later that year in Nicaragua. *El Libertador*'s editors seized on this as "a betrayal of Nicaragua."[67] Monitoring elections held under the guns of US troops ran counter to the solidarity efforts LADLA and others had been engaged in for several years. In their view, Sandino's forces had been fighting precisely for the right to decide their country's destiny free of US influence. A few weeks later, Haya reaffirmed APRA's support for Sandino and announced that it would send a "legion" to fight alongside him; in the end, the "legion" consisted solely of Pavletich, who worked as Sandino's secretary for a few weeks before returning.[68]

These disagreements over Nicaragua and over Haya's insurrectionary plans for Peru may have had few immediate material consequences, but the larger strategic questions they raised were profound. Terreros and Hurwitz felt APRA had placed itself on the wrong side of these key issues, and that membership in the movement was no longer compatible with their anti-imperialist commitments. This was only the first in a series of zero-sum disputes that emerged over the following months, and which contributed to a growing sense that Communists and *apristas* were engaged in political projects that were not only distinct, but in many ways opposed.

JUPITER VS. EARTH

In April 1928, the gap between Communists and *apristas* widened when Mella published a pamphlet titled *¿Qué es el ARPA?*[69] It pulled no punches, identifying APRA as "objectively and collectively, elements of continental reaction."[70] Mella made a number of ad hominem attacks on Haya and other *apristas*, and his deliberate mangling of APRA's initials in the title, turning the acronym into the Spanish word for "harp," laid the basis for several music-themed jokes at APRA's expense. Behind the biting rhetoric, Mella's critique of APRA represents with unusual clarity the widening divergences between the two movements.

First, Mella was highly skeptical of APRA's program. Not only was it not especially novel—Mella claimed most of its basic points were already enshrined in the 1917 Mexican Constitution—it was not necessarily revolutionary. The demand for nationalization of land and industries might sound radical in Latin America, but as Mella observed, the bourgeoisie in many other countries was in favor of it. For Mella, the key question was who was in charge of the state doing the nationalizing.[71] That meant, in turn, that it was crucial to consider the social composition of the movement that aimed to seize control of the state. Power, he argued, "cannot be seized in any manner and with any element whatsoever. . . . If you want power for any reason other than enjoying it and exploiting those at the bottom, you must take it with progressive social forces."[72]

What was missing from APRA's conception, according to Mella, was a clear understanding of the centrality of class. He criticized Haya's idea of a "united front of manual and intellectual workers" for its vagueness. Without taking account of the balance of forces between the different classes in the alliance, it risked turning into a front for advancing the interests of the bourgeoisie.[73] For Mella, moreover, recent events such as the KMT's slaughter of Chinese Communists and the Nicaraguan elite's opposition to Sandino had shown that the bourgeoisie had no intention of ceding any power to the workers and peasants. On the contrary, once its back was against the wall the bourgeoisie in each place had effectively aligned itself with imperialist powers. Haya's idea that Latin American intellectuals, lawyers, and students could form the basis for a revolution was too optimistic, argued Mella; with rare exceptions, these groups tended to support the status quo.[74]

The example of China also showed, for Mella, the dangers of taking a distance from Communism in the name of expediency. The problem, as he put it, was that "any revolutionary movement, if it really is one, no matter its [social] base, is labelled 'communist'" simply because it challenged local elites and US interests. In Mexico, both Calles and Obregón had been tarred with the same anti-Communist brush despite having nothing to do with the Comintern or PCM. APRA's attempts to avoid the same fate would, in Mella's view, lead beyond mere verbal compromises: "In order for it to be useful, not calling oneself communist as a matter of 'tactics' can only have one corollary: never acting as a communist, and not only that, but even [acting] against the communists."[75]

Mella also took issue with APRA's attachment to the concept of Indoamerica. There was nothing wrong with the term itself, given that the vast majority of Latin America's population was at least partly of Indigenous descent. "That's fine," Mella declared, "we accept this baptism." But in holding up the Indigenous as the foundation of the anti-imperial struggle, APRA accepted a racial framing of the question that he found troubling. "They forget," he argued, "that the penetration of imperialism is putting an end to the 'problem of race' in its classical conception by turning *indios, mestizos*, whites, and blacks into workers, that is to say, by giving the problem an economic rather than a racial basis."[76] For Mella, the racial gradations and divisions specific to Latin America were already being replaced by class categories shared across the globe.

The premise underpinning Mella's reasoning here was that Latin America was a full participant in global developments, not a region apart. As he put it, "América is not a continent on Jupiter, but on Earth."[77] Imperialism, he argued, was a global phenomenon, and while its local manifestations could vary, its basic characteristics were the same in the Americas as in Asia. The same logic allowed him to counter assertions by some *apristas* that Communism was "exotic" and alien to Latin America. Across the region, workers' movements and parties were emerging "autochthonously" thanks to the process of capitalist development. This rising tide of radicalism included labor unions in Argentina, Mexico, and Chile, and strikes by oil workers in Colombia, tenants in Panama, and sugar workers in Cuba. The attribution of these events to interference by Bolsheviks or to "Moscow gold" was no more than "petty bourgeois and jingoistic Latin Americanist shouting."[78]

Mella's criticisms of APRA highlight another important divergence, at once political and epistemological, over whether concepts and categories developed elsewhere were applicable to Latin America. *¿Qué es el ARPA?* makes the case that they are: Mella repeatedly cites Lenin's writings and Comintern resolutions and compares APRA itself to the Russian *narodniks* of the late nineteenth century.[79] The *narodniks* had insisted on the specificity of the Russian peasant commune and argued that it would be possible to make a direct leap to socialism from these communal forms, bypassing the normal path of capitalist development.[80] In Mella's eyes, APRA was repeating this error by romanticizing Indigenous communities as a kind of "Incaic communism," which Mella held was too rudimentary a basis on which to build modern socialism.[81] (Mariátegui, as we will see in chapter 5, was at this very moment developing an argument than ran parallel to Haya's, seeing the Indigenous *ayllu* as the basis for a future socialist society. But like Mella, Mariátegui deployed European examples and categories to build his case.)

Mella's polemic was a landmark in the history of the Latin American left. It has often been seen as crystallizing the opposition between, on the one hand, a radical wing loyal to the precepts of the Comintern, and on the other a nationalist and anti-imperialist left convinced that solutions to Latin America's problems could only be found within the region.[82] Yet to frame the Mella–Haya debate in these terms is to overlook the degree to which both sides were deeply imbricated in global transnational networks. The Communists were by definition committed to the Comintern's project for world revolution, and as we have seen in chapter 1, APRA emerged out of a transnational convergence of Latin American exiles in Europe and drew on the examples of postrevolutionary Mexico, the Bolshevik Party, and the KMT.

The key contrast between APRA and Communism was not so much between a regional anti-imperialist movement and a global class-based one, but rather between two transnational projects with different strategies. Both Communists and *apristas* adopted a transnational framing of Latin America's political problems; neither believed solutions lay within the confines of any single nation-state. For APRA, continental unity was to be achieved by first seizing power in individual nation-states and then melding these states into a pan-regional confederation, although as Haya argued, this second step could only take place once each country's wealth had been national-ized and its sovereignty consolidated.[83] The Communists, by contrast, were committed to a worldwide proletarian revolution that would from the out-set overflow national frontiers, demolishing existing states in the name of a global workers' republic. At the core of this divergence lay distinct attitudes to the problem of state power: how to obtain it, who should wield it, what the priorities should be, and above all how to relate to existing states. From mid-1928 onward, the gaps that had opened up between Communists and *apristas* on these questions widened further under the pressure of Mexican domestic politics.

AFTER OBREGÓN

On July 17, 1928, president-elect Obregón was shot and killed by José de León Toral, a Catholic extremist. The event threw the Mexican political landscape into turmoil, as the postrevolutionary elite scrambled to hold the system together. The Mexican authorities responded to the crisis with a wave of surveillance and repression directed principally against the left. Given the different relationships each component of the anti-imperial milieu had with the Mexican state, this repressive turn played out very unevenly.

Mexico's nascent security apparatus was centrally involved. Formed as "Confidential Services" under President Venustiano Carranza in 1918, by the mid-1920s it had morphed into the office of Investigaciones Políticas y So-ciales (IPS; Political and Social Investigations).[84] It kept tabs on the left from early on; starting in 1925, agents filed numerous reports on PCM and LADLA activities.[85] But it did not view them as serious threats; indeed, in select cases it saw some members of the anti-imperial milieu as allies. According to IPS files, Úrsulo Galván filed reports for the government from Monterrey and Texcoco in 1927.[86] This is not to classify Galván as a government agent; rather, as Sebas-tián Rivera Mir has argued, it points to the fluid and cooperative relationship between the Mexican state and parts of the left in the mid-1920s.[87]

After Obregón's assassination, the mood shifted. In July 1928, the Mexi-can consulate in Antwerp forwarded to the Secretariat of Foreign Relations a massive file of materials about Comintern agents supposedly on their way to Mexico to sow subversion.[88] As it turned out, the documents were forg-eries, but they fed a growing paranoia on the part of the Mexican authori-ties, and the anti-Communist tide began to swell. *Apristas* were mostly unaffected, but IPS agents stepped up surveillance of PCM and LADLA events and of associated individuals, gathering details on their movements and their daily lives.

Even as the Mexican state was putting increased pressure on the Communist left, the Comintern was pushing the PCM into a major strategic shift. The organization's Sixth Congress, held in Moscow in July 1928, initiated a worldwide turn away from the United Front policy of the previous years, toward a more aggressive strategy of "class against class." Capitalism, the Comintern announced, was headed for imminent crisis and collapse. The time was ripe for Communists to forge an independent path, dropping any idea of collaboration with nationalist and social-democratic forces, whom they now dubbed "social-fascists."[89]

For the PCM, the consequences of this shift were quickly apparent. A few months earlier, the party had backed Obregón for the presidency, but by early 1929 it had set up its own electoral vehicle, the Bloque Obrero y Campesino (BOC; Workers' and Peasants' Bloc).[90] The PCM also began to set up its own trade union organization, creating the Confederación Sindical Unitaria de México (CSUM; Unitary Trade Union Confederation of Mexico). Both of these initiatives were a direct challenge to the Mexican authorities, who were looking to tighten their grip on the political system and on organized labor. In 1929 frictions between the Communist movement and the Mexican state flared into open conflict, and the anti-imperial milieu was shattered.

DISINTEGRATION

At 10:00 p.m. on the night of January 10, 1929, on the Calle Abraham González in Mexico City's Colonia Juárez, Julio Antonio Mella was shot by two unknown assailants. He had been walking down the street accompanied by his partner, the Italian American photographer and PCM militant Tina Modotti, when the two men shot him from behind. His friends and fellow Cuban exiles Sandalio Junco and Rogelio Teurbe Tolón rushed to the offices of *Excélsior* to spread news of the attack, even as Mella was taken to San Jerónimo hospital for treatment.[91] But he died from his injuries later that night.

Mella's death marked a watershed for the radical left in Mexico City. Thousands thronged the streets for the funeral, held on January 12 (see

FIGURE 5. Procession for Julio Antonio Mella's funeral, Mexico City, January 1929. From Archivo General de la Nación, Fondo Enrique Díaz Delgado y García, 30/1/3.

figure 5). The Mexican press ran lengthy reports on the event accompanied by many photographs of the procession, pallbearers, and funeral orators.[92] Among those to give speeches were Junco, Diego Rivera, Úrsulo Galván, PCM leaders Rafael Carrillo and Hernán Laborde, and several Mexican student leaders. On the one hand, the funeral was an occasion of great unity: Almost the entire anti-imperialist milieu was present, including *apristas* with whom Mella had recently sparred.[93] But on the other hand, the assassination set a grim tone that only deepened in the following months. Amid a series of interlinked crises that gripped Mexico during 1929, the divisions that had become apparent the previous year deepened, creating irreparable rifts within Mexico City's radical left.

The first of these crises occurred in March and April, with a revolt by disgruntled factions of the Mexican military; led by General José Gonzalo Escobar, it unfolded principally in the north of the country. A PCM manifesto published soon after it began condemned the insurrection. But this time the party did not instruct its supporters to back the government. Instead, it put forward a maximalist platform: Workers and peasants should be given arms to fight "reactionaries" themselves; *latifundios* should be broken up and land redistribution accelerated; and factories should be put under workers' control, among other demands.[94] This radicalized stance was in line with the Comintern's new strategy, which encouraged the PCM to adopt a much more confrontational attitude toward the Mexican state. That February, *El Machete* had framed the alternatives facing Mexico in uncompromising terms: The choices were "fascist government, or government of workers and peasants?"[95] In March, the paper called on Mexico's peasants to seize the opportunity of the Escobar revolt to crush not just the "reactionaries" but the government as well.[96]

The PCM's response to the Escobar revolt brought an immediate rupture with the peasant leagues. Galván sided with the government and urged his supporters to help defeat the insurrection. The majority of the National Peasant League followed his lead, mobilizing militias to defend the government as they had done during previous revolts in 1923–24 and 1927. Since the PCM had by this time taken to describing the Mexican authorities as "fascist," the League's decision put it firmly on the other side of a sectarian divide. The break between Communists and peasant leagues was swift: Galván was expelled from the PCM in May 1929 and thereafter subjected to a stream of vitriol in *El Machete*, which even published a special supplement on Galván's expulsion.[97]

Haya sensed an opportunity in the League's rupture with the Communists. From a distance—by this time he was in Berlin—he tried to win over the peasant leagues to APRA, hoping that they might form the kernel of a continental peasant movement, effectively creating a Latin American rival to the Krestintern. Haya wrote to Julio Cuadros Caldas in August 1929 urging him to meet with Galván: "It is extremely important that you try to get him to agree to form the Aprista International of Indoamerican Campesinos. . . . It is necessary for Úrsulo to be persuaded of the necessity for immediate, *aprista* and Américan action."[98] The fact that Haya was still thinking in these pan-continental terms suggests the continuing force of the transnational framing from which APRA had originally emerged.

Nothing came of Haya's efforts to forge an alliance with the National Peasant League, but the consequences of the League's break with the PCM were profound. The rupture led to a wave of resignations and expulsions of leading *campesino* figures from the PCM. This cut the party off from what Barry Carr describes as "the single most important site of Communist influence" during the 1920s. At the same time, the fallout from these developments brought increasing acrimony between the PCM and its former sympathizers within official circles, as the party began to denounce erst-while allies such as Tejeda and De Negri. As Carr puts it, "In one fell swoop the party's main channels of communication with the left-wing current of the Mexican Revolution were broken."[99]

The PCM's stance during the Escobar revolt also provided the pretext for a fierce anti-Communist campaign by the Mexican government. Starting in April 1929, the authorities began to make scores of arrests, with a notable spike coming at labor rallies held on May 1 in Mexico City.[100] Soon after this came an event that prompted a significant escalation: On May 14, Durango peasant leader Rodríguez Favela was extrajudicially executed by the Mexican army.[101] Though he had helped put down the Escobar revolt, he had also confiscated local landlords' estates and cattle, even branding the latter with a hammer and sickle, according to Siqueiros.[102] In response to Rodríguez Favela's killing, the PCM organized protests in Mexico City, Monterrey, and Jalapa.[103] The party appealed for solidarity outside Mexico, calling for demonstrations outside Mexican consulates in Latin America, the United States, and Europe.[104] The government responded with another turn of the screw: After a wave of further arrests, on June 5 the police seized the PCM's headquarters and the premises of *El Machete*.[105]

Amid this turmoil, many Mexican Communists were gunned down or imprisoned, and the PCM was forced underground; it would operate clandestinely for the next five years. But far from prompting a rethink of its radical line, the repression only hardened the PCM's commitment to it. The bitter lesson the party drew from Rodríguez Favela's death was that he should not have fought alongside the government against Escobar's forces. Perhaps thinking of the Chinese Communists' fate at the hands of the KMT two years earlier, the PCM argued that Mexican government leaders who appeared progressive today were "the reactionaries of tomorrow."[106] In late May, barely two weeks after Rodríguez Favela's death, Siqueiros argued that "at this time the Party's slogan cannot be anything other than revolution. . . . The Party's hour has sounded. We have the weapons and everything is ready. . . . Our task shall be to create a Sandino in every state."[107]

The Comintern, too, was unbending: In its July 1929 "Manifesto on Mexico," its Executive Committee declared that siding with the Mexican government amounted to support for imperialism.[108] Both the PCM and the Comintern now formulated an even more ambitious program for Mexico that called for the creation of worker and peasant militias to prepare for a seizure of power.[109] These shifts went hand in hand with deteriorating relations between the Mexican and Soviet governments. Mexico's ambassador to Moscow, Jesús Silva Herzog, observed that after Rodríguez Favela's death, the Soviet press began denouncing the Mexican government as "fascist."[110] He wrote to his superiors: "We are treated with suspicion and with the same lukewarm courtesy that they reserve for countries considered their enemies."[111] In January 1930, Mexico broke off relations with the USSR entirely; they were not restored until 1943.[112]

DEPARTURES

If 1929 had begun with the burial of one man, it ended with the interment of the hopes of the entire radical milieu. By the end of that year, Mexico City's role as a transnational hub had ended. Having served as a prime venue for anti-imperialist exiles from across Latin America for a decade, it had now become much more forbidding terrain. In November 1929, the Mexican authorities arrested a slew of foreign-born Communists, including Sandalio Junco and Alejandro Barreiro, and deported them all from Veracruz on January 2, 1930, on a boat bound for Bremen.[113] Tina Modotti was arrested in early February and deported a few weeks later.[114] Jacobo Hurwitz avoided the same fate only because he lent his papers to the Italian Comintern operative Vittorio Vidali, who left with Modotti.[115] Esteban Pavletich, who had broken with APRA in mid-1929, was also arrested by the Mexican authorities in June 1930, along with the Salvadoran revolutionary Agustín Farabundo Martí, and both were deported from Manzanillo on the Pacific Coast.[116] Hurwitz was eventually rounded up in 1932 and sent to the penal colony in the Islas Marías.[117]

In early November 1929, the PCM wrote to the Comintern lamenting the drastic change in Mexico's political climate. Previously it had been "one of the only countries where we enjoyed the legal status necessary to develop, coordinate, and direct continental activities and where the government, under the disguise of anti-imperialism, favored such action." Moreover, "the bulk of the Latin American political revolutionary emigration was concentrated in Mexico," which enabled the creation of an anti-imperialist organization that was "broad and with representatives well known by the worker and peasant masses of the continent."[118]

Conditions had now changed, however—and in the PCM's assessment, the radical left's relationship to the Mexican government had been central to that shift. Both the party and LADLA became vulnerable to repression "from the moment when the anti-imperialist struggle in Mexico, as in all the countries of Latin America, became closely linked with the struggle against national governments."[119] Once LADLA and the PCM were in direct conflict with the state, in other words, it became "almost completely impossible" for them to operate. They could no longer print and circulate materials, and "most of the revolutionary political émigrés who constituted [LADLA's] Continental Committee . . . have left the country or are preparing to leave, in order to avoid certain deportation by the government."[120] In a crowning irony, given previous tensions over where LADLA's headquarters should be, the PCM recommended that its offices be moved to a place where it was easier for people to gather and communications with the rest of the world were faster: New York City, the belly of the imperial beast.[121] The move was completed in 1930, but by that time LADLA had fallen apart, its components set on divergent and antagonistic paths.[122]

What explains the speed and thoroughness of this disintegration? Many accounts have focused on the negative influence of the Comintern's increasingly sectarian turn after 1928, arguing that the strategy of "class against class" drove a wedge through the broader left unity of the 1920s.[123] The PCM's handling of the Escobar revolt is a prime example, since it led to definitive ruptures between the Communists and many of their allies. On this reading, it was the Communists' fealty to Moscow that undermined the possibility of a more durable Latin American anti-imperialist coalition; one form of transnationalism overpowered another.

Yet as I have argued in this chapter, there were many other factors at work. While the PCM's turn to the "class against class" strategy certainly aggravated relations with the rest of the left, divergences between apristas, Communists, and campesino organizations had already begun to emerge long before mid-1928. These arose over a range of issues—China, Nicaragua, the question of class alliances—but at their core were differences over how to relate to Latin America's existing governments. For the apristas, the Mexican government was an ally in the struggle against US imperialism and the herald of a coming revolutionary transformation of the rest of Latin America. For the LNC, Mexico's postrevolutionary state was the campesinos' best means of protecting their gains and of keeping alive the hope of a more radical agrarian reform in future. The PCM had an ambivalent relationship to the Mexican state under Calles, but in the tense climate that developed in 1928–29, the two entered into a more adversarial relationship.

The radicalization of the Comintern line then coincided with a period of turbulence for the postrevolutionary regime.

It was this combination of circumstances that made the disintegration of Mexico City's radical transnational milieu so swift: the temporal coincidence, that is, of sharpening polarization within the left, crises for the Mexican state, and the Comintern's lurch toward confrontation. In 1929, a string of emergencies presented the different components of the radical left with stark strategic dilemmas. In each case, the transnational framing to which they had previously been wedded came into conflict with a nationally bounded perspective, forcing them to choose between alignments that had previously been complementary but were now incompatible: either with the Comintern or with the Mexican state; either APRA or LADLA; either the *campesino* movement or the PCM. These options led in divergent directions, both for the individuals and organizations concerned and ultimately for the Latin American left. Over time, the trajectories that branched in 1928–29 became defining features of segments of the left that were solidly antagonistic, with conflicting views on how best to combat imperialism and fundamentally incompatible visions of revolution. As we will see, each came to offer distinct perspectives on race and nation, too, but those developed out of fractures that had already emerged in Mexico City's anti-imperial milieu.

The Communists' and the *apristas*' responses to the Mexican state were motivated by contrasting ideas about what the Latin American state itself was. The distinction is captured in an article written by Pavletich in mid-1929, coinciding with his departure from APRA and his joining Mariátegui's Peruvian Socialist Party.[124] Pavletich was responding to an as-yet-unpublished text by Haya, "The Anti-Imperialist State." Written as a direct response to Mella's *¿Que es el ARPA?*, Haya's text built on the analysis he had laid out in his Mexico City lectures of 1927, though it was not published until 1936.[125] In Latin America, Haya argued, the state was not only, as Marx had it, a tool used by one class to oppress the rest, but could also serve as an "instrument for the defense of the peasant, working, and middle classes united against the imperialism that threatens them." Class conflict between these groups was "subordinated to the great conflict with imperialism, which is the greater danger."[126] This was an argument Haya had made before during his public appearances. Drawing on his personal knowledge as a former *aprista*, Pavletich noted that Haya often made use of a resonant image to illustrate his point: that of passengers on a ship—"aristocrats, bourgeois, and proletarians"— uniting to save it from shipwreck. In Pavletich's paraphrase, "Faced with imminent catastrophe . . . they drown class prejudices and set aside resentments, in order jointly to devote themselves, in a noble and human gesture, to the task of salvation."[127]

The problem with Haya's argument, according to Pavletich, was that it blurred the very real clashes of interest between the different classes. It also assumed that one could simply capture the state and turn it into "an instrument to balance the interests of diverse national hierarchies," "representing equally the contradictory and opposed interests of those who forged it."[128] Returning to the ship metaphor, Pavletich suggested a more realistic scenario: At the moment of crisis, the wealthier passengers would escape in the lifeboats to which their social positions would grant them access. From a safe distance, they would then watch the ship sink beneath the waves, together with the last of its proletarian passengers.

Pavletich himself may have had cause to ponder this metaphor one year later as he sailed away from Manzanillo, deported from Mexico as a "pernicious foreigner." The disintegration of Mexico City's radical milieu sent many of its key figures into new exiles. Some fled to other parts of Latin America, while several of the Communists, including Junco and Modotti, ended up taking refuge in the USSR. Their dispersal across the globe coincided with a series of Comintern debates in which the nation-state became the explicit object of contention, and which had surprising repercussions for Latin America.

PART TWO

Moscow/Buenos Aires/ The Caribbean/Lima (1928–1932)

FOUR

Black Radicals, Bolsheviks, and Self-Determination

CONVERGING STRANDS

At the end of the 1920s, the handful of spaces where Latin American radicals had been able to debate, publish, and organize in relative freedom all but disappeared. The combination of government crackdown and rising sectarian tensions in Mexico was repeated across much of the region. Communists were forced into exile or underground, as were some of the Mexico City–based *apristas*. But while this reduced the radical left's room for maneuver, it did not diminish its energy or imagination. Nor did it curtail its geographical horizons. If anything, both the creativity and transnational scope of radical left debates increased in the late 1920s, even as the physical sites for these debates changed. The conceptual terrain also shifted: Race and ethnicity became more prominent within discussions of revolutionary strategy.

In this chapter and the following two, the scene moves to a string of locations—Buenos Aires, Moscow, the Caribbean—as I track the evolution of radical debates around race, empire, and sovereignty. I devote particular attention to contention within the Communist movement around race and self-determination. From 1928 to 1930, Latin American Communists engaged in far-reaching discussions on race, including racism's role in shaping the present and how to redress its systemic consequences.

The scope and depth of these discussions have not been fully explored or appreciated. In large part this is because they coincided with the onset of the Comintern's Third Period. As we saw in chapter 3, the Comintern's adoption of a more confrontational stance put an end to alliances with social-democrats or bourgeois nationalists, widening rifts between Communists and other parts of the left. The new line was laid out at the Sixth Comintern Congress, held in Moscow in 1928 and attended by over five hundred Communist delegates from more than fifty countries. Occurring at the same time that Stalin was consolidating his grip on power in the Soviet Union, the 1928 Congress is widely seen as confirming the Comintern's transformation into a top-down, ideologically conformist entity, in which the project of global revolution was increasingly subordinated to the foreign policy priorities of the Soviet state.[1]

Yet while the Third Period brought a narrowing of ideological horizons, it paradoxically created some openings. These included attempts to address racial inequality and discrimination, closer engagement with movements for national liberation, and wide-ranging debates about the validity and political repercussions of the category of race itself. All of these strands converged in Comintern deliberations over the idea of self-determination.

At the end of the Sixth Congress, the delegates approved a program that included a call for "the recognition of the right of all nations, irrespective of race, to complete self-determination, that is, self-determination inclusive of the right to State separation."[2] Yet during the congress itself there had been heated discussions over which groups this policy should apply to—and in particular, whether groups usually identified as racial minorities should instead be treated as "nations," with a corresponding right to territorial self-determination. During deliberations on the United States, a subcommittee adopted a policy doing exactly that: Majority-Black areas in the southern United States were to be given the right to territorial self-determination—what became known as the "Black Belt thesis." As several scholars have observed, this had a notable impact on the trajectory of US Communism for several years thereafter; the party began organizing efforts in the South that were transformative both for its militants and for the Black popular movements they encountered there.[3]

Much less well known, however, are the consequences of the Black Belt thesis for Latin America. In this chapter I argue that debates around Black self-determination at the Comintern's Sixth Congress also refashioned Communists' thinking about race in the rest of the Americas, including their approach to Indigenous populations. It was through discussions of race in the United States and the colonial world that the Comintern arrived at the idea that Indigenous groups and people of African descent in Latin America were "nationalities" rather than racial or ethnic minorities—and that they therefore had the right to self-determination.

In what follows, I explore the origins of the Comintern's Black self-determination policy and the process through which it was applied to Latin America. In much of the scholarship to date, the self-determination policy has been portrayed as an aberration that Moscow briefly imposed on the region's Communists, transferring Bolshevik ideas about the "national question" to the Western Hemisphere without regard for local realities.[4] Yet the archival evidence tells a different story. I argue that far from being a crude transplantation of Soviet thinking to the Americas, the self-determination policy took shape through a complex and multisided dialogue that unfolded between venues as far flung as Moscow, Harlem, Buenos Aires, and Brussels, and that involved a range of participants: Bolsheviks, anti-colonial activists, and US and Latin American radicals.

Black radicals from the United States and the Caribbean were critical to the formulation of the self-determination policy, which emerged, as we will see, out of a confluence of Pan-Africanism, anti-colonialism, and Soviet thinking about "nations" and "nationality." This chapter focuses in particular on US Communist Harry Haywood, coauthor of the Black Belt thesis. In portraying the adoption of the self-determination policy as an outlandish imposition—one historian labeled it "bizarre"—previous scholarship has tended to disregard its transnational origins and at the same time downplay Haywood's role in shaping it.[5] I see the policy as the product of a more complex and contingent process, in which Haywood was an active participant.

The adoption of the Black Belt thesis paved the way for delegates to the Sixth Congress to apply the idea of self-determination to Indigenous peoples in Latin America. Discussions of the Indigenous and people of African descent have often been sundered, both historically and in scholarly literature.[6] But in Moscow in the summer of 1928 they were closely intertwined. Deliberations on the Black Belt thesis spilled over into sessions on Latin America and the colonial world. I show how, in the midst of vocal commitments to anti-colonialism and the struggle against racism, delegates began to frame the movement's relation to the Indigenous as a matter of "national" liberation. In the process, they recategorized what had previously been viewed as racial oppressions as national ones—and territorial sovereignty became the central means for redressing them. Drawing on first-person recollections and Comintern archival materials, I not only bring together neglected moments in the history of US and Latin American Communism; I also link Latin American radical debates to Black internationalism and anti-colonial thought, reconnecting the Comintern's self-determination policy to the broader context in which it emerged.

THE MAKING OF A BLACK BOLSHEVIK

The first time Harry Haywood heard about the Russian Revolution was toward the end of the First World War, while he was serving in the US Army in northeastern France. In August 1918, as his regiment stopped by a roadside, they saw men in unfamiliar uniforms huddled behind barbed wire. They were Russian Cossacks, and in the wake of the Bolshevik Revolution their French allies considered them unreliable and withdrew them from the fighting. In Haywood's recollection, the incident made little impression on him: "At the time, I was not even sure of the meaning of the word revolution."[7] But a decade later, Haywood found himself in Moscow debating the Comintern's policy on race with leading Bolsheviks and members of Communist parties from around the world. His personal and political journey over that span embodies the transnational mix of ideas behind the Comintern's Black self-determination policy.

Born in Omaha, Nebraska in 1898, Haywood's original name was Haywood Hall.[8] His parents had both been born slaves in the 1860s, his father in Tennessee, his mother in Missouri. Though he experienced plenty of racism in his youth, the moment that radicalized Haywood came in July 1919 with the nationwide eruption of white supremacist violence. By that time, Haywood was working on the railroads in Chicago. "Bewilderment and shock struck the black community" on the South Side, Haywood wrote. "I began to see that I had to fight," he recalled: "I had to commit myself to struggle against whatever it was that made racism possible."[9]

In 1922, Haywood was drawn into Communist circles through his brother, Otto Hall, who had joined the US Communist Party a year earlier.[10] Like many Black radicals, the brothers had been impressed by the Bolsheviks' success in overthrowing the old tsarist order, but they were also drawn by the Comintern's early concern with people of African descent in the United States. The "Theses on the National and Colonial Question" adopted at the Comintern's Second Congress in 1920 insisted that "communist parties must give direct support to the revolutionary movements among the dependent nations and those without equal rights (e.g. in Ireland, and among the American Negroes), and in the colonies."[11]

There was another reason Black radicals in the United States were attracted to the Soviet regime. As Haywood put it: "Most impressive as far as blacks were concerned was that the [Bolshevik] revolution laid the basis for solving the national and racial questions on the basis of complete freedom for the numerous nations, colonial peoples, and minorities formerly oppressed by the czarist empire."[12] The Jamaican socialist journalist Wilfred Domingo expressed similar sentiments in 1919, describing the USSR as "a country in which dozens of racial and lingual types have settled their many differences . . . a country from which the lynch rope is banished and in which racial tolerance and peace now exist."[13] This idea of the Soviet Union as a champion of racial and ethnic equality exerted a powerful influence on Black radicals in the United States, as it did on radicals in Latin America and elsewhere. It is therefore worth clarifying what the Soviet view of the "national question" was, before then seeing how Haywood and others took up its key principles and adapted them to their own ends.

DEFINING BOLSHEVIK POLICY

From early on, the Bolsheviks had supported the rights of the Russian empire's national minorities. The 1903 program of what was then called the Russian Social Democratic Labor Party (RSDLP) envisaged toppling the tsar and putting in place a new constitution that would guarantee the "right of self-determination for all nations included within the bounds of the state."[14] But what this meant in practice remained rather abstract. Bolshevik policy on the national question only fully crystallized ten years later, in a series of texts Lenin published in 1913–14.[15]

Lenin was responding to two alternative views of the "national question" laid out by socialists elsewhere in Europe; on one side were the "Austro-Marxists," and on the other Rosa Luxemburg of the Polish Social Democrats. In the former camp, Otto Bauer had in 1907 put forward the idea of "national cultural autonomy," arguing that the best way to manage differences within a multinational state was to encourage their expression in cultural forms and to give communities limited autonomy over affairs in this realm.[16] Luxemburg, meanwhile, had in 1908–9 argued against the idea of granting national minorities self-determination, since this obscured the more fundamental class divisions in capitalist societies.[17] In her view, supporting self-determination for minorities would give free rein to bourgeois nationalists among them, rather than encouraging workers to unite across national lines against their common oppressors.

In his 1913–14 texts, Lenin articulated a position distinct from both these standpoints. Against the Austro-Marxists, he argued that their concept of "national cultural autonomy" would mean the segregation of schools, workplaces, and so on along national lines, which would only fuel reactionary forces. Still more importantly, for Lenin "cultural autonomy" failed to address the fact that national movements inherently tended toward taking a territorial form.[18] Against Luxemburg, meanwhile, Lenin argued that the fear of empowering bourgeois nationalism among minorities only played into the hands of the larger oppressor nations. Fighting for equal rights for all nations, and for the right of self-determination in particular, was not only morally consistent; it was also the most effective way to combat the most dangerous and reactionary forms of nationalism—those of powerful empires such as Russia and Britain, for example.[19]

These arguments were combined in a resolution Lenin's party adopted in 1913. (Having emerged as a faction within the RSDLP in 1903, the Bolsheviks formed a separate organization in 1912.) The resolution urged support for the right of all oppressed peoples in the Russian Empire to self-determination, "i.e., the right to secede and form independent states."[20] This enshrined a crucial feature of Bolshevik nationalities policy that would recur in Comintern discussions of self-determination in the Americas fifteen years later: the assumption that territorial sovereignty was the best way to counter the effects of national oppression.

It was also at around this time, in 1913, that Stalin produced the canonical Bolshevik definition of what constituted a nation. As a Georgian, Stalin was himself a member of a national minority within the empire. His essay "The National Question and Social Democracy," written during a stint in Vienna, defined a nation as "a historically constituted, stable community of people, formed on the basis of a common language, territory, economic life, and psychological make-up manifested in a common culture."[21] This multicomponent description was hugely influential throughout the Communist movement across the twentieth century and was repeatedly cited by participants in Comintern debates in the 1920s.

Thanks to this work on the "national question," Stalin was appointed commissar of nationalities on the day after the October Revolution—a post from which he oversaw the new regime's efforts to hold together the former Romanov empire. In principle, the new Soviet state was to be a voluntary union of peoples who had exercised their right to self-determination. In practice, however, what took shape between 1917 and the formation of the USSR in 1922 was a system of centralized control from Moscow with a nominally federal structure.[22] As we will see in subsequent chapters, the gap between the idealized image of Bolshevik nationalities policy and the hard reality of centralism rarely troubled advocates of Soviet-style self-determination.

The "national question" was not only pivotal to the Bolsheviks' domestic politics; it also loomed large in their relations with the rest of the world. One of their earliest statements on national issues, published in December 1917, was titled "To All Muslim Toilers of Russia and the East."[23] From its foundation in 1919, the Comintern, too, encouraged movements for national liberation in the colonial world. In July 1920, Lenin and M. N. Roy presented theses on "national and colonial questions," to which the organization's Second Congress devoted two entire days.[24] This marked the beginning of a more concerted focus on colonized peoples, notably those under British rule in India and Africa. Two months later, the Bolsheviks held the Congress of the Peoples of the East in Baku, drawing together eighteen hundred delegates from across the Middle East and Central and South Asia. The Baku Congress's manifesto exhorted them to join a *ghazavat* or "holy war"—but this time "under the red banner of the Communist International"—for "the liberation of the Peoples of the East . . . for complete equality of all peoples and races, whatever language they may speak, whatever the color of their skin and whatever the religion they profess."[25]

By the time Haywood joined the US Communist Party in 1925, he was convinced that "Moscow had now become the focus of the colonial revolution." In joining the party, he felt he would not so much be joining a national political organization as becoming "part of a world revolutionary movement uniting Chinese, Africans, and Latin Americans with Europeans and North Americans."[26] Internationalism of the kind expressed here by Haywood was one key ingredient in the growth of Communism worldwide; but in the case of Black US radicals, there were also other varieties of internationalism in play.

PAN-AFRICAN PERSPECTIVES

Haywood joined the Young Communist League in 1923 and then the US Communist Party two years later.[27] But his first organizational affiliation was a six-month spell in the African Blood Brotherhood (ABB) in 1922–23. Founded in Harlem in 1919, the ABB was driven by a combination of socialism and anti-colonialism, seeking an end to racial oppression in the United States and independence from Britain for the Caribbean homelands of many of its members. Though Haywood's passage through the ABB was brief, its brand of Black internationalism had a shaping influence on the Comintern's stance on race and on its self-determination policy.

The ABB was markedly cosmopolitan: As well as its Nevis-born founder, Cyril Briggs, members included the Jamaicans Wilfred Domingo and Claude McKay; Otto Huiswoud, originally from Suriname; and Lovett Fort-Whiteman, born in Texas, who had been radicalized by working in Yucatán during the Mexican Revolution.[28] Within two years of its founding, almost all the ABB's members had also joined the US Communist Party. As well as being drawn to the Bolsheviks' revolutionary example, as Briggs later put it their "interest in Communism was sparked by the national policy of the Russian Bolsheviks and the anti-imperialist orientation of the Soviet state birthed by the October Revolution."[29]

Two other currents of thought circulating in the aftermath of the First World War left their imprint on the ABB, and on Haywood too. One was the drive toward national self-determination that was accelerating in Europe near the end of the war. This raised the question of whether people of African descent should have similar rights. In September 1917, Briggs wrote an editorial for the Black newspaper *Amsterdam News* asking rhetorically: "Security of Life for Poles and Serbs—Why Not for Colored Americans?"[30] A few months later in the same venue, he framed the question in territorial terms, calling for a "colored autonomous State" to be established in "one-tenth of the territory of the United States."[31] According to Haywood, Briggs did not have a specific location in mind for this Black homeland, at various times suggesting Washington, Oregon, Idaho, California, and Nevada.[32] Though Briggs's views did not become ABB policy at the time, they set a precedent for Black territorial self-rule on which Haywood could draw a few years later.

The second major influence on the ABB's outlook was Pan-Africanism. Aspirations for unity among people of African descent had been growing since the end of the nineteenth century; in 1919 W. E. B. Du Bois organized the First Pan-African Congress in Paris.[33] But the organization the ABB and the Communists came to see as their direct rival was the Universal Negro Improvement Association (UNIA). Founded by Marcus Garvey in

Jamaica in 1914 but based in Harlem after 1916, it called for unity among all people of African descent and encouraged its members to migrate "back" to Africa, where the UNIA would establish a sovereign Black state. By the second half of the 1920s, the UNIA claimed several million members and nearly one thousand branches; most of these were in the United States, but around a quarter were scattered across the Caribbean, South and Central America, and West and South Africa.[34]

As a transnational movement for Black liberation, the UNIA was competing for the loyalty of Black workers on similar terrain to the ABB and Communist parties. Initially relations between the movements were friendly—Wilfred Domingo was the first editor of the UNIA's newspaper, *Negro World*, and ABB members attended and spoke at UNIA congresses until 1921—but over time they became more antagonistic.[35] Still, Black radicals remained keenly aware of the support Garveyism enjoyed in the United States and Caribbean—and of the magnetic appeal of the concept of Black self-rule. It may have been in response to Garvey's Back to Africa movement that Briggs modified his views on Black sovereignty: By 1921, he was no longer calling for a Black homeland on US soil, instead echoing the UNIA platform by advocating the creation of a "strong, stable, independent Negro state . . . in Africa."[36]

Though ABB members were critical of Garveyism on several counts—among them its hostility to organized labor and what they saw as the unrealistic nature of the Back to Africa program—their engagement with Pan-Africanism had a powerful impact on the Comintern's view of race.[37] It was largely due to the presence in Moscow of ABB members McKay and Huiswoud that race received sustained attention at the Comintern's Fourth Congress in 1922.[38] Huiswoud presented a "Report on the Black Question" in which he called for the Comintern to organize Black workers for a worldwide struggle against capitalism and imperialism.[39] McKay, meanwhile, laid out an ambitious vision of a global movement for Black liberation—what he termed "a Negro International."[40] He proposed a conference that would gather "representative American, South African, West African, and West Indian Negros of Revolutionary spirit" and establish sections for coordinating their efforts.[41] The resemblance between his proposal and the UNIA is plain.

Within this Pan-Africanist perspective, McKay recognized that demands would vary from place to place. In the United States, the demand was "for full citizenship rights," while in Puerto Rico, Haiti, and the Dominican Republic "the movement is for independence"—the latter two countries were under US occupation at the time—and in Africa it was "to defend . . . native rights against the growing encroachments of the Whites."[42] But McKay still saw an overarching, racial commonality between these struggles. In that respect, his proposal reinforced a tendency in Comintern thinking to view all people of African descent as part of a single oppressed group spanning both colonized and noncolonized realms.

This linkage between the oppressions suffered by Black people in the United States and by colonized peoples in Africa would become critical to the self-determination policy. Yet the idea that Black people should have the right to form a separate state, raised by Briggs in 1917, would not coalesce as Comintern policy until 1928. One of the reasons for the timing of this shift is that, after extensive debates in 1927–28, the Comintern began to identify racial and ethnic minorities as incipient nations.

ENCOUNTERS IN MOSCOW

Haywood played an integral part in these discussions. In 1926 he left the United States for the USSR, where he would spend the next four years studying in the Comintern's cadre schools. This was a crucial interval in his life; it was during his sojourn in Moscow that Haywood became a member of the US Communist Party's Central Committee and its leading spokesperson on race. Part of the reason for his increased prominence was his advocacy of Black self-determination. The story of how that policy took shape is bound up with the ideas, forces, and movements that Haywood encountered in the Bolshevik capital.

On his way to the USSR, Haywood Hall acquired the name by which he would be known for the rest of his life. Seeking to avoid the attentions of the Federal Bureau of Investigation, before leaving the United States he applied for a passport under an alias combining his mother's first name, Harriet, with his father's, to produce "Harry Haywood."[43] He had to take a roundabout route to get to the USSR, traveling first to Canada via a network of comrades—he compared it to the Underground Railroad—then by boat from Quebec to Germany, and from there to the Soviet capital by train.

In the spring of 1926, the city Haywood arrived in was a place of wild dreams as well as material hardship.[44] The center of Soviet power, Moscow was also a magnet for traders and migrants, with commerce reviving under the Bolsheviks' New Economic Policy, as well as being the scene of remarkable creativity in the arts. The German Marxist thinker Walter Benjamin, who experienced its febrile intensity from December 1926 to January 1927, described it as a place where "each day, each thought, each life lies . . . as on a laboratory table."[45]

Haywood was greeted on his arrival by his older brother Otto, who had preceded him by a few months.[46] Both studied at the Comintern's cadre schools, through which many key figures in twentieth-century Communism also passed: Ho Chi Minh, Deng Xiaoping, Nazim Hikmet, Josip Broz Tito, and Erich Honecker, to name only a few.[47] Haywood and his brother were initially at the Kommunisticheskii Universitet Trudiashchikhsia Vostoka (KUTV; Communist University for the Toilers of the East). As Haywood recounts in his autobiography, the KUTV, founded in 1921, was divided into two sections, "inner" and "outer."[48] While the inner section encompassed the USSR's Caucasian, Central Asian, Siberian, and Far Eastern territories, the outer section included students from China, South and Southeast Asia, the Middle East, and Africa. It also included a handful of Black students from the United States.[49] The overarching category that ostensibly bound these disparate places together, as per the institution's name, was the "East." That category in turn rested on a conception of the "East" as a colonized space.[50] The fact that the Comintern counted US citizens of African descent among colonized peoples was consistent with its views to date; recall Lenin's pronouncement at the 1920 Second Congress. But it also pointed to a crucial ambiguity that would recur in the ensuing years: To what extent did the "racial" and "colonial" questions overlap, and how was racial liberation tied in with anti-colonialism?

Haywood's time in Moscow coincided with a renewed attention to these questions on the Comintern's part. The Pan-Africanist idea of a collective racial oppression endured by people of African descent was still present, but the means proposed for redressing it differed. The 1927 Brussels Congress of the League Against Imperialism, for example, adopted a "Common Resolution on the Negro Question," which called for "complete equality between the Negro race and all other races" and the "complete freedom of the peoples of Africa and of African origin."[51] In some cases, the resolution tied struggles for freedom and equality to the attainment of sovereignty. In Africa, it called for "control of the land and governments of Africa by the Africans"; in the cases of Haiti, Cuba, Puerto Rico, and the Dominican Republic, it demanded "complete political and economic independence and the immediate withdrawal of imperialist troops," while advocating "self-government" in the rest of the Caribbean. In the United States, however, while the Brussels resolution referred to "disfranchisement, legal injustice, debt and convict slavery, and lynching and mob violence," there was no sense that people of African descent had a right to self-determination by virtue of their racial origin.[52] At the time, this was also Haywood's view: "To me, the idea of a black nation within U.S. boundaries seemed far-fetched," he recalled. Instead, his preferred solution was "the incorporation of blacks into U.S. society on the basis of complete equality."[53] How and when did Haywood's and the Comintern's thinking begin to shift?

Three factors converged over the course of 1927–28 to tilt Haywood toward supporting Black self-determination. The first was the salience of the "national question" in 1920s Moscow. At this point, the Soviet authorities were dedicating considerable resources to counting and classifying their own far-flung populations and to subsidizing a wave of publications and radio broadcasts in non-Russian languages. Soviet linguists produced dozens of dictionaries and developed alphabets for languages that had previously lacked scripts. These efforts contributed to making the USSR—temporarily—into what Terry Martin terms an "affirmative action empire."[54] In 1926, the first comprehensive Soviet census allowed those surveyed to self-identify their nationality; as a result, the number of officially recognized groups ballooned from ninety or so in 1920 to around two hundred.[55] Indeed, the late 1920s saw a flowering of national identities; according to Yuri Slezkine, this was "the most extravagant celebration of ethnic diversity that any state had ever financed."[56]

In this context, it is not surprising that national questions loomed large for Haywood. He first encountered many of the USSR's nationalities at KUTV—"Uzbeks, Tajiks, Bashkirs, Yakuts, Chuvashes ... and many other national and ethnic groups I had never heard of before."[57] During his summer vacations in 1927 and 1928, Haywood also "observed ... firsthand in the Crimea and the Caucasus" how the use of languages suppressed under the tsars was now being officially encouraged. Still more crucially, Haywood's time in the USSR supplied him with a conceptual schema for defining what a nation was. As Francine Hirsch has demonstrated, early Soviet ethnographers deployed a cluster of terms to describe the USSR's myriad ethnic groups.[58] These implied a hierarchy of size and significance, ranging from large *natsii,* "nations," to smaller *natsional'nosti,* "nationalities," and *narodnosti,* "peoples." For the Bolsheviks, this continuum of terms mapped onto the line of humanity's historical development, from the tribal identities of "primitive communism," through the prenational phase of feudalism, to the development of national consciousness under capitalism. The French, Italians, and Germans were full-blown nations, while the many peoples of the Russian empire were distributed at various points along the continuum. The Bolsheviks' idea of a spectrum of national consciousness provided a framework for establishing which groups were "nations," and it surfaced repeatedly in Comintern discussions.

The KUTV curriculum reproduced this framework. As Haywood put it, "The starting point for us was to understand that the formation of peoples into nations is an objective law of social development." Some of the peoples inhabiting the new Soviet state "had not yet fully matured" by the time the Revolution took place; now, however, "the Soviet system itself... became a powerful factor in the consolidation of these nationalities into nations."[59] The idea of a transition from "nationalities" to "nations" implies the same continuum of national development noted previously, but this time with the Soviet state rather than capitalism as the catalyst for the shift.

A second crucial influence on Haywood's thinking came into play in the fall of 1927 when he began studying at another of the Comintern's cadre-training institutions, the Mezhdunarodnaia Leninskaia Shkola (MLSh; International Lenin School), founded in 1925. Here classes were organized along linguistic lines, and Haywood was grouped together with British, US, Australian, New Zealand, Canadian, and South African Communists. But he was particularly struck by his encounter with Irish radicals. "As members of oppressed nations, we had a lot in common," Haywood observed. What impressed him most of all was "their sense of national pride—not of the chauvinistic variety, but that of revolutionaries aware of the international importance of their independence struggle."[60] The idea that nationalism could have a radical internationalist slant gave Haywood food for thought; he "became deeply interested in the Irish question, seeing in it a number of parallels to U.S. blacks."[61] Could Black nationalism play an equivalent role in the United States, rallying people of African descent to an anti-colonial, internationalist banner? In retrospect, he continued, "I am certain that this interest [in Ireland] heightened my receptivity to the idea of a black nation in the United States."[62]

The third shaping influence on Haywood's thinking was conversations he had with friends in late 1927 and early 1928, and in particular with Nikolai Nasanov. A native of Siberia, Nasanov had met Haywood in the mid 1920s in Chicago, where he briefly worked for the US Communist Party's youth league.[63] When they met again in Moscow, they debated the US party's stance toward people of African descent. Why, Nasanov asked, did the party not advocate for their right to self-determination? Haywood raised objections he had voiced in the past: Black people in the United States were an oppressed race rather than a national group, and there was no territorial basis for any claim to self-determination. As well as being impracticable, the idea would get in the way of cross-racial unity, diverting Black and white workers from the joint struggle for socialism.[64]

But in the course of their discussions, Haywood's views changed. Nasanov argued that if Black people in the United States lacked some of the characteristics of a nation, according to Stalin's canonical 1913 definition, this was because "imperialist policy . . . is directed towards artificially and forcibly retaining the economic and cultural backwardness of the colonial peoples."[65] Black people in the United States, in other words, had been halted in their progression along the continuum of national development. To support their right to self-determination was merely to call for their path to be unblocked. Nasanov raised two further arguments that resonated with Haywood. One was that self-determination was not solely a concern for Black people; on the contrary, obtaining justice for them was "a constituent part" of the struggle for socialism for whites, too. Nasanov also agreed with Haywood that the US Communist Party was guilty of serious "underestimation of the importance of work among blacks." But whereas Haywood believed this derived from "the persistence of remnants of white racist ideology within the ranks of the Party," Nasanov argued that it was the other way around: Racist attitudes persisted because the party still had the incorrect line, refusing to see the question in national terms.[66] From this perspective, support for self-determination could in itself become an instrument for combating racism within the party.

Another key shift occurred when Haywood revised his earlier opinion of Garveyism. In dismissing it as petty bourgeois Black nationalism, he recalled, he had failed to see that "the Garvey movement was the U.S. counterpart of the vast upsurge of national and colonial liberation struggles" of the 1910s and 1920s.[67] In Moscow, having absorbed Soviet ideas about the national question and been exposed to radical internationalist forms of nationalism, he saw Garveyism in a new light: as a misguided but nonetheless authentic Black nationalism. For Haywood, this was, as he put it, "the clincher." Communists had to seize hold of the sentiments behind Black nationalism and redirect them against capitalism and US imperialism, and the best way to start was to call for the "right of self-determination in the South, with full equality throughout the country."[68]

By early 1928, Haywood was fully in favor of Black self-determination, and it was he and Nasanov who drew up this new policy and made the case for it at the Comintern's Sixth Congress. But there was still considerable opposition to the idea, both in the Comintern and in the US Communist Party. For this resistance to be overcome, a further convergence of factors would have to take place.

THE HAYWOOD–NASANOV THESIS

Why did the 1928 Comintern Congress take up the issue of Black oppression again? For Haywood, the answer lay in "the changed world situation: the sharpened crisis of the world capitalist system . . . the beginning of a deepening economic depression in Europe; and the continued upsurge of the colonial revolutions in China, India, and Indonesia." Globally, this was "a period in which the national and colonial question was to acquire a new urgency." But he also pointed to a further factor specific to the United States: "the low status of the [Communist Party's] Negro work" and the lack of progress made on this front, "despite the prodding of the Comintern."[69] It was the combination of the Comintern's intensified anti-colonial stance and its denunciations of racism—often referred to as "white chauvinism"— that ultimately pressured the US Communist Party into endorsing Black self-determination.

The initial prospects for the policy were not good. Haywood's and Nasanov's ideas received a first airing in June 1928, in the run-up to the Comintern Congress, at a meeting of the "Negro Commission" of the Anglo-American Secretariat, the section of the Comintern responsible for the English-speaking world. Haywood demanded that the US Communist Party pay greater attention to people of African descent and that it launch serious organizational efforts in the US South. Then, in a move that reflected his conversations with Nasanov, he quoted Stalin's definition of a nation to argue that Black people in the South possessed many of the characteristics of a nation, and that there was a basis for a national revolutionary movement among Black peasants in the South.[70] Otto Hall poured scorn on his brother's analysis, dismissing the idea that the US party should support a

Black nationalist movement in the South as "criminally stupid" and tantamount to "revolutionary Jim Crowism."[71] He also pointed out that even Haywood himself admitted that Black people in the United States did not meet *all* of Stalin's criteria for nationhood—they notably lacked a language distinct from that of the white population—and were therefore not a national minority.

The same commission met again a few weeks later, during the Comintern's Sixth Congress. This time a few more US Communist Party members who had arrived in Moscow for the congress attended. On August 2, Haywood presented a revised version of his and Nasanov's thesis. He explicitly framed it as an attempt to redress the US party's neglect of racial questions. The party should aspire to be "the emancipator of the oppressed Negro race," and should adopt the slogan of "full social and political equality."[72] Haywood then made a key assertion: In its approach to race, the US party should be guided by Comintern resolutions on national and colonial questions. This, he argued, was because people of African descent should be considered a national group: "Although there are some peculiarities in the Negro question in the United States . . . nevertheless the sum total of the economic, social, and political relations existing between the Negroes and the white population make this question one of an oppressed national (or racial) minority."[73]

The commission's response to the "Haywood–Nasanov thesis" was decidedly mixed. Several of its members objected strongly to what they saw as the misidentification of people of African descent as a national group. US Communist Party member and Sixth Congress delegate Sam Darcy said the thesis showed "no understanding of the difference between a national minority and a race minority."[74] Others, while not convinced of Haywood's arguments, were at least willing to discuss whether people of African descent in the United States were a nation. At the commission's meeting the next day, several attendees put forward alternative terms: an "oppressed race," a racial group "made up of many nations," a "national-racial minority," or a group "developing slowly towards a nation"—the latter concept recalling the historical continuum described earlier.[75]

The sheer range of categories being entertained here suggests that many on the commission were grappling with a genuine conceptual problem. One of its members, however, sought to sidestep the debate altogether: Alexander Bittelman, a Russian Jewish emigre who had joined the US Communist Party in 1919, observed that "on the question of nation and race, there is no difference between the two. . . . The real question is, what kind of a race and what kind of a nation."[76] Bittelman's concerns were of a tactical nature: "The question of self-determination is not so terrible. It is not a question as to whether we should issue this slogan [i.e., the demand for Black self-determination], but what concrete forms we should give it."[77]

This emphasis on the tactical utility of self-determination complemented Haywood's and Nasanov's call for a stronger commitment to the struggle against racism. Adopting the self-determination policy would bolster the US Communist Party's reputation and lay the groundwork for an organizing push in the South, while at the same time making clear to white members the party's opposition to "white chauvinism." It is worth noting this dual character of the self-determination policy—directed outward, toward the Black population the party was courting, and inward toward its own white members—since, as we will see in chapter 7, this same pattern would recur in 1930s Cuba.

On August 4, 1928, the Negro Commission passed a draft resolution that attempted to split the difference between Haywood's position and that of his opponents. It affirmed that, "while fighting for the cause of the Negroes as an oppressed race, and while underlining the international race character of the Negro movement, the Party must also bear in mind that in the South of the USA there are certain prerequisites which lead to the future development of a national revolutionary movement among the Negroes."[78] In other words, the Black population of the South was not yet a nation but might still become one. But Haywood's proposal to include a demand for self-determination was voted down, and opposition to the idea still prevailed.

RACE AND NATION IN THE COLONIAL FRAME

Within days, Haywood's luck changed. Rather than being confined to US Communist Party members, the question of Black self-determination was now taken up by a Comintern Congress subcommittee on the "Negro question" created on August 7.[79] This new subcommittee included US party members who had taken part in previous discussions, but it also had a broader and more international profile. Chaired by Comintern functionary David Petrovsky, it included other Comintern staff such as Finnish Communist Otto Kuusinen and representatives from South Africa, Colombia, France, and Belgium, as well as Haywood and Nasanov.

The changes in personnel meant that the US Communist Party members who had opposed the Haywood–Nasanov thesis found themselves in the minority. But more than this, the new context brought a shift in framing. Petrovsky set the tone at the commission's first meeting by observing that "the Negro problem is an international one and is not confined to America only."[80] In practice, the commission set tight limits to its deliberations: On August 11 it decided to restrict its work to South Africa and the United States, "in as much as there is such a lack of material on this question."[81] Among the few materials it had concerning other places was a brief comment from the Colombian delegate, known only as "Cárdenas," who flatly stated, "There is no race hatred in Latin America towards the Negroes."[82] This kind of denial of racism's existence recurs in many discussions of race in Latin America to this day; at the time, the effect of Cárdenas's comments was to block off any discussion of Latin America within the Negro Commission—though as we will see, its deliberations would soon affect the region in other ways. Yet even with its remit narrowed to the United States and South Africa, the shift in the focus of the Negro Commission proved decisive: Over the next few days, the commission discussed the politics of race in the United States through the prism of colonialism. This in turn gave a boost to Haywood's idea of Black self-determination as a form of "national" liberation.

The crucial deliberations on Black self-determination began on August 11. A discussion of South Africa brought together the questions of racism and Black self-determination. The Comintern had previously been critical of the South African Communist Party (SACP) for its inaction on the issue of race—and in particular, the refusal of its (largely white) leadership to take up the Comintern's recommendation, articulated in March 1927 by leading Bolshevik and Comintern Executive Committee member Nikolai Bukharin, that it raise demands "for a Negro republic independent of the British empire"—meaning that all of South Africa should gain sovereignty under the democratic rule of its Black majority.[83] At the time, the SACP had objected that this would divide the working class along racial lines. But in August 1928, the Comintern renewed its criticisms and insisted once more that the SACP take up the demand for "an independent Native South African Republic."[84]

The South Africa discussions were significant in two respects. First, they established a connection between the struggle against racism and the demand for sovereignty. Overcoming the resistance of the SACP's leadership on the latter front was directly tied to putting pressure on it to address the former. Self-determination was both a demand in its own right and an instrument for countering racism among white Communists. The same logic was then applied to the US Communist Party. Petrovsky had made the link a few days earlier: "When we fight for self-determination in the program of the American Party, we are fighting against the principle of white chauvinism."[85] Many of the opponents of the self-determination thesis agreed that racial prejudices within the US party had to be combated; a few days earlier, Otto Hall had told a plenary session of the Congress that there was "more chauvinism in the American Party than in any other Party in the Comintern," arguing that this explained its relative lack of Black members.[86] By the time the Negro Commission discussed the United States on August 11, Haywood's opponents had unwittingly bolstered his position.

Second, the Comintern's approach to South Africa involved a symptomatic blurring of the distinction between race and nation. At the March 1927 meeting mentioned earlier, Bukharin conflated the two, referring to "the national question, or in other words the race question."[87] As well as pushing the SACP to take up the demand for a "Negro republic," Bukharin had proposed the party demand "autonomy for the national white minorities etc."[88] The implication that whites would occupy a distinct "autonomous" territory nested inside a sovereign Black republic echoed the Soviet model, in which many national minorities were allocated autonomous territories within the majority ethnic-Russian RSFSR (Russian Soviet Federative Socialist Republic). But more importantly, the idea of allotting territories along racial lines identified white and Black people *as such* as legitimate subjects for "national" self-determination. The categories of race and nation collapsed into one another. The apparent malleability of these categories underpinned the Comintern's insistence on the "Native Republic" thesis, which the commission now obliged the SACP to adopt.

Immediately after the conversation about South Africa, the commission turned once more to the Haywood–Nasanov thesis. It began by holding a vote "on the principle of self-determination," with the exact "formulation [to] be made afterwards." Haywood's view won out, by ten votes to two. The new wording the commission then approved called on the US Communist Party to "fight for the full rights of the oppressed Negroes and for their right to self-determination." An amendment went further, adding words that made clear what the policy potentially involved: "to the point of separation and organization of a separate state."[89]

This was the resolution that would become the US Communist Party's Black Belt thesis, committing the party to support Black territorial self-rule in the US South. As we have seen, it emerged out of a confluence of Pan-Africanism, Soviet ideas about "nationalities," and a renewed anti-colonial upsurge. The process of its drafting and approval owed much to the contingencies of the Comintern's Sixth Congress—the mix of personnel attending particular meetings and the framework and sequence in which issues were discussed. The debates on Black self-determination in the United States also spilled over into sessions on colonial issues and on Latin America, where they had a marked impact on delegates' views of race and nation.

SOVIETS AND SEMICOLONIALS

In his speech at the opening of the Comintern's Sixth Congress on July 17, 1928, Bukharin observed that "South America is for the first time widely entering the orbit of influence of the Communist International."[90] More Latin American countries than ever before sent representatives to Moscow—there were delegates from Mexico, Brazil, Argentina, Ecuador, Colombia, Uruguay, and Paraguay—and they played an active role in discussions. The region's new visibility in Comintern discussions went hand in hand with increased attention to the geopolitical and economic power of the United States, which the organization saw as the main rival to the British Empire.[91] As a result, a wide range of delegates and Comintern officials weighed in about policies Communists should adopt in the region. There was also much discussion of whether categories used with regard to other parts of the world could be applied to Latin America. The proceedings in Moscow thus offered a preview of debates that would recur in the ensuing decades over the character of Latin American societies, as well as foreshadowing tensions between Communists within the region and the global movement to which they belonged.

For some time, the Comintern had put Latin America in the category of "colonial and semicolonial" countries, placing it alongside both formal colonies and independent territories such as China that remained de facto under the sway of foreign powers. At the Sixth Congress, Latin American delegates objected to this designation. On August 9, Ricardo Paredes, founder of the Ecuadorean Socialist Party, argued that the term "semicolonial" did not account for Latin America's peculiar status as a region mostly made up of independent states in which the dominance of US capital was growing.

He therefore proposed "a new category," consisting of "the 'dependencies' which have been penetrated economically by imperialism, but which retain a certain political independence."[92]

The question of how to categorize Latin America had far-reaching strategic implications, as became clear when Jules Humbert-Droz presented his report on the region on August 16.[93] A former Protestant pastor and founder member of the Swiss Communist Party, Humbert-Droz was based in Moscow for most of the 1920s and was a member of the Comintern's Executive Committee; he would head its Latin American Secretariat in 1929–30.[94] He presented his report in French, the lingua franca for many Comintern deliberations; many of the Latin American delegates would have spoken in French too, while others followed through the efforts of a corps of translators (one of the few areas of the Comintern's activities in which women predominated).[95]

According to Humbert-Droz, there could be no doubt that Latin America was effectively becoming a colony of the United States. He cited the different forms in which US power was penetrating the region, from Wall Street investments to military interventions in Nicaragua and Haiti. He went on to make another argument that resembles an early version of what would become known as dependency theory—the idea, articulated by economists Raúl Prebisch and Hans Singer in the late 1940s, that the worsening terms of trade between "peripheral" countries and the advanced capitalist "core" kept the former in a state of dependency. Humbert-Droz argued that "the more capital imperialism invests in Latin America, the more it develops industrialization, the more also develops the colonization of Latin America." The growth of industry in the region, though it might seem to indicate a modernizing tendency, was in fact part and parcel of the colonization of Latin America by US capital. And since "the capitalist regime is only developing as a colonial regime," this in turn meant local elites could at best play a subordinate role to foreign capital; as Humbert-Droz put it, "there is no base for the development of an independent national capitalism."[96]

The strategic upshot of this was that the struggle against capitalism was tightly bound up with the battle against foreign imperialism. Humbert-Droz urged Latin America's Communists to adopt a radical program: expropriation and nationalization of land, confiscation of foreign-owned enterprises, bringing down landowners and the Church, and the creation of "workers', peasants' and soldiers' soviets."[97] This was similar to the agenda the Comintern was proposing for the colonial world. But Humbert-Droz added two further recommendations. First, to "overcome the nationalism which impe-rialism has fostered in most of the Latin American countries," Communists should call for a "Federal Union of the Workers' and Peasants' Republics of Latin America"—that is, a pan-regional confederation along Soviet lines. Second, he urged them to endorse the idea of "Latin Americanism," that is, pan-regional unity to counter divisions along national lines. For Humbert-Droz, this seemed an easily attainable goal, since there was actually "nothing in the race or language which separates the peoples of Latin America into different nationalities."[98]

These proposals drew the ire of many delegates, in large part because the concept of Latin Americanism smacked of APRA's pan-regional rhetoric. Bertram Wolfe insisted that "we cannot slavishly accept the general pro-posals for Latin American unity which are made by petty bourgeois intel-lectuals," singling out his former friend Haya as a "dangerous careerist."[99] Without mentioning APRA by name, PCM delegate Vittorio Vidali simi-larly decried Latin Americanism as "the ideology of a clearly petty-bourgeois anti-imperialist movement."[100]

But at issue here was a more basic question: What kind of revolution should be pursued? A struggle for liberation from imperialism, which would then develop in a socialist direction, or on the contrary, a struggle in which anti-imperialist and socialist agendas were intertwined? At its core, the di-lemma was the same as the one that had divided Communists and *apristas* in Mexico City. Should existing nation-states be defended and consolidated in the face of US dominance, or dismantled and remade in order to make a direct leap into the socialist future?

"INDIGENOUS ELEMENTS"

In the midst of these discussions, several delegates highlighted a group that had largely been missing from deliberations so far: Latin America's Indig-enous population. On August 9, Paredes, the Ecuadorean delegate, observed that in Latin America "the revolutionary problem is linked up with that of the oppressed races such as the Indians," who were in many countries "the biggest section of the rural population" and were potentially "very revolu-tionary elements." He therefore urged that "this problem of oppressed races must be dealt with in the [Comintern] program."[101] In subsequent sessions on the "colonial question," chaired by two Communists from Indonesia and

Brazil, delegates from Latin America repeatedly returned to the Indigenous theme, pressing the Comintern to address it more substantively. On August 18, Vidali observed that "the colonial and semi-colonial thesis paid very little or hardly any attention to the native [Indigenous] problem."[102] Yet there were twenty-five million Indigenous people in Latin America, he said, "a mass of exploited and enslaved people who are not even entitled to a plot of land."[103]

Vidali then made a radical proposal. He argued that the Comintern's program should insist that "under a regime of workers' and peasants' democratic dictatorship they [Indigenous people] will have the right of self-administration and of developing their own culture, etc." He added that this was not only a question for the future: "Also under the present regime we must struggle for the recognition of these rights."[104] Later that same morning, Wolfe echoed Vidali's recommendation, insisting that Latin America's Communist parties "must work out a whole series of special measures" for the Indigenous population. These should include "such matters as self-determination for the indigenous races, special propaganda in their own languages, special efforts to win leading elements among them, special educational activities for those Communists who are of Indian origin and who speak the Indian dialect so that they can go back into the inner regions of the country and organize the indigenous elements."[105]

These are the first instances I have found of Communists using the term "self-determination" with reference to Indigenous peoples in Latin America. The Soviet context no doubt had an influence. Wolfe's recommendations clearly drew on Bolshevik nationalities policy: The idea that Indigenous cadres should be trained and then return to their home territories directly echoed the strategy of *korenizatsiia*, "taking root," pursued by the Bolsheviks in the 1920s.[106] Vidali's stress on the fostering of Indigenous cultures likewise bore a marked resemblance to the burgeoning of national identities in the USSR of the 1920s. Yet there were two other important factors that influenced their thinking: continuing discussions on Black self-determination in the United States and an intensification of the Comintern's anti-colonial stance.

Vidali himself linked the fate of the Indigenous in Latin America to the plight of people of African descent: "Side by side with this [Indigenous] problem we have that of the black race."[107] He was surely encouraged to draw the parallel by the sustained attention given to the "black question" in the United States over the previous few days. US Communist Party delegates Otto Hall and James Ford had spoken out about persistent "white

chauvinism" within their party, and veteran Japanese militant Sen Katayama had referred to the "criminal neglect of the Negroes on the part of the
American Party."[108]

After the adoption of the Haywood–Nasanov thesis, Black self-determination resurfaced several times in sessions devoted to colonial issues
and to Latin America. Following Humbert-Droz's August 16 report,
Katayama once again upbraided the US Communist Party for its inaction on racial issues, insisting that it "should put up a propaganda slogan—
self-determination and complete independence of the American Negroes,
pointing to the living example of the Soviet Union."[109] Petrovsky echoed
his suggestion: "The American Party must come out openly and unreserv-
edly for the right of national self-determination to the point of separation
and the organization of a separate state of the Negroes in the South."[110] The
US party delegate Charles Phillips agreed, but emphasized that the United
States was just one part of an international picture. In his view the Communist movement needed to "link up the struggle of the Negroes as an
oppressed minority in the United States with anti-imperialist struggles in
Haiti, Santo Domingo, etc. This includes propagation of the right of self-
determination for the Negroes in the United States."[111]

Black self-determination had gone from being a minority position within
the US Communist Party to being taken up by an array of Comintern
delegates—and crucially, it was programmatically linked to combating racism within the movement. Even staunch opponents of the idea seemed to
have yielded. James Ford and Otto Hall repeated their objections to Black
self-determination on August 17 and 18—Ford insisting that "any nationalist movement on the part of the Negroes does nothing but play into the
hands of the bourgeoisie."[112] But Hall conceded that "there is no objection
on our part on the principle of a Soviet Republic for Negroes in America."[113]
Ford meanwhile linked the fate of "Negroes throughout the world" to a
rising "national aspiration"—accepting Haywood's framing of Black self-
determination as a matter of national liberation.[114]

The demand for national liberation was also central to Comintern discussions of the colonial world. Anti-colonialism, as we have seen, had
been part of the organization's program from its foundation in 1919.
With the Sixth Congress, however, national liberation became even more
prominent—and it was now accompanied by a new emphasis on the right
to self-determination. On August 13 Pierre Semard, general secretary of the
French Communist Party, noted the absence of "a paragraph dealing with

the national question" in the draft program Bukharin had presented a few days earlier. "It seems," added Semard, "that we have forgotten about the defense of the national minorities and the fight . . . to secure to them the right of self-determination."[115]

Within the next few days, support for the right to self-determination became one of the red lines separating Communists from social-democrats and other forces worldwide. As the Third International, the Comintern had been founded with the aim of succeeding and replacing the social-democratic Second International. But the latter still existed, and Communists continued to define many of their stances in antagonistic contrast to it. In the summer of 1928, that contrast could be made in real time: While the Comintern's Sixth Congress was happening in Moscow, a meeting of parties and trade unions affiliated with the Second International took place in Brussels on August 5–11. Delegates to the Comintern Congress followed that meeting closely. On August 15, Italian Communist Palmiro Togliatti denounced the European social-democrats gathered in Brussels for refusing to contemplate independence for the territories under their countries' flags: "Negation or limitation of the right of nations to self-determination is the general rule." He posed the alternative in stark terms: "The entire world is today divided in two: On the one side there are the peoples that are struggling for the right of self-determination and on the other side there are their oppressors, whose domination is being more and more shaken." This was a global struggle for liberation, according to Togliatti: "There are barricades which divide the entire earth."[116]

By the time Vidali and Wolfe were floating the idea of Indigenous self-determination on August 18, then, the link between countering racial oppression and supporting a right to sovereignty had been firmly established in the minds of Congress delegates. In the case of South Africa and the US South, "national" self-determination had been established as policy with regard to people of African descent—blurring the categories of race and nationality. But elsewhere, the categories seemed to remain distinct, as in the program the Comintern adopted at the end of the Sixth Congress, which enshrined as a guiding principle the "recognition of the right of all nations, regardless of race, to complete self-determination, i.e. going as far as political secession."[117] These inconsistencies point to an ongoing confusion over how to conceptualize race, both as a social fact and as a political question, uncertainties that would linger as Communist parties across the world debated what the Comintern's new emphasis on self-determination meant.

The Comintern's take-up of the idea of Black and Indigenous self-determination in the Americas was not a unidirectional extension of the Soviet approach to nationalities to the Western Hemisphere. On the contrary, this chapter has argued that the policy developed out of a more complex and multisided process, in which Soviet thinking melded with Black radicalism and anti-colonialism. This convergence took place through figures such as Harry Haywood, whose efforts led to the adoption of the Black Belt thesis. Though this directly concerned people of African descent in the US South, deliberations on it were interwoven with discussions of Latin America and of national liberation in the colonial world. In that context, some Congress delegates applied similar logic to the peoples of Latin America—for the first time raising the idea of Indigenous self-determination. There is thus a clear link between the transnational activism of Black US radicals and Latin American Communism's attempts to address the question of race.

The connections I have drawn in this chapter point to a paradox. At a moment when the Comintern was marked by mounting ideological conformity, it took up the themes of racism, colonialism, and Black and Indigenous liberation in a more serious and sustained manner than ever before. Growing rigidity coincided with openings within the movement to raise concerns about racial prejudice and to imagine alternative political forms that might begin to redress the balance of centuries of oppression. The idea of territorial, "national" self-determination for Black and Indigenous peoples has generally been dismissed as a delusion. Yet it cannot be so easily brushed aside. In Latin America, as we will see, it catalyzed some of the radical left's most substantive discussions to date on the questions of race, nation, and sovereignty.

FIVE

Race, Class, and the Making of the Present

SOUTHERN CROSSINGS

In mid-1929, two crucial gatherings of Latin American Communists took place on the shores of the Río de la Plata. The first, held in Montevideo from May 18 to May 26, was the founding congress of the Confederación Sindical Latino Americana (CSLA; Latin American Trade Union Confederation). Sponsored by the Profintern, the Comintern's trade union body, the CSLA was to be an umbrella organization for Communist-aligned unions across the region. The second was a conference of Latin American Communist parties, held in Buenos Aires from June 1 to June 12. This was the first time that representatives from all the region's parties gathered in one place, and the first Comintern event to focus specifically on conditions in Latin America and on the strategic dilemmas facing its revolutionary movements.[1]

Between them, these gatherings were a measure of how far Communism had come in Latin America in the space of a decade. They brought together scores of delegates from more than a dozen countries as well as several Comintern envoys. Unlike at Comintern meetings in Moscow, where the main lingua franca was French, most of the proceedings were conducted in Spanish or Portuguese. Many of the attendees at the gatherings in Montevideo and Buenos Aires were the same, with delegates shuttling across the Río de la Plata. Making the journey to attend was a perilous undertaking: Many had to use aliases and false papers to avoid arrest by local authorities along the way, their credentials printed on scraps of silk sewn into their clothes.[2]

The gatherings were also highly contentious. Delegates expressed profound disagreements on a range of issues, with the Comintern's views being forcefully countered by the Latin Americans.[3] Many of these objections revolved around a familiar problem: Could concepts and categories developed for other parts of the world be applied to Latin America? This was not an abstract question: The answers pointed to very different political strategies—and ultimately to divergent visions of revolution. Amid this broader contention, one particular focus of dispute was the "problem of race." Latin American Communists pushed back against the Comintern's call for Black and Indigenous self-determination, issued at its 1928 congress in Moscow. Many Latin American delegates also questioned the idea of defining racial minorities as "national" groups. In the process, they offered their own analyses of race and indigeneity in the Americas, grounded in the region's history but also geared toward the politics of the present.

Taken together, the Buenos Aires and Montevideo conferences produced some of the Latin American left's most substantive reflections on race and nationality. Yet these discussions have seldom been situated within their original context, or in relation to the Communist debates of the time.[4] One reason for this may be the ideological climate of the Comintern's Third Period: Given the increasing conformism within the organization, few would imagine its deliberations could generate any genuine insights. A second reason is that the self-determination policy in particular has been widely dismissed in Latin America as an outlandish fantasy, imposed on the region's parties by a Comintern apparatus that was ignorant of local realities.[5]

My research shows that such interpretations overlook the complexity of the 1929 debates. The archival record reveals some surprisingly nuanced attempts by Latin American Communists and Comintern envoys to grapple with what they termed the *problem of race*. As we saw in chapter 4, the idea that self-determination for "national" minorities might apply to Indigenous groups and people of African descent was strongly influenced by Haywood's Black Belt thesis and by a resurgence of anti-colonialism within the Communist movement. Yet the conceptions of race and nation underpinning the Comintern's thinking on the "national question" in the Americas were hazy at best. In Buenos Aires and Montevideo, delegates addressed those ambiguities head-on, giving more sustained attention than they previously had to Black and Indigenous oppression: its origins, its character and manifestations in the present, and its strategic implications.

This was not the first time the region's radicals had considered these issues. From the turbulent struggle for independence to postrevolutionary Mexico, the link between liberatory politics and ending racial oppression had often been made. What was new in 1929 was that the terms of the discussion were shaped by the Comintern's call for self-determination for "national" minorities. Even though many Latin American radicals opposed the idea, the Comintern's framing of the issue prompted them to respond in equivalent terms, setting out their own views of race and nation and exploring how class interacted with, but also cut across, these categories.

Throughout these conversations, the fate of Latin America's existing nation-states was centrally at stake. The Comintern's self-determination policy would have involved redrawing the map of the Americas, creating a patchwork of ethnic republics nestled within larger entities. This in turn would only have been the prelude to a revolutionary transformation of the hemisphere: The Comintern's ultimate vision for the region was a Soviet-style federation from the Rio Grande to Patagonia, in which current national boundaries would cease to have meaning. For the Comintern's envoys, the region's existing states were little more than fictions. But for many of the Latin American delegates these states, for all their flaws, were indispensable bulwarks against US and European imperialism. This disparity in attitudes was rooted in contrasting versions of radical transnational politics. One was the Comintern's vision, premised on a willingness to destroy existing nation-states; the other was a Latin American anti-imperialism that sought to consolidate those states in the face of US dominance. In effect, the terms of the disputes between Communists and *apristas* analyzed in chapter 3 now resurfaced within the Communist movement itself.

In reconstructing the Buenos Aires and Montevideo debates, this chapter focuses on contributions from two key participants: the Peruvian Marxist José Carlos Mariátegui and the Afro-Cuban trade unionist Sandalio Junco. Mariátegui was not physically present at either meeting—he had been confined to a wheelchair since 1924 and was unable to make the journey from Lima—but the Peruvian delegation presented theses in which he laid out a highly influential interpretation of race in the Americas. Mariátegui's arguments rested on a materialist analysis, in which economic exploitation took precedence over racialized forms of oppression. While he recognized the reality of racism, he drew a distinction between its impact on the Indigenous and on people of African descent. He also opposed the idea of Indigenous self-determination: For Mariátegui, creating separate sovereign states for speakers of Quechua, Aymara, and other Indigenous languages would do nothing to address the fundamental problems besetting these populations.[6]

Junco, for his part, laid out a historically grounded account of "the black question" in Latin America. In contrast to Mariátegui, he drew parallels between Black and Indigenous oppression, decrying the racism endured by both groups and pointing to shared elements that could feed into a common struggle against capitalism. But while he diverged from Mariátegui in that respect, the two were united in their opposition to the Comintern line. Junco's arguments against Black self-determination were similar to those made by Mariátegui: As Junco put it, racial oppression could not "be resolved by creating one more bourgeois republic, even if it is a black one."[7]

Both Junco's and Mariátegui's interventions prompted heated discussion, and I highlight the principal threads of the contention that ensued. After attempts to arrive at a synthesis in Buenos Aires failed, the Comintern envoys returned to Moscow, where they gave a detailed and fairly balanced account of the disagreements aired in Buenos Aires. I retrace the process through which, at the beginning of 1930, the Comintern—despite the resistance it had met six months earlier—reaffirmed its commitment to Black and Indigenous self-determination in Latin America, and in the process challenged the region's parties to reshape their approach to race.

VERY BOLSHEVIK AND VERY PERUVIAN

The problem of race was not originally going to be on the agenda for the gatherings in Montevideo and Buenos Aires at all. It was included thanks to the Ecuadorean Ricardo Paredes, who in April 1928 took part in a Profintern meeting in Moscow devoted to early preparations for Montevideo. Paredes observed that the draft agenda included a point on organizing among migrant workers but said nothing about either women or Indigenous people. While observing that "the question of women has not yet been accepted"—it is unclear by whom—he called for "a point on the indigenous" to be added to the agenda.[8] This conversation in Moscow was the reason Mariátegui was invited to draft his theses on race in Latin America. And it was thanks to the Sixth Congress's deliberations on Haywood's Black Belt thesis that Mariátegui was obliged to organize his remarks as an argument against self-determination.

Mariátegui wrote his Buenos Aires theses at a critical moment in his political and intellectual evolution. They offer an exceptionally clear summation of his ideas about Peru's history, the specificity of Latin America's social formations, and the Indigenous question.[9] Born in the southern Peruvian province of Moquegua in 1894, Mariátegui began his journalistic career in Lima in the mid-1910s, writing sly commentaries on national politics and *limeño* society. His radical sympathies were readily apparent: In December 1917, when the conservative press accused him and his friends of being "Peruvian Bolsheviks," he responded, "Well! Very Bolshevik and very Peruvian!"—before adding an important qualifier: "But more Peruvian than Bolshevik."[10]

In 1918–19, Mariátegui was an outspoken supporter of a general strike in Lima and of student protests calling for university reform. In July 1919, Augusto Leguía seized the presidency in a coup. Moving quickly to sideline his critics, Leguía offered Mariátegui a stipend to go abroad. That October Mariátegui left for Europe, where he would spend three and a half years, most of them in Italy. By his own account, it was in Europe that he acquired a Marxist formation, fueled by encounters with militant workers' movements and with the work of leading Marxist thinkers.

After returning to Peru in 1923, Mariátegui focused increasingly on Peruvian themes, and in particular on what he termed "the problem of nationality."[11] How should the internal contradictions and deep divisions of Peruvian society be understood, and what role might the marginalized peasantry and Indigenous population play alongside workers in the construction of a socialist future? Between 1925 and 1928, Mariátegui developed a systematic view of his country's history, its economy, society, politics, and culture, writing a series of articles that he then assembled in book form as *Siete ensayos de interpretación de la realidad peruana* (*Seven Interpretive Essays on Peruvian Reality*).[12] While applying the principles of Marxist analysis to Latin America, Mariátegui also drew on a range of other influences, including the *indigenista* literary currents then active in Peru and the work of scholars such as Hildebrando Castro Pozo, who in his 1924 book *Nuestra comunidad indígena* (Our indigenous community) described the survival into the present of Indigenous communal economic forms. The result was a distinctive view of the region's history and present—and one that pointed to political diagnoses that were at odds with the Comintern's prescriptions.

For Mariátegui, the key difference between Latin America and Western Europe was that the feudal system and its ruling class had not been superseded by a fully capitalist society. Rather, the feudal class had simply "camouflaged" itself: Beneath Peru's republican forms, landowning families from the colonial era remained dominant.[13] Since capitalist development along European lines had been blocked, there was no "national bourgeoisie" in Peru, only a "semifeudal" class linked to, and indeed dependent on, international capital. From this, Mariátegui drew far-reaching conclusions about the nature of revolution in Latin America as a whole. The semifeudal structure of Latin American societies meant that they could not march through the same historical progression envisaged in Europe, from the bourgeois-democratic revolution to the proletarian. Not only was there no national bourgeoisie; the proletariat was dwarfed in scale by the peasantry. While Mariátegui continued to insist on the proletariat's leading role, from the mid-1920s onward his analyses placed increasing emphasis on the revolutionary potential of the peasantry.

In foregrounding the peasantry, Mariátegui was at the same time giving a prominent place to the Indigenous rural masses. As he put it in 1927, "Our socialism would not be Peruvian—would not even be socialism—if it did not stand in solidarity, first and foremost, with the demands of the indigenous."[14] The reason for this was that Peru's system of agrarian exploitation weighed most heavily on its Indigenous majority. From this flowed a second argument that set him apart from many of Peru's *indigenistas* at the time. The "indigenous problem," in his view, derived from the country's agrarian property regime and its labor system; it was fundamentally socioeconomic in nature, rather than a matter of culture or education.

The Indigenous became crucial to Mariátegui's political project in another sense. He saw the persistence of the Indigenous Andean community, the *ayllu*, as a potential basis for socialism. In July 1927, he argued that "the *ayllu*, the cell of the Incaic state, which has survived into the present despite the attacks of feudalism . . . still possesses sufficient vitality to become, over time, the cell of a modern socialist state."[15] This complex of ideas found its fullest expression in the *Siete ensayos*, published in October 1928, just after Mariátegui and a group of comrades founded the Peruvian Socialist Party.[16] A few months later, the delegates of that party went to the Montevideo and Buenos Aires conferences, where they presented Mariátegui's theses on race.

MARIÁTEGUI'S THESES

The theses Mariátegui drafted for the CSLA congress focused solely on the Indigenous question; those he prepared for the Buenos Aires gathering were broader and more substantial, addressing the problem of race as a whole. From the outset, his argument sought to reframe that problem as fundamentally an economic and social one. He began by observing that in

Latin America, most discussions of race unfolded in the realm of "bourgeois intellectual speculation" and only served "to obscure or disregard the real problems of the continent." A Marxist analysis, by contrast, had to put the problem "in its real terms": "Economically, socially, and politically, the problem of race, like that of the land, is at bottom that of the dissolution of the feudal system." For Mariátegui, focusing on race itself was a distraction: "The thesis that the indigenous problem is an ethnic problem does not even merit discussion." The very notion of racial hierarchy was a mechanism that enabled "feudal exploitation of the natives" to take place.[17]

Yet while he denied the existence of racial hierarchy, Mariátegui acknowledged the ideological and cultural weight of racism. In Latin America, in his view, racial distinctions mapped onto class ones. The "feudal" and bourgeois classes in these countries "feel for both the Indians and the blacks and mulattos the same disdain as the white imperialists," a sentiment that reached into the middle classes, too.[18] This sense of racial affinity only compounded the elite's feelings of class solidarity and made them the willing tools of imperialist powers. For this reason, Mariátegui argued, the "struggle for national independence in the countries of [Latin] America with a large indigenous population" could not be directly compared to that in Asia or Africa.[19] The use of the term "national independence" to refer to countries that were already formally independent is striking here, echoing the ideas of Haya and others in Mexico City's anti-imperialist circles. It was also a response to the discussions held in Moscow the year before over whether Latin America could be deemed semicolonial in the same way as China, for example. While for others the argument hinged on the contrast between de jure independence and de facto dependence on US capital, for Mariátegui the problem was a historical one, grounded in the centuries-long exploitation of the Indigenous by European and mestizo landowners. Racialized structures of economic inequality were thus central to Mariátegui's view of what set Latin America apart.

Yet within Latin America itself, Mariátegui argued, the problem of race did not present itself everywhere in the same way. His Buenos Aires theses surveyed the region as a whole, identifying three extremely broad racial groups. Just two covered the entire Indigenous population: on the one hand "Incan and Aztec Indians," comprising the highland peoples of South America—Peru, Bolivia, Ecuador, part of Chile—and the majority populations of Mexico and Guatemala; and on the other "forest-dwelling" peoples, which included various nomadic groups in the Amazon Basin and

Central American rainforests.[20] This was of course a drastic oversimplification of the continent's ethnolinguistic variety—and a politically problematic one, subsuming hundreds of groups under just two of the region's historic imperial polities. But Mariátegui didn't dwell on the implications of his schema; his priority was to highlight overarching categories of economic exploitation. He described the Incan and Aztec category as being locked in agricultural subservience, while the forest-dwelling groups were small in number and structurally marginal to those systems, and therefore "of reduced importance."[21]

The third racial category Mariátegui addressed was people of African descent. Here his arguments rested on a series of contrasts between their fate and that of the Indigenous. Equally schematic but much briefer, his treatment of Black people in Latin America involves some startling logical twists, in which the Indigenous are accorded weight as a distinct racial category but people of African descent are not. Having been "imported by the colonizers," Mariátegui argued, Black people in Latin America "have no roots in the land like the Indian, possess almost no traditions of their own, lack their own language, speaking Spanish or Portuguese or French or English."[22] Furthermore, he argued, people of African descent were fully integrated into the same socioeconomic structures as everyone else; they were not exploited separately from other racial groups, but alongside them. This was one cardinal contrast between the Indigenous and Black populations in his schema: While he identified the Indigenous as not only racially but also socioeconomically distinct, people of African descent were subsumed into broader class categories. This had strategic and political implications, too: Mariátegui viewed Indigenous people as an exploited group who were potential allies of the proletariat, while those of African descent were apparently already within its ranks. A class-based agenda would be sufficient to address the exploitation of the latter, but a different kind of politics would be required to forge an alliance with the former.

The central sections of the Buenos Aires theses fleshed out the political vision that followed from Mariátegui's picture of race in Latin America. Focusing on Peru, they drew on the analysis he had recently published in the *Siete ensayos*. Mariátegui stressed the link between the condition of the Indigenous and the system of agrarian exploitation and insisted once again on the socialistic tendencies contained within the Andean *ayllu*. These communities, with their collective economic organization, represented what he called a "primitive agrarian communism." The idea of a preexisting

Indigenous basis for socialism led Mariátegui to celebrate the radical potential of the Indigenous as political actors. "An indigenous revolutionary consciousness may be slow to take shape," he claimed, "but once the Indian has made the socialist idea his own, he will serve it with a discipline, a tenacity and a strength that few proletarians in other settings will be able to better."[23]

Mariátegui insisted that Communists should stress "the fundamentally economic and social character of the problem of race in Latin America." While they should certainly work to "destroy racial prejudices," it was the bourgeoisie that sought to give Black and Indigenous struggles "an exclusively racial character." Communists should oppose these "self-interested deviations" and try to link Indigenous and Black struggles with those of white and mestizo proletarians.[24]

At this point, Mariátegui took aim specifically at the Comintern's self-determination policy. Having noted earlier that "the struggles carried out by blacks in Latin America have never had, and never can have, the character of a national struggle," he dismissed the idea of Black self-determination. The Comintern had previously opposed what he termed "black Zionism"—a reference to Garveyism—and should now likewise resist any "utopian solutions." The same applied to the Indigenous: In his view, "the constitution of the Indian race in an autonomous state would not lead at the present time to the dictatorship of the Indian proletariat, nor much less to the formation of a classless Indian state, as some have sought to affirm, but rather to the constitution of a bourgeois Indian State with all the internal and external contradictions of bourgeois States."[25]

There are clear parallels here between Mariátegui's reasoning and that of Rosa Luxemburg in 1908–9: Both argued that national self-determination for minorities would only empower their respective elites. It is not clear whether the Peruvian would have read Luxemburg's writings on the national question, though he would have been familiar with Lenin's 1913 polemic against her. Mariátegui's emphasis on class as the primary division certainly echoed Luxemburg's views, but his acknowledgment of class divisions among the Indigenous was in tension with his depiction elsewhere of the Indigenous as a coherent exploited category. When seeking to drive home his argument against self-determination, he returned to the idea of the Indigenous as radical political subjects. In his view, it was only "the revolutionary classist movement of the indigenous masses" that could expand the "possibilities for their political self-determination."[26]

Here, Mariátegui seemingly counterposed *national* self-determination to a more genuine *political* variety. Yet there is an ambiguity in his logic: While insisting that Indigenous struggles not be given a racial character, he argues that a class-based movement will enable the self-determination of the Indigenous *as a race*. As he put it, an anti-capitalist movement of Indigenous proletarians and peasants, allied with whites and mestizos, would foster "the free development of indigenous racial characteristics (and especially the institutions with collectivist tendencies) and may create a link between Indians in different countries, across the current borders which divide ancient racial entities, leading them to the political autonomy of their race."[27]

Having argued against the dissolution of existing nation-states to form smaller Indigenous republics, Mariátegui ends up evoking a border-spanning Indigenous political community. While this might seem comparable to Haya's concept of Indoamérica, Mariátegui did not envisage a confederation of existing states, but rather a transcendence of them. In that sense his thinking has more in common with the Austro-Marxists' concept of "cultural autonomy"—except that he does invoke the kind of ethnically based political community that the Austro-Marxists ruled out. The idea is not fleshed out, but even in this brief form it points to an underlying tension in Mariátegui's thinking. His opposition to self-determination rested on a denial of the Comintern's assertion that Indigenous groups constituted nations. But Mariátegui did recognize the existence of Indigenous collective identities rooted in shared racial oppression and clearly agreed that these did not map onto current national boundaries. For Mariátegui, too, existing borders should not ultimately define the struggle for Indigenous liberation. The difference between his thinking and that of the Comintern was thus not so categorical as it might have seemed.

In arguing against Indigenous self-determination, Mariátegui also made some significant omissions. His ideas about the problem of race were largely based on Peru. Applying the same logic to other parts of Latin America, Mariátegui ended up arguing that in countries where the agrarian structure was different, there was no racism against the Indigenous. He claimed that in Mexico, "there is no hostility towards the Indian," and that in Central American countries such as Guatemala, "the indigenous problem, in the 'racial' sense of the word, does not exist."[28] The key point here is not the inaccuracy of Mariátegui's views.[29] Rather, it is that his version of a materialist argument did not address the racial discrimination that Indigenous people living under very different socioeconomic systems endured in common.

This was an important weakness, since it enabled those arguing for self-determination to present themselves as being more cognizant of racism than their opponents.

On what he termed the "black problem," meanwhile, Mariátegui's arguments rested on a denial of racism's existence. In Latin America, he asserted, "In general, the black problem does not present a marked racial aspect." The basis for this claim was that "the Negro . . . does not suffer the same contempt as in the United States," and that "the prejudice of inferiority or incapacity for certain occupations has never taken root." Elsewhere in the theses he did acknowledge that such forms of discrimination existed—but then argued that they be given a reduced priority. Across the region, he asserted, "Blacks must struggle for the proletarian demands more than against the prejudices and abuses of which they are the victims as blacks."[30] The idea that people of African descent suffered little or no discrimination was (and is) a recurrent theme in discussions of race in Latin America. While its stubborn persistence is perhaps not surprising overall, its recurrence within the Communist left is remarkable, given that another of the delegates to the Buenos Aires conference refuted it at length that same day, directly after Mariátegui's theses were presented.

FROM MATANZAS TO MONTEVIDEO

Like Mariátegui, Junco opposed the Comintern's self-determination policy, arguing forcefully against applying to Latin America the same remedy that Haywood and Nasanov had proposed for the US South. But at the Buenos Aires conference, Junco offered an account of the Black experience in the Americas that differed starkly from Mariátegui's. Both the overlaps and the divergences between the two expressed a set of tensions over race that the Latin American radical left would consistently struggle to address, or at times even acknowledge.

Junco's route to the Río de la Plata had been a circuitous one. Born in 1894 in Cuba's Matanzas province, he moved to Havana in his teens, where he began working as a baker.[31] In 1916 he joined the Havana baker's union, and by 1919 he had risen to become its leader as well as editor of its newspaper, El Productor. In the early 1920s, Junco was prominently involved in labor politics in the Cuban capital, and when the Confederación Nacional Obrera de Cuba (CNOC; National Workers' Confederation of Cuba) was founded in 1925, he was designated its international secretary. That same year, he joined the newly established PCC.

Enrique de la Osa, a Cuban member of APRA, knew Junco in Havana in the 1920s and described him as "very intelligent, very sensitive [*delicado*], very agreeable and very correct."[32] De la Osa also noted, somewhat enigmatically, that Junco was "a man with a lot of energy but full of misery." Perhaps this was a reference to the hardship and instability he often had to endure: As a trade unionist and a Communist, he lived most of his life on the run or in hiding. To the psychological pressures of clandestine activism and exile we can surely add the constant burdens of racism. His visibility as a Black Communist and labor leader drew the attention of the Machado regime: In November 1925, he was briefly imprisoned for "sedition," and in early 1927 he was among a range of activists, labor leaders, and intellectuals who were repeatedly rounded up.[33]

In January 1928, Junco went into exile in Mexico City.[34] He would spend most of the next two years in the Mexican capital, joining the PCM on arrival and later serving on LADLA's Continental Organizing Committee.[35] Alongside Mella, he was also active in ANERC. When Mella was fatally wounded in January 1929, it was Junco who rushed to notify the press. Junco also spoke at the funeral, denouncing the Cuban government and calling on all those present to pursue Mella's cause.[36] In a photograph taken just prior to the burial at the Panteón Dolores, his anger at Mella's death is plain to see (figure 6).

In the spring of 1928, before he was even settled in Mexico City, Junco had traveled to Moscow to represent the Cuban labor movement at the Profintern Congress. There, under the pseudonym "Saturnino Hernández," he was elected to the Profintern's Executive Committee.[37] Over the next few weeks, he took part in deliberations over Latin America—including those noted previously in which Paredes raised the Indigenous question—and preparations for the CSLA congress in Montevideo.[38]

Junco was seemingly no longer in Moscow by late July 1928, since there is no record of his involvement in the Sixth Comintern Congress. Yet at this time—most likely in absentia—he was elected to the governing body of the Profintern's newly created International Trade Union Committee of Negro Workers (ITUCNW).[39] The ITUCNW immediately drew up a "program of action" that included calls for civil rights, an end to racial discrimination, and support for Black self-determination in the United States and South Africa.[40] By the time Junco came to argue against the latter policy in Montevideo and

FIGURE 6. Sandalio Junco speaking at Mella's funeral, Mexico City, January 1929. From Archivo General de la Nación, Fondo Enrique Díaz Delgado y García, 30/1/2.

Buenos Aires, then, it had been enshrined by the Comintern as a demand for which the international labor movement should be fighting.

Three months after Mella's death, in April 1929, Junco left Mexico to make his way to Montevideo. He traveled in the company of fellow Cuban Communist Alejandro Barreiro and two Mexican trade unionists: Manuel

Rodríguez Cerrillo, representing the Liga Nacional Campesina, and the railway worker Elías Barrios, whose memoir records their journey.[41] First they traveled by boat from Veracruz to New York, where they stayed in a bedbug-ridden boarding house on 42nd Street, sleeping two to a bed, and surviving on free meals from canteens run by the US Communist Party.[42] While in New York, they met with Enrique de la Osa, who saw the tattered state of Junco's clothes and gave him a suit.[43] They left New York on April 22, arriving in Montevideo on May 8. More than a hundred delegates crammed into a hotel near the docks, sharing meals at a large table. Barrios recalled hearing "all the accents of Spanish," as well as the Portuguese and Creole spoken by Brazilian and Haitian delegates respectively. Across these linguistic differences, as Barrios put it, "we all understood each other like men united by a single problem and a common aspiration."[44] But while that unity may have been clear in Montevideo, it proved more tenuous at the Communist gathering in Buenos Aires.

JUNCO'S ARGUMENTS

Junco presented reports on the "black question" both at the Montevideo CSLA congress and then, a few days later, at the Buenos Aires meeting. A photograph taken from stage left in Montevideo shows him standing with his left hand tucked casually into the trouser pocket of his three-piece suit (see figure 7). His right hand is a blur of motion as he gestures mid-argument, chin thrust confidently outward. While Junco's remarks in Montevideo were longer and more substantive, giving us greater insight into his views, his speech in Buenos Aires was markedly different in tone and seems to capture his frustration with his Latin American comrades. He found himself contesting the Comintern's advocacy of "national" self-determination while at the same time having to push other Latin American Communists to even acknowledge the existence of racism in the region. This must have been all the more disheartening because he otherwise agreed with their view of the material and economic origins of the "problem of race." Taken together, Junco's interventions constitute a fascinating document of the unenviable position Black radical leftists found themselves in at this time, as well as of the blind spots and insights on race evidenced by the rest of the Latin American left.

Junco's remarks in Montevideo offered a historical and geographical overview of Latin America's Black populations. He began by drawing a direct

FIGURE 7. Sandalio Junco addressing the CSLA Congress in Montevideo, May 1929. From Russian State Archive of Social and Political History, fond 534, op. 3, d. 1171, 8.

parallel between Black and Indigenous peoples: Both were "equally oppressed and humiliated by capitalism," and together they constituted "the bulk of the continental proletariat."[45] Indeed, whereas Mariátegui's theses had distinguished the Indigenous from people of African descent, presenting the latter as unfortunate tools of the exploiting classes, Junco portrayed both groups as similarly shaped by enduring structures of oppression that had their origins in conquest and colonization.[46]

Junco briskly took his audience from Haiti, Jamaica, Cuba, and the rest of the Antilles down through Central America to Venezuela, Colombia, Ecuador, Peru, and Brazil, and on to Argentina and Uruguay, where he noted the maintenance of traditions and social clubs among the Black population. He also drew on testimony from Isaiah Hawkins, a Black US delegate from the National Miners' Union who had traveled with Junco's group from New York, to depict conditions in the United States, where Black workers suffered discrimination in the workplace and a range of oppressions outside it, from segregation to physical violence.[47]

Where Mariátegui had drawn a contrast between the treatment of Black people in the United States and in Latin America, Junco highlighted similarities. In Panama, the government had repressed a tenants' strike in 1925 in a highly racialized manner, and in his native Cuba, "the situation of blacks is not much better." Junco expounded at length on the gap between the promises of Cuba's independence struggle and the lived reality for the island's Black population: "Liberty and equality remained on paper." People of African descent were excluded from many professions and jobs and discriminated against by a bourgeoisie that "constantly tries to deny the existence of the problem of race in the country and especially its hatred and contempt for blacks, [which] its own deeds disprove all the time." He insisted, moreover, that Cuba and Panama were by no means exceptional: "What we have just described in those countries exists, with very few differences, in nearly all the others in which there are [people of] the black race, black workers."[48]

How had people of African descent responded to these conditions? Here Junco sought to counter the myth of Black passivity. Far from accepting their lot, Black people had "always and throughout history struggled against the oppression of which they were the victims." Moreover, these rebellions were closely tied to larger, systemic questions. In the "age of bourgeois revolutions" a century earlier, enslaved people "instinctively put the problem of their liberation in the foreground of political and social struggles." Junco's thinking here foreshadows the argument—most famously substantiated a few years later by C. L. R. James—that rebellions of the enslaved, far from being marginal to the Age of Revolutions, were central to its unfolding.[49]

The prime example Junco offered for this was the Haitian Revolution, which he described as "a great revolution of agrarian character" against both "the French metropolitan power" and "the feudal lords of Haiti." Having redistributed the land and proclaimed their independence, Haitians successfully fought off Napoleon's attempts to subdue them. Yet this page of history "is very little known," Junco observed, and the bourgeoisie had taken advantage of this to "distort the real social and agrarian character" of the Haitian struggle, presenting it as "simple 'manifestations of black savagery against whites.'" For Junco, this racialized misinformation obscured the true character of the Haitians' struggle, which was "against the feudal lords, whatever their color."[50]

Junco's second major example was "the heroic episode of the black republic of Palmares in Brazil." In the seventeenth century, waves of enslaved people left the sugar plantations of northern Brazil for the mountains, where they established "a republic that had a population of 35 to 40,000 black inhabitants." This cluster of communities was brutally suppressed by an army sent by the Portuguese crown. Junco described Zumbi, the leader of the "republic," as "a genuine black Spartacus," and Palmares itself as comparable to the rebellion of Roman slaves Spartacus had led, dubbing it "similar . . . in its social significance, in [having] its own government."[51]

Strikingly, Junco's counterhistory of Black struggles in Latin America celebrated instances not simply of rebellion, but of Black sovereignty. Yet when it came to the present, he strongly opposed the idea of Black self-determination. He denounced Garveyism as a current that had emerged "among a group of black intellectuals in the United States" that was "similar to Zionism among the Jewish bourgeoisie." Not only was it impossible to "return . . . blacks from the United States and Latin America to Africa"; for Junco, such a project would "not represent any kind of solution to the specific problem of black workers." He went on to elaborate, in terms very similar to those used by Mariátegui for the Indigenous, that "the question cannot be resolved by creating one more bourgeois republic, even if it is a black one." Worse still, Junco argued, the creation of a Black state in Africa could even serve as a tool of US imperialist expansion to that continent, since it "would naturally be under [the United States's] well-known protection and control."[52]

What, then, was the right way to address the problem of race? Having diverged from Mariátegui both in his historical presentation and in his emphasis on the prevalence of racism in Latin America, Junco returned to the key point on which they agreed. Just as the Peruvian's theses had done for the Indigenous question, he affirmed that "the black problem . . . also has profound social and political roots." It was not to be understood as "a solely racial problem, or a merely administrative or philanthropic one." What was needed, in Junco's view, was "a proletarian conception" of this issue. This meant an internationalist and class-based approach, designed to demonstrate to working people of African descent that "their place is alongside the continental and world proletariat." The only way for Black people to secure their "full and effective liberation," as "a class and as a race that is oppressed economically, socially and politically," was through "open struggle for their immediate and political demands against imperialism and against all the exploiters, whatever their color or origin."[53]

Junco's framing of Black liberation in many ways ran parallel to Mariátegui's arguments about the Indigenous. While Junco rejected the idea that people of African descent constituted a nation, he did see them as a single oppressed race. But rather than advocating a pan-regional political project rooted in shared racial oppression, he instead called for a strategy in which class had primacy.

Junco ended by calling on the CSLA congress to produce a resolution on the Black question, "to orient our comrades across the Continent in their action."[54] The language of the final text clearly reflects Junco's influence: It describes the many obstacles to racial equality across the Americas and highlights the discrimination endured by Black workers in Cuba, Panama, and elsewhere. In a further echo of Junco's language, it urges the CSLA to persuade Black workers that "the cause of their social liberation, as a race and as a class, is indissolubly linked to the cause of the general redemption of the proletariat."[55] According to the congress proceedings, Junco's speech was greeted with "much applause and cheers for the black proletariat." This was followed by an enthusiastic singing of the "Internationale," "as an act of homage and solidarity towards the black proletariat and towards the indigenous *campesino* workers"—binding the two groups together symbolically, as Junco had done analytically.

But if the Montevideo event seemed to emphasize what Black and Indigenous peoples had in common, the Buenos Aires proceedings brought forth exactly the kinds of distinction Junco had been trying to overcome. Junco had opened his remarks in Montevideo on an optimistic note: As he put it, the fact that the CSLA was addressing the question of race would show Black workers that it was "the best standard bearer and defender of [their] rights and demands."[56] But a few days later on the other shore of the Río de la Plata, he found himself in a less positive frame of mind. He began by commenting that "up till now no Latin American party has posed the question" of race. Worse still, he observed that "on many occasions when we have discussed this question, some comrades . . . have denied the existence of this problem in many Latin American countries." Yet, as Junco insisted, "the problem exists and compels us ever more urgently to address it."[57]

In Buenos Aires, then, Junco found himself first having to show that racism even existed, before he could suggest how to counter it. It seems clear that the spur for the change in his approach was Mariátegui's theses, read out by Peruvian delegate Hugo Pesce directly before Junco's intervention. The text Mariátegui prepared for Montevideo had been devoted solely to the Indigenous, and it was only in the longer Buenos Aires theses that he discussed Latin America's Black population. This included the assertions described previously that "in general, the black problem does not present a marked racial aspect," and that in Latin America, "the Negro . . . does not suffer the same contempt as in the United States."[58] Directly contradicting this, Junco insisted at Buenos Aires that "the black problem exists in every country in Latin America." True, it did not exist in the same form and with the same severity everywhere, but again seeming to take issue specifically with Mariátegui's theses, he observed that "what some comrades have expressed on this question is not the reality in many countries of Latin America."[59]

Junco then underscored once again the interlinked fates of the Indigenous and people of African descent—countering the distinctions Mariátegui's theses had made. Under colonialism, Junco argued, enslaved Africans "suffered the same condition of servitude that the indigenous had previously suffered": a "servitude and slavery that gave rise to an identical treatment of both, and which over time has not undergone any essential modifications."[60] For that reason, Junco insisted that "in addressing the problem of the Indians . . . we are obliged to address simultaneously or in parallel the problem of the blacks." For both people of African descent and the Indigenous, the ultimate source of their oppression was the same: the "capitalist regime." What was needed was "an active and systematic struggle for the equality of all beings."[61]

Junco's remarks in Montevideo and Buenos Aires offered a historically grounded picture of the Black experience in Latin America—one that sharply contrasted with that laid out in Mariátegui's theses. The disparity between the two signaled many of the tensions that would plague discussions of race in Latin America for decades to come: the clash over whether the Black and Indigenous questions should be considered parallel or distinct, and still more fundamentally the struggle by Junco and other leftists of African descent to get their comrades to acknowledge the existence of racism in Latin America. The interventions by these two men, however, were not the only contributions on the themes of race and nationality at these gatherings. The ensuing discussion at Buenos Aires—including one further report on race and comments by more than a dozen delegates—revisited many of the same contested issues, as well as broaching questions about the desirability of maintaining Latin America's existing nation-states.

CONTENTION IN BUENOS AIRES

Following on from Mariátegui's theses and Junco's remarks, a third brief report on race was given by a Brazilian delegate, Leôncio Basbaum. Born in Recife to Jewish parents, Basbaum trained as a doctor and joined the

Brazilian Communist Party in 1926.[62] His remarks at the Buenos Aires conference were at odds with both preceding presentations. First, he went still further than Mariátegui in stressing the material causes of the Indigenous problem, claiming that it should simply be relabeled the "agrarian problem." He also disagreed with Mariátegui over the political potential of the Indigenous community, arguing that basing any future socialism on the *ayllu* would be a step backward from Latin America's existing level of development. Moreover, he insisted that to even present the Indigenous question in ethnic terms was to veer toward an acceptance of APRA's ideas, which he deemed "an absurd program" that "takes no account of social reality."[63] For Basbaum, what was needed instead was an unwavering emphasis on class struggle.

With regard to people of African descent, meanwhile, Basbaum gave voice to exactly the kind of assumptions against which Junco had just been arguing. In Latin America as a whole, he insisted, one could not speak of "a race question similar to that in the United States, since among Latin Americans . . . the preconception of color does not exist." In Brazil, he claimed, racism "does not exist at all" among the proletariat, although "those prejudices can be seen" among the bourgeoisie. But overall, "prejudice against blacks is of reduced proportions." In his view it was therefore "unnecessary" to combat racism, since "it rarely manifests itself."[64]

One can only imagine what Junco's reaction to this would have been. In the ensuing discussion, he limited himself to pointing out the omission of migrant workers—in particular, Chinese communities in several countries—from the conversation so far.[65] But Junco's Cuban comrade Alejandro Barreiro did respond to Basbaum. Racial discrimination certainly did exist in Latin America, he said, pointing to an "alarming" degree of prejudice in Cuba. People of African descent were banned from many occupations on the island, and transport was de facto segregated. He also criticized Basbaum directly: The problem of racism existed in Brazil too, "contrary to the information given by the comrades from that country."[66]

More than a dozen other delegates also contributed to the broader discussion, including David Siqueiros, the Peruvians Julio Portocarrero and Hugo Pesce, as well as delegates from Argentina, Bolivia, El Salvador, Guatemala, Panama, the United States, and Venezuela. Most of them gave additional information, rather than directly contesting the interpretations previously offered—providing details on the Indigenous population in Bolivia and Guatemala, for example, or the situation in Panama.[67] But there was intense debate on two interlinked questions: the relationship between race and nationality, and self-determination.

The key interventions here came from two Comintern envoys: Jules Humbert-Droz, representing the Latin American Secretariat, and a twenty-five-year-old delegate of the Kommunisticheskii Internatsional Molodezhi (KIM; Communist Youth International) named Zakharii Rabinovich. Born in Tbilisi to a Jewish family in 1903, Rabinovich joined the Bolshevik Party in 1918 and worked for the KIM in France, Uruguay, Brazil, and Argentina from 1925 to 1931.[68] In Buenos Aires he began by pointing out a general confusion in all the presentations between "the question of race and the national question." These were not the same thing at all, he said: "There are nations made up of different races, and different nations composed of a single race." In his view, this confusion led to mistaken analyses—and therefore to errors in political strategy. While the Peruvian comrades were right to insist on the material, class basis of the problem, Rabinovich argued that they had fallen into the error of "*denying the national character* of the indigenous struggle." Yet there was no necessary contradiction between class and national perspectives; as Rabinovich put it, "One thing does not exclude the other, but rather completes it."[69]

For Rabinovich, it was a mistake to reduce the national question to one of class. This was why the Comintern had put forward, "*alongside* class demands, the slogan, which is fundamental for us, of 'the right of people to dispose of themselves, going as far as the right of separation.'" Yet many Latin American comrades seemed opposed to the idea. Why? In a conversation on the sidelines of the conference, Pesce had apparently told Rabinovich that advocating Indigenous self-determination would foment racial hatred and empower Indigenous "chauvinism"—which then brought the risk that the Indigenous would slaughter white workers. But Rabinovich argued that the opposite was true: Supporting Indigenous self-determination was "the only path to solidarity between the indigenous and white workers" and the best way to advance the common struggle against their oppressors.[70]

Here Rabinovich raised a concern that had featured in discussions of the Haywood–Nasanov thesis in Moscow the year before, and that would continue to run through debates on Black and Indigenous self-determination in Latin America over the next few years. Was the reluctance of some Latin American comrades to take up the idea of self-determination itself a sign of unconscious "white chauvinism"? There was no necessary connection between the two; Junco had firmly opposed self-determination while assailing his comrades' blindness to racism. But in giving priority to cross-racial class-based organizing, Junco had also offered no specific strategy for countering racism as such. In a context in which many other delegates seemed unwilling to concede that racism was a genuine problem, the self-determination agenda took on a new valence: It became a shibboleth measuring the movement's willingness to push for the liberation of oppressed groups. In this form, as we will see in the case of Cuba in chapter 7, the policy was directed as much at the party's own members as beyond its ranks.

In Buenos Aires, the Latin American comrades' resistance to the self-determination policy pointed to another concern. For Rabinovich, it signaled an unhealthy "fetishism of *current* borders." Yet the lines dividing states in Latin America *"are not national borders,"* he argued. The process of nation formation, driven by the development of capitalism, was not yet complete. This meant that "Peru, for example, is not *a nation*." Moreover, the process of nation formation would never be completed: When the revolution came, it would do away with national borders altogether.[71] As part of that process, an Indigenous republic might well emerge; in any case, Communists should support the right of the Indigenous to decide their own fate. Rabinovich cited the Soviet Union as a successful example: The Bolsheviks had redrawn the internal boundaries of the old tsarist empire to create territories for dozens of national minorities. He also cited Lenin's polemic with Rosa Luxemburg, to show that objections to self-determination similar to those raised by the Latin American comrades had already been addressed and overcome.

Rabinovich's remarks drew some support, but they also sparked strong dissent. The Venezuelan Ricardo Martínez was among those who agreed with the call to support Indigenous self-determination. He quoted at length from the Comintern Sixth Congress resolution on South Africa to raise the idea of a "native republic" with guaranteed rights for white minorities.[72] Siqueiros offered more qualified backing, saying that the self-determination line was correct, "without that implying the formation of a separate government in every case." He proposed a list of demands in which a radical agrarian agenda would be coupled not with Indigenous self-determination, but with a "struggle for autonomy on their lands."[73] As we will see in chapter 8, this shift from self-determination to autonomy—the former meaning fully sovereign self-government, the latter something short of that but not clearly specified—would recur with regard to Mexico's Indigenous peoples in the 1930s.

The two Peruvian delegates, for their part, pushed back against Rabi-novich's arguments and against the idea of self-determination. Portocarrero reiterated his opposition to Indigenous self-determination, on the grounds that the demand could easily be distorted by the left's enemies. He also pointed out that class differentiation was taking place among his country's Indigenous populations, giving rise to landowning "castes of caciques"—the implication being that, as Mariátegui had argued, the creation of an Indig-enous republic would mainly empower this class.[74] Portocarrero then took issue with Rabinovich for bringing in Lenin's polemic with Luxemburg: The "translation" from Eastern Europe to Latin America could not be made so easily, he said. (As with the polemic between Haya and Mella, the nub of contention was whether concepts developed elsewhere could be applied to Latin America.) Pesce, meanwhile, answered Rabinovich's accusation that he had confused race and nation. On the contrary, he had sought precisely to distinguish the two, in order to "separate the 'racial' concept from the 'national' concept, negating the present-day importance of the latter." He then underscored his point concerning the Indigenous: "The Indian racial problem is not necessarily, at the present time, a national problem."[75]

Yet while Pesce claimed he had been trying to dispel confusions over race and nation, he introduced some new arguments that only emphasized how little clarity there was among the delegates on the distinctions between the two. Pesce now described nation as contingent and complex, conditioned by a series of geographical, ethnic, linguistic, religious, historical, and even climatic factors. On this front he actually agreed with Rabinovich: "The present-day limits of the countries of Latin America, which enclose large in-digenous majorities, as they were ratified at the end of the wars for so-called independence, are completely arbitrary." Race, by contrast, was for Pesce "simpler and purer," "less conditioned" than nation.[76] His logic seemed to accord race a more fundamental solidity than nation—as if race were not it-self conditioned by, and indeed constructed in dynamic interaction with, all the factors Pesce enumerated. The political payoff from this line of reason-ing might seem to be that race trumped nation as a source of mobilization. But Pesce went on to say that the racial problem must be subordinated to a class agenda. According to this new framing, then, class had primacy over race, which in turn had primacy over nation.

Amid such frontal disagreements, it was not possible to arrive at a consen-sus, and the Buenos Aires gathering did not produce a resolution on race. In his closing remarks, Humbert-Droz appeared to congratulate the gathering for being the first to devote an entire session to the issue of race in Latin America. But he pointedly observed that, when previously asked about it in Moscow, comrades from the region had denied that race posed any problems. The discussions in Buenos Aires had clearly shown that such problems did exist, and that they were "of an extreme complexity."[77] Humbert-Droz's attempts to grapple with these complexities are apparent from his handwritten notes from the Buenos Aires conference, archived in Moscow. Mixed in with jottings of key details from Junco's remarks and Mariátegui's theses, we see scattered phrases that testify to his attempt to process what he was hearing: "The problem does not pose itself as in the United States + differentiate"; "racial question not separate from historical and social developments"; "Race—not used" followed by "Social category"; and perhaps most tellingly, the words "Denied by the Latin American com[rades]."[78]

Recognizing the depth of the differences that had been aired, Humbert-Droz called for further study of this issue. He also conceded that "given the situation we have just analyzed, the slogan of self-determination for oppressed nations . . . will not be sufficient to solve the racial problem in Latin America."[79] It needed to be supplemented, he said, with a radical agrarian program for the Indigenous, but also with demands for Black people, mestizos, whites, and Chinese and other immigrant workers. In effect, Humbert-Droz was trying out a grand synthesis, combining the proletarian internationalism expressed by Junco with Mariátegui's attention to the agrarian dimensions of the Indigenous question, while maintaining the commitment to self-determination for oppressed nations that had emerged from the Sixth Congress. Yet in Buenos Aires, it was clear that such a synthesis would not command support from all the Latin American delegates. With his call for deeper study, Humbert-Droz deferred the question for the time being. It was in Moscow, rather than Buenos Aires, that the synthesis took shape.

SELF-DETERMINATION AFFIRMED

On New Year's Day 1930, just yards away from the Kremlin in a gray four-story building at No. 1 Vozdvizhenka Street, Humbert-Droz delivered a report on the question of race to a meeting of the Comintern's Latin American Secretariat. The gathering was designed to resolve the impasses reached in Buenos Aires a few months earlier. As well as Humbert-Droz himself, a dozen others attended, including Latin Americans living in Moscow and Comintern functionaries with direct experience of Latin America, such as Edgar Stirner and Lev Khaikis.[80] Those present also included Communists who had never spent time in the region but who worked on Latin American affairs in the Comintern's Moscow apparatus, such as the Italian Communist Ruggiero Grieco and August Guralsky, a Bolshevik who had worked for the Comintern from its founding in 1919.[81] Another key participant was Genrikh Yakobson, a Bolshevik who had led the Far Eastern section of the KUTV from 1922 to 1928. Yakobson began working on Latin America in the late 1920s, somehow acquiring fluent Spanish despite seemingly never leaving Russia; in the 1930s he taught Spanish-speaking students at the International Lenin School.[82] This disparate, highly cosmopolitan group would debate and eventually agree on the policy of Indigenous self-determination for Latin America.

Humbert-Droz began by once again criticizing the parties from the region for their neglect of race. "Many Latin American comrades," he observed, "believe ... that this question does not exist in Latin America and it is in Moscow that the question of race in Latin America was invented."[83] But the session on race at the Buenos Aires conference had clearly shown otherwise. Carefully summarizing that discussion, he concluded that it was impossible to reduce the race question in the region to a single cause. It was tied up with many other interlocking forms of oppression and discrimination, including not only labor exploitation but also "the national problem, of oppressed and exploited races and nationalities," as well as "the problem of racial prejudices which aggravate the other problems.[84]

Yet for all these complexities, it was clear enough where the main disagreements lay. Humbert-Droz noted that the Buenos Aires conference had not produced a final resolution on race "because there were great struggles around this question of the right of the indigenous to dispose of themselves."[85] The same divisions loomed large again in Moscow. A preparatory document for the New Year's Day meeting, drawn up on December 19, 1929, contained two parallel wordings on this question, proposing diametrically opposed approaches. One draft argued that "one cannot and should not pose the problem of national self-determination of the indigenous and black races in the continental part of Latin America," while the second stated that Communists should support "the struggle of the Indians to claim their liberty as an oppressed nation" and "their rights to decide their own destiny as a nation."[86]

At the New Year's Day meeting, Humbert-Droz initially suggested a compromise. "We should differentiate the question according to region," he argued, distinguishing areas "where the Indians had a nationality, a culture, social, economic, and political traditions" from those "where the Indians at the time of the Conquest were not at such an advanced stage of development"—where they had "not yet arrived at the state of nationality," as he put it.[87] Again we see the concept of a continuum of national development, described in chapter 4, in which peoples are propelled to nationhood by the unfolding of capitalism. The distinction Humbert-Droz drew here also seemed to enshrine the hierarchy proposed in Mariátegui's Buenos Aires theses, in which areas dominated by Indigenous empires were seen as "advanced" while more dispersed or nomadic societies were "backward." Humbert-Droz's handwritten notes from Buenos Aires clearly echoed Mariátegui's theses. One fragment reads: "Indians. 2 categories," and then identifies "Indians with culture/Nationality" as "Aztec/Inca," in contrast to the "wild indigenous."[88]

But after hedging on the idea, Humbert-Droz swung round to endorse self-determination. In Latin America, he asserted, "both in regard to the blacks and the Indians, our fundamental slogan on the question of race should be the right of peoples to dispose of themselves." He added, in case there was any doubt about what this implied for existing national boundaries, that it would mean "blowing up the artificial framework of the current South American States."[89]

This prompted opposition from many of those present, as it had in Buenos Aires. Khaikis argued that making distinctions between Indigenous and mestizo workers was divisive.[90] Stirner, too, voiced doubts, arguing that "in Latin America we don't see a national problem like in Central Europe or Yugoslavia."[91] But this time there were more voices in favor of self-determination. Yakobson asserted that "the principal slogan should be self-determination of the races going as far as separation"—mirroring the wording of the Haywood–Nasanov thesis. Yakobson also pointed to the tactical utility of self-determination: "The white workers must win the confidence of the indigenous and the blacks."[92] While Guralsky was impatient, saying, "We should put an end to the chatter about race," he agreed that a key demand for the Indigenous was "the right to self-disposition and to form their own state."[93] Grieco endorsed the idea of self-determination and added an important warning: "If the Comintern denies the problem of race and declares that there is only a problem of class, we will create trouble among our comrades and we will not succeed in putting our comrades to work among the national minorities in Latin America."[94] As with the Haywood–Nasanov thesis, a question of principle was interwoven with tactical considerations.

In the wake of these exchanges, those assembled approved a call for self-determination with a wording very close to that suggested by Yakobson: "self-determination going as far as separation."[95] Alongside this, the meeting protocol records a provisional demand for the expropriation of large land-owners and imperialist enterprises. What resulted from the Moscow discussion, then, was a synthesis of Mariátegui's emphasis on the agrarian question and the Sixth Congress's call for self-determination. But it had turned the Peruvian's historical materialist analysis into a program for agrarian revolution and combined it with calls for "national" liberation.

Why was self-determination approved in Moscow when it had met such resistance in Buenos Aires? Differences in personnel are one major factor: Those who had most articulately opposed the idea in mid-1929 were not in Moscow six months later. And even those who stood against self-determination in Moscow did so less on principle than for tactical reasons; they argued that the policy was misguided or insufficient, but not that it involved a fundamental misreading of race in the Americas. But perhaps most significantly, proponents of self-determination were able to portray opposition to it as proof that Latin American parties were unwilling to admit racism was a problem. First, the logic ran, the Latin American comrades denied the problem existed, then they opposed what any good Communist knew was the only real solution, tried and tested in the homeland of revolution, the USSR. The appeal to Bolshevik experience is one reason the self-determination policy has been portrayed as a Comintern imposition. But the Soviet example was a justification for the policy, not the impulse behind it. In the Moscow discussions of January 1930, as in debates around the Haywood–Nasanov thesis, it was racism and its structural consequences that were the core issue, and self-determination was the means of addressing it. In this context, self-determination became both the Comintern's preferred political solution and a token of the Communist movement's willingness to tackle the problem.

The Latin American Secretariat's decision of January 1, 1930, provided the foundation for extending the self-determination policy, already applied to the Black population of the US South, to Black and Indigenous peoples in Latin America. The decision was reaffirmed in a resolution reprinted in the Comintern's official South American publication, *La Correspondencia*

Sudamericana, in June 1930. It stated that "the struggle for the complete and real freedom of every people is the struggle for their right to dispose of themselves, up until separation, that is, the right to organize their own State."[96] Over the next few years, a string of Communist parties and affiliated organizations in Latin America would commit themselves to this program of Indigenous and Black sovereignty.

FORKING PATHS

The contention in Buenos Aires and Montevideo over race and self-determination has often been framed retroactively in terms of Latin American resistance to ideas developed in and for the USSR—that is, of better-informed local perspectives trying to prevent the imposition from outside of policies ill-suited to the region. Yet such interpretations obscure important features that have emerged from my reconstruction of the 1929 gatherings. First, the archival evidence reveals a relatively open and wide-ranging discussion, rather than a peremptory issuing of instructions from Moscow, and Comintern representatives in Buenos Aires were clearly listening attentively to Latin American delegates as they portrayed the region's realities. Second, while the 1929 debates prompted Latin American Communists to devote more attention to race than they had done to date, they also exposed a number of blind spots—including an insistence by many delegates that the problem of race did not exist. It was often the Comintern's representatives who were more willing to address racial oppression than local Communists, and as with debates around the Haywood–Nasanov thesis, Comintern support for self-determination was partly driven by a desire to combat racism within the movement.

These features of the 1929 debates shed new light on the Comintern's subsequent decision to push Latin America's Communist parties to take up the self-determination agenda. Far from being an arbitrary imposition, the policy was part of a serious attempt to grapple with the problem of racial oppression. As we have seen in chapter 4, it initially developed out of a transnational dialogue between Bolsheviks, Black US radicals, and anti-colonial activists. In this chapter we have seen how Latin American leftists such as Mariátegui and Junco raised substantive and well-founded objections to the self-determination policy. Yet amid wider contention over the extent of racism within the region, and indeed over the very definitions of race and

nation, the policy's supporters could often—and with some justification—
paint its opponents as unwilling to recognize the realities of discrimination.

The Buenos Aires and Montevideo debates constitute a neglected chapter
in the evolution of the Latin American left's thinking on race, nation, and
sovereignty. But more than this, they also offer insights into how interwar
radicals tried to address ethnic and racial inequalities without embracing
the essentialist race thinking of the time, and how they imagined redressing
the consequences of racism while simultaneously advancing a class-based,
anti-imperialist politics. Many of the blind spots the debates exposed would
persist decades later. But these shortcomings coexisted with some perceptive
analyses that were in many ways ahead of their time. Returning to the 1929
debates allows us to reconnect them to the wider discussions of race, nation,
empire, and sovereignty that took place in the interwar period. Within that
ferment, different analyses opened up divergent strategies, leading the components of the radical left down contrasting paths. The Communists' embrace of self-determination and of a program that would dismantle existing
nation-states was one such path; as we will see in the next chapter, APRA's
drift in the opposite direction, toward nationalism, was another.

SIX

Continental Nationalism

IN THE LION'S MOUTH

At the end of May 1929, as Communist trade union delegates were gathering in Montevideo, the Peruvian poet and leading APRA militant Magda Portal arrived in Cuba at the start of a three-month Caribbean tour. After engagements in Havana and Santiago de Cuba, she would go on to give lectures in Puerto Rico, the Dominican Republic, and Barranquilla on Colombia's Caribbean coast, galvanizing audiences with her denunciations of US imperialism and appeals for continental unity. Her choice of destinations was more than appropriate: "Our peoples are in the mouth of the lion," an editorial in the Dominican newspaper *El Mundo* put it, adding: "That lion is Yankee imperialism, an avaricious lion, hungry despite all the food it has already taken . . . from other very weak animals."[1] Portal herself noted that the Antilles and Central America had suffered both US military invasions and financial pressures "in the service of the plutocracy," describing the Caribbean as a place where "imperialism wears no disguise."[2]

Portal's presence in US-ruled Puerto Rico evidently unsettled local officials; the original venue in San Juan for a lecture titled "Latin America Against Imperialism" reportedly withdrew permission on the orders of the island's Department of Education.[3] When she eventually gave the talk in a new location, she pulled no punches: After laying out all of the region's vulnerabilities before the might of US capitalism, she concluded with a rousing exhortation: "We have a single and great enemy; let us form a single and great union."[4]

Portal's words reprised one of APRA's key slogans, emphasizing the need for Latin America to coalesce around an anti-imperial agenda. Her

Caribbean tour was itself a demonstration of *aprismo* in action: Roving from one location to the next, Portal was broadcasting the movement's ideas and sowing the seeds of future APRA cells, working toward continental unity on both an intellectual and a practical level. Yet even as she did this, APRA's character was changing. Indeed, her tour came at a pivotal moment in its evolution. Amid the disintegration of the anti-imperialist milieu described in chapter 3, significant differences emerged between APRA and the Communists. At the turn of the 1930s, the trajectories of the two movements diverged still more dramatically. The Communists, as we saw in chapter 5, radicalized their stance, envisaging a revolution that would bring about the demolition of existing nation-states. APRA moved in the opposite direction, changing from a continent-wide revolutionary movement to a specifically Peruvian party focused on achieving state power within a single country.

From the 1930s onward, APRA became a political force to be reckoned with in Peru, winning sizeable shares of the popular vote in elections and forming part of governing coalitions in 1945–48 and 1956–62; it eventually secured the presidency in 1985. This evolution has shaped the scholarly literature on the movement, which until recently framed discussion of it largely in national terms.[5] Its overseas origins tended to feature as an incidental detail in the early biography of a movement seen as an exemplar of Latin American populism, combining progressive nationalism with anti-imperialism. In the past decade, however, several scholars have highlighted the importance of transnational networks and experiences of exile to APRA's development and have pointed to the decisive importance of Communism in shaping its ideology from the outset.[6] As well as reinserting the movement into the broader context that formed it, these contributions offer a more nuanced view of APRA's ideological evolution.

One of the central ongoing tensions within APRA was between the transnational and the national. Did APRA have to draw back from its project of continental unity in order to win power in Peru, or, on the contrary, were strong transnational ties the best way to advance its cause within the national realm? The project of pan–Latin American unity was a key part of the movement's ideological self-positioning into the 1930s and 1940s, and transnational connections were crucial to the party's survival in what its militants called the "Era of the Catacombs," a period of enforced clandestinity from 1933 to 1945.[7] But continental appeals were increasingly subordinated to the pursuit of power within Peru, the idea of pan-regional confederation delayed over an ever more distant horizon as the movement shed its revolutionary garb and drifted rightward.

What explains this change? Political expediency was one factor; as we will see, Haya and his comrades adjusted the movement's program in key respects, believing that moderation would bring them closer to power. But these decisions were not improvised. Rather, they emerged out of deeply held ideas about what kind of revolutionary transformation Latin America should undergo. To a large extent, I argue, APRA's outlook in the 1930s was defined by its convergences and clashes with the Communists in the 1920s. After a period of anti-imperial consensus between the two, APRA literature began repeatedly to insist that "aprismo is not Communism"—a negative identity that became central to its self-definition.[8] As we saw in chapter 3, the two movements differed markedly in their relationship to the Mexican state and in their interpretations of the Mexican Revolution. APRA's version of transnational politics also took shape in deliberate contrast to the class-based, global vision of the Communists. Seeing itself as the standard-bearer for a regional anti-imperial project, APRA promoted what the editors of the Mexico City aprista magazine Indoamérica called "continental nationalism."[9]

The term encapsulates the tension in APRA's outlook between the transnational and the national. This chapter traces the movement's gradual drift from prioritizing the first of those two terms toward a predominant focus on the second. I chart APRA's evolution by following the trajectory of Magda Portal.[10] One of the movement's most prominent figures, Portal was at once representative and exceptional. She stood out most obviously as the only woman in the leadership of the Partido Aprista Peruano (PAP; Peruvian Aprista Party), which she cofounded in 1930. This in itself drew curiosity and attention, in a time and place where very few women were able to take leading political roles. At the same time, Portal embodied the transnational blend of experiences and influences that were so constitutive of APRA itself, moving from Peru's vanguard literary and political circles in the early 1920s to exile in revolutionary Mexico.

Most crucially, however, it was Portal who produced the earliest and most systematic articulation of APRA's ideas on two key themes: Latin America's urgent need to confront US imperialism and the example set for the region by the Mexican Revolution. Haya de la Torre's book El Antimperialismo y el APRA (Anti-imperialism and APRA), though often seen as the canonical statement of the movement's views during this period, was not published until 1936. Portal's arguments preceded it by several years: Published in book form in 1931 as *América Latina frente al imperialismo* (Latin America against imperialism), they were first laid out in the lectures she gave in the Caribbean in 1929.

In what follows, I reconstruct Portal's analysis and situate it within APRA's ideological evolution. Her thinking was traversed by the same contradictions that ran through APRA as a whole: While Portal was critical of Communists for embracing "distant internationalisms," she was concerned by APRA's increasing focus on Peruvian domestic politics and remained an important voice within the party seeking to maintain both its transnational and revolutionary commitments.[11] Her attempts to reconcile these tensions allow us to see the paradoxes of continental nationalism with unusual clarity. In chapter 5, we saw how Latin America's Communists edged toward a revolutionary agenda that implied the dismantling of existing nation-states; in retracing APRA's ideological evolution, we can follow the other strand of the strategic divergence that began in 1920s Mexico to its denouement.

DARK POWERS, CONTRARY TRUTHS

By the time she set off on her Caribbean tour, Portal had undergone many kinds of exile. Born in 1900 into a middle-class family in Barranco, just south of Lima, she grew up in Callao in "a huge rambling house on the far edge of town," nestled by the Pacific.[12] By the early 1920s, Portal had entered the Peruvian capital's bohemian circles and gained a reputation as a poet. Her literary entrée coincided with an important political discovery; she joined the student protests of 1923 and briefly met their leader, Haya de la Torre. This, she recalled, was when she "got a glimpse of Peru's social problems."[13]

In 1924 Portal married the writer Federico Bolaños, but the following year she left him for his brother Reynaldo, better known under his pseudonym Serafín Delmar. Possibly in a bid to flee the ensuing scandal, the couple left for Bolivia, where they stayed until late 1926, joining the literary vanguard in La Paz and helping produce a newspaper titled *Bandera Roja* (Red flag).[14] Their activities got them deported back to Peru, where they rejoined the capital's literary circles. In Lima, Portal regularly attended gatherings at Mariátegui's one-story house on Jirón Washington, where factory workers rubbed shoulders with literati and journalists. Portal's poems appeared in Mariátegui's journal *Amauta*, and her early works drew Mariátegui's praise; describing her in 1928 as "already one of the leading poetesses of Indoamérica," he hailed her "original and autonomous temperament." His characterization of her work suggested a personality beset by contradictions: "Who knows," he asked, "how many dark powers, how many contrary truths make up a soul like hers?"[15]

In June 1927 the conservative Lima newspaper *El Comercio* announced the discovery of a "Communist plot" to topple Leguía. Mariátegui was imprisoned in a military hospital, and Portal was also among those rounded up. Deported to Cuba, she arrived just as the Machado regime was conducting its own anti-Communist sweep. Rifling through her luggage, the customs police confiscated books by Russian authors or with red covers (inherently suspicious, it seems). Portal was placed under house arrest, while her husband was jailed alongside Cuban leftists such as Juan Marinello, Raúl Roa, and the writer Alejo Carpentier. A few weeks later, Portal was released on condition that she depart immediately, and in July she sailed from Havana to Veracruz.[16]

THE INDOAMERICAN HOUR

"Mexico marked fundamental changes in my life," Portal recalled in later years.[17] On arriving in the country in 1927, she found that "one still breathed the revolutionary atmosphere." The encounter with Mexico was transformative not only for her view of that country, but also for her understanding of Peru and of Latin America as a whole. "It was in Mexico," she wrote, "that I began to discover the indigenous man of Peru and of the Americas."[18] As it had done for Haya before her, Mexico prompted Portal to become more aware of Latin America's Indigenous heritage and to link the concept of Indoamerica to an anti-imperialist politics.

Indoamérica was the title of the monthly organ of APRA's Mexico City cell, of which Portal was one of the founders, along with fellow Peruvian exiles Esteban Pavletich, Nicolás Terreros, and Jacobo Hurwitz. Its first issue, published in July 1928, carried a manifesto by Portal titled "The Imperative of the Indoamerican Hour," in which she argued for the unification of Latin America's "vast mosaic of small republics" as the only means of resisting the economic might of the United States.[19] "The future of IndoAmerica," she wrote, "is in the hands of the plutocratic class of the United States"; regional unity was the only way to avoid being "drained by the economic forces of the most powerful people on earth." To achieve this, what was needed was "a great IndoAmerican nationalist party."[20] Other articles in the same issue described the ideology of the pan-regional movement APRA aspired to lead as "continental nationalism."

How could the two parts of this apparent oxymoron be reconciled? How could a supranational category such as Indoamerica be the container for any kind of nationalism? Part of the answer is that, for Portal and the other Mexico City *apristas*, Indoamerica itself was already unified on many levels. "We are one people," Portal argued in her 1928 manifesto, "united by a common tradition, by a common race and by a common danger that identifies us in the future."[21] APRA saw itself as a project for transferring this preexisting unity to the state level, where fragmentation stubbornly persisted, despite the fellow feeling of the populace. Continental nationalism was the patriotism of a country that did not yet exist but that was coming into being.

The anti-imperial consensus described in chapter 2 was part of the evidence *apristas* found for this tendency toward unity. Another example was Senator Álvarez's proposal for continental citizenship, passed by the Mexican Senate only a few months before. Underlining the link between the two, the first issue of *Indoamérica* reprinted, on the page facing Portal's article, a letter to Álvarez from Augusto Sandino praising his proposal. Sandino promised that once he had formed a new Nicaraguan government, "your initiative of continental citizenship will be one of the first measures approved by it."[22]

This "IndoAmerican nationalism" was still framed in revolutionary terms, and Mexico City's *apristas* expressed admiration for the most famous of the world's recent examples. The November 1928 issue of *Indoamérica*, with a woodcut of Lenin on its cover (see figure 8), paid tribute to the Russian Revolution as "the first total and indisputable victory achieved over imperialism"—hence "its importance for us, colonial peoples."[23] But it was Mexico that took center stage for Portal and for APRA, as a Latin American model for social and political transformation, anti-oligarchic in its consequences and anti-imperialist in its orientation to the world.

The postrevolutionary Mexican state's embrace of *mestizaje* was crucial in inspiring Portal's adoption of the concept of Indoamerica. In a 1928

FIGURE 8. Cover of *Indoamérica*, no. 5, November 1928. From New York Public Library.

pamphlet titled *The New Poem and Its Orientation Toward an Economic Aesthetic*, she used Vasconcelos's term "cosmic race" to refer to the demographic outcome of the encounter of Spanish colonialism with "the heap of Indians piled together in the cruelest slavery, barbarically decimated [by the Conquest], illiterate and fanatical." For Portal, the mestizos who had emerged over the centuries—"the product of all the importations, but now for the most part of Indian blood"—were the progenitors of a continent-spanning, "new Latin American culture" to come.[24]

Portal's less than flattering depiction of Latin America's Indigenous population points to the ambiguity—if not hypocrisy—at the heart of APRA's notion of Indoamerica. Ostensibly a celebration of the region's Indigenous identity, the term was employed first and foremost by mestizos; and while APRA paid homage to historic Indigenous traditions, at this point the movement paid little attention to present-day Indigenous peoples.[25] Much as the Mexican state in the 1920s treated the Indigenous as a legacy of the past to be "incorporated" into the mestizo mainstream, APRA viewed indigeneity more as a historical marker of a shared pan-regional identity than as a focal point for solidarity in the present.

As well as inspiring Portal's framing of Latin America's racial destiny, Mexico was where she began to develop her materialist analysis of the region. The spur for this, in her retelling, came from Haya, who returned to Mexico City from Europe in late 1927. "Half-joking and half-serious," Portal said, Haya told her to stop writing poetry and study economics. In response, Portal took the manuscript of her new collection of poems to a park, tore up the pages one by one, and dropped them into a stream—to the horror of Esteban Pavletich, who was accompanying her.[26]

Portal's new interest in economics bore fruit a year later in the *New Poem* pamphlet, which synthesized her vanguard literary stance with an economic analysis of Latin America. While devoted to contemporary Latin American poetry, its arguments were shaped by readings that included Scott Nearing's and Joseph Freeman's *Dollar Diplomacy*, recently translated into Spanish and frequently cited by others in Mexico City's anti-imperialist milieu. Portal would draw on their analysis of US economic dominance in her Caribbean lecture tour.

Portal labeled her discussions of poetry in *The New Poem* with the heading "Songs to the Future," adding that "All of América is in the future."[27] The combination of pan-regional unity and messianic overtones was characteristic of APRA, and Portal's pamphlet loudly proclaimed her adherence to the movement. The text was bookended by APRA slogans, concluding with a call for the "manual and intellectual workers of Latin America" to form "the united front of justice" and opening with the phrase Portal would repeat in San Juan a year later: "We have a single and great enemy; let us form a single and great union."[28]

In May 1929, Portal left the Mexican capital for Yucatán, and from there she would begin her Caribbean tour. The trip was ostensibly carried out on the instructions of the Mexico City APRA Committee, which tasked Portal with mounting an "anti-imperialist campaign" as well as forming APRA cells in new locations.[29] The timing was fortuitous; as we saw in chapter 3, by this point Mexico was a much less welcoming place for radical exiles, and several of Portal's friends and colleagues were soon to be arrested or deported. Though Portal herself was not targeted, she did not return to Mexico after her three-month voyage around the Caribbean. Her departure thus marked a new phase in her life of exile.

Portal arrived in Cuba in May, visiting Havana and Santiago de Cuba. From there she went to Puerto Rico in June, and to the Dominican Republic in July, briefly returning to Puerto Rico at the end of the month before moving on to Barranquilla, Colombia, in early August.[30] In each place, she gave ticketed public lectures in large venues, such as the Teatro Municipal in San Juan, where she spoke on June 8 and 25, and the Teatro Colón in Santo Domingo, where her talk took place on July 14. In Santo Domingo, as many as two hundred people braved torrential rain to hear her speak, applauding enthusiastically both before and after her two-hour lecture. She also made free appearances in workers' clubs and union halls, including one at the Association of Trade Employees in Barranquilla on August 16.[31]

The local press was enthused by Portal's presence: Puerto Rican journalist José Abad Ramos described her as "a force in action, a tremulous wellspring of dynamism, a liquid metal in continuous fusion."[32] Several newspapers ran profiles of Portal, with reporters impressed by her forceful personality, though perhaps also by the novelty of a woman playing such a prominent political role. The San Juan paper *El Mundo* observed incredulously that "this woman, fragile and slight like a schoolgirl, carries hidden in her breast the battle-hardened heart of a man."[33] The people who met her off the boat in Puerto Rico were surprised by her appearance, too, evidently expecting someone of a different physical type; Portal joked with them: "Did you think I was a large, older woman with her hands in her pockets, probably with a bomb in each hand?"[34]

Both the Puerto Rican and the Dominican press covered her lectures extensively, announcing them in advance and providing lengthy summaries of her arguments afterward. *La Correspondencia de Puerto Rico* republished one talk in its entirety.[35] Her lectures focused on two principal themes: the penetration of Latin America by US imperialism and the origins and achievements of the Mexican Revolution. These topics formed the two halves of the book that appeared in 1931 under the title *América Latina frente al imperialismo*. They offered a cogent summary of *aprista* thinking at the end of the 1920s, laying out key differences from the Communists' views and clarifying APRA's strategic vision of revolution.

Early on in her tour, the Santiago newspaper *El Diario de Cuba* published an article by Portal titled "Capitalism and Colonization."[36] As well as showcasing her interest in economic questions, it laid a strongly materialist foundation for the analysis of imperialism she would provide in her lectures. Echoing Marx and Engels's celebrated opening to the *Communist Manifesto*, Portal asserted that "a new specter is roaming the world"—this time "the danger of armed aggression by the imperialist powers competing over markets." Rich European countries and the United States had overproduced manufactured goods and accumulated capital to such an extent that, in order to avoid an economic crisis, they had to find new markets for their products. For Portal, this was the impulse driving the economic carve-up of the globe after the First World War. While Latin America was insulated to some extent from European predations by the Monroe Doctrine, this left it all the more exposed to the market hunger of the United States. Only a few months before the Wall Street crash in 1929, Portal warned that "the specter of crisis threatens the equilibrium of the formidable Yankee capitalist skyscraper."[37]

In her lectures, Portal discussed the impact of US finance on Latin America, noting in particular the link between the export of US capital and the vulnerabilities of Central and South American states to intervention from the North.[38] So as to more clearly specify these effects, Portal divided Latin America into four zones. First, there was a primary zone of US penetration comprising Mexico, Central America, and the Caribbean basin. Here, US imperial influence was at its most direct and aggressive, with serial military interventions cementing Washington's economic and political dominance. Puerto Rico, one of the places where she delivered these lectures, was of course a key site of US imperial expansion, and she described it as having been ceded by Spain in 1898 as a "war trophy" without its inhabitants even being consulted.

A second zone included the "Bolivarian" countries (Venezuela, Colombia, Ecuador, Peru, and Bolivia), where US influence was mainly financial and took the form of loans or ownership of mines, oilfields, railroads, and public works. In a third region, comprising Argentina, Chile, and Uruguay, competition between British and US capital lessened the dominance of either; at the time, these were also the most industrially developed countries in Latin America. A fourth zone consisted solely of Brazil, where the sheer scale of the country meant imperialism took a different form. But in Portal's view, the Brazilian government's pursuit of an "open door" policy toward foreign investors posed a real threat to regional unity.[39]

Portal's focus on the financial aspects of US power echoed Mella's views, discussed in chapter 2, about what distinguished US imperialism from its predecessors. But her arguments took those ideas a step further by causally linking the export of US capital to Latin America's continuing status as a provider of natural resources. The financial sway of Wall Street and its copious investments in the primary goods sector blocked Latin America's ability to pursue any alternative paths. These arguments resonated with the points that the Swiss Comintern operative Jules Humbert-Droz and the Ecuadorean Communist Ricardo Paredes had made about Latin America's "dependent status" at the Sixth Comintern Congress the previous summer; not coincidentally, Portal's biographer Kathleen Weaver argues that in these lectures Portal was laying out an early version of dependency theory.[40] The congruence between the Communists' and Portal's analyses is not surprising, given the avowedly Marxist nature of her approach. At one point she noted that until recently, Latin America's problems had not been seen clearly because "no one went to the Marxist root of the question." Portal argued that "the fundamental problem of our peoples . . . is an economic problem." Later she asserted that "economic causes are what determined the sociological, political, and moral process of peoples."[41] In this respect, Portal was actually more unwavering in her materialism than the Communists; at this very moment, as we saw in chapter 5, the delegates to the 1929 Buenos Aires conference were debating the relationship between racial and class oppressions, and while they ultimately agreed on the primacy of class, they proved willing to bring in a wider range of factors than Portal considered.

There were other significant differences between Portal's views and those of the Communists. One was her emphasis on the specificity of Latin America. While she described the region using terms similar to those the Comintern did—"semi-colonial," "agrarian and semi-feudal"—Portal argued that its situation was unlike that of the rest of the world, with the possible exception of China. This meant that "imported methods" would not work: "APRA cannot propose the solution to [Latin America's] problems in accordance with systems alien to its reality." This necessarily implied a different strategy from that pursued by the Communists. As Portal put it, "Our struggle is not against the oppressive power of a national bourgeoisie which in most of our countries does not exist, but rather against the advance of foreign capital."[42]

Here, Portal's analysis matched that of Mariátegui: In Latin America, there was no national bourgeoisie, because the people who might otherwise play that role were tied to foreign capital. But from similar premises Portal arrived at a quite different strategic payoff: Whereas Mariátegui concluded that the proletariat and peasantry should carry forward the revolution, Portal insisted on the need for a cross-class "united front." Local elites, however, were not to be included in this front; according to Portal, they had "no feeling of responsibility . . . for the problem of national sovereignty," and she described them as "foreignizing" (*extranjerizantes*), due to their willing subordination to imperial interests and disdain for the region's "truly native races."[43] With elites excluded, there was only one place left for popular classes to look for allies. As in the 1928 controversy between Haya and Mella, the crux was the role of the middle classes. Would they align with local and international elites, or could they be drawn to the side of workers and peasants?

In Portal's view, the second scenario had unfolded in revolutionary Mexico. In her lectures on Mexico, Portal didn't explicitly refer to an alliance between middle and popular classes, but it was heavily implied in her references throughout to a singular "people" (*pueblo*), which had risen up as one against landowners and foreign capitalists. For Portal, the Mexican Revolution was "the first movement of a social character carried out in Latin America, with clearly defined goals, the destruction of latifundism and the emancipation of the great masses of indigenous workers of the countryside." Though the revolution's gains were far from consolidated or evenly distributed, it had set an example for the rest of the region. Portal placed particular emphasis on the Mexican Constitution of 1917, which had nationalized land and natural resources. This, for Portal, was an important step in establishing "the basic principle of the economic sovereignty of a people."[44] Yet for the moment, Mexico was alone: The rest of the continent, still dominated by oligarchic governments, "had done nothing to support [its] struggles." This had to change; according to Portal, only through pan-regional unity could Latin America withstand the pressures of imperialism. Tellingly, she praised Mexico's 1927 "continental citizenship" law as a major step toward creating a sense of shared destiny.[45]

The motif of continental unity—the centerpiece of APRA's founding ideology—recurred several times in Portal's lectures, and with good reason: It was ultimately the sole means of opposing empire. Citing José Martí and Simón Bolívar, Portal observed that "in face of the advance of economic Imperialism which, like a gigantic wave, threatens to swallow the shaky sovereignty of our peoples, there is a single dilemma: either we unite or we perish." What was needed was the formation of a "Federation of Latin American States"—a union that would be "strong, respectable, harmonious, and capable of facing up to the enormous power of Yankee imperialism." The foundations for this already existed, in Portal's view: Latin America's population was "a conglomerate of peoples identified [with each other] on various ethnic, ethical, ideological, and traditional grounds, and above all on economic grounds."[46] There is a faint echo here of Stalin's list of criteria for defining a nation, and Portal would certainly have been aware of Communist debates on the national question. Her goal, however, was not to separate out smaller sovereign groups, but to bind larger ones together into a pan-regional bloc.

Continental nationalism was the term Portal used to describe APRA's program for realizing that unity. It had previously been used by the Mexico City *apristas* to promote an expansion of solidarity beyond national frontiers, to the continental level. But another layer of meaning to the term began to emerge in Portal's 1929 lectures, signifying a retreat from a global horizon to a regional one. While APRA stood in solidarity, she claimed, with people struggling for liberation from imperialism everywhere, it was now "urgent to concentrate all our anti-imperialist activity in Latin America . . . without wasting energy in distant internationalisms." The criticism of the Comintern's global aspirations is plain. Portal's project for continental integration would help realize "our absolute independence" and thus "fulfill the dream of Bolívar."[47] But the world beyond Latin America was not APRA's concern.

Portal's Caribbean lectures provide the clearest and most substantial exposition of APRA's views at the end of the 1920s. They offer a materialist interpretation of contemporary Latin America, identifying the different mechanisms of imperial dominance at work in different parts of the region and highlighting the example set by Mexico in overturning those structures. They also mark a further development of the disputes between APRA and the Communists, cementing the divergences in political strategy that emerged out of analyses that initially had much in common. Moreover, although Portal called for a pan–Latin American, cross-class unity, her emphasis on national sovereignty as the first building block in that strategy reflected APRA's increasing focus on the national realm. That shift became still more marked once the movement's members were able to reassemble in Peru in 1930.

But Portal first had to endure a further interval of exile. Though well received by the press and public, her lectures in San Juan were not viewed favorably by the US authorities; they were probably also not pleased that she met with Puerto Rican nationalists and took part in anti-US demonstrations while there.[48] After her talk on July 31 at the University of Puerto Rico, she was summoned for questioning and, after four hours of interrogation—conducted in English, much to Portal's irritation—was ordered to leave the island within twenty-four hours.[49] After a brief visit to Colombia, she spent several months in Costa Rica, working closely with Joaquín García Monge, publisher of the magazine *Repertorio Americano*.[50] In early 1930 Portal transplanted to Chile, where she was reunited with other Peruvian exiles. But conditions there soon proved inhospitable, too; accused of being a Communist agent, she was briefly imprisoned by the government of Carlos Ibáñez.[51]

During her brief stay in Santiago, there had been talk of a meeting to reconcile *apristas* and Mariátegui's supporters. But Mariátegui's death in April 1930 ended those hopes.[52] The leadership of the Peruvian Socialist Party was taken over by Eudocio Ravines—himself a former *aprista*, ironically—who renamed it the Peruvian Communist Party and set aside his predecessor's heterodox ideas, fully adopting the Comintern line. By the time Portal returned to Lima a few months later, the battle lines had hardened, and the *apristas* were firmly focused on creating their own national political party.

DOMESTICATING APRA

In August 1930, Peruvian president Augusto Leguía was deposed by a military junta led by Lieutenant-Colonel Luis Miguel Sánchez Cerro. The end of Leguía's eleven-year rule brought an amnesty that allowed many of those previously exiled to return. The brief political opening also enabled the *apristas* to establish the PAP in Lima on September 21, 1930. Portal describes its first meeting taking place in a room lent to the group by a trade union. There was no electricity, and only a dozen people huddled around the light of "a slender sperm candle by which we could barely write the minutes or recognize each other."[53] From these modest beginnings emerged a party that would become one of Peru's main political forces.

Portal would be one of the PAP's most visible and dedicated militants in the 1930s and 1940s, enduring five hundred days of imprisonment in 1934–36 and a further period of exile from 1939 to 1945, before finally breaking with the party in 1948. Many of her reservations about its changing path were apparent from early on, and these frequently created frictions within APRA's leadership. Both Portal's activities on behalf of the movement and her discontents with it illustrate *aprismo*'s uneasy journey from transnationalism to a political horizon bounded by a single nation-state.

The political opening under Sánchez Cerro lasted less than three months, till November 1930. For the next three years, bursts of repression alternated with periods in which it was possible to organize legally. Portal later described that interval as "a nightmare owing to the brutal persecution of which I was the object." As a member of the PAP's Executive Committee, she was one of its better known leaders and was repeatedly imprisoned in the early 1930s. She was a highly active campaigner, speaking at rallies across the country. This was how she got to know "what is now called deep Peru," discovering "the deep misery endured by its malnourished children, its women exploited by the landlord, its suffering men." As Portal recalled, repeated contact with these crowds made her into an orator: "In my tours of the Antilles and Central America I read out lectures, but faced with concentrations of people there was no other way to act than to speak directly." Portal also described this as the first time APRA was able "to get closer to the people and speak to them face to face, many times with translators for native languages."[54] Indeed, this was APRA's first prolonged encounter with the Indigenous people its rhetoric had celebrated—this time not as abstract signifiers of pan-regional identity, but as concrete political actors.

Yet while Portal was a committed and disciplined *aprista*, tensions nonetheless emerged between her and Haya. Some of these stemmed from Haya's insistence on placing her in charge of the PAP's "Women's Command," to which Portal reluctantly agreed—perhaps sensing an attempt to marginalize her.[55] Haya certainly paid little heed to women's capacity to contribute to his movement in anything more than an auxiliary role. Portal recalled him telling a congress of *aprista* women in the early 1930s that their tasks were simply to be mothers and wives. Portal furiously whispered to him that this wasn't what they wanted to hear, but he continued in the same vein before departing the stage angrily. What happened next tells us much about the continued radicalism of APRA's base, even as its leadership led the party rightward: When Portal asked the women what they'd like her to speak about, they replied, "About Marxism, *compañera*."[56]

Portal's concerns over machismo within the movement were wrapped up with growing alarm over Haya's personalistic style of leadership and the direction in which he was taking APRA. Haya had returned to Peru triumphantly in 1931, greeted by large crowds. In his absence, the PAP had drafted an electoral platform calling for a radical transformation of the country's socioeconomic structures. Among other things, it envisaged an agrarian reform and redistribution of land. For Haya, it went too far: "No! This can't be done here," he told Portal. She recalled him objecting to the platform's proposed moves against some of Peru's wealthiest landowners: "You've got too many expropriations of haciendas here," he said, "the country will collapse."[57] For Portal, the purpose of APRA remained a radical one: "We all dreamed of a genuinely revolutionary, socialist organization," she later noted. Impatient with Haya's bid to steer a moderate course, at one point she wrote to him, "We are still on the rose-colored paths," referring to APRA's watering down of its earlier radicalism. "When are we switching to the red paths?" she asked.[58]

Another source of discord was Haya's focus on electoral politics. For Portal, this implied a troubling shift in APRA's overall strategy. "It was not a question of engaging in party-political action," she remembered thinking, "but rather of preparing the masses for a continental struggle against the national oligarchies and foreign imperialism."[59] Shortly before returning to Peru in September 1930, Portal had insisted that "in speaking of Peru we cannot separate it from its common Latin American roots."[60] She would retain this continental framing of Peru's political fortunes even as the rest of APRA, and Haya in particular, increasingly set it aside.

In February 1932, Haya produced a manifesto laying out APRA's program at length. This made clear how much his views had changed in the six years since APRA's founding. Having launched his movement by proclaiming a world-spanning radical anti-imperialism, Haya now insisted that the revolution he was advocating was a peaceful *evolution*, citing Christ, Galileo, Tolstoy, Gandhi, and the British industrial revolution as examples of revolutionary ends being achieved without violence. *Aprismo* was not communism, he insisted.[61] He also sought to reassure the public about the nature of APRA's internationalism. Its "Latin Americanism" merely reflected existing tendencies toward unification across the region, such as those embodied in calls for a customs union. And while the movement remained committed to the ideal of "Latin American political and economic union" contained in its "maximum program," Haya noted that "the realization of the great Bolivarian principle is still far away." Moreover, this program for the unification of Latin America's peoples in any case "did not exclude the profound and heroic desire of each group for ... national defense." On the contrary, he insisted that *aprismo* was the true vehicle for the realization of national goals: "*Aprismo* is nationalism, in its most authentic, most restorative and constructive sense."[62]

Haya's identification of *aprismo* with nationalism—*as* nationalism— showed how far the movement had traveled from its transnational origins. Committed, as of 1930, to the pursuit of power within Peru, APRA had shifted its horizons firmly to that single nation-state. From advocating "continental citizenship," it became a zealous defender of national sovereignty and increasingly expressed skepticism about "international" movements such as Communism. Even during subsequent periods of persecution and exile— especially those that followed the assassination of President Sánchez Cerro by an APRA member in 1933 and a failed *aprista* uprising in 1934—transnational connections served more as leverage to advance APRA's cause within Peru itself than as the basis for a continental struggle.[63]

In the course of its ideological journey, then, APRA came to define itself against the Communists' global, class-based internationalism twice over: first in regional terms, as a specifically Latin American anti-imperial movement, and then in national terms, as the representative of a nationalist populism that would meld middle classes with workers and peasants. To some extent these shifts were the result of the PAP's maneuvering within the Peruvian political landscape. But more than a matter of opportunism, they stemmed ultimately from the strategic commitments that had divided *apristas* and Communists in Mexico City. Haya's pursuit of an alliance with the middle classes and national bourgeoisie, which he had deemed essential to his anti-imperial agenda, prompted a series of compromises with Peru's ruling elites that led APRA to shed its radicalism and drift to the right. APRA's anti-Communism likewise bore out one of Mella's arguments in his 1928 polemic with Haya. The Cuban had predicted that if APRA began by insisting on its non-Communist credentials, it would sooner or later end up taking an anti-Communist line. By the mid-1930s it was doing precisely that, framing itself as a counter to both fascism and communism: "Neither with Rome nor with Berlin nor with Moscow, only *aprismo* will save Peru," ran one of its slogans.[64]

Portal was increasingly alarmed by APRA's rightward shift, which continued into the 1940s and eventually led her to leave the party. In 1945, APRA was a major component in the electoral coalition that brought centrist lawyer José Luis Bustamante to power. Portal watched Haya give a speech in Lima's Plaza San Martín in which he reneged on key components of APRA's program. There was "no mention of any struggle against imperialism," she later recalled, "No mention of taking back the wealth controlled by the transnationals."[65] Over the next three years, with a majority in the Senate and only a handful of seats fewer than that in the Congress, APRA played what Portal characterized as a double game, making deals with the country's traditional elites behind closed doors while publicly claiming the mantle of a popular movement. What had started as tactical maneuvering became self-justifying political praxis, or as Portal later put it, "the mendacious disguise became the normal and obligatory clothing for *aprista* leaders."[66]

In 1948, Portal broke with the party for good. Her frustrations had been building for some time, but the immediate trigger for the rupture came at the party's Second Congress that May–June. According to Portal, the APRA leadership showed no respect for internal democratic processes, and there was little sense of accountability to its members. Worst of all, the leadership decided to deny women *apristas* the right to vote on internal party matters, on the grounds that they couldn't vote in Peru anyway. This, Portal wrote two years later in a furious denunciation of her former comrades, was how the party "repaid more than twenty years of loyalty from a woman who made no distinctions of age or sex in the struggle to attain liberty, justice and democracy for all Peruvians."[67] She walked out of the congress and left the party there and then. A few months later, in October 1948, APRA militants led a failed rebellion that was quickly disavowed by its leadership—an act that Portal saw as the culmination of "a series of transactions, surrenders and . . . betrayals of doctrine and of the people's hopes."[68]

APRA was no longer the movement Portal had joined in the 1920s. In her view, it had turned its back on its radical origins, renouncing any intention of redistributing wealth and even going so far as to deny the existence of US imperialism: Haya referred instead to an "Indoamerican inferiority complex."[69] Portal's disappointment was profound. But twenty years after she parted ways with *aprismo*, she would recommit to the ideas that APRA had abandoned and that had been so foundational for her politics. This involved making an ideological journey back across the rift that had opened up in 1920s Mexico: In 1967, Portal joined the Peruvian Communist Party.[70]

The divides that had developed between *apristas* and Communists in Mexico City in the 1920s were formative for APRA's subsequent evolution in Peru. In many cases, the contention revolved around the same issues, and to some extent the rivalry that developed between the two movements in 1930s Peru was a direct continuation of the trajectories that had diverged in Mexico. After the formation of the PAP in 1930, APRA and the Communists vied bitterly for the loyalties of Peru's trade unions. Against the Communists' internationalism, APRA claimed to be the authentic representative of Peruvians, independent of foreign ideological influences.

The idea that Communism was alien to Latin America echoed the 1928 dispute between Haya and Mella, as well as arguments made in APRA's magazine *Indoamérica* later that year by Colombian *agrarista* Julio Cuadros Caldas: The Communists, he argued, had "lost their sense of reality and wish to forcibly ignore our idiosyncrasy and our problems in order to apply texts that communist orthodoxy wrote for a corrupted and senile Europe."[71] In his book *El Comunismo criollo*, published in Mexico in May 1930, Cuadros Caldas argued that Communism was simply inapplicable to Latin America, since it was fundamentally at odds with "the social conditions of IndoAmerica."[72] In October 1930 Manuel Seoane, who on his return from exile in Buenos Aires became one of the PAP's best known leaders, used the same line of argument, asserting that the Peruvian Communists' policies had been devised by "the European leaders of creole Communism." This was a double insult, since it implied that Latin American Communists were not only ideologically non-native to the region, but also willingly subordinated to foreigners.[73]

The playing out in Peru of arguments originally aired in Mexico also involved former *apristas* such as Esteban Pavletich, who had joined the Communists in 1929. Even prior to his deportation from Mexico in 1930, he was working on a critique of the Mexican Revolution's outcomes.[74] Published in 1934, *El mensaje de México* (The message of Mexico) provided a counter to APRA's insistence on seeing that country as a model for the rest of Latin America. According to Pavletich, the Mexican Revolution was "useful only for its errors, its vacillations, its explorations and defeats"; at best it offered "lessons and experiences on how . . . a revolution neither can nor should be carried out successfully." For Pavletich, the reason Mexico's revolutionary impulse had been "sterilized," as he put it, was simple: Whereas the proletariat had directed the revolution's course in Russia, in Mexico the bourgeoisie had held sway. After a period of radicalism sustained by "vague nationalist sentiment," this bourgeoisie had opted to make a deal with foreign imperialists and to rein in the social upsurge the revolution had unleashed.[75]

Yet for all that, Pavletich insisted that the Mexican Revolution was not over. Its historic tasks had simply passed into other hands: The workers, peasants, and Indigenous would carry out the transition to socialism. Mexico's message was not one of success, but rather of incompletion.[76] What remained to be done in Mexico, in Pavletich's view, could be summed up in a three-point agenda that also applied to the entire region: expropriation of latifundios without compensation, nationalization of imperialist-owned enterprises and repudiation of the ancien régime's debts, and recognition of the right of Indigenous national minorities to self-determination.[77]

The emphasis Pavletich placed on self-determination points to a new feature of the contention between Communists and apristas. The adoption of the self-determination policy had been highly disputed within the Communist movement, as we saw in chapter 5. For APRA, it was yet another instance of "creole Communists" mistakenly applying European notions to Latin America. As Seoane argued in 1930, whereas European national minorities were indeed "persecuted by a different race that maintains them in slavery because they are minorities," in Peru Indigenous people "are in the majority and their slavery is in essence economic." Mirroring the objections Mariátegui had raised a year earlier, Seoane insisted, "It is ... not a problem of race but a problem of class." Besides, he went on to observe, "geographically the initiative is absurd": Indigenous people were scattered all over Peru, mixed together with whites and mestizos. "The line of difference that we apristas establish," Seoane concluded, "is that of the exploitation of man by man, and not the color of their skin pigments."[78] At this moment, it was APRA that was insisting on the primacy of economic factors, and the Communists who were attending to the specificity of racial domination.

This contrast between the apristas' and the Communists' approaches to race emerged out of the two movements' differing relationships to the nation-state. In the 1920s, APRA had emphasized the need to bolster existing nation-states against imperialism, while the Communists sought to overturn and remake them. In the 1930s, each movement took its stance to its logical conclusion: APRA focused increasingly on the conquest of power within a single nation-state, while the Communists debated whether to re-draw the political map of the Americas.

In the 1930s, several of the region's Communist parties adopted versions of the self-determination policy. A pamphlet published in Bolivia in 1931 by the Latin American Trade Union Confederation promised that the coming worker and peasant revolution "will give full national independence to all the Indians creating INDEPENDENT QUECHUA AND AYMARA REPUBLICS."[79] In 1934, the Chilean Communist Party called for the establishment of a "Republic of Araucanía" for the Mapuche.[80] In Mexico, the PCM's 1932 congress passed a resolution calling on the party to "support, organize, and direct the struggle for the right to self-determination of the indigenous, up to the right of the tribes to separate from Mexico and constitute independent indigenous states, if they so desire."[81] In Cuba, it was the island's Black population that were held to be legitimate subjects for self-determination, and from 1932 onward, the PCC identified the majority-Black regions of Oriente province as the territory where the party should support the exercise of that right. In the Mexican and Cuban cases, the self-determination policy had divergent and uneven impacts, and it is to these that I turn in the chapters that follow.

PART THREE

Cuba/Mexico
(1932–1940)

SEVEN

Another Country

Anyone who wishes to see another country, without going abroad, should go to Oriente.

—Pablo de la Torriente Brau, "Realengo 18"
(*Ahora*, 16 November 1934)

A NEW APPROACH

In September 1932, two Cuban Communists in Moscow reframed their party's entire approach to race. Ramón Nicolau and Aggeo Suárez Pérez had been sent from Havana to the USSR the previous year to study at the International Lenin School. Writing under the pseudonyms "Justo Ríos" and "Simón Álvarez," they denounced the racism and discrimination endured by people of African descent in Cuba.[1] Overturning these injustices, however, would require more than simply acknowledging the long shadow of slavery and its present-day legacies. According to Nicolau and Suárez Pérez, a two-track policy was in order. On the one hand, the party needed to push for full equality and an end to discrimination across the island. On the other, in the eastern province of Oriente, where Black Cubans were the majority of the population, the party should call for them to be granted the right to self-determination—that is, the right to form their own separate, sovereign state if they so desired.

The PCC would adopt precisely this dual approach just three months later. A document drawn up for internal discussion in December 1932 was emphatic: "For our Party it should be clear once and for all that BLACKS IN CUBA CONSTITUTE AN OPPRESSED NATIONALITY and that our duty is . . . to demand self-determination."[2] For the next three years, the PCC would describe the country's Black population as an oppressed "national" group and call for self-determination in Oriente. At the same time, the party began to advocate energetically for racial equality. For the rest of the 1930s, the PCC was actively engaged in the struggle against racism in Cuba and forged alliances with Black social clubs and civic organizations, known as *sociedades de color*, as well as recruiting many people of color into its own ranks.[3] Indeed, by the end of the decade the PCC had become the most prominent Cuban political party working for Black rights, taking up demands for equality in the workplace and for access to public spaces. Communists also played a prominent part in getting an antidiscrimination provision included in the island's new 1940 Constitution.[4]

How should we understand the relationship between the PCC's advocacy of Black self-determination and its calls for racial equality? Most of the scholarship on Cuban Communism in the 1930s has seen the two components of the PCC's agenda as separate, if not counterposed. In this view, the self-determination policy was a brief, externally imposed delusion, prompted by the PCC leadership's desire to toe the Comintern line. Originally devised by the Bolsheviks to address tensions between the patchwork of ethnic groups in the USSR, the policy was adopted by the US Communist Party in 1928, to be applied to the southern "Black Belt."[5] In the standard version of the story, this idea was then imitated by the PCC—a conceptual debt betrayed by the Cuban party's use of the term *faja negra* to refer to Oriente. In 1935 the PCC set the self-determination policy aside, and thereafter—"freed from its erroneous framing of the black problem," as the Black Cuban historian and PCC member Pedro Serviat put it in 1986—devoted its energies instead to a campaign for racial equality.[6] From this perspective, the PCC's self-determination policy appears as a passing folly, of little consequence to Cuban Communism's larger trajectory.[7]

My findings, based on research in Cuba and in the Comintern archives in Moscow, directly contradict this interpretation. First, the self-determination policy was not an alien intrusion; although it was forged through a series of transnational debates, as we saw in previous chapters, the version put forward in Cuba was most clearly articulated by Cubans and was debated extensively among the rank and file as well as the leadership. The text cited earlier by Nicolau and Suárez Pérez was the first sustained argument for Black self-determination in Cuba; to my knowledge, it has not been discussed in the literature on Cuban Communism to date. Neither of its authors were of African descent, but after 1932, the key spokesman for the policy was Martín Castellanos, a Black Cuban from Oriente who joined the party precisely because of its nascent commitment to racial equality and who moved into a leadership role as the policy was being formulated.

Second, I argue that the PCC's abandonment of the policy in 1935—depicted in much of the literature as a return to common sense—was neither inevitable nor uncontested. The move away from Black self-determination was inter-linked with the party's adoption of the Comintern's new Popular Front strategy, announced at the organization's Seventh Congress in Moscow in the summer of 1935. Setting aside the confrontational approach of its previous "class against class" strategy, the Comintern now advocated unity with social-democratic and progressive nationalist forces in the name of anti-fascism. In this context, the PCC adopted an increasingly nationalist stance, jettisoning Black self-determination as too frontal a challenge to national unity. At the same time, there were fierce internal debates over whether the party should abandon its anti-racist commitments for the same reason. It was only in the wake of considerable contention that the PCC decided to keep one part of its dual agenda, subsequently emerging as the Cuban political party most actively promoting racial equality.

Finally, I argue that far from being a short-lived anomaly, the PCC's advocacy of Black self-determination had long-lasting political and institutional effects. The policy was integral to the party's first coherent attempt to address the problems of racism, prompting energetic internal debates. Indeed, it was consciously conceived as a means of combating racism both in the country at large and within the party's ranks. It also spurred active moves to recruit Black members, thus helping to transform the PCC's composition for the rest of the 1930s and beyond.

In what follows, I reconstruct the PCC's adoption of the Black self-determination policy in 1932 and then analyze how the party most fully articulated that policy in 1933–34, during the turmoil that followed the fall of dictator Gerardo Machado. In this period of crisis, a web of contradictions formed around class, race, and nation that the party struggled to navigate, and I address the clashes that developed between the PCC's internationalist class solidarity, its understanding of race, and a new iteration of Cuban revolutionary nationalism. While the PCC framed its self-determination policy as part of an expansive program for Black liberation, it was not always successful in explaining that policy, either to its own rank and file or to the wider Cuban public, resulting in frequent misunderstandings.

In 1935, the PCC formally set aside the Black self-determination policy. That shift was accompanied by heated arguments over the rest of the party's agenda on race, and I explore the tensions laid bare by these disagreements. A compromise position ultimately emerged from these discussions in favor of continuing to push for racial equality. In the late 1930s, the PCC cemented its role as a prominent supporter of Black Cubans' interests, and

I conclude by analyzing the party's advocacy for the inclusion of antidiscrimination measures in the island's new 1940 Constitution. While most discussions of the Black self-determination policy tend to dismiss it as ill-conceived or outlandish, I maintain that in its bid to radically reframe the struggle for racial equality in Cuba, it merits much more serious and sustained attention than it has received to date.

THE PCC, THE COMINTERN, AND RACE

How did the PCC come to adopt the Black self-determination policy in the first place? Before 1932, the concept did not appear in the PCC's publications or internal documents—and neither did racial equality. Two major factors were likely behind this reticence. First, as Ada Ferrer and others have shown, the Cuban independence struggle had given rise to an "ideology of a raceless nationality," in which racial distinctions had purportedly been transcended.[8] In the postindependence era, this ideology solidified into a consensus that Cuban national unity required the avoidance of explicit discussions of racial difference. This limited the space for public debate around the effects of racism and the legacies of slavery, implying that to even raise such issues would summon the specter of national disintegration. It was often those voicing concerns about racial discrimination who were denounced as "racists," rather than those defending a highly racialized and unequal status quo.[9]

Second, and partly as a result of this, the early Cuban republic harshly suppressed any attempts at independent Black political mobilization. The 1910 Morúa Law banned race- or class-based parties, but its principal target was the Partido Independiente de Color (PIC; Independent Party of Color), founded in 1908 by Evaristo Estenoz, a Black veteran of the war of independence. Excluded from the political system, the PIC planned a protest in Oriente in 1912 that the press rapidly labeled a "racist uprising." Thousands of Black Cubans were killed in the ensuing repression by a combination of regular troops and white vigilantes.[10] The crushing of the PIC starkly demonstrated the potential consequences of challenging Cuba's "raceless" ideal.

In its early years, the PCC seemed constrained by this same concept of "racelessness." The party's August 1929 program proclaimed equal rights for men and women, and for foreigners and Cuban nationals, but made no specific reference to race.[11] It was only after repeated prompting from the

Comintern that the party began actively to address the question of race. Since its founding in 1919 the Comintern had viewed Black liberation as part of its broader anti-colonial efforts, and as we saw in previous chapters, in 1928 the organization began to pressure parties in the Americas to take up the question of race. In the United States, this led to the adoption of the Black Belt policy. However, initial attempts to extend the idea to the rest of the Americas encountered resistance. At the 1929 Buenos Aires conference, many Latin American Communists rejected Black and Indigenous self-determination on the grounds that this would simply create new bourgeois republics, leaving fundamental inequalities unaddressed. Some delegates also argued that in Latin America, "in general, the black problem does not present a marked racial aspect," as José Carlos Mariátegui put it.[12] The Comintern's envoys saw such denials as symptoms of lingering "white chauvinism" and pressed the Latin American parties to take racism more seriously.

It was in this context that the Comintern began to urge the Cuban party to change its policy. In August 1929, the Political Secretariat in Moscow told the PCC's Central Committee that the party should "search for practical means of putting itself in contact with the black masses." A little over a year later, the Comintern's Moscow-based Latin American Secretariat reiterated the message, calling on the PCC to "agitate among the blacks on the question of their demands as an oppressed and particularly exploited race."[13]

Yet these prompts seemingly went unheeded. In early 1932, an internal party report noted that only the Santiago de Cuba section had done any recruitment work "among the blacks," and that none of the sections did "anything to attract the Haitians and Jamaicans" working on the sugar plantations.[14] That July, a visiting representative of KIM reported that "there exists a very serious underestimation of Negro work accompanied by a dangerous amount of white chauvinism in the ranks of our movement."[15] The KIM delegate, known only as "Eduardo," noted some extreme examples in local branches of the PCC's Youth League: "In Havana no dances have been held for years because Negroes would have to be allowed to come in." "Eduardo" also reported that "there exists a widespread opinion that in Cuba there is no discrimination against Negroes and that it is even wrong to address our leaflets to white and Negro workers, since 'That divides them.'"[16] Within the PCC, this same assumption continued to generate resistance to the creation of structures dedicated to organizing Black Cubans. In 1933, for example, the Camagüey District Committee claimed that the party's establishment of a "Departamento Negro" was itself an act of discrimination.[17]

By the time "Eduardo" visited Cuba in 1932, Black self-determination had been Comintern policy for four years. Yet as he put it, "The majority of the leading comrades opposed this slogan and think that it does not apply to Cuba."[18] Within a few months, however, the PCC would radically revise its stance—and when it did take up Black self-determination, it also finally began more actively to address the issue of racial discrimination.

RETHINKING RACIAL OPPRESSION

Transnational connections were instrumental to the process through which the PCC adopted these interwoven agendas. From late 1931 through the middle of 1932, the Comintern's New York–based Caribbean Bureau wrote to the PCC Central Committee several times urging the Cuban party to pay greater attention to organizing among Black workers, especially in the sugar and tobacco industries and in Oriente province.[19] In August 1932, it wrote again about the PCC's platform for the Cuban elections due that November. As well as economic demands for the working class as a whole, the Caribbean Bureau suggested: "Equal rights for blacks. Against all forms of national oppression and discrimination. For the right to self-determination."[20] The program the PCC drew up a few weeks later duly called for a struggle "against all forms of economic, political, and social discrimination against blacks" and "for the complete equality of blacks"—but it left out self-determination.[21]

Six thousand miles away in Moscow, Ramón Nicolau and Aggeo Suárez Pérez were at this same moment rethinking the so-called Black problem in Cuba as a version of the "national question." Born in Havana in 1907, Nicolau joined the PCC in 1928 and was sent to study in the USSR in 1931; Suárez Pérez was born in Pinar del Río in 1910, joined the party in 1929, and left for the Soviet Union the same year as Nicolau.[22] During their time at the International Lenin School, the two men would have been steeped not only in the Marxist canon but also in Bolshevik ideas about the national question.[23] The text they wrote as "Ríos" and "Álvarez" established two key features of what would become the PCC's stance. One was a complementarity between Black self-determination in Oriente and equality in the rest of the island; the second was an emphasis on the policy's value as a means of combating racism within the party itself.

Nicolau and Suárez Pérez devoted more than half their text to the history of slavery in Cuba and the struggle for abolition. They also highlighted the importance of the PIC, hailing its 1912 rebellion as a popular anti-imperialist revolt. The two authors claimed that the rebellion had called for a "Black Republic for the Eastern Region [República Negra para la Región Oriental]."[24] Though there is little evidence the PIC actually put forward this demand, the rumor supplied a local precedent for Black self-determination and would often crop up in subsequent Communist debates.[25] As well as these historical arguments, Nicolau and Suárez Pérez cited an array of present-day burdens weighing on Cuba's Black population, including discrimination, segregation, and lack of access to jobs and education.[26]

But these were not the main reasons they described that population as an "oppressed national minority." For that, they followed Haywood in turning to Stalin's 1913 definition of a nation: "a historically constituted, stable community of people, formed on the basis of a common language, territory, economic life, and psychological make-up manifested in a common culture."[27] According to Nicolau and Suárez Pérez, Black Cubans fulfilled these criteria especially well in Oriente province, in some parts of which they accounted for three-quarters of the population. In this territory, they argued, the Black population should have the "complete and unlimited right . . . to exercise governmental authority"—that is, the right to "self-determination." Crucially, the exercise of that right could mean the creation of a new state—"a complete separation," as the authors put it—but it could also take a number of forms short of full sovereignty. The point was for Oriente's Black majority to have the right to decide what form that should be.[28]

Nicolau and Suárez Pérez did not confine themselves to arguing for Black self-determination in Oriente, however. "The struggle for self-determination," they wrote, "will be accompanied by a struggle in the rest of the territory for equal social rights, for their specific demands and against any form of national oppression."[29] Equality and Black self-determination, then, were not alternative paths, but complementary strategies to be pursued in different parts of Cuba, in response to differing social and demographic conditions.

Nicolau and Suárez Pérez also framed Black self-determination as a strategic question within the ranks of the PCC. In their view, the party's failure to recognize the "right of the black nationality to self-determination" had led to an "almost total absence of blacks in the ranks of the Party." The policy was in part intended to draw in more recruits. But they insisted that the party go further: It had to wage an internal battle against "expressions of white chauvinism."[30] This motif would recur in subsequent PCC debates:

The Black self-determination policy would advance the party's struggle against racism within its own ranks as well as outside them.

In late September 1932, an ocean—literally and figuratively—still separated the PCC's views on Black self-determination from those of Nicolau and Suárez Pérez. Yet within weeks, the gap closed. In mid-December 1932, the internal PCC document quoted previously took stock of the party's poor performance in the November elections. Among a range of factors, it pointed to the PCC's inability to secure the support of Black Cubans. "It is clear," the document explained, "that, having failed to understand the black problem in Cuba, the Party has also not been able to mobilize the black masses around its electoral program during the campaign." The PCC had failed to see that what it called *el problema negro* was a national issue: Black people in Cuba were an oppressed "nationality," and as such the party had a duty to fight "for equal rights for blacks, against all forms of national oppression, and for the right of self-determination."[31] The proximity of the slogans and reasoning here to those of Nicolau and Suárez Pérez suggests that the document's authors had taken on board the ideas laid out by their Cuban comrades in Moscow.

By the end of 1932, then, the PCC had recognized the need to address racial inequality and discrimination. At the same time, it had begun to see Black Cubans as a "nationality," whose right to self-determination the party should uphold. Yet the content and meaning of equality and self-determination remained unclear. Nor was it evident how these policies would be combined in practice. The answers to these questions would be hammered out on the ground in 1933–34, when the PCC strove to clarify its stance even as Cuba entered a period of sustained turbulence.

ENTWINED AGENDAS

The early 1930s were a time of escalating political and economic crisis in Cuba. Loló de la Torriente, a young PCC militant at the time, recalled that "events followed upon each other, enfolding us in a whirlwind."[32] The country's dependence on sugar exports had tied its fortunes tightly to those of US corporations and banks, which left it disastrously exposed to the effects of the Wall Street crash and the ensuing depression. Faced with rising discontent, the Machado government jailed many of its opponents, yet their will to resist only hardened.

After months of mounting pressure from a broad opposition movement, in August 1933 a nationwide general strike administered the coup de grâce to Machado's regime.[33] "In the public squares it seemed like there was a festival," according to de la Torriente.[34] One month later, a progressive government took office under Ramón Grau San Martín, and it quickly produced legislation for an eight-hour day, women's suffrage, and the beginnings of a land redistribution program. Grau's "Government of a Hundred Days" only lasted until January 1934, in large part thanks to US pressure. (Washington withheld recognition, and its ambassador worked behind the scenes to put together a new government more amenable to US interests.)[35] Yet despite its short span, Grau's administration unleashed a political ferment that continued for much of the decade, putting the key questions of sovereignty, democracy, and national liberation firmly on the agenda.

Even as many Cubans hailed the Grau government's progressive measures, however, it enacted labor and migration laws that were punitive for the country's foreign-born population. On October 18, Grau authorized the forcible repatriation of unemployed foreigners.[36] Then, on November 8, he introduced a law on "nationalization of labor" that required half of employees in agriculture, industry, and the mercantile sector to be "native Cubans."[37] This became known as the "50%" law, and it was highly popular. This was partly due to the dire economic situation and widespread unemployment. But there were longer-term factors, too: Over the previous decades, several thousand Spanish migrants had come to Cuba as part of an officially promoted process of "whitening," in many sectors occupying skilled posts from which Cubans were excluded. Grau supporters' slogan of "Cuba for the Cubans" was mainly directed at these better-placed Spanish workers; but in practice, its heaviest impact fell on Haitian and Jamaican sugar workers, large numbers of whom had been recruited to work on plantations in the country's east, and who were now targeted for deportation.[38]

At this critical juncture, the PCC became entangled in a series of contradictions. It had been caught off guard by the fall of Machado; just before his ouster it had been negotiating with the government and had tried to call off the general strike. The PCC then tried to compensate for this miscalculation, known within party lore as the "August mistake," by radicalizing its stance. It vehemently opposed the Grau government and sent cadres to organize among striking sugar workers in September–October 1933, enthusiastically promoting the creation of "soviets" in Camagüey and Oriente.[39] By November the PCC was calling for all of Cuba to be transformed into a "soviet republic" and labeling the Grau government a "defender of the system of colonial-bourgeois-landlord exploitation and oppression."[40] Yet at the same time, conscious of the threat of US intervention, the PCC refrained from calling for any direct confrontation with US interests. As a party circular from October 1933 explained, the task was "not to prioritize the struggle against imperialism in the current moment."[41]

The PCC was also caught up in contradictions on race and migration. It continued to demand "absolute political, social, and economic equality for blacks," and in October 1933 spoke out against a recent spike in racist attacks.[42] It also opposed Grau's "50%" law, denouncing it as part of a "divisionist campaign."[43] But the party's calls for solidarity with Haitian and Jamaican migrants pitted it against a newly ascendant Cuban nationalism and against a gathering constituency behind the "50%," which was especially popular among Cubans of African descent, who formed a disproportionate share of the unemployed. This created a tension between different parts of the PCC's agenda: its calls for social and economic justice for Black Cubans and its defense of all workers on class grounds regardless of nationality.

The PCC's initial solution was to frame its policies on race and the "50%" as integral parts of Cuba's anti-imperialist struggle. Party materials spoke of the need to "win Cuba's national independence" and to struggle for the "national liberation of Cuba's oppressed people."[44] At the same time, the party exhorted its members to "liberate the black masses and give them the right of self-determination [going] as far as separation and their constitution as an independent state in the 'black belt' in Oriente."[45] Cubans in general and Black Cubans specifically were identified as collectives with the right to exercise a sovereignty that had been truncated. In the PCC's framing, the demand for Black "national" liberation was part of the demand for Cuban national liberation.

The PCC adopted this stance at a moment when racialized tropes were circulating with increasing frequency. In September 1933, an internal PCC report on Oriente and Camagüey referred to attempts by the local bourgeoisie to discredit the party: "They say that the communists want to install an empire of disorder . . . that [communists] wanted to make white women marry blacks, and this campaign was being run by Spaniards."[46] Similar rumors surfaced in October in Tacajó, a sugar mill town in Oriente: The PCC cell there reported that its opponents told local peasants that the Communists would take away their cows and force their daughters to marry Black men, that they mistreated the Cuban flag, and that all of the PCC's members were foreigners.[47] The same combination of motifs—fears of forced miscegenation, accusations of anti-patriotism—would crop up repeatedly over the following months.

These tensions were present across Cuba, but they were felt with special force in Oriente. The island's easternmost province, with a proportionally larger Black population than the rest of Cuba, Oriente also contained many remote and deeply deprived areas whose distance from Havana, metaphorical and literal, was captured by journalist Pablo de la Torriente Brau in the 1934 text cited in the epigraph to this chapter. Not only the scene of the 1912 massacre of PIC supporters, Oriente was also one of the main areas for the expansion of US sugar companies in the early twentieth century, as well as housing the US naval base at Guantánamo. Here the issues of labor, race, nationalism, and anti-imperialism were closely intertwined, as the Comintern's envoy discovered when he traveled there in late 1933. His experience is worth expanding on, since it condenses many of the contradictions that ran through the PCC during 1933–34.

LOVSKY'S JOURNEY

By November 1933, Witold Lovsky had already been in Cuba for several months. Born Mendel Mikhrovsky in Poland in 1894, he had been a member of a Marxist–Zionist party in his youth before joining the Polish Communist Party in 1921. After fleeing into exile in the USSR in 1925, he took the name "Lovsky" and began working for the Comintern's trade union arm. In the late 1920s he was dispatched as its clandestine envoy to Latin America.[48] By the time he arrived in Cuba, he had acquired fluent Spanish and had adopted the rather generic codename "Juan."

During his first few months on the island, Lovsky quickly became frustrated with the PCC's leadership in Havana. The party had completely misjudged the mood of the country during the August general strike, but as he reported back to Moscow in September, there was a "sad lack of self-criticism" among the leadership.[49] He bemoaned the leadership's "low political level," describing its meetings as "awfully tiresome."[50] By early November, Lovsky was more than ready to leave; he wrote to the Comintern complaining that he had run into severe health and money problems.[51] Both his and the PCC's prospects looked bleak.

But Lovsky's view brightened after he traveled the length of the island to attend a PCC gathering in Santiago. On the way there, he reported seeing PCC slogans painted on the walls of every town between Havana and Santiago: denunciations of the government, anti-imperialist slogans, and calls to emulate the sugar workers' "soviet" at Mabay. Lovsky was well aware of Oriente's importance, as a place where "multiple political problems that the Party must solve" were conjoined. In his report he noted its "39 sugar *centrales*, 18 ports, manganese mines, [and the] Yankee imperialist naval base in Guantánamo." As a majority-Black province, he noted, it was also "the place where the burning question of self-determination must be resolved."[52]

Some forty delegates attended the meeting in Santiago. They included nine sugar workers and handfuls drawn from a range of other occupations: cobblers, peasants, carpenters, and students. Lovsky also made a careful note of the racial breakdown of the delegates, classing seventeen as *blanco*, eleven as *mulato*, and ten as *negro*—including one Haitian—and leaving two unspecified.[53] His understanding of Cuba's racial landscape thus seemed to involve three categories rather than two. By this measure, just over half the Santiago delegates were of African descent, but only a third were classed as *negro*.

The comrades Lovsky met were not only dedicated but also well-informed: They were able to discuss Bolshevik tactics during the 1917 revolution and ideological disputes within the Bolshevik Party over the 1918 Treaty of Brest-Litovsk and the New Economic Policy of 1921. "One gets the impression that the comrades from this region have read much more than the workers in the capital," Lovsky observed.[54] But while this left him feeling more optimistic about the party's future, he also found considerable discontent with the party leadership. Lovsky referred to a "state of rebellion" within the District Committee, adding that "it must be said that the majority of this bitter criticism . . . is entirely justified."[55] There was confusion about some of the PCC's policy shifts, such as the October instruction "not to prioritize the struggle against imperialism." Some delegates pointed out that so much of Oriente's land belonged to US companies that in some places, "for hundreds of leagues you can't see a single bit of grass that is Cuban." Telling party members not to prioritize the struggle against imperialism was "the same as telling all the workers and peasants not to struggle in general."[56]

But the major surprises that awaited Lovsky in Oriente concerned the problem of race, which was "much more acute than we had considered till now."[57] He was taken aback to find that "in Oriente in the black belt itself there is perhaps less clarity on the black question than in other parts of the country." Comrades in Santiago complained that the self-determination slogan had been launched without sufficient explanation, either to Black workers or to white ones. The result was that "no one really knows what self-determination is." This lack of clarity made it easier for the local bourgeoisie to turn the slogan against the PCC, spreading rumors that "self-determination is the preparation of a massacre of whites by blacks, that self-determination will decree laws saying that every black man should marry a white woman." Here again we see echoes of the racialized fearmongering that accompanied the repression of the PIC in 1912; in Oriente, the specter of "race war" still lingered barely a generation later. Even within the PCC, Lovsky learned, there were "white workers who say, 'what is self-determination, I myself don't like it when a black governor gets elected.'" Self-determination, then, had become both a lightning-rod for racialized opposition outside the PCC and a sticking point for racists within it.

A second troubling discovery Lovsky made concerned prejudice against migrant workers. "It might seem a little incredible," he wrote, "if I tell you that in Oriente in the black belt there is . . . an indifference towards the persecution of blacks."[58] Across the region hundreds of Haitians and Jamaicans who had stood "in the front lines of struggle" in the recent strike wave were now being "hunted like dogs" by the army and then deported in crowded, unsanitary ships. Yet to Lovsky's astonishment, none of the PCC's local organizations had raised any protest. The apparent explanation was that Black Cubans "consider these blacks to be a *race inferior to their own*."[59] At this, Lovsky threw up his hands: "I don't know what to call this kind of chauvinism."

Lovsky clearly expected there to be racial solidarity between Black Cubans and Haitian and Jamaican migrants. But in Oriente and elsewhere, that expectation was confounded, partly thanks to the popularity of Grau's nationalization of labor law. Over the next few months, the PCC would insist that there was no contradiction between its opposition to the "50%" and the rest of its agenda, and that racial solidarity and worker solidarity were one and the same. It also tried to clarify the self-determination policy, which remained a source of confusion within its ranks.

FORMULATING SELF-DETERMINATION

At two PCC gatherings held in December 1933 and April 1934, among the issues most extensively debated were the self-determination policy and the

"50%." The most substantive interventions on these themes came from Martín Castellanos, who would be the PCC's main spokesman on race over the next few years. Born in Santiago in 1901, Castellanos was the son of a carpenter of African descent who had fought in the war of independence.[60] He trained as a doctor, a profession he would maintain alongside his political activism after he joined the PCC in 1932. By 1933, he was in Havana heading the national committee of Defensa Obrera Internacional (DOI; Workers International Defense), a Communist-affiliated group that helped organize campaigns for solidarity with the "Scottsboro Boys."[61] Jailed for four months under Machado, he was then centrally involved in the radical upsurge among sugar workers in Oriente in September–October 1933, addressing rallies in Manzanillo, Holguín, Santiago, and at several sugar mills.[62] That December, he was elected to the party's Central Committee, and would go on to serve as the PCC's general secretary for six months in 1935–36. As both a middle-class professional in Havana and an itinerant Communist militant in Oriente, Castellanos had direct experience of very different realms of Black Cuban experience, and until his expulsion from the party in 1938, he would spend several years bridging them to the PCC's benefit.

The arguments Castellanos made for Black self-determination positioned the PCC as part of an ongoing conversation around the forms and goals of Black political participation in Cuba. Since the 1920s, a range of public figures—from anthropologist Fernando Ortiz to the poet Nicolás Guillén and the journalist Gustavo Urrutia—had been highlighting Black Cubans' role in national culture and political life. The 1930s produced a broader upsurge of Black political activism, driven by Black social organizations and intellectuals.[63] In formulating the self-determination policy, Castellanos actively engaged with this ferment, both by defining the PCC's stance in contrast to those of other political forces and by building bridges to movements whose priorities might align with the PCC's. It was Castellanos who forged initial ties between the PCC and progressive *sociedades de color* and spoke at their joint rallies. He wrote for Black publications such as *Adelante* (Forward) as well as for *Masas* (Masses), the organ of the Cuban chapter of LADLA; in May 1934 the latter published a text of his on Black self-determination that made similar arguments to those he had deployed in PCC internal discussions (see figure 9).[64]

Castellanos's influence on the PCC policy's is apparent in a resolution adopted at a party conference held on December 7, 1933. The resolution framed demands for Black self-determination and racial equality as

maſaſ

revista mensual
editada por la
Liga Anti - Imperialista de Cuba

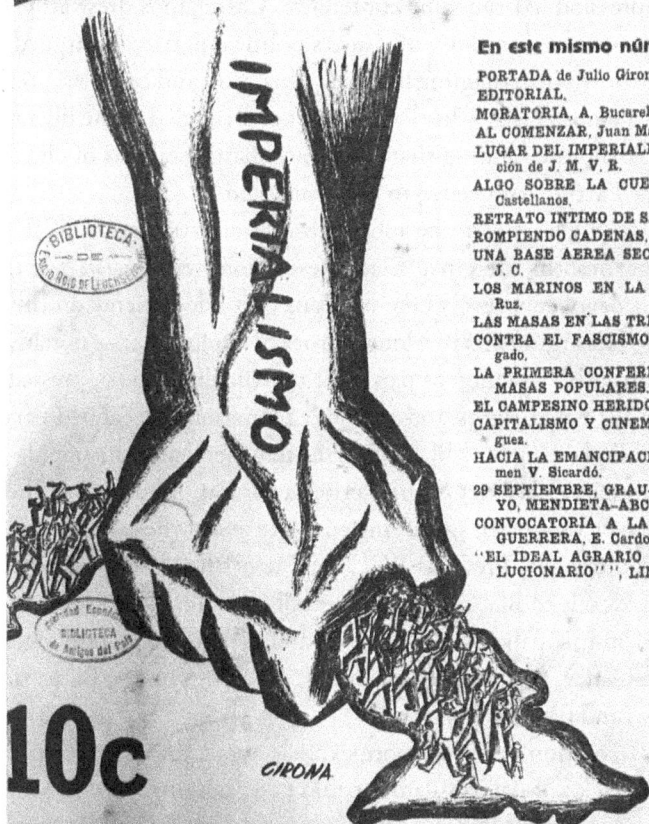

En este mismo número:

IMPERIALISMO

10c

GIRONA

LEA

algo sobre la CUESTION NEGRA

por el Dr. Martín Castellanos

FIGURE 9. Cover of *Masas*, no. 1, May 1934. From Instituto de Historia de Cuba.

not only complementary but sequential: "*The struggle for the right to self-determination of the black population in the Black Belt of Oriente* is not a separate thing, but rather a culminating form [*una forma culminante*]."[65] In other words, giving the Black population of Oriente the right to decide their own destiny was not an addition to the demand for racial equality. Rather, it flowed logically from demands for equality and autonomy and was indeed their ultimate expression. At the same conference, Castellanos drew attention to the PCC's uneven record. Of all Cuba's political parties, he argued, the PCC was "the only one struggling for black liberation and equality." Yet at the same time, he noted that "this Party does not struggle for the liberation of blacks as it should," adding that "there are manifestations of chauvinism within our Party" that needed to be "unmasked."[66]

It was Castellanos who wrote the most substantial articulation of the PCC's stance a few months later, in a "Black Resolution" (*Resolución negra*) for the April 1934 party congress.[67] Like previous party documents on this theme, it grounded its arguments in a long history of exploitation—notably referring to the 1912 PIC rebellion as part of "the struggle of the oppressed black nationality for equal rights and for their liberation." It echoed earlier documents in explaining how Black Cubans in general and the population of Oriente in particular met Stalin's criteria for nationhood. But the Resolution broke new ground in specifying concrete areas where Black self-determination would apply. Previous PCC statements had used the term *faja negra* to refer loosely to Black-majority areas of Oriente. The Resolution named a series of municipalities in the south and center of the province: Songo, La Maya, Caney, San Luis, Palma Soriano, Guantánamo, Baracoa, Santiago de Cuba, and parts of Bayamo.[68]

Castellanos's Resolution was also more explicit about the different political forms that Black self-determination could take, ranging from full independence to the status of a "federal autonomous region."[69] The PCC was not, the Resolution stressed, actively recommending separation; rather, it was advocating the "complete and unlimited right of the black majority to exercise governmental authority in the black Territory of Oriente."[70] The point of the self-determination policy was for decisions to be made by the inhabitants themselves; in other words, the core of the idea was not territorial sovereignty, but democracy.

The Resolution directly linked Black oppression to US imperialism: "The struggle against one implies the struggle against the other at the same time." Self-determination was the means for conjoining the two. It listed actions a self-governing Black territory could take, many of which would directly clash with US interests, such as the expropriation of large landholdings for redistribution to Black peasants and the withdrawal of US troops from Guantánamo and the demolition of its naval base, "the greatest instrument for the national oppression of blacks."[71]

The Resolution situated the PCC's views on race relative to other Cuban political forces, as Castellanos used his knowledge to distinguish the party's views from theirs. Bourgeois political parties, it argued, insisted on a fictitious unity that only obscured the oppression of Cubans of African descent. Black petty bourgeois organizations, meanwhile, aimed for a "harmonization" between races that would leave the current socioeconomic framework intact, overlooking class distinctions within the Black population. Elsewhere on the left, the Partido Bolchevique Leninista (PBL; Bolshevik Leninist Party)—a new Trotskyist organization established in late 1933 by Sandalio Junco and others—committed the opposite mistake: It emphasized the class character of Black oppression in Cuba, denying its "national" dimension.[72]

The PCC's articulation of its differences with the PBL represents a recurrence, within the Cuban context, of arguments aired at Buenos Aires. Should racial distinctions be understood in "national" terms? Should class have primacy over race and nation within the left's political strategy? Junco himself had parted ways with the PCC in 1932. He had gone back to the USSR after the Buenos Aires gathering, remaining there for another two years working for the Profintern and studying at the International Lenin School.[73] After returning to Cuba in March 1932, he became increasingly critical of the PCC leadership and cofounded an internal opposition faction; that September, he was expelled from the party.[74] He harshly criticized the PCC during the strikes of August 1933 and cofounded the PBL the following month together with other ex-PCC members. The new party gained a foothold in the Federación Obrera de la Habana (FOH; Havana Labor Federation)—notably among Junco's former comrades in the bakers' union—and in Oriente, especially among Black workers in Guantánamo.[75] It was thus competing with the PCC for the loyalties of workers, and it directly attacked the PCC's self-determination policy.

The PBL's platform, published in January 1934, reprised many of the points Junco had made in Buenos Aires in 1929.[76] But it went still further in arguing that "there does not exist, nor can there exist, a race struggle, but rather a class struggle." It voiced support for Black rights—but "as part of the rights of the proletariat in general." Indeed, for the PBL, this was the only true form of self-determination, and it condemned the PCC's version as "criminal and demagogic," a provocation that would only serve to heighten racial tensions. There is an echo here, from the left, of the fears of "race war" that were being stirred by the right at this time.

As well as engaging with the views of rival political formations, the PCC's April 1934 Resolution addressed the question of "white chauvinism" within its own ranks. It argued that white workers needed to struggle for Black liberation "until the ultimate consequences"—which included the possible separation of a piece of eastern Cuba.[77] A commitment to racial equality and to Black self-determination was thus to become a shibboleth within the party, testing the depth of its members' commitment to their own principles. The Resolution also criticized the inadequacy of the PCC's efforts to recruit Black members, noting in particular "an intolerable delay" in winning Black women to the party.[78] The Cuban party was overwhelmingly male at this time, and although figures close to the PCC, such as Ofelia Domínguez Navarro and Rosa Pastora Leclerc, led efforts to mobilize women "of all races, of all social classes" from the late 1920s onward, it took until later in the 1930s for this work to bear fruit in terms of PCC policy.[79]

Over the rest of 1934, the PCC put many of the April Resolution's recommendations into practice, and in the process raised its profile and prestige among Cuba's Black population. As well as condemning a wave of racist attacks by whites in early 1934, the PCC sent a commission to the town of Trinidad to investigate the killing of the journalist José Proveyer and the antiblack violence that ensued. The PCC held public events in collaboration with *sociedades de color* there and in Havana.[80] It denounced the Cuban KKK and the right-wing ABC party and joined calls for an end to segregation, demanding Black Cubans have access to parks, hotels, and cinemas.[81] The PCC also took up Black labor demands, including equal pay for equal work and the right to occupy any post within a given workplace (there was often a de facto color bar on skilled positions).[82] In Oriente, it organized dances involving both Black and white workers and opposed the Santiago city authorities' ban on public conga dances.[83] At the same time, the PCC leadership raised the problem of "white chauvinism" in its own ranks, urging lower levels of the party to combat it more actively. PCC Central Committee circulars singled out particular sections for criticism; one noted the Santa Clara section's "weak struggle against white chauvinism," while another called for an "energetic struggle" against "discriminatory tendencies" in the party in Matanzas, Cienfuegos, and Caibarién.[84] These problems evidently persisted: In October 1934, a meeting of the PCC's Politburo noted that in Ciego de Ávila there was "great racial discrimination" within the party, to the extent that there was one local section of the party in which "everyone is white and another where everyone is black."[85]

SHIFTS IN PCC MEMBERSHIP

The racial makeup of the party within which these concerns were resonating had changed markedly. For a few years after 1932, the party kept very partial records of how many Black members it had. Such figures raise many questions: It is not clear, for instance, whether racial categorizations were made by a minute-taker or whether members were surveyed, nor is it clear whether the structuring racial assumptions were binary or multiple. The PCC data mostly do not record the number of whites, so those not classed as *negros* could include whites, *mulatos*, and *mestizos*; conversely, those who might have identified as *mulato* could have been classed as *negro* by whoever did the tallying. Yet even though the figures cannot serve as a reliable measure of any empirical reality, they nevertheless offer some sense of the PCC's evolving membership and of how those shifts were perceived within the party.

In early 1932, Black militants were a small minority within the Party's tiny membership of just under five hundred; to judge by the few sections that provided information, the proportion ranged between a tenth in Banes to a fifth in Santiago.[86] A year and a half later, thanks largely to the PCC's organizing efforts in the sugar sector, the party had doubled in size. The growth was especially strong in the sugar-producing provinces of Las Villas, Camagüey, and Oriente. Las Villas went from having just 8 PCC members to having 352—more than any other province, overtaking Havana and Oriente. In the three aforementioned provinces, the party had established cells not only in cities such as Santa Clara and Cienfuegos, but also in several sugar *centrales* and towns at important railroad junctions such as Cabaiguán and Placetas. However, the overall proportion of Black members—once again, where information was given—was broadly the same as before, at 16 percent.[87]

Yet at a more granular level, some important trends emerge. Many of the newer cells in sugar-producing areas had a higher proportion of Black members than the nationwide average.[88] Moreover, the proportion of *negros* in the Liga de Juventudes Comunistas (LJC; League of Communist Youth) was often higher than in the party proper: a third in Placetas, and almost half in the case of Morón. This is important because many LJC members would soon move rapidly up the ranks of the party. If the PCC was still predominantly white in August 1933, its future was already looking decreasingly so.

Confirmation of these trends came quickly, with a shake-up of the PCC's leadership between December 1933 and April 1934.[89] Many of those promoted to key positions were of African descent. Castellanos was appointed editor of the party newspaper, *Bandera Roja*, as well as being placed jointly in charge of the PCC's Black Department (Departamento Negro). Alongside him was Antolín Dickinson, a sugar worker from Encrucijada who had joined the party in 1932; Dickinson was also assigned to the party's new Sugar Workers' Bureau (Buró Azucarero), and would soon be promoted to the PCC's Politburo.[90] Serafín Portuondo, a former tobacco worker from Santiago and the son of a PIC member who had survived the repression of 1912, had joined the PCC in 1929, running its Santiago branch by 1931; he was now promoted to the party's Central Committee.[91] Lázaro Peña, a tobacco worker from Havana who played an active role in the strikes of 1933, was assigned to represent the LJC, alongside Remigio Calderío, a *mulato* shoemaker from Manzanillo.[92] Most prominent of all, however, was the latter's brother, Francisco Calderío—also a former shoemaker—who had joined the party in 1929 and was closely involved in its growth in Oriente. During the turmoil of 1933, he had helped organize the sugar workers "soviet" in Mabay. He was now appointed the party's new general secretary and soon afterward took the name "Blas Roca."[93] He would remain the PCC's leader for most of the next three decades.

By the time the PCC met in Havana for its second congress in late April 1934, it had become a nationwide party with just under ten thousand members. More than two-thirds were from outside the capital, including twenty-three hundred in Oriente, more than eighteen hundred in Las Villas, and a thousand each in Camagüey and Matanzas provinces.[94] Its demographic profile had also been transformed. The claim—made in a resolution of the April 1934 congress—that the "immense majority" of the party's members were Black workers seems hyperbolic, to say the least.[95] But it is clear that by early 1934, the PCC had significantly more Black members in absolute terms than it had prior to 1933. Crucially, many of those members had now moved into leadership roles. The new Central Committee approved by the April 1934 congress included eight *negros* and two *mulatos* out of a total of twenty-five members.[96] The period when the PCC adopted its twin agendas of Black self-determination and racial equality, then, coincided with a demographic reshaping of both the overall membership and the core decision-making structures of the party. These shifts laid the groundwork for the PCC's transformation into the leading political proponent of Black rights in the second half of the decade.

RACE, NATION, AND THE POPULAR FRONT

In an October 1935 speech, Blas Roca painted the PCC as the heirs to Cuba's independence struggle. Enthusiastically embracing Cuban nationalist imagery, he even appropriated icons of the insurgent pantheon. "If [Antonio] Maceo were alive today," he intoned, "he would be in our ranks, he would be our leader." In the same speech, Blas Roca announced a U-turn in the PCC's stance on the nationalization of labor: The party should actively support the "50%" because it was actually an antidiscrimination measure. In Cuba, Blas Roca said, native-born workers were often underpaid relative to foreigners—a situation that amounted to "national discrimination . . . against Cubans in general, and particularly against blacks."[97] The new line on the "50%" thus tied together Cuban nationalism and anti-racism, casting the defense of native-born workers as a means of promoting racial equality.

It was also in this speech that Blas Roca announced the PCC's abandonment of the Black self-determination policy. He criticized the party for "disseminating abstract slogans" that had not been well understood, even within the party. The PCC should instead focus on "the daily demands of blacks"— the struggle for jobs, for the right to walk freely in public places, for political representation. Here the PCC should learn from previous successes—Blas Roca cited the party's activities around the Proveyer case in Trinidad and the campaign against the ban on conga dances in Santiago—as well as establishing closer relations with Black social organizations.[98]

The PCC's abandonment of the Black self-determination policy has often been framed as a return to common sense. In the words of Cuban historian Caridad Massón, "The PCC came to understand how wrong its stance was and discarded it, opening the way for a platform of struggle for absolute equality between whites and blacks."[99] Yet my findings suggest that the picture is more complicated. As we have seen, the party took up demands for racial equality in tandem with the Black self-determination policy from 1932 onward and saw the two as complementary. Moreover, the PCC's change of heart on the "50%" and on Black self-determination did not immediately lead it to focus on equality. The process through which it set aside Black self-determination was by no means an uncontested one: During 1935–36 there was intense debate within the PCC over whether it should put forward demands in favor of Black Cubans at all.

The shifts in the PCC's stance on Black self-determination and on the "50%" took place amid heated internal discussions during which the party's policies on race—including demands for racial equality—were put into question. This was not because they were deemed erroneous, but because they were seen as obstacles to unity. From the end of 1934 onward, the PCC attempted to arrive at a common platform with other Cuban political forces—an early sign of a change in Communist strategy that would take effect globally in 1935, with the turn to the Popular Front strategy. The PCC's overtures were mainly directed at the Auténticos, led by the exiled former president Ramón Grau San Martín, and the "Guiteristas," supporters of Antonio Guiteras, Grau's former interior minister.

Throughout 1935 and 1936, the problem of how to forge a united front with these forces dominated PCC discussions—and it was clear that several party leaders worried that their policies on race might be a sticking point. In February 1935, the party's Central Committee discussed a draft program to be shared with prospective allies. It included elements from Grau's and Guiteras's programs: nationalization of foreign enterprises, land redistribution, a minimum wage, and an eight-hour workday.[100] The PCC added a demand for "absolute equality of economic, political, and social rights for blacks on the entire territory of the island" and "severe punishment for those who carry out acts of discrimination against blacks"—the latter point being an early formulation of what would eventually become Article 20 of the 1940 Constitution. Notably missing, however, was Black self-determination, as Castellanos pointed out.[101] In the face of Castellanos's insistence, Blas Roca agreed to include it once more, but said "it depends how we pose it": The PCC had not articulated the policy well to date, in his view. Later in the same discussion, Blas Roca suggested there was actually no need to include specific demands for Black Cubans in the common program, "since the whole program is in favor of the blacks."[102]

In his speech to the Comintern Congress in September 1935, Blas Roca listed "slogans such as the self-determination of the black nationality" among the "conditions that made it difficult to form the united front."[103] It was on returning from Moscow the following month that Blas Roca affirmed the party's abandonment of the Black self-determination policy. But the pressure to form the Popular Front coalition continued to impact the PCC's discussions on race. In February 1936, Jorge Vivó—who had briefly been general secretary of the party in 1932–33—suggested that the PCC limit itself to calling for "equality of rights for all Cubans," and that it should not "pose 'equality' for the blacks as a separate thing." The reason he gave was that the other parties in the embryonic Popular Front would not agree.[104]

Some leading members of the party demurred. For comrade "Danton," it was a tactical matter: "If we don't go about this tactfully, the PC will lose the black members it has." But for Castellanos—at this point leading the party as interim general secretary, since Blas Roca had been jailed—it was "a question of principle": Without the demands for equality for Black Cubans and women, the proposed program "is not a completely democratic program for the revolution."[105] Castellanos's objections became increasingly serious as the meeting went on. The PCC should not, he said, make an alliance with other parties if they did not agree to include racial equality in the program. If the PCC went ahead without that demand, he would "lose faith in the Party."[106] He himself had joined "precisely because it put forward the slogan of equality for blacks," adding that "it was the same for many blacks in the party." With tensions clearly mounting, Vivó asked Castellanos if he would consider the revolution to have ended if the PCC did not demand racial equality. Castellanos replied that he would. He noted that Cuba's independence fighters of 1868 and 1895 had raised demands for equality, and even bourgeois parties paid lip service to the idea. In his eyes, omitting this basic demand amounted to "a shameful surrender."[107]

Castellanos's arguments proved persuasive. In the wake of the February discussion, the PCC adopted a new negotiating position. It would "struggle until the last moment for the inclusion of the slogan 'black equality.'"[108] If the other parties did not agree, the PCC would put forward another proposal: A future Popular Front government "will introduce a constitutional reform and legislation to guarantee the equality of all Cubans without exception, and to prohibit any restriction on the rights of blacks and women." If the other parties did not agree to this either, the PCC would still join the Popular Front, but "reserve its position of struggling for the slogan [of] black equality." This new stance is strikingly close to the PCC's positions for the rest of the 1930s. The party became an energetic advocate of Black rights, and as we will see, it was prominently involved in the push for an antidiscrimination clause to be included in the 1940 Constitution.

Having pulled back from calling for Black self-determination, then, the PCC briefly considered a retreat on equality as well. Fears of losing Black support were probably the major factor in dissuading the party from making that second retreat, but the strength of objections by prominent Black members—Castellanos above all—played a vital role in convincing the PCC leadership to keep pushing for Black rights. Having compromised on Black sovereignty in Oriente, advocates for self-determination such as Castellanos were not willing to yield further ground on the question of equality.

REFRAMING *AUTODETERMINACIÓN*

From the end of 1935 onward, the PCC would combine Cuban nationalism with anti-racism. The party no longer described Cubans of African descent as a distinct "nationality," instead portraying them as an integral part of the Cuban nation. And rather than resting on a recognition of Black Cubans' "national" rights, the PCC's stance promised the realization—finally, after decades of frustration—of long-standing ideals of equality. A PCC manifesto from April 1936 listed Black heroes of the War of Independence—Antonio Maceo, Flor Crombet, Guillermo Moncada—and insisted that Black Cubans were an integral part of the current struggle for liberation. "To liberate itself," the manifesto added, "the Cuban people needs the help of the black who is and feels himself to be Cuban, but who wishes to be so on the basis of justice and equality."[109]

This stance brought the PCC's views much closer to those of the *sociedades de color*. The PCC remained conscious of the class character of many of these organizations: In June 1936, Castellanos cautioned against seeing them as socially representative, insisting that "black workers are not in those *sociedades*."[110] Nevertheless, the PCC consistently supported the *sociedades*, in particular their efforts to hold regional and national conventions. Castellanos was prominently involved; in July 1936, a missive went out to all levels of the PCC over his signature urging the party to take part in conventions due to be held in Oriente and Santa Clara.[111] Among the issues he recommended that delegates raise at these events were better access to education, establishment of libraries, equal wages for equal work, and an end to the de facto segregation of public spaces. The list also included a call to cease immigration and implement the "50%" law, while ensuring "black predominance [*predominio negro*] in the black territory of Oriente." In effect, the PCC was combining the nationalization of labor with the makings of an affirmative-action policy in Oriente.

Was this idea of a "black predominance" in Oriente all that was left of the self-determination agenda? Even after the PCC formally dropped the policy in October 1935, the term *autodeterminación* did not disappear entirely. Instead, the party redefined its scope and content, arguing that support for Black equality was actually what self-determination meant. In late 1935, the PCC delegates who had attended the Comintern Congress earlier that year wrote to the Central Committee that "the RIGHT of self-determination in current conditions means above all the struggle against all forms of national oppression, for equal rights for the black people, [for] respect for the customs, culture, and social life of blacks." The PCC should, it argued, "support those demands that direct their cutting edge against national and racial oppression."[112] The characterization of Black Cubans' oppression as simultaneously "national" and "racial" suggested some continuity with the PCC's previous thinking. But in practice, as of late 1935 the party emphasized only the second of these forms of oppression, defining Black Cubans as a marginalized but nonetheless integral component of the Cuban nation.

From this point onward, the term *self-determination* fell out of use in Cuban Communists' discussions of race. Yet the idea repeatedly resurfaced outside the party's ranks in the late 1930s, as Black intellectuals used self-determination as a foil against which to set out their own views of race and nation. In March 1936, Alberto Arredondo argued against Black self-determination in the Havana-based Black progressive magazine *Adelante* on the grounds that "in Cuban society NATION AND BLACK cannot be separated from each other."[113] A member of the Cuban Aprista Party, Arredondo was certainly familiar with the debates between Communists and *apristas* of the preceding years. He took up the standard criteria by which Communists defined a nation to argue that, on the contrary, Black Cubans were not only an integral part of the Cuban nation but had been central to its formation.

Arredondo and others returned to this theme several times in the pages of *Adelante*, rejecting self-determination in the name of a Cuban nationalism in which the contribution of Black Cubans would be duly recognized.[114] While discussions about race and nationality took place in many parts of Cuban society in these years, it is striking that *autodeterminación* kept cropping up as a possibility that had to be rejected long after the PCC had set the policy aside. Several years later, Arredondo was still arguing against Black self-determination, devoting an entire chapter of his 1939 book *El negro en Cuba* to it.[115]

The idea of Black nationhood was also implicitly present in the enthusiasm with which the PCC took up the cause of Abyssinia, invaded by Italy in October 1935. That month, in the same speech in which he announced that the party would be dropping the Black self-determination policy, Blas Roca argued that the defense of Ethiopia "should now be a major center of our work among blacks, who feel a great sympathy with the Abyssinian people."[116] Such calls for solidarity were consistent with the PCC's internationalism, but there was a clear racial dimension to its support for what a Central Committee circular named "the only independent black State in Africa."[117] Another PCC circular that month drew a parallel between Abyssinia's situation and "that of our Cuba: victim of the imperialist rapacity not just of Italy, but also of other countries."[118] Supporting Abyssinia's cause, then, implied an affinity between Black sovereignty in Africa and Cuba's struggle for "national liberation." It is, of course, only a coincidence that the Italian invasion should have taken place at precisely the moment the PCC was shelving the idea of Black self-determination in Cuba. But the fact that the PCC specifically emphasized Abyssinia's status as a sovereign Black state does seem meaningful: It allowed the dream of Black self-determination to be maintained while projecting it outside Cuba's own borders.

In setting aside Black self-determination within Cuba, the PCC moved away from the possibility of redrawing the island's political map in a bid to address racial injustice. Instead, the party melded calls for equality with a patriotic agenda, defining Cubans of African descent as integral components of a national unity that was yet to be realized and that was contingent upon Cuba's own national liberation. In the process, they accepted the existing nation-state as the framework within which equality would have to be realized. If the PCC was to make another country out of Cuba, it would have to do so by transforming the island as a whole.

IN THE NAME OF EQUALITY

Over the second half of the 1930s, the PCC became the most prominent Cuban political party working in support of Black rights.[119] It vocally opposed racism and discrimination and raised demands for equality in the workplace and for access to public spaces. It also called for improvements in the living conditions of Black neighborhoods and more opportunities for Black Cubans to gain public office. Many of these demands had originated with the *sociedades de color*, and the PCC built on the ties it had previously forged with them, for example playing an active part alongside them in the National Permanent Committee against Racial Discrimination, established in 1939.[120] At the local level, Communists were active in campaigns against discrimination and segregation. In oral interviews conducted in the 1970s and 1980s, Communist militants from Holguín province described taking part in public meetings and labor organizing work against racism from the late 1930s onward.[121]

The PCC's efforts in the cause of racial equality made it stand out within the Cuban political landscape of the time. The party itself was clearly aware of this: As Central Committee member Serafín Portuondo put it at a PCC gathering in July 1939, "we are in a better position than any other party to reach the black masses, because we have struggled for their rights more consistently than any other party."[122] Portuondo was integral to those efforts: In 1936 he cofounded the National Federation of Black Societies, an umbrella organization for the *sociedades de color*, serving as its president through the 1940s.[123] He was part of a levy of Black cadres who rose to the top of the party in the second half of the 1930s. Castellanos was expelled in 1938 after prolonged disagreements with the party's line, but several other Black leaders emerged in the meantime.[124] Among those to speak at the July 1939 meeting were Lázaro Peña, Antolín Dickinson, and Marcelino Hernández, a trade union leader from Santiago who had joined the PCC in 1934 and was made a member of the Central Committee the following year.[125]

The public visibility of the PCC's efforts to counter racism was boosted by the number of prominent Black public figures who were identified with the party in the late 1930s. These included the poets Nicolás Guillén and Regino Pedroso, as well as educator and writer Salvador García Agüero, who was closely involved in the National Federation of Black Societies.[126] Less visibly but more crucially, large numbers of Black Cubans joined the party in these years, helping to swell its numbers dramatically from 2,256 in 1937 to 23,300 in 1939.[127] At the time, Cuban sources told US officials that more than three-quarters of the party's membership was Black, claims that are surely exaggerated.[128] But the very fact that they were made is evidence that the PCC was widely *perceived* to be a "Black" party, which would only have reinforced its appeal among Black Cubans.

By 1939 the PCC's commitment to racial equality was increasingly being channeled into a campaign to include antidiscrimination provisions in the new Cuban constitution. The demand had originated a few years earlier with the *sociedades de color*, and the PCC became an early supporter of it. A party communiqué from mid-July 1936 called for "a Sovereign Constituent [Assembly] in which blacks can defend an article that punishes discrimination and assures their equality in all spheres."[129] The PCC stuck with this demand over the following years and helped foreground the theme of discrimination in the run-up to elections for the Constituent Assembly, held in November 1939. Earlier that year the Club Atenas, an elite Black social club in Havana, invited all the major political parties to present their views. While the representatives of other parties either minimized the severity of discrimination or denied it even existed in Cuba, Blas Roca emphasized its pervasiveness, and the well-known Communist writer Juan Marinello reiterated that message, adding, "It does not matter that some people have come here to deny it. Daily experience confirms it more than enough."[130]

The Communists carried this stance into the deliberations at the Constituent Assembly, which began in February 1940. In the elections for delegates the previous November, six Communists had won seats, out of a total of seventy-six delegates. Communists accounted for three of the assembly's five Black or *mulato* delegates: Blas Roca, Salvador García Agüero, and Esperanza Sánchez Mastrapa, a member of the PCC as well as of the Oriente federation of *sociedades de color*.[131] During the proceedings, Communist delegates spoke about the widespread and structural nature of racial discrimination in Cuba. They argued forcefully for the inclusion of an antidiscrimination provision in the new Constitution, with García Agüero putting forward an amendment calling for additional legislation to establish penalties for violations of this new article.[132] As Alejandra Bronfman has observed, dozens of ordinary Cubans wrote to the Constituent Assembly to support this idea, and there were public rallies outside the Capitol in Havana where proceedings were being held.[133] It was García Agüero's wording that was unanimously adopted as Article 20, which stated "All Cubans are equal before the law," and declared "illegal and punishable any discrimination on grounds of sex, race, color, or class."[134]

The new Constitution, which entered into force in October 1940, enshrined many of the original demands of the 1933 Revolution, codifying the political struggles of previous years and establishing what Robert Whitney calls "a new political and economic consensus."[135] Yet it was by no means certain that this would include recognition of racial equality and sanctioning of discrimination. The fact that it did so was in large measure thanks to the Communist delegates at the Constituent Assembly, whose party had become the principal political force backing these demands. This legislative landmark was thus the most tangible outcome of the decade-long evolution of the PCC's stance on race and nation.

TRANSFORMATIONS

In 1930, the PCC had barely addressed the question of race. Ten years later, it had become known as a staunch advocate of racial equality. As Alejandro de la Fuente has noted, "Whereas labor rights and land distribution were supported by many other political parties, the Communists' vigorous anti-racist campaign contributed to singling them out as the true champions of Afro-Cuban rights."[136] How do we account for this transformation?

The PCC's support for racial equality in the 1930s is generally depicted as coming after its advocacy of Black self-determination in Oriente. Yet as I have demonstrated, Black self-determination was much more organically linked to the PCC's advocacy of racial equality than is commonly recognized. The party only began seriously to take up the cause of equality once it had endorsed Black self-determination in 1932. For several years thereafter, the party viewed both agendas as complementary. When the PCC set the self-determination policy aside in 1935, it also considered dropping demands for racial equality—underscoring the link between the two. Moreover, the PCC's adoption of an anti-racist stance was far from preordained; it was only after considerable internal debate that it decided to maintain its commitment to that cause.

The idea of Black self-determination was crucial in shaping PCC discussions between 1932 and 1936, prompting the party to address the nature and causes of Black oppression and pushing it to publicly clarify its views on race. De la Fuente has argued that "the Comintern's directives had at least one positive effect: They turned the struggle for racial equality into a centerpiece of the PCC's work."[137] The party's advocacy of Black self-determination was integral to that process. Yet contrary to de la Fuente, I argue that the policy was not imposed on the PCC from the outside. The clearest arguments in favor of it came from party members of African descent, who saw self-determination as a way of going beyond the existing liberal constitutional framework, which had left persistent racial injustices untouched.

Posterity has tended to treat the PCC's Black self-determination policy with a mixture of bafflement and condescension. A range of misconceptions about it persist to this day, including the belief that the PCC planned to "deport" Cubans of African descent from the rest of the island to Oriente.[138] At least some of the confusion stems from a misunderstanding of the basic nature of the policy. Rather than a proposal to partition Cuba, it represented a commitment to a democratic principle: the right of the Black majority in Oriente to decide their own destiny.

There are instructive parallels to be drawn between the Cuban case and the US Communist Party's Black Belt policy. In his study of US Communism and race, Mark Solomon argued that the self-determination policy, though often dismissed as "a musty relic handed down from Moscow," had a significant positive impact. It instilled a strong commitment to anti-racism within the party's ranks and pushed it to organize among a population it had previously neglected—a move that in turn profoundly altered the culture and composition of the party itself. Just as important was the fact that, through the self-determination policy, "the Communists had touched a fundamental issue: democracy as independence, and independence as the right of choice."[139]

All of these considerations apply to Cuban Communism in the 1930s. Far from being an aberrant interlude, the PCC's Black self-determination policy had important practical consequences. It posed crucial questions of principle more sharply than before and catalyzed a shift in Cuban Communists' views on race that transformed the party's composition and public reputation for decades to come. By that metric, though Oriente did not gain self-determination, the wider anti-racist shift of which the policy was an integral part was a success.

EIGHT

A Plural Nation

"MEXICANIZING THE INDIAN"?

In April 1940, dozens of delegates from across the Americas gathered on the shores of Lake Pátzcuaro, Michoacán, for the first Inter-American Indian Congress. The event, which brought together policymakers, anthropologists, linguists, and other scholars from nineteen countries, was front-page news in Mexico.[1] As host to the conference, Mexico dominated proceedings numerically: In addition to thirteen official delegates, it sent thirty-seven advisers and thirty-two Indigenous representatives from more than a dozen ethnolinguistic groups.[2] It also dominated the gathering in other ways: Throughout the proceedings, in one resolution after another Mexican Indigenous policy was held up as the model to be emulated.

President Lázaro Cárdenas summed up the essence of that model in his address at the opening of the Pátzcuaro Congress. "Our indigenous problem," he said, "does not lie in keeping the Indian 'Indian,' nor in indigenizing Mexico, but in Mexicanizing the Indian."[3] For much of the twentieth century, Mexican Indigenous policy was premised on the idea that the country's ethnic heterogeneity was an obstacle to progress, and that Indigenous peoples therefore had to be "incorporated" into the broader population through state action. Referred to collectively by the term *indigenismo*, the goal of these efforts was that of creating a unified Mexican nation— "forging the *patria*," according to the title of a celebrated 1916 book by Manuel Gamio, widely seen as the founder of Mexican anthropology.[4]

That future unity was commonly framed in racial terms, to be achieved through a process of mixing or *mestizaje* that would ultimately fuse all of its peoples into a harmonious new whole—what José Vasconcelos, secretary of education in the early 1920s, termed a "cosmic race." But the incorporation of the Indigenous was also a socioeconomic and cultural project in the here and now, and Mexico's postrevolutionary state undertook a variety of initiatives to speed along the process. The best known of these came in the realm of education: In 1921 the SEP created the Department of Education and Culture for the Indigenous Race, and the following year it began opening schools in rural, predominantly Indigenous areas; starting in 1924, it also organized "Cultural Missions" to spread Spanish-language literacy.[5]

The 1940 Pátzcuaro Congress is often framed as a crowning moment for Mexican *indigenismo*.[6] As well as enabling Mexico to tout the successes of its model, the congress provided a platform for Mexican *indigenistas* to transfer their prescriptions to the international stage. In the wake of the Pátzcuaro Congress, Mexico was chosen as the location for the Instituto Indigenista Interamericano (III; Interamerican Indigenista Institute), established in November 1940 to coordinate research and policy at the continental level. Over the following decades, the Mexican state claimed a central role in hemispheric exchanges on Indigenous affairs, making its approach to these issues an important component of Mexican foreign as well as domestic policy.

Yet even at Pátzcuaro, the assimilationist version of *indigenismo* was not the only model on offer. In the 1930s, space began to open up for alternative visions of how the Mexican state should relate to its Indigenous populations. Criticisms of the assimilationist approach gained a wider hearing as many policymakers and ethnographers defended the intrinsic value of Indigenous cultures and languages.[7] This chapter focuses on a radical strand of *indigenismo* that coalesced in the second half of the 1930s and offered an alternative to the Mexican state's assimilationist policies. Drawing on Communist discussions of the "national question," and influenced in particular by the encounter between Bolshevik thinking and Latin American Communists discussed in previous chapters, a cluster of *indigenistas* argued that Mexico should adopt the same approach the Soviet Union had to its national minorities: that is, to offer Indigenous populations the right to "national" self-determination.

Advocates of this policy included the ethnographers Miguel Othón de Mendizábal, Alfonso Fabila, and Jorge Vivó; the labor leader and public intellectual Vicente Lombardo Toledano; and the historian Luis Chávez Orozco. These figures were mostly not members of the PCM, but their understanding of Mexico was rooted in a Bolshevik-influenced conception of

FIGURE 10. John Collier addressing the Pátzcuaro Congress, April 1940. Seated to Collier's right is DAI chief Luis Chávez Orozco, and to the right of Chávez Orozco is President Cárdenas. From Archivo General de la Nación, Fondo Enrique Díaz Delgado y García, 75/4/1.

the country's Indigenous peoples as "nationalities" at various stages of his-torical development—that is, as nations or proto-nations within a compos-ite Mexican nation.

All of these figures were actively involved in debating and formulating Indigenous policy, and many of them worked in the Mexican state appara-tus. From 1939 to 1940, Chávez Orozco was director of the Departamento de Asuntos Indígenas (DAI; Department of Indigenous Affairs), a new arm of government created by Cárdenas in 1936 to handle Indigenous policy. In that capacity, Chávez Orozco convened the Pátzcuaro Congress and chaired the proceedings; in a photograph from the first day, he appears seated between President Cárdenas and John Collier, who headed the US delegation as commissioner for the Bureau of Indian Affairs (see figure 10). Besides Chávez Orozco, other advocates of Indigenous self-determination were centrally involved in the Pátzcuaro Congress: Mendizábal worked on the program committee, Lombardo was part of the official Mexican delega-tion, and Vivó and Fabila were among the Mexican delegation's advisers.[8] As we will see, Vivó used the platform at Pátzcuaro to call for Indigenous self-determination, while Lombardo proposed a redrawing of Mexico's internal boundaries that would have led to Indigenous territorial autonomy.

In retracing the effect of the Soviet nationalities model on Mexico's radical *indigenistas*, I am arguing that *indigenismo* was far from monolithic, and that it contained dissident currents that questioned many of its basic premises. I am also arguing for an alternative mapping of transnational influences in the interwar period. Much scholarship on *indigenismo* and anthropology in this period has focused on cross-border links between the United States and Mexico—and with good reason, given the subsequent sway of US scholars, foundations, and institutions over the discipline in Mexico.[9] Yet this outcome has retroactively obscured the degree to which other possibilities were still in play in the 1930s. The Soviet approach to its myriad ethnic groups offered Mexico's radical *indigenistas* another paradigm—distinct from both the assimilationist mainstream and the US approach—for thinking about their country's internal diversity.

The Mexican case offers a contrast with that of Cuba, discussed in the previous chapter. Whereas the PCC's advocacy of Black self-determination had a marked effect on the policies and makeup of the party itself, in Mexico the main impact of Indigenous self-determination came outside the ranks of the PCM, in broader discussions around Indigenous rights. In what follows, I explore the largely neglected presence of Marxist ideas of self-determination in Mexican *indigenismo* through portraits of key figures. I then analyze the peak of these radical *indigenistas*' institutional reach in 1939–40. The Pátzcuaro Congress marked a turning point, after which the assimilationist line once again reasserted its dominance. I begin, however, with a puzzle: The figures at the center of this chapter began advocating Indigenous self-determination more or less at the moment that the PCM set aside the idea. When and how did the PCM first take up the policy, and why did it then abandon it?

THE PCM AND THE NATIONAL QUESTION

The PCM seems to have given little specific attention to Indigenous people as such until the turn of the 1930s. At the Comintern's Sixth Congress, as we saw in chapter 4, support for the self-determination of "national" minorities became official Communist policy, and in the early 1930s several Latin American Communist parties did take up the self-determination agenda. But in each case, there was a delay. In Mexico, the take-up was gradual. Starting in 1929, there were scattered references to Mexico's Indigenous populations in PCM documents and its newspaper, *El Machete*. A July 1929 internal report referred to land struggles by Indigenous *campesinos* in Quintana Roo, and later that year the electoral platform of the PCM-led BOC expressed support for the demands of "indigenous tribes."[10] Two years later, an appeal from *El Machete* to "Support the Struggle of the Indians" insisted on the right of the Indigenous to "their own social organization which will autonomously administer justice."[11] But these documents stopped shorted of backing territorial self-determination.

This began to shift in 1932. That January, an item in *El Mauser*, the organ of the PCM's cells in the Mexican army, criticized the long-standing repression of Indigenous groups such as the Yaqui people of Sonora, the Tarahumaras in Chihuahua, and the Maya in Yucatán.[12] Against this legacy of dispossession and violence, the PCM championed these peoples' "right of self-determination [*derecho de propia determinación*]," defined as "their right to organize themselves and govern themselves as they wish." It was no coincidence that this came in a publication aimed at the armed forces; as the text noted, "the great majority of soldiers come from indigenous tribes."

Two months later, in March 1932, the PCM's national conference adopted a "Resolution on the Indigenous Question" which called for Mexico's Indigenous peoples to be granted the right to territorial self-determination.[13] The resolution argued that Mexico's Indigenous peoples had been exploited and oppressed by centuries of colonial domination and then by Mexican landowners, yet they remained "resistant to incorporation." The text described groups such as the Maya, Yaquis, Zapotecs, and Tarascans as each possessing a shared language, culture, traditions, forms of social organization, and territory that distinguished them from the rest of the Mexican population. According to the criteria laid out by Stalin in 1913, they thus constituted "several oppressed nationalities." It was the PCM's duty to "support, organize, and direct the struggle of the indigenous for self-determination," clarifying that this went "as far as the right of the tribes to separate from Mexico and constitute independent indigenous states, if they so desire."[14]

The 1932 resolution not only closely followed the formulations used at the 1928 Comintern Congress; it was also clearly responding to the Buenos Aires debates. Implicitly countering Mariátegui's arguments, the resolution explained that the PCM should support self-determination despite the possibility that an Indigenous bourgeoisie might end up leading any independent states that emerged.[15] At the same time, it added—seemingly taking on board the emphasis Mariátegui, Junco, and others had laid on class—the PCM's support for self-determination should be accompanied by class struggle among the Indigenous. To that end, the resolution listed a series of demands that should be advanced alongside self-determination: restitution of Indigenous lands, an end to forced labor, an easing of taxes, equal wages and employment rights, and "absolute respect for their traditional forms of government."[16] There were also demands for education and for legal proceedings to be conducted in Indigenous languages—for which alphabets should be developed where needed. These proposals echo Soviet nationalities policy in its 1920s "affirmative action" phase.[17] The prominence of language and education in the PCM's agenda is worth underscoring, since it stood in marked contrast to the methods of the Mexican state at this time and foreshadowed the views of the radical *indigenistas*.

Why this shift from neglect of the Indigenous to support for their right to self-determination? The PCM's take-up of the self-determination agenda needs to be understood against the backdrop of the turbulence besetting both Mexico and the party in these years. The Wall Street crash of 1929 had plunged much of the world into economic crisis, bringing rising unemployment and poverty. In Mexico, these effects were compounded by the deportation of perhaps a million Mexican workers from the United States in the early 1930s.[18] As we have seen in chapter 3, this was also the period when the PCM identified the Mexican postrevolutionary regime as "fascist" and called for its replacement by a "soviet government of workers and peasants."[19] The Mexican authorities responded with fierce repression, and between 1929 and 1934 the PCM was forced to operate underground. Its membership correspondingly shrank: Barry Carr estimates a drop from fifteen hundred members in mid-1929 to a mere six hundred in late 1934.[20]

In these years of crisis, the PCM strove to distinguish itself from the country's other political forces. In May 1932, the BOC published its electoral program in *El Machete*. Among the many areas where it claimed to stand against the false promises of the governing "fascist regime" was in its support for "the Right of Self-Determination for indigenous tribes."[21] A month later, in June 1932, *El Machete* assailed the Mexican government for "forcing [the Indigenous] to abandon their languages, customs, and traditions," "stealing their land and reducing them to the condition of inferior economic, social, and national beings." It reiterated its support for "the struggle for full self-determination for indigenous races, for their rights to constitute independent states, national indigenous republics that would have the right to separate from Mexico." Recognition of Indigenous sovereignty was part of what the article defined as "the central task of the Party": "to break up the Mexican semi-colonial State."[22]

The PCM's adoption of self-determination coincided with efforts to extend its reach in rural areas and to Indigenous communities. The June 1932 *El Machete* article referred to the formation of BOC committees in Oaxaca, and that year and the next, the paper published a string of items on issues affecting Indigenous people: debt burdens in Chiapas, killings of Mayan *campesinos* in Yucatán, land struggles in Michoacán, and government repression in Orizaba.[23] Yet the PCM's outreach efforts seem to have had little impact. A Central Committee resolution from August 1934 referred to an "alarming situation": The PCM's work among the Indigenous in Puebla had "yielded no positive results," and attempts to use its one Indigenous cell in Oaxaca as a basis for further organizing had failed.[24] Due to the party's clandestine status at the time, the documentary record is fragmentary at best. But it seems that—unlike in Cuba—there was relatively little internal debate on the self-determination policy, at either the national or local level.

An internal party document from October 1934 on "the national question in Mexico" referred to the "enormous variegation and complexity" of the country's Indigenous groups, adding that "the question of self-determination ... would have to be posed concretely before each of this great conglomerate of nationalities."[25] Yet barely a year later, in late 1935, the PCM set the self-determination policy aside without much ceremony or contention. A major factor in this shift was the worldwide reorientation of Communist policy in the wake of the Comintern's Seventh Congress, held in Moscow in July–August 1935. Once the organization adopted its Popular Front strategy, Mexico's Communists underwent an evolution comparable to that of their Cuban counterparts. When Lázaro Cárdenas had taken office in 1934, the PCM had initially denounced him as yet another "fascist." In October 1935 it changed its tune entirely. In a letter to the party's Central Committee laying out the new line, the PCM's delegation to the Comintern Congress said the party should support Cárdenas in his struggle against imperialism and criticized the party's previous views as "sectarian errors."[26] It now envisaged forming a Popular Front with progressive forces in Mexico, including the Cárdenas government. But in the platform it proposed, Indigenous self-determination was replaced by a demand for "effective equality of civil and political rights for the indigenous" and "teaching of the indigenous in their own languages."[27] In Mexico as in Cuba, the adoption of the Popular Front brought the abandonment of territorial self-determination for "national" minorities.

The link between the PCM's Popular Front turn and its abandonment of Indigenous self-determination was not made explicit at the time. But the fact that these changes in policy coincided so closely means that, as in the Cuban case, they have been portrayed as part of a return to common sense after the fever dreams of the Comintern's "Third Period."[28] The PCM itself certainly contributed to this impression, since its leaders and chroniclers showed little interest in discussing the policy thereafter; it goes unmentioned in internal histories and in memoirs by leading figures such as David Siqueiros and Valentín Campa.[29] Yet to depict Indigenous self-determination as a passing folly is to ignore the wider influence that the idea enjoyed in Mexico in the second half of the 1930s. Even as the PCM was abandoning it, self-determination acquired a number of advocates outside the party, in particular among people working on Indigenous issues. This is where the Comintern-inspired view of the "national question" had its greatest impact in Mexico, and it is to the constellation of figures who adapted self-determination to the Mexican context that I now turn.

MARXISM AND MEXICAN *INDIGENISMO*

During the 1930s, criticisms of *indigenismo*'s assimilationist model began to emerge among Mexican ethnographers and policymakers. Some had second thoughts after running into difficulties when trying to implement that model; for others, encounters in the field with Indigenous cultures and languages encouraged them to rethink the assumption that these were symptoms of backwardness. Many scholars have noted the emergence of a minority current within Mexican *indigenismo* at this time, often referred to as "pluralism." Seeking to preserve Indigenous cultures rather than erase them, the "pluralists" envisaged some degree of heterogeneity within an integrated national whole.[30]

The figures at the center of this chapter have previously been identified as "pluralists," since they too were critical of assimilationism and emphasized Mexico's internal variety.[31] Yet their views were more distinctive than this label would suggest, and their specific contributions to debates on Indigenous issues have not been fully recognized. I define their outlook as *radical pluralism*, founded on three basic principles. First, the radical pluralists held that Mexico's myriad Indigenous peoples constituted national minorities in their own right, with distinct cultures, languages, traditions, patterns of social organization, and forms of government. This might seem unremarkable today, but it would have been more surprising in Mexican *indigenista* and governmental circles of the 1930s, where Indigenous groups were identified according to racial categories and the persistence of Indigenous cultures was seen as an obstacle to be overcome. For the assimilationists, Mexico itself was still struggling toward nationhood because of its mixed racial makeup. The pluralists rejected this racial framing, preferring to see Mexico as a nation that contained many nations.

A second key point was that Indigenous peoples had a legitimate right to maintain their cultures and ways of life and thus to be shielded from aggressive projects of incorporation. Here the radical pluralists differed from other critics of official *indigenismo* in seeing the maintenance of Indigenous cultures not as a means toward a more gradual, consensual assimilation, but as a permanent commitment. The radical pluralists differed still more dramatically on a third principle: In their view, each Indigenous group had the right to a degree of autonomy and self-government. Crucially, this involved recognizing existing Indigenous political structures—that is, forms of self-rule that were independent of the Mexican state. Radical pluralism thus challenged not only official *indigenismo*, but also the authority of the country's postrevolutionary governments.

At the heart of the radical pluralist view lay the concept of *autodeterminación*. What did they mean by this? Up to this point the word had tended to imply separate territorial sovereignty. In 1930s Mexico, the meaning of the term shifted, instead connoting a right to greater autonomy. It is in this form that the idea of self-determination ultimately had its strongest influence there: as an insistence on the political right of Indigenous groups to determine their own destinies, within the existing confines of Mexico but independent of its mestizo-dominated structures of rule.

"The World of the Future": Vicente Lombardo Toledano

The most visible of the figures who took up the idea of Indigenous self-determination was Mexican labor leader Vicente Lombardo Toledano. In October 1935, on his return from a trip to the Soviet Union, the Mexican press asked his opinion of "the solution to the problem of nationalities in the USSR and what lessons it might hold for Mexico."[32] He replied that the Soviet model was "brilliant" and praised the way it had "lifted large and small nuclei of populations, distinct in race and language from the Russians and Western Europeans, out of poverty, illiteracy, religious fanaticism, and superstition." This model could not simply be transferred to a capitalist country, Lombardo noted, but "certain aspects" of it could be implemented in Mexico "immediately, and with great success." These included economic development, fostering vernacular languages, and "absolute respect for the right to self-determination and government for defined ethnic groups."

Lombardo's enthusiasm for the Soviet model was surprising for several reasons. Prior to his trip to the USSR, he had been the target of many sharp polemical attacks from the PCM. Born in Teziutlán, Puebla, in 1894, Lombardo played a prominent role in Mexican political and intellectual life until his death in 1968.[33] Closely connected with the capital's intellectual circles in the 1920s, he became a key player in Mexican national politics in the 1930s as a labor leader, first in the CROM and then as head of the Confederación General de Obreros y Campesinos de México (CGOCM; General Confederation of Workers and Peasants of Mexico), formed in 1933. His role in mediating between organized labor and the government earned him the enmity of the PCM, which frequently accused him of "betraying" the working class.[34] But in 1934 and 1935, Lombardo's CGOCM organized a series of strikes that demonstrated labor's power to the new president, Cárdenas.[35] Lombardo's leftward evolution opened the way for a rapprochement with the PCM, sealed by his 1935 trip to the USSR.

Together with his friend the economist Víctor Manuel Villaseñor, Lombardo left Mexico for Moscow in mid-July 1935.[36] He described the Soviet capital as "an apiary of four million inhabitants," humming with purposeful activity and endless construction.[37] While there Lombardo attended sessions of the Seventh Comintern Congress, including the gathering at which Comintern Chairman Georgi Dimitrov laid out the new Popular Front line. Lombardo praised it for setting aside "sectarianism" to forge a mass movement against fascism.[38] He and Villaseñor then spent a month traveling within the USSR, including trips to Ukraine and the Caucasus. After returning to Mexico in mid-October, the two men gave a series of lectures recounting their impressions of the Soviet Union. Given in November 1935, these were published in book form in 1936, under a title that made plain the authors' sympathies: *A Journey to the World of the Future.*[39] In the fourth of these lectures, Lombardo laid out his views of Soviet nationalities policy and its applicability to Mexico.

This was not Lombardo's first foray into the Indigenous question. In the 1920s he had addressed the problem of Indigenous education—including during a brief stint as governor of the state of Puebla, which had some of the country's largest Nahuatl- and Totonac-speaking populations—and in 1931 he earned a doctorate from UNAM with a thesis on the Indigenous languages of the Sierra de Puebla.[40] At this time, his view seems to have been very close to that of official *indigenismo*: At a CROM conference in 1924, for example, he insisted that the Indigenous population had to be taught Spanish in order to foster national cohesion.[41] Lombardo's 1931 thesis also had a strongly assimilationist bent, referring to "the racial and social unification of Mexico" as "the supreme task of the State."[42]

In the wake of his 1935 trip to the USSR, however, Lombardo expressed very different views. The title of his fourth lecture signals his admiration for the Bolshevik approach: "How the Soviet Regime Solved the Problem of Oppressed Nationalities."[43] He began by describing how the Bolsheviks had addressed the national tensions bequeathed to them by the tsarist empire. Among the key measures they applied was "recognition of the right that Russian nationalities possess to self-determine [*autodeterminar*] their destiny, up to the juridical capacity to separate from the Soviet Union: full autonomy, absolute sovereignty, right of joining or not joining the ensemble of Soviet Socialist Republics."[44] Lombardo then praised the Soviet regime's initiatives during the 1920s to foster the use of native languages, including through education, literacy campaigns, creating alphabets, and publishing books and newspapers. He also lauded Soviet efforts to train cadres from each of the nationalities and moves toward economic development, including through industrialization and the collectivization of land.[45]

There are many bitter ironies here. At the time of Lombardo's visit to the USSR, the policies he extolled were a thing of the past, the "affirmative action" of the 1920s having given way to a brutal crackdown on expressions of "bourgeois nationalism." Russification was increasingly the dominant trend in education, accompanied by large doses of repression.[46] Moreover, the forms of economic development Lombardo praised were often of scant benefit to national minorities. Industrialization generally brought an influx of ethnic Russians rather than employment for the local population, and the collectivization of agriculture in 1929–30 and the ensuing famines in 1931–33 were devastating in their human toll; conservative estimates put the total number of "excess deaths" at 5.7 million.[47] Like many other visitors to the USSR at the time, Lombardo seems either to have been unaware of these facts or to have overlooked them in his desire to hold up the Soviet model as an alternative to capitalism.

When it came to self-determination, he and the other radical pluralists tended to abstract the Soviet model from its original context, taking up and adapting select features. In his 1935 lecture Lombardo proposed measures that certainly bore a resemblance to the USSR's experience. They included redrawing municipal and federal boundaries in areas inhabited by Indigenous peoples, "in order to create homogeneous districts, rather than arbitrarily dividing the indigenous masses into different jurisdictions." Within these new boundaries, there should be "absolute political autonomy for entities populated by indigenous people," and Lombardo added that "the authorities [governing] the indigenous must invariably, in all cases, be indigenous"—an echo of the Bolshevik policy of *korenizatsiia*, "taking root." He also recommended a "fostering of vernacular languages" and the creation of alphabets for languages that lacked them. Finally, Lombardo recommended a policy of economic development in Indigenous areas, including the collectivization and industrialization of agriculture.[48]

But there were also some notable differences between Lombardo's proposals and the Soviet model. First, he made a significant modification to one of the basic premises of Bolshevik self-determination. Lombardo proposed redrawing internal boundaries to make the administrative map of Mexico better reflect its ethnic composition, but he did not advocate a right to territorial separation. For him, *autodeterminación* signified political autonomy for Indigenous territories that would remain a part of Mexico. The reach of the term was thus circumscribed. Second, there was a symptomatic blurring in Lombardo's usage of the terms "nation" and "nationality." On the one hand, he described Mexico's Indigenous groups as "oppressed nations" within a Mexican "nation" that was still not fully formed. Mexico was in that sense "an ensemble . . . of diverse beings within one country." But on the other hand, Lombardo described Mexico as "a semi-colonial country" with "all the characteristics of an oppressed nation, which must fight vigorously against its natural enemy which is international imperialism." Here, he defined Mexico as a single "oppressed nation" relative to imperialism, and thus as possessing precisely the internal coherence he previously denied it. In the same passage, Lombardo further confused things by stating that his goal was to foment the "class consciousness of the oppressed nations that still weigh on our nationality."[49] The implication was that the incompleteness of Mexico's "nationality" was due to the presence of multiple nations within it.

These incongruities point to a core dilemma faced by all the figures discussed in this chapter: how to reconcile their appreciation of Mexico's internal heterogeneity and recognition of the provisional character of Mexican nationhood with the need to bolster Mexico's sovereignty in the face of external pressures. The answer, for Lombardo as for others, was that there was no necessary contradiction between their support for Indigenous aspirations and the definitive coalescence of Mexico as a nation; indeed, one was the necessary path to the other.

A Scholar in the Field: Miguel Othón de Mendizábal

In September 1935, a month before Lombardo returned from the USSR, Mexico City hosted the Fourth Pan American Scientific Congress, a gathering of scholars and government officials from across the hemisphere. Among the presentations were some remarks by ethnographer Miguel Othón de Mendizábal on the Cárdenas administration's plans to create a new department dedicated to Indigenous matters. Mendizábal explained that its goal would be to "promote the improvement of indigenous groups who have remained at the margin of national life in economic, social, and cultural terms, as well as supplying the means to accelerate their incorporation."[50] Mendizábal's description was consistent with the Mexican state's assimilationist agenda. But he opened his remarks with a revealing set of international comparisons, contrasting Mexico's policies favorably with those of European colonial powers, who sought knowledge of Indigenous peoples in order to dominate them, and with those of the United States, whose Bureau of Indian Affairs he dismissed as "a resounding failure." The only country he praised was the USSR, whose policy toward its "small nationalities . . . seeks to accelerate, through the development of local economies, the evolution of their particular cultural forms."[51]

Although he was trained squarely within the mainstream of Mexican *indigenismo*, in the mid-1930s Mendizábal became a prominent supporter of the Soviet nationalities model. Born in Mexico City in 1890, he studied at the National Museum of Archeology, History, and Ethnography in the early 1910s and then joined its staff.[52] In the 1920s he produced historical studies of Mexico's Indigenous groups, including an analysis of the economic role of salt in pre-Columbian societies.[53] He also worked for the SEP, attending the founding congress of the Liga Nacional Campesina in 1926 as its official delegate, and was involved in the capital's anti-imperialist circles; in 1927, he addressed LADLA meetings on the subject of intellectuals and imperialism.[54]

Though he seems never to have been a member of the PCM, Mendizábal was avowedly materialist in his approach.[55] Both in his historical scholarship and in his work for the SEP and, later, the DAI, he consistently stressed the importance of economic factors. This emphasis went hand in hand with his critique of the Mexican state's predominantly cultural approach to Indigenous matters. In 1932 the prominent *indigenista* and former deputy secretary of education, Moisés Sáenz, invited Mendizábal to take part in an "Experimental Station" in Carapan, Michoacán, where he spent several months studying the local people's daily lives, their culture, and their language. From this experience, Mendizábal recalled three years later in his presentation at the Pan American Scientific Congress, "I drew the firm conviction that it is absolutely useless to attempt to further the prosperity of any indigenous region by cultural means, without previously making a judicious economic intervention."[56]

In emphasizing the insufficiency of cultural approaches, Mendizábal was by extension criticizing the SEP-led assimilationist effort as a whole. From the mid-1930s on, he repeatedly endorsed Soviet nationalities policy as an alternative model. As well as comparing the Bolshevik approach favorably to those of the United States and Europe at the Pan American Scientific Congress in 1935, he hailed the Soviets' encouragement of the use of native languages as an example for Mexico to follow at a November 1938 gathering devoted to linguistics.[57] He continued to voice admiration for the USSR's nationalities policy in texts written in the early 1940s.[58]

For Mendizábal, the appeal of the Soviet model was that it offered a more holistic and seemingly successful approach to ethnic and linguistic diversity than the dominant *indigenista* paradigm. He did not advocate for the right of Mexico's Indigenous peoples to territorial separation, instead adapting other features of the Soviet model to the Mexican context. The promotion of Indigenous languages was one key premise, and it was central to his work: In 1928 he published a linguistic map of Mexico, and in the 1930s he drew on census data to create several comprehensive and up-to-date charts of the distribution of different languages, as well as of the prevalence of bilingualism.[59] He would go on to become a key advocate of Indigenous-language education, in the belief that maintaining linguistic variety was not a threat to Mexico's cohesion.

A second Bolshevik premise also seems to have informed Mendizábal's thinking: the idea of a continuum of historical development running from "tribes" to "nationalities" to "nations." In a 1930 work on Mexico's northwest, he noted that at the time of the Spanish Conquest the Indigenous peoples of the region were still going through the critical period of the "formation of nationalities."[60] In 1935, in a lecture on Mexican history given at the Palacio de Bellas Artes, Mendizábal referred to the Indigenous groups of the northwest constituting "genuine States that were entirely independent" of the central government for centuries.[61] At different moments in history, Mexico's Indigenous groups were thus located at different points along the continuum, in some cases even exercising de facto sovereignty.

Both of these premises—the importance of Indigenous linguistic diversity and the historical contingency of processes of "national" development— were central to the radical pluralists' thinking. Behind them lay a belief that many of Mexico's Indigenous groups formed distinct communities that were either already or incipiently "nations." While Lombardo initially took up the Soviet idea of territorial self-determination for these groups, Mendizábal and others focused their efforts in different areas, such as expanding Indigenous-language education. The role of the Soviet precedent here was to strengthen their case for state policies that aimed not to forcibly "Castilianize" the Indigenous, but on the contrary to support the free expression of their cultures.

From Havana to Tamazunchale: Jorge Vivó

At the very end of 1935, President Cárdenas decreed the establishment of the DAI, the official functions of which were to "study the fundamental problems of the aboriginal races," and to "promote and manage before the federal and State authorities, all those measures and dispositions concerning the general interest of the aboriginal nuclei of the population."[62] Over the next few years, the DAI was at the center of government policy on Indigenous questions, helping the state to address such basic needs as agrarian reform, irrigation, labor rights, and access to education.[63] Between 1936 and 1939, the DAI also organized a series of Indigenous congresses. The first, held in Ixmiquilpan, Hidalgo, in late 1936, gathered more than seven hundred Otomí delegates. It was followed by meetings of the Tarascans in 1937;

of the Nahuas and the Mixtecs in 1938; and of the Tzotzil, the Huastecs, and the Chontal Maya in 1939.[64]

These congresses were a concrete demonstration of the Cárdenas government's new approach to the Indigenous question. The president himself gave the opening address at Ixmiquilpan, asserting that "the government of the Revolution considers it an obligation to give first priority to the indigenous race of the Republic."[65] The congresses received extensive press coverage; the government newspaper *El Nacional* splashed an entire page of photographs of Cárdenas at Ixmiquilpan, for example.[66] The purpose of these events was to create dedicated forums for the articulation of Indigenous demands, and hence further the incorporation of previously marginalized groups into Mexico's national political life. Yet the very form these congresses took—regional gatherings of specific ethnolinguistic groups—fostered the assertion of precisely the distinct identities Mexican officialdom had previously sought to assimilate. As far as mainstream Mexican *indigenismo* was concerned, there was a troubling tension here. As Alexander Dawson perceptively put it, "Even if the promotion of ethnic affinities did not challenge the nation, they nonetheless would create another layer of power directly oriented to protecting the interests of a community that defined itself as parallel to the national polity."[67]

But for anthropologist and geographer Jorge Vivó, there was no tension at all. In a series of articles titled "Mexico and the Indian" published in *El Nacional* in May 1937, Vivó commented enthusiastically on Cárdenas's Indigenous policy. In his view the Mexican government was "teaching the Americas, and without exaggerating we can say the world," a great deal about the handling of ethnic questions.[68] According to Vivó, only one country exceeded Mexico in its "audacity in addressing ethnic-national problems": the USSR. Like Mendizábal, Vivó saw Soviet nationalities policy as a potential model for Mexico, in particular because of its apparent capacity to combine economic development with protection of Indigenous cultures and its provision for political autonomy within a broader unity.

In the literature on Mexican *indigenismo*, Vivó features mainly as an anthropologist and geographer who happened to advocate Soviet-style self-determination for Mexico's Indigenous people.[69] In the 1940s he became a household name in Mexico as the author of a geography textbook.[70] But Vivó was an unusual scholar: Prior to taking up anthropology, he had been a prominent Communist militant, and his transnational trajectory intersects with the debates discussed in earlier chapters, all of which shaped his understanding of the "national question" in the Americas.

Born in Havana in 1906, Vivó studied law at the University of Havana in the early 1920s before working as a teacher.[71] He took part in student protests, was a key member of the Cuban section of LADLA, and joined the Cuban Communist Party in 1927. Soon after that, he was forced into exile. Vivó was an itinerant militant in Costa Rica, Panama, Colombia, and Guatemala, working as a linotypist and journalist. Expelled from Colombia and then Guatemala, he arrived in Mexico in 1929, where he joined the PCM and, in the wake of Mella's death, took over as leader of ANERC, the Cuban exiles' organization. But in 1930, amid the Mexican government's crackdown on the left, he was deported to the United States, where he worked for the US Communist Party's Centro Obrero de Habla Española (Spanish-Speaking Workers' Center) in New York.

In 1930, almost the entire leadership of the PCC was arrested by the Cuban authorities. With Mella dead and other leading Cuban Communists absent from the island, it fell to Vivó to take up the post of general secretary. He returned to Cuba in 1931 and remained the PCC's leader until 1933. As we saw in chapter 7, it was during this interval that the Cuban party grew rapidly and expanded its geographical reach across the island; this was also the period when the PCC took up the idea of Black self-determination.

Vivó was removed as PCC leader in late 1933, as part of the internal reckoning with the party's "August mistake." But even after Blas Roca took over his role, Vivó remained a prominent member of the Central Committee. In the internal debates of 1933–34, he was among the strongest supporters of Black self-determination, though as we have seen, he would later spar with Martín Castellanos over maintaining the policy. Vivó also represented the PCC at the Comintern Congress of 1935. But tensions between Vivó and his successor contributed to his removal from the Central Committee in 1937. Disenchanted, Vivó left Cuba for Mexico. In March of that year, Mexican Communist Rafael Carrillo—who had spent time in Cuba in 1933—wrote to Blas Roca mentioning Vivó's arrival and his distant attitude toward his former comrades. According to Carrillo, Vivó had "got into 'science' up to his neck," adding dismissively: "Just imagine [*Figúrate*], he has set himself to studying indigenous dialects."[72]

This was no passing fancy, as Vivó's later career demonstrated, nor was it an entirely new interest. In an autobiographical statement he wrote during a stint in Moscow in 1934–35, Vivó listed the subjects in which he was best read as "the trade union question, the colonial question, and the national question."[73] There was a clear continuity between Vivó's earlier support for Black self-determination in Cuba and his interest in Mexico's Indigenous groups—and the hinge between the two was Soviet nationalities policy, which he learned about firsthand in the USSR.

Vivó laid out his impressions of the Soviet model in a series of articles for *El Nacional* published three years later, between August and November 1938.[74] After giving readers a sketch of the former tsarist empire's ethnic diversity, Vivó described how the Bolsheviks had addressed the "national question" by applying the principle of self-determination to national minorities. For Vivó, the attraction of the Soviet model went beyond its provision of the formal right to territorial separation. As he explained, certain national minorities could also gain autonomy within the territories of others—that is, form "autonomous republics" nested, *matryoshka* doll–style, within formally sovereign Soviet Socialist Republics. Vivó recounted his experiences of a trip to the Caucasus, where he visited the Autonomous Republic of Abkhazia, embedded within the Georgian Soviet Socialist Republic.[75] Here, according to Vivó, the Bolsheviks had overseen a remarkable national rebirth, turning the Abkhaz from a "people in decline" into a "thrusting, hardworking nationality."[76]

Vivó's praise of Soviet literacy and cultural efforts echoed that of Lombardo and Mendizábal. He also shared their blindness to the increasing coercion involved in Soviet nationalities policy in the 1930s. As in Lombardo's case, the model Vivó praised was at best an idealized vision of what Bolshevik policy had been in the 1920s. But his approval of Soviet efforts in Abkhazia also brought an important modulation in the meaning of self-determination. Vivó was referring to groups that had "autonomous" status rather than a right to territorial separation. In this framing, self-determination did not necessarily imply the formation of separate sovereign entities; it could also mean the establishment of "autonomous" units within a nation-state.

Vivó had another, more surprising reason for visiting Abkhazia: The region was home to a small community of people of African descent. Numbering only a few dozen by 1935, they descended from people who had been enslaved and taken to work on plantations in Abkhazia between the seventeenth and nineteenth centuries. According to Vivó, "My status as an Américan, where more than 40 million blacks live . . . imposed on me the task of visiting the region where this black population lived."[77] He reported conversations with one of these "Ethiopian natives of the Soviet Union," a Red Army veteran named Shaavan Abash who had married a white Russian woman and who insisted he had never suffered the slightest discrimination since the Revolution. Abash was a member of the Communist Party of the Soviet Union, and it seems likely his contact with Vivó would have been vetted in advance, adding further to the need to treat Vivó's account with caution. But for Vivó, Abash's life story was an example of how the Soviet system had "liberated all the peoples oppressed by Tsarism, even [this] small population of black Africans." Among the Soviet populace as a whole, Vivó found "an atmosphere of surprising interracial cordiality," in stark contrast to the "suffocating atmosphere" of racism in the capitalist world. For Vivó, then, the Soviet model reinforced the link between making revolution and ending racism.

The remaining articles in Vivó's *El Nacional* series were devoted to Soviet efforts to study the USSR's myriad national groups, focusing on the work of linguists and ethnographers.[78] The depth of Vivó's interest in languages is plain, and he would carry it over into his subsequent anthropological work. But what is especially striking about these articles is how close their themes and concerns are to those of the texts in Vivó's "Mexico and the Indian" series from the previous year. There, Vivó had drawn attention to the linguistic and ethnographic work being done by Mendizábal and others at the DAI, the SEP, and UNAM, and he had argued strongly in favor of state support for education in Indigenous languages.[79] The parallels with his account of the Soviet model, written in 1938 but based on his experiences three years earlier, are clear.

For Vivó, the Cárdenas government's Indigenous policy was not as ambitious or as extensive as that of the USSR, but both seemed to be adopting similar means to foster diversity within a broader unity. The creation of more systematic knowledge about the Indigenous and state support for Indigenous languages were two obvious commonalities. Yet where previous discussions of the Soviet model had emphasized the right to territorial separation, Vivó deployed it in pursuit of a different goal: greater Indigenous autonomy within the existing confines of Mexico. This mostly seemed to mean a right to organize politically and to maintain their cultural distinctiveness—both goals that were notably furthered by the Indigenous congresses to which Vivó devoted such enthusiastic coverage, including a Nahua gathering in Tamazunchale in March 1938.[80] But while the notion of territorial separation seemed to fade into the background, the idea of *autodeterminación* was still supposed to apply to specific pieces of land, as another leftist ethnographer's advocacy for the Yaqui people made clear.

Yaqui Self-Determination: Alfonso Fabila

In 1938 the SEP commissioned Alfonso Fabila to write a report on schools among the Yaqui people of Sonora. Fabila then wrote an extensive ethnographic study of the history, beliefs, culture, and customs of this Uto-Aztecan people. Titled *The Yaqui Tribes of Sonora*, it was published by the DAI in 1940. But it was the book's subtitle that conveyed what was most distinctive about his account of the Yaquis: It referred to *Their Culture and Desired Self-Determination*.[81] Fabila's book was the most concrete and sustained argument made for Indigenous self-determination in Mexico in these years, and it exemplified the shift in emphasis from a demand for territorial separation to greater autonomy within the confines of a plural Mexico.

Like Mendizábal, Fabila had moved toward supporting self-determination from within the mainstream of *indigenismo*. Born in Amanalco, Mexico State, in 1897, he came from a family of peasant origins that moved to the capital during the Revolution.[82] In 1921 he began working for the SEP, taking part in its literacy campaigns and "cultural missions." In 1928 he spent several months in the United States, and after his return published a pamphlet decrying the suffering endured by his compatriots there.[83] At the end of the 1920s he worked for the National Repatriation Committee, a Mexican government body established to foster return migration from the United States.[84] In the early 1930s he began working once more for the SEP, including fieldwork with Manuel Gamio in Hidalgo State and postings in Michoacán and the Sierra de Puebla. Alongside his ethnographic work, Fabila also had creative aspirations, publishing fiction with a marked *indigenista* tinge.[85]

It's not clear exactly when Fabila joined the PCM, but he very likely knew several of its militants in the 1920s, whether through the SEP or through his association with Mexico City's literary circles. His work on the Yaquis, moreover, shows that he was very familiar with Communist debates around self-determination. Although Fabila does not make direct reference to the Soviet model, the Bolshevik influence is plain: The text is littered with terms drawn from Soviet and Comintern debates on the "national question." In the book's preamble, Fabila echoes the criteria for defining a nation that Stalin laid out in his 1913 essay "Marxism and the National

Question." As Fabila puts it, before the Spanish Conquest, the Yaquis "possessed their own language, territory, economic regime, government, culture, and psychological habits."[86] He refers to "the self-determination of small nationalities" and describes the Yaquis as an "oppressed nationality and a mistreated race" with "the right to self-determination."[87]

Fabila's argument for self-determination was grounded in the Yaquis' distinctive history of resistance to settler encroachment and state repression.[88] He evoked the Yaquis' recurrent rebellions against Spanish colonial and then independent Mexican rule, revolts that the authorities of the day barely suppressed through the use of overwhelming force.[89] Yet despite this onslaught, the Yaquis had "been able to defend their autonomy as a people and as a race."[90] The Mexican state had responded with further violence, culminating in a long military campaign under Porfirio Díaz that involved the mass deportation of Yaquis to Oaxaca and Yucatán between 1890 and 1910. During the Revolution, many Yaquis fought alongside the Constitutionalist army of Álvaro Obregón. But by 1917 Mexico's new rulers had resumed the forcible removal of the Yaquis from their lands, now to the benefit of Sonoran generals rather than foreign corporations.[91] Further rebellions in the late 1920s were met with the same punitive response. In the 1930s, many Mexican officials continued to view the Yaquis as an obstacle to progress requiring a militarized solution. In 1936 the military commander for the region submitted to Cárdenas his plans for solving "the Yaqui agrarian problem": army supervision of the continued colonization of the Yaqui Valley.[92]

In October 1937, however, Cárdenas transformed the Mexican state's policy toward the Yaquis. That month he reached an agreement with Yaqui tribal authorities that recognized their claim to the lands on the right bank of the Yaqui River and the Sierra del Yaqui—an area totaling 400,000 hectares, or roughly the size of Rhode Island.[93] This was the first in a series of accords between the government and the Yaquis over the next two years, and it was an exceptional document in several ways. First, it recognized the Yaquis' own, independently constituted tribal authorities as legitimate interlocutors for the Mexican state. Second, it recognized their collective right to the lands in question as a tribe, rather than as holders of parcels registered with the Mexican agrarian bureaucracy, which had been the main form of obtaining rights to land since the Revolution.[94] This notably included Yaquis not currently residing in the region, such as the fifteen hundred families who had migrated across the border to Arizona, about whom Cárdenas had expressed his concern to the governor of Sonora a few months earlier.[95] Third, the agreement conceded these lands to the Yaquis in accordance with their traditional claims to them as a people, rather than any prior legal title; that is, it recognized the Yaquis' claim on an ethnic basis.

The Cárdenas government's 1937 accords with the Yaquis are an outlier; they are the only "tribal" land grant ever made in Mexico. As such, they testify to a relative opening in Mexican *indigenismo* in the late 1930s, a flexibility that stands in marked contrast to the assimilationism of the 1920s. But remarkable as this was, for Fabila it was insufficient. The 1937 agreement only "restored" part of the land the Yaquis considered theirs. In his book he included a hand-drawn map showing the much larger area that they claimed, as he put it, "because they consider it a sovereign nation by tradition, titles, and religious beliefs."[96] Indeed, between the time of his research and the publication of the book, Fabila lobbied Cárdenas on behalf of the Yaquis in order to extend the 1937 settlement. In August 1938 he wrote to the president conveying their claim to the villages of Bácum and Cócorit.[97] Fabila argued that their claim was justified because "traditionally they are eight tribes and eight villages," and therefore, "lacking two villages they feel incomplete and discontented." He stressed his "firm conviction" that "the Yaquis are in the right." When he came to publish his book in 1940, Fabila reiterated the Yaquis' desire for "restitution" of these two villages, out of respect for "the sovereignty of their land."[98]

Yet even as Fabila made a strong case for Yaqui self-determination, he was clear that this would not mean separation from Mexico. The Yaquis, he argued, "consider themselves part of the Mexican *patria*"; indeed, according to Fabila, "at the end of the day they are the real Mexicans, fighting for their own honor and that of the different ethnic groups in chains in Mexico." What Fabila recommended was comparable to the autonomous status some minorities in the USSR enjoyed. But rather than citing the Soviet example, he drew on precedents closer to home. The Mexican Constitution, he observed, gave sovereignty to its federal states and frequently redrew the boundaries of municipalities, and this did nothing to diminish Mexico's national unity. "Why then," he asked, "do we not use this same established, liberal criterion to grant to the Indian something that historically belongs to him?" He sketched out a proposal for "relative self-determination," in which the Yaqui region would be turned into "a state experimental indigenous zone," governed by the Yaquis themselves and monitored through a "supervisory organism" that would cooperate closely with federal officials.[99]

Fabila's scheme was light on details. Who would run the supervisory organism, and what would its powers be? Exactly how much latitude would the Yaquis have? Then there is the question of whether he intended this "experimental indigenous zone" to be a one-off or, if it were successful, to be replicated elsewhere. But in arguing for some version of Yaqui autonomy, Fabila pointed out that their situation was already very different from that obtaining elsewhere, and it should simply be properly codified.

Fabila then added a much broader justification that reflected his conception of Mexico as being composed of myriad national groups. "It is time," he wrote, "for the governments of Mexico to occupy themselves not only with building works . . . but also with something transcendent, which is the construction of a more just world." In order to do this, "we must fully realize that Mexico is a mosaic of small nationalities, which until today have not had the right to enjoy the most basic human prerogatives, simply due to the prejudices of racial inferiority and jingoism."[100] For Fabila, there was no contradiction between self-determination for the Yaquis and Mexican national unity; on the contrary, the one was integral to the success of the other.

Even as Fabila was writing his study, the Cárdenas government made further agreements with the Yaquis. In June 1939 the president visited the region, meeting with the tribal leadership in Pótam, where he reaffirmed the government's 1937 land grant.[101] He also promised to provide greater resources for Yaqui agriculture, education, sanitation, and health. However, he did not recognize the Yaquis' claim to Bácum and Cócorit, effectively curtailing their bid for sovereignty over all of their traditional domain. But in the same agreement, Cárdenas made an extraordinary concession, agreeing to withdraw Mexican military detachments from the Yaquis' homeland and leave the "maintenance of order" in the hands of the Yaquis themselves. The Yaquis' territory was thus distinguished from the rest of Mexico in a series of ways, both legally and de facto.

What was the relationship between Fabila's arguments and the Mexican state's policy toward the Yaquis? Cárdenas would certainly have known of his work. After visiting the Yaqui region, he asked the head of the DAI to find an expert who could write a study of the Yaquis. Chávez Orozco replied by telegram, recommending Fabila: "HIS INTERPRETATION IS SCIENTIFIC AND REVOLUTIONARY."[102] But it is not clear when or if Cárdenas read Fabila's report, and the chronology of the Mexican government's agreements with the Yaquis—concluded between October 1937 and June 1939—suggests Fabila had no direct influence on these. There seems rather to have been a transitory alignment between the Mexican government's treatment of the Yaquis and the views of the radical pluralists.

The 1930s agreements between the Mexican state and the Yaquis were a remarkable break from previous practice—not only toward the Yaquis, but toward any Indigenous group. The Indigenous congresses described earlier, for example, provided forums for collective political representation, but they did not involve effective recognition of separate jurisdiction over any pieces of Mexican territory. The Yaquis, by contrast, were granted extensive lands on the basis of a collective ethnic claim, through a process that recognized their traditional tribal authorities as legitimate treaty partners for the Mexican state. While the rights accorded to the Yaquis were not explicitly described as self-determination, they nonetheless amounted to a surprising degree of autonomy, granted to an Indigenous group on terms they had shaped themselves.

There remained, however, a gap between the views of Cárdenas and those of the radical pluralists. While in Pótam in 1939, the president said he was seeking to "put a definitive end to the differences that have existed between the Tribe and the rest of the Mexican population, in order to maintain the ensemble in perfect harmony, and thus give greater strength to our nationality."[103] For Cárdenas, there was only one "nationality" in Mexico, and while his treatment of the Yaquis points to a new flexibility on the part of the Mexican state, he did not consider the Yaquis or any other group a distinct "nation." Fabila and the other radical pluralists continued to insist on that distinctiveness and tried to reshape the state's Indigenous policy to take account of it.

A Socialist at the Helm: Luis Chávez Orozco

In May 1939, Luis Chávez Orozco addressed a gathering of linguists in Mexico City. "We all agree," he said, "that, whatever the economic, racial, and historical factors that have shaped the spirit of the contemporary indigenous [people], that spirit . . . must be respected in all its higher manifestations, without attempting to denature or even redirect them."[104] This was the radical pluralist view in its most basic form, and it stood in sharp contrast to the assimilationist goals of mainstream *indigenismo* up to that point. Crucially, the statement came from the head of the Mexican government agency devoted to Indigenous policy. Chávez Orozco took over as head of the DAI at the start of 1939. Though his tenure was brief, lasting only until 1940, during that span he offered institutional support for radical pluralist views, granting them greater public visibility and resonance than they might otherwise have obtained.

Born in Irapuato, Guanajuato, in 1901, Chávez Orozco is principally known today as an economic historian. Focusing mainly on the colonial era, he was one of the pioneers in applying materialist methods to Mexican history. He began working in the Mexican state apparatus in 1930, first in the Secretariat of Foreign Relations, then from 1933 onward at the SEP, where he rose to become undersecretary in 1936.[105] During that time he also published scholarly works on the Maya and Nahua civilizations and a two-volume history of Mexico.[106] Though not a PCM member, Chávez Orozco was avowedly Marxist in his approach and was a vocal supporter of Cárdenas's "socialist education" policy.[107] His leftist convictions played a role during his tenure as head of the DAI, too. Chávez Orozco not only promoted the work of radical *indigenistas*—as we have seen, he brought Fabila's study of the Yaquis to Cárdenas's attention and published it—he also sponsored a series of initiatives that influenced state policy.

Prominent among these was his support for bilingual education. In the 1930s, mainstream *indigenismo* frowned upon bilingualism, since it delayed the process of *castellanización*—meaning not just Spanish-language literacy, but the use of Spanish as the primary language. In May 1939, Chávez Orozco convened the First Assembly of Philologists and Linguists. Among those attending were the French anthropologist Jacques Soustelle, the US linguist Morris Swadesh, and William Cameron Townsend, a US Protestant missionary and personal friend of Cárdenas. There were also European émigrés based in Mexico, such as Paul Kirchhoff.[108] Mexican attendees included radical pluralists such as Mendizábal and Vivó, who wrote a series of articles on the Assembly for *El Nacional*.[109] There were also seventeen Indigenous delegates, including speakers of Maya languages and representatives of the Mixtec, Nahua, Otomí, Zapotec, Yaqui, and other peoples.[110]

The spread of attendees partly reflects the increasingly transnational nature of Indigenous expertise at this time. But it was also a strategic choice on Chávez Orozco's part, specifically intended to bolster the position of the radical pluralists. Years later, when he recalled organizing the Assembly, Chávez Orozco referred to "an awkward circumstance": "Anyone in Mexico who advocated the use of [native] languages for education of the indigenous was automatically denounced as someone who was imitating Soviet methods."[111] The remark suggests that the radical pluralists were pushing against the current on two counts: because of their critique of mainstream *indigenismo*, but also because of their apparent endorsement of a Communist model.

These ideological headwinds would grow stronger in the 1940s, but for now, Chávez Orozco was able to maneuver around them. As he later recalled, "To get around the natural obstacle that [anti-Communist] attacks of that kind implied, I assembled the specialists and asked them the question, telling them I was perplexed, I didn't know what to do . . . and that I was inviting them to study the issue and resolve it."[112] Inviting foreign specialists to the Assembly allowed support for Indigenous-language education to emerge as a scientific consensus across ideological lines. When someone like Mendizábal supported bilingual education, it might come across as suspect; he spoke highly of the Soviet nationalities model at the Assembly.[113] But most of the foreign specialists could scarcely be accused of Communist sympathies; Townsend, for instance, saw native-language education as being useful for missionary purposes. The Assembly's final resolutions mainly focused on scholarly endeavors, calling for further study of alphabets and dialects, as well as recommending the creation of a Council for Indigenous Languages. But the Assembly also strongly endorsed the need for literacy in Indigenous languages and for rural teachers to be drawn from among Indigenous groups.[114] In effect, the Assembly produced an undeclared alliance between Mexican Marxist *indigenistas* on the one hand, and US and European anthropologists and missionaries on the other. In practical terms, the main result was that the Mexican state began to encourage bilingual education programs. The best known of these was Swadesh's Proyecto Tarasco, which was launched after the 1939 Assembly and became the prototype for many subsequent efforts.[115]

Chávez Orozco's support for bilingual education was part of a broader emphasis on scientific expertise during his tenure at the DAI. In the late 1930s, both the DAI and the radical pluralists were closely involved in new institutions created for the study of Mexico's Indigenous peoples—and thus in the formation of Mexican anthropology as a discipline. Among the most important of these was the Instituto Politécnico Nacional (IPN; National Polytechnic Institute), founded by Cárdenas in 1936. Mendizábal played an active role in its establishment and was among its first teachers of anthropology.[116] As well as having a strong focus on Indigenous linguistics, the IPN's anthropologists devoted significant attention to present-day material conditions. Mendizábal founded the School of Rural Medicine at the IPN, arguing for faster training and a massive expansion in the number of doctors in Indigenous areas. (The proposal was greeted with hostility by medical professionals and the Department of Public Health, which complained that it would only produce "folk healers.")[117]

The link between ethnographic research and the practicalities of state policy was, of course, not new. But previously, under the aegis of the SEP, it had taken highly assimilationist forms, focusing on forced-pace cultural and linguistic transformation. The creation of the DAI in 1936 signaled a weakening of this impulse. Under Chávez Orozco, the DAI's relationship with the IPN and outside experts created an alternative pole for knowledge and policymaking around Indigenous issues. In the short term, the collaboration between Chávez Orozco's DAI and the leftists at the IPN opened up spaces for the radical pluralist view. One such space was the linguists' Assembly of May 1939. But the most significant platform by far was the Pátzcuaro Congress of 1940.

ZENITH AND ECLIPSE

The Pátzcuaro Congress marked the peak of the radical pluralists' institutional reach. But it was also a turning point, signaling the start of a steady reassertion of mainstream *indigenismo*'s assimilationist line. Cárdenas himself was pivotal to that shift; in his speech at the opening of the congress on April 14, he spoke of the paramount need to "Mexicanize the Indian" and reaffirmed the singularity of the country's national destiny. To mix two astronomical metaphors, Pátzcuaro was radical pluralism's zenith but also the moment when its eclipse began.

It was somewhat fortuitous that the congress was held in Mexico at all. When the idea of a hemispheric gathering of *indigenistas* had been raised in 1938 at the Pan-American Conference in Lima, Bolivia had volunteered to host it in La Paz in late 1939.[118] However, with the death of Bolivian president Germán Busch that August, the prospective host country took a sharp conservative turn, and the congress could no longer rely on state support. Mexico stepped into the breach, with Cárdenas offering to host a rescheduled congress the following April.[119]

The Mexican government was well placed to take charge of the arrangements: One of its leading *indigenistas* had been closely involved in organizing the abortive La Paz event. As Mexican ambassador to Peru, Moisés

Sáenz had attended the 1938 Pan-American Conference in Lima and had strongly backed the idea of an *indigenista* congress, persuading representatives from the United States, Guatemala, Colombia, Ecuador, Peru, and Bolivia to sign a draft resolution to that effect.[120] When Mexico took over hosting duties, Sáenz initially took the lead in shaping his country's interventions at the congress.

Sáenz had been a key figure at the SEP, replacing Gamio as undersecretary of education from 1925 to 1930, and throughout the 1930s he continued to do ethnographic research for the SEP and other institutions. For most of that time, he took a strongly assimilationist stance. In 1935 he sent Cárdenas a memo outlining ideas for what would eventually become the DAI. Among the names Sáenz originally proposed were the "Department for the Incorporation of the Indian" and the "Department for the Nationalization of the Indian."[121] In the same memo Sáenz gave a brutally succinct summary of the assimilationist view, arguing that "the Indian, as an Indian, has no future in Mexico." For the Indigenous, therefore, the "logical exit is to become Mexican."[122]

Yet within a few years, Sáenz's views had moved closer to those of the radical pluralists. In 1939 he published *México Íntegro* (Integral Mexico), a book of essays in which he described the country as "a living panorama of peoples and cultures."[123] The Mexican state had so far taken the wrong approach to this diversity, he argued. "We are unilateral," wrote Sáenz: "We approach the Indian as *Mexicans*, in order to impose on him a national theory and even a social creed; we carry a predetermined program." Besides criticizing *indigenismo*'s existing approach, Sáenz argued that Indigenous forms of political organization were an untapped resource. "Has it occurred to us, for example, that certain Indian institutions . . . might serve as effective and permanent forms of government . . .? Has it occurred to us that perhaps it would be possible to establish a kind of 'indirect government' through which the Indian would preserve his own organization, articulating it with that of the rest of the country?"[124] In posing these questions, Sáenz was effectively advocating what would later be called Indigenous autonomy. The resemblance between his views and those of the radical pluralists is striking. For Sáenz, respect for Indigenous political institutions would help, rather than hinder, the cause of Mexican national unity.

Sáenz's shifting views exemplify the relative openness of mainstream *indigenismo* to radical pluralist ideas in the run-up to Pátzcuaro. In practical terms, Sáenz was also partly responsible for radical pluralism's visibility at this pivotal moment. In January 1939 he wrote to Cárdenas suggesting that a special committee be set up to strategize for the forthcoming *indigenista* congress, at that moment still due to be held in Bolivia. The president agreed, replying that he had put Chávez Orozco in charge of that committee.[125] The DAI chief in turn delegated much of this work to Mendizábal; in April 1939 he informed Cárdenas by telegram that "committee chaired Mendizábal and charged with drafting presentation working very actively."[126] Radical pluralists were thus centrally involved in the preparations for the congress even before Mexico had agreed to host the event.

PLURALISM AT PÁTZCUARO

At the Pátzcuaro Congress itself, although the radical pluralists were a minority within the Mexican delegation, it is striking how prominent they were. Chávez Orozco presided over the entire event, Mendizábal was head of the program committee, and Fabila and Vivó were both advisers to the Mexican delegation. The latter three all presented papers, as did Lombardo Toledano and leftists linked to the IPN's new anthropology program, such as Kirchhoff. Several of the radical pluralists used their platform at Pátzcuaro to push for one or other component of their shared agenda, in one case making an overt case for Indigenous self-determination.

Lombardo Toledano referred to the need to "respect . . . the nuclei of indigenous [people] and all their characteristics, helping them to develop with the aim of their incorporation into the economy of their country."[127] Lombardo used *incorporation* here in a purely economic sense, rather than implying sociocultural assimilation. The goal was a more harmonious form of Mexican national unity, in which diversity would be maintained. A few months earlier, in December 1939, he had addressed the National Education Conference, laying out the same logic more explicitly: "It is not the forcible unification of language that will create the *patria*, but the voluntary unification of consciousnesses."[128]

Lombardo's most surprising intervention at Pátzcuaro, however, was a proposal for a "new political-territorial division of zones inhabited by the indigenous." He argued that the current structure of the Mexican state imposed an "arbitrary division" on Indigenous communities, separating "what geography, economics, and history have united." To that end, he suggested that legislation be adopted "to form municipalities or homogeneous districts rather than arbitrarily dividing the indigenous masses into different jurisdictions."[129]

Though little remarked on in the scholarly literature, perhaps because of its apparently technical character, Lombardo was quietly calling for the map of Mexico to be redrawn. The idea of forming homogeneous Indigenous districts resembled the Soviet system of "autonomous republics" embedded within the USSR's subunits. These entities had been created to consolidate minority groups into territorial blocs, rather than splitting them across units created by the tsarist authorities. Lombardo's Pátzcuaro proposal similarly aimed to reconfigure Mexico's internal boundaries based on the spatial distribution of Indigenous groups.

Yet it left critical questions unanswered. How would these Indigenous territories be governed, and by whom? Would they be added to Mexico's existing political architecture or stand apart from it? Though modest in its stated ambitions, Lombardo's Pátzcuaro proposal could have raised far-reaching questions about the political relationship between Indigenous groups and the Mexican state, perhaps even setting in motion rival claims to sovereignty. Yet none of these issues were addressed in the bland administrative language of the proposal or in the final version of it approved as Resolution XL by the congress.[130]

Others presenting at Pátzcuaro also raised the idea of Indigenous self-determination. María de los Ángeles Azcárate, chairwoman of the National Committee for the Aid of Indigenous Children (and also Chávez Orozco's wife), did so indirectly in her presentation on Indigenous children's welfare. Adopting the same basic framing and terminology as the radical pluralists, she referred to Indigenous groups as "national minorities" and praised the Cárdenas government for "really giving the Indians their rights to exist and to self-determine [*autodeterminarse*]."[131]

When Jorge Vivó took the podium, he made a more direct call for self-determination. He gave two presentations at Pátzcuaro. The first focused principally on economic questions affecting Indigenous groups, suggesting a range of measures to improve their material situation—from the provision of irrigation and electricity to the protection of Indigenous handicrafts.[132] Vivó's second presentation, titled "Tribal and National Features of the Indigenous Problem," set out the principles underlying his previous recommendations and in the process returned delegates to the same fundamental questions with which Comintern delegates had grappled in Buenos Aires and Moscow over a decade earlier.[133]

Vivó began his remarks with a series of questions: Were Indigenous people a race, a class, or a caste? Or did they constitute national minorities, or nations in their own right? His answers revealed some curious modulations in his thinking, even as the broad framework remained consistent. First, in arguing against the idea that Indigenous people were a distinct race, Vivó drew on contemporary anthropologists' classification of humanity into three broad racial groups—"white," "yellow," and "black"—and placed Indigenous peoples within the second of these, alongside people from East Asia. This kind of crude race thinking was common enough at the time, but Vivó deployed these racial categories only to assert their irrelevance in understanding what was specific to Indigenous people. The same was true of the concepts of class and caste. The latter in his view only applied to the hierarchies of the colonial period, while class could not account for Indigenous oppression as such, since Indigenous people belonged to different class categories—mainly the peasantry and the proletariat. And while the Indigenous were certainly subject to "a specific form of discrimination" that placed them in worse conditions than their class peers, in his view this did not "exclude them from the classes to which they belong."[134]

Were Indigenous peoples, then, national minorities or nations? For Vivó these two categories were interlinked: In order to constitute national minorities, they had to at least potentially be nations in their own right. According to Vivó, not all Indigenous groups met the criteria—and the reasons for this were mainly historical. Colonization, *mestizaje*, the spread of the Spanish language, and successive forms of economic exploitation had in his view obstructed the development of Indigenous groups into fully fledged nations. The advent of capitalism, meanwhile, had widened imbalances between groups, marginalizing many while accelerating the national development of others. The result, as Vivó saw it, was that some groups "had not gone past the tribal stage of social organization" while others—he named Mexico's Maya people, the Quechuas and Aymaras of the Andes, and the Guaraní in Paraguay—possessed "national features" that might lead them to become nations "in a not-too-distant future."[135]

Vivó's arguments drew on the same idea of a continuum of national development that had underpinned Comintern debates on race and nation, and Bolshevik nationalities policy before that. Following a similar logic to that deployed by Haywood with regard to Black people in the United States, Vivó argued that Indigenous peoples would have moved smoothly along that same continuum if their progress had not been blocked by colonialism.

But it was not only Indigenous national development that Vivó sought to historicize. Across the Americas, nation formation was still in progress, with processes of "national integration" unfolding at different speeds since independence—and with differing degrees of success, in terms of arriving at a common identity and a shared economic life. In effect, Vivó was arguing that many Indigenous groups were incomplete nations within larger nations that were themselves often still unfinished.[136]

For Vivó, the starting point for addressing the Indigenous question had to be "recognition of the right the indigenous have to their free determination." But he recommended a differentiated approach. For Indigenous groups still at what he called the "tribal" stage, in socioeconomic and technological terms, he recommended "if not a full self-determination . . . [then] full respect for their social organization." For groups he identified as "advanced," he called for self-determination, which he then defined as a suite of enhanced rights. These included the right to elect their own local authorities and representatives to national bodies, the right to conduct their political affairs in their own languages, the right to "adopt the measures for social improvement they deem necessary for their progress and wellbeing," the right to form organizations to advocate for their rights, and civil rights equal to those obtaining in the rest of the country.[137]

What Vivó outlined here—on a selective and highly paternalist basis, to be sure—was a program for Indigenous autonomy. Setting aside the territorial component of earlier Communist thinking, he did not call for separate Indigenous republics, focusing instead on what self-determination could mean within the confines of Mexico. As we have seen, his proposals spanned the realms of politics, economics, and culture, but their common core was a more fundamental principle, unnamed yet implicit throughout: that of the right to democratic representation.

THE TIDE TURNS

Reflecting on the Pátzcuaro Congress in its immediate aftermath, Chávez Orozco claimed that the event had shown that "the old theory of the 'incorporation of the Indian into civilization,' a pretext for better exploiting and oppressing aboriginal peoples, has been rejected." Instead, "there was a recognition of the existence of the personality of the indigenous as something positive and capable of turning into a creative force."[138] In other words, he felt that the assimilationist approach had yielded to a new consensus about the intrinsic value of Indigenous societies.

Yet even as Chávez Orozco was writing these words, the tide had begun to shift back toward assimilationism. The push to "incorporate" the Indigenous that had previously predominated within Mexican *indigenismo* received an unequivocal boost at Pátzcuaro from President Cárdenas. In his address at the opening of the congress, Cárdenas seemed to give some space for a pluralist perspective, insisting that the Indigenous have "the right to demand the recognition of their social personality" and criticizing previous attempts to "de-Indianize and impose foreign customs" on them. Yet while he deemed such methods high-handed, he endorsed the ultimate goal of incorporating the Indigenous in the name of Mexican patriotism. "By respecting his blood, by winning over his feelings, his love of the land and his unyielding tenacity, we will ensure that national sentiment takes root [in the Indigenous]." It was in this context that Cárdenas gave as concise a definition of the assimilationist approach as one could wish for: "Our indigenous problem does not lie in keeping the Indian 'Indian,' nor in indigenizing Mexico, but in Mexicanizing the Indian."[139]

Cárdenas's speech in many ways set the tone for the Pátzcuaro gathering. Many of the presentations praised the Mexican state for advancing the project of *mestizaje* and for its efforts at incorporating the Indigenous into modernity. Delegates from other Latin American countries admired Mexico's efforts, seeing lessons for addressing their own racial and ethnic disparities.[140] In that sense Pátzcuaro was the launch pad for Mexico to project its version of *indigenismo* as a hemispheric model—a process that gathered pace with the foundation of the III, headquartered in Mexico City, in November 1940.

The Pátzcuaro Congress and establishment of the III were the Cárdenas government's last major initiatives on Indigenous issues; in December 1940, Manuel Ávila Camacho succeeded to the presidency. Though Cárdenas had become increasingly cautious since 1938—the nationalization of oil that year marked the high point of his radicalism—the arrival of Ávila Camacho signaled a more conservative turn in Mexican politics. In ideological terms, this meant increased hostility to "foreign" ideas, especially ones with a Marxist or socialist stamp. Those espousing such ideas were no longer welcome in the state apparatus. At the DAI, senior official Ángel Corzo quickly launched an anti-Communist campaign. In February 1941 he wrote to Ávila Camacho promising to expel "all exotic communist theories" and "Soviet agents" from the DAI.[141] One of his main targets was Chávez Orozco, forced out that same year. Elsewhere, anti-Communists targeted initiatives such as Indigenous-language education. In April 1941, teachers at Swadesh's Proyecto Tarasco were accused of being Communists, and although a delegation of Tarascans leapt to their defense, the project was shut down.[142]

This conservative turn went hand in hand with a reassertion of *indigenismo*'s assimilationist strand, albeit now in a revised form. Cárdenas had emphasized economic inequalities and material conditions, breaking with the predominantly cultural approach of the SEP in the 1920s and early 1930s. But from 1940 onward, there would be no equivalent to Cárdenas's redistributive agenda in the countryside. Official *indigenismo* would instead combine the SEP's cultural thrust with a developmentalist impulse, often tied to state-led infrastructural projects that aimed to "integrate" the Indigenous into the national economy.

A combination of patriotism and developmentalism was soon put into action. The DAI's annual report for 1941–42 proudly records the department's "nationalist work," which included handing out two hundred Mexican flags to isolated communities in an attempt to better connect them to "the nationality"—meaning the unitary Mexican nation.[143] In 1943, Ávila Camacho reestablished the SEP's Cultural Missions, and in 1946 he disbanded the DAI, folding its functions back into the SEP. Two years later, Mexico's new Instituto Nacional Indigenista (INI; National Indigenista Institute) began to take the lead on Indigenous policy. For the next four decades, the INI largely worked to support the state's combined agenda of national integration, economic development, and sociocultural incorporation.

"THE PEOPLE ARE ALWAYS CREATORS"

From the 1940s to the 1960s, the figures at the center of this chapter remained involved in Indigenous policy, and in some cases still played prominent public roles. But they no longer stood out as advocates of greater Indigenous autonomy. Lombardo Toledano remained highly visible as a labor leader, while Chávez Orozco, after leaving the DAI in 1941, served as Mexican ambassador in Honduras and then became the first general secretary of the powerful teachers' union, the Sindicato Nacional de Trabajadores de la Educación (SNTE; National Union of Education Workers).[144] Mendizábal died in 1946, having been closely involved in the foundation of the Escuela Nacional de Antropología (ENA; National School of Anthropology) in 1942. Vivó was among the new faculty there, remaining active until only a few years before his death in 1979.[145] Fabila worked for the SEP's Cultural Missions again and in 1954 became a researcher at the INI, conducting fieldwork in many parts of Mexico until his death in 1960.[146]

But the moment for expressing their alternative vision for Mexico's Indigenous people had passed. The eclipse of the radical pluralists meant, among other things, that their contributions to Mexican *indigenismo* and anthropology for a long time went largely overlooked. This chapter focused on their novel adaptation of Communist ideas about self-determination to Mexican conditions. Taken up by the PCM in 1932, the idea of Indigenous self-determination had its greatest resonance outside the party's ranks in the late 1930s, acquiring prominent supporters in Mexican political and intellectual life, in particular among anthropologists and ethnographers. For them, the Soviet "nationalities" model came to signify less a right to territorial separation than recognition of the integrity and autonomy of Indigenous peoples. This involved a rejection of any homogenizing, assimilationist vision of Mexico, seeing the country as a mosaic of peoples and nations, each of which should possess the right to develop according to its own lights. As Fabila put it in the 1950s, reflecting on his work for the SEP in Hueyapan, Puebla, "No people or human grouping, however ignorant and poor it may be, lacks its own aspirations for progress." Taking his distance from the SEP's paternalism, Fabila emphasized instead the need to learn from the Indigenous themselves: "The people are always creators [*El pueblo es siempre creador*]."[147]

In their own time, the radical pluralists' ideas remained a minority current within Mexican *indigenismo*. Nevertheless, by the end of the 1930s they had achieved a certain visibility and had clearly influenced state policy, notably in the realm of bilingual education. Yet although it emphasized Indigenous political agency, radical pluralism wasn't a movement for fomenting or organizing that agency. It was an internal critique of the Mexican state's top-down assimilationist policy, made from within the realm of state policy. While the radical pluralists provided a repertoire of ideas on which later movements could draw, at the time these concepts remained severed from the collective agency that might have given them real substance.

At least one of the radical pluralists seemed aware of the disjuncture between their advocacy of Indigenous autonomy and an approach that was still premised on paternalist, state-led action. In 1941 Fabila published a short text titled "Mexico's Indigenous Problem," in which he warned against forcibly integrating the Indigenous. Directly contradicting Cárdenas's dictum from the previous year, he argued that "the native will not be incorporated into the country's rhythms by trying to Mexicanize him." What was needed, rather, was for the Indigenous "to bring about his own liberation." It should be Indigenous people themselves who managed their day-to-day affairs; the state's role, as Fabila put it in somewhat patronizing terms, was simply to "facilitate, morally and materially, the development of the creative forces lying dormant within our poor Indian."[148]

He then added a cautionary note: If the state was not willing or able to take on this task, "those Indians would have to make their own revolution, to liberate themselves."[149] Fabila seemed to foresee that the Mexican state's approach to the Indigenous question was storing up future challenges, and that the right of Indigenous communities to govern themselves should be a fundamental factor in their liberation, as yet distant and unrealized.

EPILOGUE

———

Afterlives

AUTODETERMINACIÓN RETURNS

On New Year's Day 1994, Alfonso Fabila's prediction that the Indigenous would make their own revolution came to pass. A predominantly Indigenous guerrilla movement seized the town of San Cristóbal de las Casas in Chiapas and launched a rebellion against the Mexican state. With its choice of name, the Ejército Zapatista de Liberación Nacional (EZLN; Zapatista Army of National Liberation) harked back to Mexico's revolutionary past in order to reshape its present. Timed to coincide with the entry into force of the North American Free Trade Agreement, the Zapatista revolt was in large part a protest against the neoliberal policies pursued by Mexican governments since the 1980s. But it was also the high point of a longer wave of Indigenous political mobilization, in which the EZLN was among a number of groups contesting the Mexican government's rule.

Central to that contestation was a repudiation of official *indigenismo*. At the end of 1994, an alliance of twenty Indigenous organizations occupied the Coordinating Center of the National Indigenista Institute (INI) in San Cristóbal de las Casas. Set up in 1960, the center had been at the forefront of government efforts to reach rural Indigenous communities in the country's poorest state. Yet by 1994 many of those communities vehemently rejected the state's approach, denouncing the INI's assimilationist policies and the failure of its attempts to "disappear us or acculturate us."[1]

It might seem ironic that the INI's Chiapas center was targeted by the communities it had been designed to serve. But then, as Fabila and the other radical pluralists had warned decades earlier, official *indigenismo* prioritized the "incorporation" of these communities over what they themselves may have wanted. At the time of his death in 1960, Fabila had been picked to run the INI's new Coordinating Center in Chiapas—the very same one that was occupied in 1994.[2] It is tantalizing to think about how Fabila would have run the INI's operations in Chiapas had he lived. Would he have toed the assimilationist line, or would he have insisted the Indigenous have some margin of autonomy? And by 1994, would the outcome have been any different?

Though it's impossible to know the answers to these questions, we do know where the road taken by official *indigenismo* led. From the 1940s through the late 1960s, during the decades of Mexico's economic "miracle," it focused on the acculturation of the Indigenous into the mestizo mainstream and their integration into national labor markets. Thereafter, *indigenismo*'s path was marked by a prolonged crisis that went hand in hand with the travails of the ruling Partido Revolucionario Institucional (PRI; Institutional Revolutionary Party). After the PRI regime crushed protests by students and workers in Mexico City in 1968, and with economic growth slowing down, its legitimacy began slowly to dwindle. Its *indigenista* institutions, too, became the target of searing criticism. There were two main sources for this, both inspired by the radical upsurge of 1968 and by global anti-colonial currents. On the one hand, Indigenous activists trained by the INI began to raise material demands and claim a political platform for their communities.[3] On the other hand, a new cohort of radical anthropologists rejected the INI's assimilationist policies. In 1970, several rising stars of the discipline assailed the INI's approach as paternalistic, undemocratic, and even "ethnocidal." Guillermo Bonfil Batalla asserted that "the goal of *indigenismo*, brutally put, consists in managing to make the Indian disappear."[4]

Even as criticisms of the INI multiplied, Indigenous communities voiced their grievances against the PRI regime and began to organize independently of the state's corporatist structures. President Luis Echeverría, in office from 1970 to 1976, tried to channel these pressures into manageable institutional forms. In a process brokered by *indigenista* officials, radical anthropologists, and Indigenous organizations—María Muñoz aptly calls it "participatory *indigenismo*"—the INI convened more than fifty regional Indigenous congresses between March and July 1975, and then in that same October, the National Congress of Indigenous Peoples in Pátzcuaro, Michoacán.[5] Thirty-five years after the congress described in chapter 8, this time it was not ethnographers and state officials who took center stage, but Indigenous delegates representing dozens of organizations from across the country.

A document produced at the end of this event reaffirmed the central role played by Indigenous peoples in Mexican history, but at the same time registered their continuing social, economic, and political marginalization. Dubbed the "Pátzcuaro Letter," it noted that the manner of their incorporation into national life thus far had "led to the disintegration of our communities." For that reason, the letter announced, "We proclaim the right to self-determination in regard to the traditional [forms of] government and organization that are proper to us."[6] The letter went on to clarify that the word *autodeterminación* did not imply any desire for separation: "Self-determination for us means conscious integration into the national community and full exercise of [our] democratic rights subject to the constitutional order of the Republic."[7]

There is a remarkable resemblance between the concept of Indigenous self-determination laid out here and the ideas articulated by the radical pluralists—in particular the belief that Indigenous groups should have autonomy within the confines of the existing nation-state. Put forward in the 1930s, this version of *autodeterminación* faded from view in the 1940s, displaced by the assimilationist line. Yet within little more than a generation, it had returned—and with one major difference. What had previously been a minority position had been taken up by a range of Indigenous organizations and was then put forward as the new consensus at a congress convened by the Mexican state.

The appearance of demands for *autodeterminación* in the Pátzcuaro Letter was not a one-off. From the 1970s onward, the term would recur across a wide swathe of Indigenous mobilizations. Some organizations emerged out of the state-led process that led to the Pátzcuaro Congress, including the Consejo Nacional de Pueblos Indígenas (CNPI; National Council of Indigenous Peoples), which gathered the leaders of the "supreme councils" of several ethnic groups. Increasingly, however, Indigenous actors sidestepped the Mexican state's corporatist channels, forming independent entities such as the Movimiento Nacional Indígena (National Indigenous Movement) and the Alianza Nacional de Profesionistas Bilingües Indígenas (National Alliance of Indigenous Bilingual Professionals), established in 1973 and 1976 respectively.[8] In some cases, these movements directly challenged the PRI. In 1973 Zapotec activists in Oaxaca founded the Coalición Obrera, Campesina, Estudiantil del Istmo (COCEI; Coalition of Workers, Peasants, and Students of the Isthmus), which in 1981 won municipal elections in Juchitán, Oaxaca—one of the PRI's first electoral defeats, and an early marker of democratizing pressures to come.[9]

For most of these movements, *autodeterminación* generally meant greater regional or local autonomy. Yet demands for expanded political rights were commonly accompanied by calls for recognition of the plurality of cultures within Mexico. In 1992 a reform to Mexico's Constitution did precisely that, adding an article stating that the country "has a pluricultural composition based originally on its indigenous peoples" and that its laws would "protect and promote the development of their languages, cultures, traditions, customs ... and specific forms of social organization."[10] In 2001 the Mexican Congress revised the constitution once more to recognize "the right of indigenous peoples to free determination [*libre determinación*]," which would be exercised "within a constitutional framework of autonomy." This would guarantee the right of Indigenous peoples to "decide their internal forms of coexistence and social, economic, political and cultural organization," which included electing their own authorities "for the exercise of their own forms of internal government," as well as preserving their languages, cultures, and identities.[11]

These gestures toward Indigenous autonomy were made under serious pressure from below. In the case of the 2001 reform, the spur was the Zapatista rebellion, which shook up Mexican politics and fueled intensive discussions over Indigenous autonomy.[12] The struggles that pushed these issues up the agenda emerged in turn out of long traditions of resistance and self-rule, in which the Indigenous themselves were the driving force. Yet the concrete terms in which demands for autonomy have been couched since the 1970s closely echo terminology developed in previous decades. The radical pluralists of the 1930s provided a repertoire of concepts on which subsequent actors were able to draw—including an understanding of self-determination that emphasized political autonomy within the confines of a plural Mexico. The resemblance between the 1975 Pátzcuaro Letter and the 1992 and 2001 constitutional reforms on the one hand, and some of the radical pluralists' key postulates on the other, is striking. There remains some distance, however, between official "pluriculturalism" and acceptance of the idea, expressed by the radical pluralists and rearticulated separately in 2018 by Mixe activist Yásnaya Elena Aguilar Gil, that Mexico is "not a single nation but a State in which many oppressed nations exist."[13]

This also points to an enigma behind the recurrence of the radical pluralists' ideas. Their legacy is largely overlooked, their work little cited in discussions of Indigenous autonomy from the 1960s to the present.[14] Paradoxically, this neglect may stem in part from broad agreement with their views: Previously marginal positions have now become much more mainstream. It may also be linked to the tainted legacy of Stalinism, which understandably made many scholars reluctant to revisit 1930s debates inspired by Soviet nationalities policy, let alone see them as having any relevance to Mexico's Indigenous peoples. This applies even to radical scholars such as Pablo González Casanova, whose concept of "internal colonialism," first laid out in a 1963 article with regard to Mexico's Indigenous peoples, bears a clear family resemblance to the Communist idea of the Indigenous as "oppressed nationalities" within the Mexican nation-state.[15] From the 1970s onward, on the rare occasions that Mexican scholars and intellectuals did discuss the Soviet model, they gave little indication that it had previously been promoted by the radical pluralists.[16] I have found no evidence that late twentieth-century demands for *autodeterminación* drew directly on the radical pluralists' ideas; no clearly marked trail leads from Vivó's speech at Pátzcuaro in 1940 to the Pátzcuaro Letter of 1975 or to more recent calls for autonomy. Rather, what seems to have occurred is the repeated resurgence, in new forms and put forward by new actors, of a common principle: that people should have the right to determine their own destinies.

GHOSTS OF AUTONOMY

The rising tide of Indigenous mobilization in late twentieth-century Mexico was itself part of a continent-wide phenomenon. Indigenous peoples across the Americas have long pushed for recognition of their rights and greater respect for their cultures, but since the 1970s they have increasingly done so specifically *as Indigenous peoples*. Within this upsurge, demands for autonomy have played a central role. As Dominican Mexican anthropologist Héctor Díaz-Polanco put it in his 1991 book *Regional Autonomy*, paraphrasing Marx and Engels, "A specter is haunting Indoamerica: the specter of autonomy."[17]

Internationally, one of the key markers of the advance of these struggles was the International Labor Organization's adoption, in 1989, of the "Indigenous and Tribal Peoples' Convention" (known as C169). As well as establishing that governments should consult Indigenous peoples on measures that affect them, the convention recognized "the aspirations of these peoples to exercise control over their own institutions, ways of life and economic development and to maintain and develop their identities, languages and religions, within the framework of the States in which they live."[18] Though the convention did not use the terms *autonomy* and *self-determination*, it encapsulated what many movements understood those terms to include. The convention provided Indigenous movements with an internationally legitimized tool for bolstering their claims, and it soon became a yardstick for measuring how far national governments fell short of their commitments.

The progress of Indigenous movements can best be gauged within the national realm. In recent decades, they have achieved some remarkable electoral successes. In Bolivia and Ecuador in the 2000s, Indigenous movements were central to the advent of progressive governments and have remained crucial political players ever since.[19] In 2008–9, both countries adopted new constitutions declaring themselves to be "plurinational states." "Plurinationalism" also entered public debate across Latin America in the 2010s, though the momentum behind it has stalled in recent years. In 2022 Chile's draft constitution asserted the country's "plurinational" character and proposed that Indigenous peoples be granted territorial autonomy; both these measures proved contentious, however, and were among the factors that contributed to the draft being rejected in a referendum—including by many Indigenous people themselves.[20] At the local and regional levels, however, Indigenous communities remain at the forefront of challenges to extractive development, proclaiming instead a model of stewardship of the natural environment.[21]

In parallel with the advance of Indigenous movements, the region has seen a resurgence of Afro-Latino/a organizing, as Black activists and scholars have fought for civil rights and worked to counter the structural effects of racism. In Brazil these efforts built on longer histories of Black political organizing and on the continued example of Black autonomy embodied by *quilombos*, communities historically built by escaped slaves.[22] While contemporary *quilombos* have defended community self-rule and access to land and resources, both in Brazil and elsewhere Black struggles have also taken cultural forms, seeking greater recognition of the roles played by people of African descent. Demands for affirmative action have achieved some notable successes, for example in Brazil through the 2012 enactment of racial quotas in higher education.[23] Despite severe funding cuts to education and the far right's repeated verbal attacks on quotas, especially during Jair Bolsonaro's government in 2019–23, the system remains in place and was even extended in 2023 under pressure from social movements.[24]

In Cuba, the question of race remains highly sensitive. The 1959 Revolution made dramatic early strides in addressing racial disparities, including desegregation of public spaces and nationalization of private schools. The literacy campaign of 1961 opened paths for social advancement for many thousands of poor Cubans, among whom Black people were disproportionately represented.[25] Over time, the socioeconomic transformations wrought by the Revolution had remarkable equalizing effects. As Devyn Spence Benson puts it, "By the 1980s, black and *mulato* Cubans had virtually the same life expectancy, high school education rates, and percentage of professional positions as white Cubans—in sharp contrast to the United States and Brazil."[26]

Yet there are still many ambiguities in the Cuban Revolution's relationship to race. After an initial burst of government action and public debate around racism, the consolidation of the new order was increasingly held up in official discourse as evidence that racism had been overcome. In 1962 Fidel Castro claimed that the Revolution had "eradicated discrimination because of race or sex."[27] Thereafter it became difficult to address racial discrimination without seeming to criticize the Revolution's record. In effect, the "raceless" ideal of Cuban nationalism, as famously articulated by José Martí at the end of the nineteenth century, had been reinstated.[28] In the post-1959 vision of *cubanidad*, the Revolution had finally realized the promises of equality made during the island's long struggle for independence. By the same token, it claimed to have resolved the tension between Black aspirations for equality and the prerogatives of Cuban nationalism, described in chapter 7. But this new unity came at a cost: From now on, to broach the issue of race was to risk accusations of "divisiveness."

In the 1990s, with the fall of Communism and the advent of the "Special Period" in Cuba, racial inequalities began to widen once more on the island. The liberalization of the Cuban economy in the 2010s, combined with uneven flows of remittances from outside the island, followed by a tightening of the US blockade, augmented those disparities, prompting renewed debates on race and inequality. These have been accompanied by a steady increase in positive affirmations of Afro-Cuban identity, especially in the realm of culture and religion. Yet even implicit challenges to the "raceless" ideal continue to cause discomfort—pointing to an underlying disquiet around Black political agency that remains equally common beyond Cuba's shores.

MEANINGS OF FREEDOM

In different ways and in varying circumstances, Black and Indigenous movements in Latin America have ultimately been seeking to redefine the contours of citizenship and to reimagine the nation-state. These movements have had uneven, often uneasy relationships with the radical left. Yet as this book has shown, they share a history of contestation of the nation-state that stretches back to the 1920s, and the questions that animated the radical transnational debates at the center of my study clearly resonate with contemporary contentions over race, nation, equality, and sovereignty.

In the preceding chapters I reconstructed a series of transnational convergences that took place under the dual impact of the Mexican and Russian Revolutions, bringing Latin American leftists into contact with Comintern emissaries, anti-colonial activists, and Black Communists from the United States. Chapter 1 focused on Mexico in the 1920s and described the distinctive brand of internationalism to which these convergences gave rise. In chapter 2 I analyzed the novel anti-imperialist politics that emerged as a result. Premised on the understanding that the major problems besetting Latin America were global and systemic in nature, this radical anti-imperial consensus brought together a range of political currents, from Communists to *campesino* leagues to the exiled members of APRA. However, as chapter 3 recounted, this consensus was pulled apart by a combination of pressures. As well as having divergent attitudes to the Mexican postrevolutionary regime, the components of the anti-imperial milieu also differed fundamentally over questions of political strategy, and above all over how to relate to existing nation-states. Were they to be consolidated in the face of US imperialism or dismantled and remade from below in the name of equality?

These alternatives led in very different directions. At the turn of the 1930s, as I showed in chapter 6, the *apristas* drifted toward an increasing embrace of nationalism and of the nation-state as the main arena for political action. The Communists, meanwhile, questioned the nation-state in increasingly radical terms. The peak expression of this came with the adoption of a policy advocating "national" self-determination for Black and Indigenous peoples.

The idea that the Indigenous and people of African descent should have the right to sovereign self-rule is commonly described as, at best, a piece of Comintern eccentricity, through which Moscow imposed Soviet ideas on the Americas with little regard to local realities—and, ultimately, to little effect. My findings directly contradict this standard picture. In chapters 4 and 5 I analyzed the debates over Black and Indigenous self-determination that ran through the Communist movement in the late 1920s. In chapter 4 I demonstrated that the policy was itself the product of a transnational convergence between Soviet thinking on "nationalities," anti-colonialism, and a Black radicalism informed by Pan-Africanism. First applied in relation to the Black population of the US South, the self-determination policy was the source of heated debates on the problem of race within Latin American Communist parties, which I reconstructed in chapter 5. Far from involving any straightforward imposition of a Comintern line, these debates prompted substantive and often nuanced discussions of race and racism in Latin America, in which delegates tangled not only over questions of strategy but also over their understandings of the past and present of their societies.

Moreover, the self-determination policies adopted by several Latin American Communist parties in the early 1930s were not the outlandish fantasies depicted in many accounts. In chapters 7 and 8 I traced the adoption and consequences of these policies in Cuba and Mexico. In Cuba, the Communist Party's take-up of Black self-determination was inextricably linked to its embrace of anti-racism; indeed, I argued that without the former, the party may not have espoused the latter as fully as it subsequently did. The PCC's advocacy of the right of the Black majority in Oriente to territorial self-determination was a clear indication of the party's commitment to Black liberation: It showed that it was willing to dismantle Cuba in the name of equality. While the PCC dropped the policy in 1935, I argued that it nonetheless had a transformative effect on the party and hence on its role within the island's political landscape.

In Mexico, the impact of the self-determination policy took a different form. Rather than reshaping the Communist Party, it had a more enduring resonance outside the ranks of the PCM, thanks to its adoption by a Marxist current within Mexican *indigenismo*. In the late 1930s these thinkers—many of them working within the state apparatus—adapted the policy to Mexican conditions. They placed less emphasis on territorial separation and greater stress on the right of Indigenous communities to political self-rule.

In this form, the Mexican iteration of the self-determination policy offered a radical vision of Mexico as a "plural nation" made up of many nations, an idea that would resurface in later debates around Indigenous autonomy.

In both the Cuban and Mexican cases, the idea of self-determination encountered many of the same obstacles and counterarguments, and their recurrence also sheds light on the broader trajectory of the Latin American left. As my findings show, many radicals objected to the policy because it involved redefining as incipient "nations" groups that had long been seen as racial minorities. By the same token, this meant recategorizing the legacies of slavery, conquest, and racial discrimination as forms of "national" oppression, to be remedied by granting these groups the right to self-determination. This proposal may have been all the more contentious because it seemed to threaten the integrity of nation-states already deemed to be fragile and incomplete, even after more than a century of independence.

In rejecting the idea of self-determination in the mid-1930s, the Communist left then attempted to develop a progressive variant of patriotism. As part of efforts to form the Popular Front, the anti-imperialist solidarities expressed in the 1920s would be blended with a defense of existing nation-states and a celebration of their discrete histories. It was only at this point—in the wake of a radical questioning of the nation-state—that the Latin American Communist left adopted what would become a characteristic combination of nationalism and anti-imperialism, which proved a potent basis for mobilization throughout the rest of the twentieth century. The names given to many of that century's most transformative events— the Mexican Revolution, the Cuban Revolution—assert their national character, implying a necessary connection between projects for radical social change and the nation-state. Yet as I hope to have shown, that link was far from exclusive or unvarying, and the Latin American left's fusion of nationalism and anti-imperialism was only one of many possible configurations. My aim has been to restore a degree of contingency to that outcome and to show that it came at a cost: The specific interests of Black and Indigenous populations would be subordinated to an ideal of national unity, in which ethnic minorities had little or no say.

The radical transnational debates of the interwar years provided precedents and rough drafts for many of the ideas that would dominate the politics of the Latin American left in the rest of the twentieth century. The anti-imperialist consensus that developed between Communists, *apristas*, peasant leagues, and others in the 1920s would return in other guises, especially in the 1960s, when the Cuban Revolution inspired a wave of solidarity across the region, much as its Mexican predecessor had done. Many of the questions debated in the interwar years—what kind of revolution to wage, what kind of state to establish, and what the rights and roles of racially dominated groups would be within that state—remained urgently relevant to a wide range of political forces. The rifts that opened up in the 1920s likewise proved enduring, evolving into a division between Communists and "populists" that structured bitter struggles within the broad left from the Cold War through the second half of the twentieth century.[29]

The interwar debates on the "national question" also reemerged in the late twentieth century, albeit in new forms, accompanied by other demands, and with better developed, more sophisticated conceptual framings. The exchanges I reconstructed in earlier chapters invoked the possibility of territorial separation, which was certainly one of the scenarios implied by the Soviet-inspired concept of self-determination. Yet to focus on this aspect alone is to miss the true core of the idea, which was to extend the right to self-rule to groups long marginalized and denied that right. Fundamentally it concerned the political right of a people to determine its own destiny. In its most basic form, another word for this idea is *democracy*.

Across a long arc stretching, in many cases, from before independence to the present, Latin American popular movements have struggled not simply to attain democracy but also to expand its reach and redefine its meaning.[30] Going beyond the abstractions of liberal constitutionalism, they have sought to acquire a range of social rights and to give substance to their own visions of justice and sovereignty, as well as to preserve their languages and cultures. Self-determination has often been a catchword encapsulating that quest, as well as a name given to the political means for advancing it, whether in the form of territorial sovereignty or of regional autonomy. The story told in this book illuminates one small part of this history, in which a wide variety of interwar radicals tried to imagine new ways of making revolution, of escaping the pressures of empire, and of outrunning the legacies of racism, in order to arrive at a fuller freedom. The contours of that radical sovereignty have continually shifted, but its light remains steady on the horizon.

ACKNOWLEDGMENTS

In undertaking a transnational project such as this one, I have been highly fortunate in having the freedom to move between several countries and in having access to the resources needed for research in two hemispheres. Thanks to doctoral funding at New York University and a CLIR/Mellon Fellowship in 2018–19, I was able to carry out fieldwork in Mexico, Cuba, Peru, Russia, and the United States. A Kayden Research Grant from the University of Colorado Boulder in the summer of 2023 allowed me to tie up some loose archival ends in Mexico City. At each step of the way, I have benefited immensely from the generosity, knowledge, and friendship of many people, and although the following words seem small next to the many debts incurred, I hope they can convey some of my gratitude.

In Mexico City, I was especially lucky to have the company of family and friends. Irving Reynoso Jaime was generous with his time and knowledge, as were Pablo Yankelevich, Daniela Spenser, Rafael Rojas, and Sebastián Rivera Mir. I also thank Paula López Caballero for highly generative conversations that led to a fruitful and ongoing collaboration. On the archival front, I am grateful to the staff at the Archivo General de la Nación and the Archivo Histórico Genaro Estrada at the Secretaría de Relaciones Exteriores; to the comrades at the Centro de Estudios del Movimiento Obrero y Socialista; to Eréndira Reyes at the Archivo Histórico of the Escuela Nacional de Antropología e Historia; to Mónica Montes Flores at the Sala de Arte Público Siqueiros; and to Enrique Gutiérrez Alonso at the Universidad Obrera de México. I also thank the staff at the Biblioteca Nacional de México; the Biblioteca Nacional de Antropología e Historia; the Biblioteca Lerdo de Tejada; the Fideicomiso Archivos Plutarco Elías Calles y Fernando Torreblanca; the Centro de Estudios Filosóficos, Políticos y Sociales Vicente Lombardo Toledano; la Fototeca Nacional; and the Biblioteca Manuel Gamio at PUIC-UNAM. Special thanks must go to Ariel Zúñiga Laborde, who kindly allowed me to spend several days working through his grandfather's back issues of *El Machete*, and to María Estela Duarte for putting me in contact with Don Ariel and with Rafael Doníz, whose photograph of Diego Rivera's mural *El Agitador* graces the cover of this book.

In Havana, I thank Belkis Quesada at the Instituto de Historia de Cuba and Marcia Peñalver Armenderos and Henry Heredia at the Instituto Cubano de Investigación Cultural Juan Marinello for making my journeys to the island possible. At the Instituto de Historia, I was lucky to draw on the archival expertise of Rosa Ana Roque Martínez; Nirma Rabal, Gloria Martínez, and Concepción Allende provided crucial assistance. Thanks also to the staff at the Archivo Nacional de Cuba and the Biblioteca Nacional José Martí. Personal thanks must also go to Julio César Guanche, Caridad Massón, Frank García Hernández, and Pável Contreras.

In Holguín, I owe a tremendous debt to the historians Mayra San Miguel Aguilar and Hernel Pérez Concepción. As well as providing excellent company and invaluable expertise, they helped set up my trips to Rafael Freyre (formerly Santa Lucía) and Tacajó, sites of sugar mill occupations in 1933. I thank Enrique Doimeadiós Cuenca for accompanying me to Rafael Freyre, and to Georgelina Noris Ochoa for her memories; in Tacajó, I thank Víctor Fernández and Gaspar Tellería San Juan for their hospitality. At the Archivo Histórico Provincial de Holguín, I am very grateful for the help of María Belén Batista Hidalgo, Leonida Torres Ledesma, and Esperanza Velázquez Toranzo. In Santiago, Julio Corbea and Reinaldo Suárez Suárez gave me a warm welcome and many ideas, energizing me for the work ahead; and I learned a great deal from Joel Mourlot and Concepción Portuondo López. I also thank the staff of the Archivo Histórico Provincial de Santiago de Cuba and the Biblioteca Elvira Cape.

In Russia, Victor Jeifets has been an extremely generous colleague, and I am grateful to Andrei Schelchkov and to Svetlana Rozental and the archivists at RGASPI. Outside the archive, I thank Ilya Budraitskis for comradely conversations, and Konstantin Kharitonov for giving me a tour of the Comintern's last headquarters in the summer of 2018. Other portions of my research were conducted in the United States and in Peru. I thank the staff of the National Archives and Records Administration in College Park, Marlyand, and the Benson Latin American Collection at the University of Texas Austin; I am especially grateful to Joan Neuberger for putting me up in Austin. I also thank the staff at the Biblioteca Nacional del Perú and at the library of the Pontificia Universidad Católica del Perú.

At NYU, I was tremendously lucky to have Sinclair Thomson as my main adviser. He immeasurably improved this project at every stage, offering perceptive comments and advice with an inspiring combination of enthusiasm and calm. It was a great privilege to work closely with scholars of the caliber of Ada Ferrer, Barbara Weinstein, and Greg Grandin, and I thank them deeply for their intellectual and professional guidance and their personal kindness. I also thank Lara Putnam for engaging so generously with my work.

I am much obliged to Claudio Lomnitz, Kris Manjapra, and Kirsten Weld for their insightful reading of my manuscript during a postdoctoral fellowship at Princeton. I am also grateful to Jeremy Adelman for his sound advice, to Gabriela Nouzeilles and the staff of the Program in Latin American Studies, and to Susana Draper, Shane Dillingham, and Karin Rosemblatt for their thoughtful comments on an early version of chapter 8.

At CU Boulder, I presented a version of chapter 1 to the History Department's Faculty Seminar and was bowled over by the generosity and depth of my colleagues' engagement; I am especially grateful to Robert Ferry for his astute comments. I also thank the two anonymous reviewers for the *Hispanic American Historical Review*, in which a version of chapter 7 appeared, and Michael Goebel, who commented on an early version of chapter 2.

Heartfelt thanks must go to my agent, Zoë Pagnamenta; to my editor, Enrique Ochoa Kaup; and to rest of the team at University of California Press. I must also thank the two anonymous reviewers for their excellent suggestions, which really helped me improve the finished manuscript. I am also greatly indebted to Sharon Langworthy for her meticulous and thoughtful copyediting work.

I remain immensely grateful for the support and comradeship I have received over the years from so many people. There are too many to list one by one, and I hope I will be forgiven for not thanking everyone by name. Special mentions, though, must go to Sara Kozameh, Cayetana Adrianzén Ponce, Kyle Shybunko, Miriam Pensack, Rachel Nolan, and David Klassen.

Finally, I thank my family for their constant support: Michael Wood, Elena Uribe, Gaby Wood, Patrick Wood, Holly Chatham, Ava Turner, and Beatrice Turner. And last but most of all, I thank Colette Perold. Words cannot convey how much I owe to your love, your generosity, and your thoughtfulness, not to mention your impeccable editorial and political judgment. Thank you for being with me on this journey and for accompanying me and Remy on all the ones to come.

NOTES

The repositories consulted for this book use a variety of systems for classifying and organizing their material, with different words denoting successive levels of the archival hierarchy. Files from the Russian State Archive for Social and Political History (RGASPI) are identified using numbers attached to three terms: *Fond* (literally "fund"), which is the highest-level term; *opis'* (register), the second highest; and *delo* (file), denoting the individual file. In the notes I follow the archive's own usage in abbreviating these terms respectively as F., op. and d. The Mexican and Cuban archives consulted generally use one of two terms for the top level of the hierarchy within a given collection: *caja* (box) or *legajo* (file). An individual file is then identified as a *ficha* or *expediente* (record/file). I abbreviate *legajo* as leg. and *expediente* as exp.

INTRODUCTION

1. See Carlos Illades, *Las otras ideas: Estudio sobre el primer socialismo en México, 1850–1935* (Ediciones Era, 2008) and Kirwin Shaffer, *Anarchists of the Caribbean: Countercultural Politics and Transnational Networks in the Age of US Expansion* (Cambridge University Press, 2020).

2. On the history of anarchism in Latin America, see Angel Cappelletti, *Anarchism in Latin America* (AK Press, 2017), and the essays in Geoffroy de Laforcade and Kirwin Shaffer, eds, *In Defiance of Boundaries: Anarchism in Latin American History* (University Press of Florida, 2015).

3. The standard work on the history of the Comintern as a whole is Pierre Broué, *Histoire de l'Internationale communiste, 1919–1943* (Fayard, 1997); on Latin America specifically, see Manuel Caballero, *Latin America and the Comintern, 1919–1943* (Cambridge University Press, 1986).

4. On the ill-fated Communist uprising in El Salvador in 1932, see Jeffrey Gould and Aldo Lauria-Santiago, *To Rise in Darkness: Revolution, Repression, and Memory in El Salvador, 1920–1932* (Duke University Press, 2008).

5. For a critical account of the Comintern's ultimate subordination to Soviet foreign-policy priorities, see Fernando Claudín, *The Communist Movement: The Crisis of the Communist International* (Monthly Review Press, 1975).

6. Deborah Yashar, "The Left and Citizenship Rights," in Steven Levitsky and Kenneth Roberts, eds., *The Resurgence of the Latin American Left* (Johns Hopkins University Press, 2011), 192. On the recurrence of this view, see Kevin Young, introduction to Young, ed., *Making the Revolution: Histories of the Latin American Left* (Cambridge University Press, 2019), 1–3.

7. See for example the essays by Marc Becker, Kevin Young and Betsy Konefal in Young, *Making the Revolution*; see also Marc Becker, *Indians and Leftists in the Making of Ecuador's Modern Indigenous Movements* (Duke University Press, 2008); Jessica Graham, *Shifting the Meaning of Democracy: Race, Politics, and Culture in the United States and Brazil* (University of California Press, 2019), ch. 1; and Margaret Stevens, *Red International and Black Caribbean: Communists in New York City, Mexico and the West Indies, 1919–1939* (Pluto Books, 2017).

8. For recent studies centering the lives of militants, see Brigitte Studer, *Travellers of the World Revolution: A Global History of the Communist International* (Verso, 2023) and *The Transnational World of the Cominternians* (Palgrave, 2015); Lisa Kirschenbaum, *International Communism and the Spanish Civil War: Solidarity and Suspicion* (Cambridge University Press, 2015); and Elizabeth McGuire, *Red at Heart: How Chinese Communists Fell in Love with the Russian Revolution* (Oxford University Press, 2018).

9. For a concise overview, see Oleksa Drachewych, "The Communist Transnational? Transnational Studies and the History of the Comintern," *History Compass* 17, no. 2 (2019).

10. Among Ricardo Melgar Bao's many publications, see notably "The Anti-Imperialist League of the Americas Between the East and Latin America," *Latin American Perspectives* 35, no. 2 (2008): 9–24; and see Daniel Kersffeld, *Contra el imperio: Historia de la Liga Antimperialista de las Américas* (Siglo XXI, 2012). As well as their own scholarly essays, Victor and Lazar Jeifets have produced an invaluable resource: *América Latina en la Internacional Comunista, 1919–1943: Diccionario biográfico* (Ariadna Ediciones, 2015; hereafter *Diccionario biográfico*.) See also the essays in Marc Becker et al., eds., *Transnational Communism Across the Americas* (University of Illinois Press, 2023).

11. See for example Benedict Anderson, *Under Three Flags: Anarchism and the Anti-Colonial Imagination* (Verso, 2005); Ilham Khuri-Makdisi, *The Eastern Mediterranean and the Making of Global Radicalism, 1860–1914* (University of California Press, 2010); Kris Manjapra, *Age of Entanglement: German and Indian Intellectuals Across Empire* (Harvard University Press, 2010); and Tim Harper, *Underground Asia: Global Revolutionaries and the Assault on Empire* (Belknap Press, 2021).

12. Minkah Makalani, *In the Cause of Freedom: Radical Black Internationalism from Harlem to London, 1917–1939* (University of North Carolina Press, 2011); Susan Pennybacker, *From Scottsboro to Munich: Race and Political Culture in 1930s*

Britain (Princeton University Press, 2009). On Paris, see Jennifer Boittin, *Colonial Metropolis: The Urban Grounds of Anti-Imperialism and Feminism in Interwar Paris* (University of Nebraska Press, 2010), and Michael Goebel, *Anti-Imperial Metropolis: Interwar Paris and the Seeds of Third World Nationalism* (Cambridge University Press, 2015). On New York as a Caribbean hub, see Sandra Pujals, "A 'Soviet Caribbean': The Comintern, New York's Immigrant Community, and the Forging of Caribbean Visions, 1931–1936," *Russian History* 41 (2014): 255–268.

13. See Sebastián Rivera Mir, *Militantes de la izquierda latinoamericana en México, 1920–1934: Prácticas políticas, redes y conspiraciones* (El Colegio de México, 2018); Christina Heatherton, *Arise! Global Radicalism in the Era of the Mexican Revolution* (University of California Press, 2022); and Thomas Lindner, *A City Against Empire: Transnational Anti-Imperialism in Mexico City, 1920–1930* (University of Liverpool Press, 2023).

14. Nancy Appelbaum et al., eds., *Race and Nation in Modern Latin America* (University of North Carolina Press, 2003); Frank André Guridy, *Forging Diaspora: Afro-Cubans and African Americans in a World of Empire and Jim Crow* (University of North Carolina Press, 2010); Karin Rosemblatt, *The Science and Politics of Race in Mexico and the United States, 1910–1950* (University of North Carolina Press, 2018); and Micol Seigel, *Uneven Encounters: Making Race and Nation in Brazil and the United States* (Duke University Press, 2009).

15. Juliet Hooker, "Indigenous Inclusion/Black Exclusion: Race, Ethnicity and Multicultural Citizenship in Latin America," *Journal of Latin American Studies* 37, no. 2 (2005): 285–310; Peter Wade, *Race and Ethnicity in Latin America* (Pluto Press, 1997); and Barbara Weinstein, "Erecting and Erasing Boundaries: Can We Combine the 'Indo' and the 'Afro' in Latin American Studies?," *Estudios Interdisciplinarios de América Latina y el Caribe* 19, no. 1 (2008): 129–144.

16. Jan C. Jansen and Jürgen Osterhammel, *Decolonization: A Short History* (Princeton University Press, 2017); Jörg Fisch, *The Right of Self-Determination of Peoples: The Domestication of an Illusion* (Cambridge University Press, 2015); and Eric Weitz, "Self-Determination: How a German Enlightenment Idea Became the Slogan of National Liberation and a Human Right," *American Historical Review* 120, no. 2 (2015): 462–496.

17. On this broader ferment, see Hakim Adi, *Pan-Africanism and Communism: The Communist International, Africa and the Diaspora, 1919–1939* (Africa World Press, 2013); Adom Getachew, *Worldmaking After Empire: The Rise and Fall of Self-Determination* (Princeton University Press, 2019); and Lara Putnam, *Radical Moves: Caribbean Migrants and the Politics of Race in the Jazz Age* (University of North Carolina Press, 2013). See also the essays in Erez Manela and Heather Streets-Salter, eds., *The Anticolonial Transnational: Imaginaries, Mobilities, and Networks in the Struggle Against Empire* (Cambridge University Press, 2023).

18. Getachew, *Worldmaking After Empire*, 2–3.

19. Alberto Flores Galindo, *La agonía de Mariátegui* (Editorial Revolución, 1991); Marc Becker, "Mariátegui, the Comintern, and the Indigenous Question in Latin America," *Science and Society* 70, no. 4 (2006): 450–479; Anne Garland

Mahler, "The Red and the Black in Latin America: Sandalio Junco and the 'Negro Question' from an Afro-Latin American Perspective," *American Communist History* 17, no. 1 (2018): 16–32; and Ricardo Melgar Bao, "La IC frente al dilema raza y nación en América Latina," *Memoria* 27 (1989): 337–342.

20. As work by other scholars shows, the issues raised in these countries were also present elsewhere: see for example Olga Ulianova, "Levantamiento campesino de Lonquimay y la Internacional Comunista," *Estudios públicos* 89 (2003): 173–223; and Jessica Graham, "A virada antirracista do Partido Comunista do Brasil, a Frente Negra Brasileira e a Açao Integralista Brasileira na década de 1930," in Flávio Gomes and Petrônio Domingues, eds., *Políticas da raça: Experiências e legados da abolição e da pós-emancipação no Brasil* (Selo Negro Edições, 2014), 353–375.

21. AHR Editors, "Introduction to AHR Forum: Transnational Lives in the Twentieth Century," *American Historical Review* 118, no. 1 (2013): 45.

22. On the intersecting scales of micro- and global history, see Francesca Trivellato, "Is There a Future for Italian Microhistory in the Age of Global History?," *California Italian Studies* 2, no. 1 (2011).

23. On the experience of navigating the differences between US and Cuban racial categories, see Devyn Spence Benson, *Antiracism in Cuba: The Unfinished Revolution* (University of North Carolina Press, 2016), 25–29.

CHAPTER 1. "OUR INTERNATIONALISM"

1. "No tuvo precedente el homenaje a Zapata," *Excélsior*, April 12, 1924, 2da sección, 7.

2. Víctor Raúl Haya de la Torre, "Emiliano Zapata, apóstol y mártir del agrarismo mexicano," in Haya de la Torre, *Obras completas*, vol. 1 (Librería-Editorial Juan Mejía Baca, 1977), 35–38.

3. Haya, "Emiliano Zapata," 37; "No tuvo precedente."

4. Haya, "Emiliano Zapata," 37.

5. On the emergence of the postrevolutionary order, see the landmark essays in Gilbert Joseph and Daniel Nugent, eds., *Everyday Forms of State Formation: Revolution and the Negotiation of Rule in Modern Mexico* (Duke University Press, 1994).

6. On Mexico's role in the interwar system, see Christy Thornton, *Revolution in Development: Mexico and the Governance of the Global Economy* (University of California Press, 2021).

7. "Vozzvanie k trudiashchimsia massam vsekh stran," 21 December 1917, in *Dekrety Sovetskoi vlasti, t. 1, 25 oktiabria 1917 g.–16 marta 1918 g.* (Politizdat, 1957), 188–190.

8. Daniela Spenser, *Stumbling Its Way Through Mexico: The Early Years of the Communist International* (University of Alabama Press, 2011), 91.

9. Dalia Muller, *Cuban Émigrés and Independence in the Nineteenth-Century Gulf World* (University of North Carolina Press, 2016), ch. 4.

10. Cappelletti, *Anarchism in Latin America*, 291–302.

11. For an intensive chronicle of this network and its participants, see Claudio Lomnitz, *The Return of Comrade Ricardo Flores Magón* (Zone Books, 2015).

12. On Roy's time in Mexico, see Daniel Kent Carrasco, "M. N. Roy en México: Cosmopolitismo intelectual y contingencia política en la creación del PCM," in Carlos Illades, ed., *Camaradas: Nueva historia del comunismo en México* (Fondo de Cultura Económica, 2017), 37–71. On the "slackers," see Dan La Botz, "American 'Slackers' in the Mexican Revolution: International Proletarian Politics in the Midst of a National Revolution," *Americas* 62, no. 4 (2006): 563–590.

13. Leticia Reina, *Indio, campesino y nación en el siglo XX mexicano: Historia e historiografía de los movimientos rurales* (Siglo XXI, 2011), 55–63. See also Victor Jeifets and Irving Reynoso Jaime, "Del Frente Único a clase contra clase: comunistas y agraristas en el México posrevolucionario, 1919–1930," *Izquierdas* 19 (2014): 15–40, and Roger Bartra, *Los herederos de Zapata: Movimientos campesinos posrevolucionarios en México 1920–1980* (Ediciones Era, 1985), ch. 3.

14. Liga de Comunidades Agrarias del Estado de Veracruz (LCAEV), *El agrarismo en México: La cuestión agraria y el problema campesino* (n.p., 1924), 23. On the Veracruz *liga*'s origins, see Heather Fowler-Salamini, *Agrarian Radicalism in Veracruz, 1920–38* (University of Nebraska Press, 1978), 25–47.

15. Jeifets and Jeifets, *Diccionario biográfico*, 233–35.

16. Benedikt Behrens, "El movimiento inquilinario de Veracruz, México, 1922–1927: Una rebelión de mujeres," *Journal of Iberian and Latin American Research* 6, no. 1 (2000): 57–92.

17. "Rafael" and "D García" to Edgar [Stirner], 21 April 1923 and 3 May 1923, Russian State Archive of Social and Political History (hereafter RGASPI), F. 495, op. 105, d. 33: 20, 30.

18. Manuel Díaz Ramírez to Comintern, 14 September 1923, RGASPI, F. 495, op. 108, d. 33: 43.

19. Galván speech in Jalapa, 27 November 1924, RGASPI, F. 535, op. 2, d. 97: 4–5.

20. Galván speech, 27 November 1924, RGASPI, F. 535, op. 2, d. 97: 7.

21. Protocols of First Krestintern Congress, 10 October 1923, RGASPI, F. 535, op. 1, d. 1: 4–6.

22. Protocols of First Krestintern Congress, 57. Ho was in Moscow from 1923 to 1924, studying at the Communist University for Toilers of the East and working for the Comintern; see Sophie Quinn-Judge, *Ho Chi Minh: The Missing Years, 1919–1941* (University of California Press, 2003), ch. 2.

23. Stenogram of Krestintern Congress, 11 October 1923, RGASPI, F. 535, op. 1, d. 2: 18.

24. Stenogram of Krestintern Congress, 16.

25. Ho's presentation at the Comintern Fifth Congress the following summer drove home this point: Ho Chi Minh, "Report on the National and Colonial Questions at the Fifth Congress of the Communist International" [July 8, 1924], in *Selected Works of Ho Chi Minh*, vol. 1 (Foreign Languages Publishing House, 1960). See also Quinn-Judge, *Ho Chi Minh*, 54–57.

26. LCAEV, *El agrarismo en México*, 55, 60, 67.

27. I have been unable to verify the provenance of the Soviet images used in the pamphlet, but it seems plausible that Galván brought them back from the USSR.

28. LCAEV, *El agrarismo en México*, 48–49.

29. "Tesis y resoluciones del 2/o congreso de la Liga de Comunidades Agrarias del Estado de Veracruz, sobre organización nacional campesina," 2 December 1924, RGASPI, F. 535, op. 2, d. 97: 33.

30. "Tesis sobre relaciones internacionales," 3 December 1924, RGASPI, F. 535, op. 2, d. 97: 61.

31. "Tesis sobre relaciones internacionales," 61. Emphasis in original.

32. On this phase of Haya's trajectory, see Pedro Planas, *Los orígenes del APRA. El joven Haya* (Okura Editores, 1986), ch. 1.

33. Haya, "La unidad de América Latina es un imperativo revolucionario del más puro carácter económico" (1923), in *Obras completas*, vol. 1, 12.

34. Iñigo García-Bryce, *Haya de la Torre and the Pursuit of Power in Twentieth-Century Peru and Latin America* (University of North Carolina Press, 2018), 20–22.

35. García-Bryce, *Haya de la Torre*, 22; Ricardo Melgar Bao, "Redes y espacio público transfronterizo: Haya de la Torre en México (1923–24)," in Marta Elena Casaús Arzú and Manuel Pérez Ledesma, eds., *Redes intelectuales y formación de naciones en España y América Latina (1890–1940)* (Ediciones de la Universidad Autónoma de Madrid, 2004), 79.

36. The literature on Vasconcelos is extensive, but see Luis Marentes, *José Vasconcelos and the Writing of the Mexican Revolution* (Twayne Publishers, 2000); and Ilan Stavans, "The Prophet of Race," in *José Vasconcelos: The Prophet of Race* (Rutgers University Press, 2011), 1–44. For a comparative analysis of Vasconcelos's thinking, see Juliet Hooker, *Theorizing Race in the Americas: Douglass, Sarmiento, Du Bois, Vasconcelos* (Oxford University Press, 2017), ch. 4.

37. See Nancy Leys Stepan, *"The Hour of Eugenics": Race, Gender, and Nation in Latin America* (Cornell University Press, 1996), ch 5.

38. Haya, "Mensaje a la Universidad Popular José Martí, La Habana" (1924), in *Obras completas*, vol. 1, 30–32.

39. Geneviève Dorais, *Journey to Indo-América: APRA and the Transnational Politics of Exile, Persecution, and Solidarity, 1918–1945* (Cambridge University Press, 2021), 65.

40. Haya, "Emiliano Zapata," 37.

41. Melgar Bao, "Redes y espacio," 82–83; Dorais, *Journey to Indo-América*, 67.

42. Haya, "La unidad de América Latina," 15.

43. Haya, "La unidad de América Latina," 15–16.

44. Luis Alberto Sánchez, *Apuntes para una biografía del APRA*, vol. 1, *Los primeros pasos 1923–1931* (Mosca Azul Editores, 1978), 35–36.

45. Dorais, *Journey to Indo-América*, 74–77.

46. See notably Víctor Jeifets and Lazar Jeifets, "Haya de la Torre, la Comintern y el Perú: Acercamientos y desencuentros," *Pacarina del Sur* 4. no. 16 (2013): 332–374.

47. *El Universal*, May 8, 1924, cited in Sánchez, *Apuntes para una biografía del APRA*, 35–36; and Haya to Jay Lovestone, 9 May 1924, cited in Dorais, *Journey to Indo-América*, 68.

48. Manuel Díaz Ramírez to Edgar Stirner, 12 January 1924, RGASPI, F. 495, op. 108, d. 41: 2; and Melgar Bao, "Redes y espacio," 85.

49. Planas, *Los orígenes del APRA*, 26–27.

50. Haya de la Torre's personal file, RGASPI, F. 495, op. 251, d. 13: 28; "Doklady delegatov Mezhdunarodnogo krest'ianskogo soveta," 11–14 July 1924, RGASPI, F. 535, op. 1, d. 14: 1–199.

51. "América Latina y el imperialismo de los Estados Unidos," July 1924, RGASPI, F. 495, op. 79, d. 7: 3. The handwritten text actually refers to "*indo-sajones*," a curious slip of the pen.

52. "América Latina y el imperialismo de los Estados Unidos," 8–9; emphasis in original.

53. Haya to Stirner, Leysin, 1 January 1925, reprinted in Victor Jeifets and Andrey Schelchkov, eds., *La Internacional Comunista en América Latina: En documentos del archivo de Moscú* (Aquilo-Press / Ariadna ediciones, 2018), 38–43.

54. Haya to Stirner, 40.

55. Haya to Stirner, 41.

56. Haya to Stirner, 41.

57. Haya to Stirner, 43, 41.

58. Haya to Pavletich, 15 April 1926, reproduced in Planas, *Los orígenes del APRA*, Anexo III, 140; emphases in original.

59. Haya to Pavletich, 142; emphasis in original.

60. Haya to Pavletich, 140.

61. Haya, "El asesinato de un pueblo," in *Obras completas*, vol. 1, 90–93.

62. Haya to Pavletich, 15 April 1926, 140; on the early development of the KMT parallel, see Planas, *Los orígenes del APRA*, 60–62.

63. Dorais, *Journey to Indo-América*, 74–77.

64. Haya de la Torre, "What Is the A.P.R.A.?," *Labour Monthly* 8, no. 12 (1926); 756.

65. Haya, "What Is the A.P.R.A.?," 756.

66. Haya, "What Is the A.P.R.A.?," 758.

67. Haya, "What Is the A.P.R.A.?," 759.

68. On Borodin's time in Mexico, see Spenser, *Stumbling Its Way Through Mexico*, 44–57; for biographical details, see Jeifets and Jeifets, *Diccionario biográfico*, 104–106. On Roy and the PCM's founding, see Kent Carrasco, "M. N. Roy en México," 58–62.

69. Barry Carr, *Marxism and Communism in Twentieth-Century Mexico* (University of Nebraska Press, 1992), 28.

70. For most of the 1920s, the US Communist Party operated legally as the Workers Party of America, eventually adopting the official name Communist Party of the USA (CPUSA) in 1929. In this book I refer to it as the US Communist Party for the sake of simplicity.

71. Beals, quoted in Daniela Spenser, *The Impossible Triangle: Mexico, Soviet Russia, and the United States in the 1920s* (Duke University Press, 1999), 99.

72. Biographical details are from Jeifets and Jeifets, *Diccionario biográfico*, 485–487. See also Daniela Spenser, "Stanislav Pestkovsky: A Soldier of the World Revolution in Mexico," *Journal of Iberian and Latin American Research* 8, no. 1 (2002): 35–56.

73. *El Machete*, no. 20, 7 November 1924, 4; and no. 21, 13–20 November 1924, 1–2.

74. Spenser, *Impossible Triangle*, 100.

75. See *El Machete*, No. 1, early March 1924; and Carr, *Marxism and Communism*, 36–37.

76. "Los sabios consejos de Zapata y Montaño," *El Machete*, no. 3, early April 1924.

77. See, among others, *El Machete*, no. 16, 9–16 October 1924; no. 18, 23–30 October 1924; no. 21, 13–20 November 1924; no. 28, 8–15 January 1925; no. 42, 3 September 1925.

78. Ricardo Melgar Bao, *Haya de la Torre y Julio Antonio Mella en México: El exilio y sus querellas, 1928* (Ediciones del CCC, 2013), 41.

79. Details in this paragraph are from Christine Hatzky, *Julio Antonio Mella (1903–1929): eine Biographie* (Vervuert, 2004), ch. 2.

80. Agrupación Comunista de La Habana, Report to First Congress of the PCC, 16 August 1925, Instituto de Historia de Cuba, Fondo Primer Partido Comunista (hereafter IHC–FPPC), 1/2:1/2, 15–20.

81. "Acta de la quinta sesión del Primer Congreso Nacional de Agrupaciones Comunistas de la Isla de Cuba," 17 August 1925, IHC–FPPC, 1/2:1/2, 73.

82. "La Liga contra las Tiranías de la América" [1925], Instituto de Historia de Cuba, Fondo Julio Antonio Mella (hereafter IHC–FJAM), 1/2:Pe2.2/6/53, 1; see also Kersffeld, *Contra el imperio*, 76–77, 79.

83. "Acta de la sesión del primer congreso nacional de estudiantes," in Julio Antonio Mella, *J. A. Mella: Documentos y artículos* (Editorial de Ciencias Sociales, 1975), 572.

84. Liga Antimperialista Comité Ejecutivo to Presidente del Kuo Min Tang [1925], IHC–FPPC, 1/2:Pe2.2/6/54. On links between Chinese Cubans and radical left circles on the island, see Kathleen López, *Chinese Cubans: A Transnational History* (University of North Carolina Press, 2013), 185, 198.

85. Mella, "Hacia la Internacional americana," in *Mella: Documentos y artículos*, 212.

86. "Audiencia de La Habana: Juzgado de Instrucción; Auto de procesamiento," 7 September 1925, IHC–FJAM, 1/2:Pe2.5/12/89, 1–2.

87. For telegrams in support of Mella from across Cuba, see Archivo Nacional de Cuba (hereafter ARNAC), Fondo Especial, leg. 6, exps. 10, 14, 18, 19, 20; see also Kersffeld, *Contra el imperio*, 80–84.

88. See Christine Hatzky and Rina Ortiz, "Julio Antonio Mella: Huelga de hambre y expulsión del Partido Comunista de Cuba. Una laguna en su biografía," *Historias* (Mexico), 49 (2001): 107–145.

89. Hatzky, *Julio Antonio Mella*, 176.

90. Mella, "Mensaje a los compañeros de la Universidad Popular," in *Mella: Documentos y artículos*, 227, 230.

91. Liga Nacional Campesina (LNC), *Primer congreso de unificación de las organizaciones campesinas de la República* (Santiago Loyo, 1927), 41–42. For more on Mendizábal's trajectory, see chapter 8.

92. LNC, *Primer congreso*, 28.

93. LNC, *Primer congreso*, 21, 24, 39.

94. Irving Reynoso Jaime, *El agrarismo radical en México en la década de 1920: Úrsulo Galván, Primo Tapia y José Guadalupe Rodríguez (una biografía política)* (Instituto Nacional de Estudios Históricos de las Revoluciones de México, 2009), 55–56.

95. LNC, *Primer congreso*, 32–33.

96. LNC, *Primer congreso*, 34–35. Born in 1885 in Cali, Cuadros Caldas lived in Mexico from 1909 to 1933, fighting in the Revolution alongside Zapata. See Guillermo Palacios, "Julio Cuadros Caldas: Un agrarista colombiano en la revolución mexicana," *Historia mexicana* 49, no. 3 (2000): 431–476.

97. LNC, *Primer congreso*, 34–36.

98. LNC, *Primer congreso*, 43.

99. Jesús Rojano to Krestintern, Cárcel Municipal de Texcoco, 28 June 1928, RGASPI, F. 535, op. 2, d. 101: 110–112. A stamp on the letter indicates that it was received by the Krestintern four weeks later, on 26 July 1928.

CHAPTER 2. AGAINST EMPIRE

1. An earlier version of this chapter appeared in Erez Manela and Heather Streets-Salter, eds., *The Anticolonial Transnational: Imaginaries, Mobilities, and Networks in the Struggle Against Empire* (Cambridge University Press, 2023), 64–88. It is reproduced here with grateful permission.

2. *El Libertador*, no. 1 (March 1925), RGASPI, F. 542, op. 1, d. 2a: 1.

3. The definitive study of the Liga is Kersffeld, *Contra el imperio*.

4. See Michel Gobat, "The Invention of Latin America: A Transnational History of Anti-Imperialism, Democracy, and Race," *American Historical Review* 118, no. 5 (December 2013): 1345–1375.

5. There is, however, considerable debate about the degree to which anti-imperial impulses drove the Revolution itself. For the latter argument, see John Mason Hart, *Revolutionary Mexico: The Coming and Process of the Mexican Revolution* (University of California Press, 1987); for a contrasting "internalist" view, see Alan Knight, *The Mexican Revolution*, vols. 1 and 2 (University of Nebraska Press, 1986).

6. Lindner argues for the "Mexican origins of Tricontinentalism" in *A City Against Empire*, ch. 4.

7. On the universidades populares in Peru, see Jeffrey L. Klaiber, "The Popular Universities and the Origins of Aprismo, 1921–1924," *Hispanic American Historical*

Review 55, no. 4 (1975): 693–715; on Cuba and Argentina, see Kersffeld, *Contra el imperio*, 41–42 and 32–34.

8. Daniel Kent Carrasco, "Breath of Revolution: Ghadar Anti-Colonial Radicalism in North America and the Mexican Revolution," *South Asia: Journal of South Asian Studies* 43, no. 6 (2020): 1077–1092; and Savitri Sawhney, *I Shall Never Ask for Pardon: A Memoir of Pandurang Khankhoje* (Penguin Books, 2008), 226–249.

9. Ricardo Melgar Bao, "Un neobolivarianismo antimperialista: La Unión Centro Sud Americana y de las Antillas," *Políticas de la memoria* 6/7 (2006–7): 149–163.

10. Rivera Mir, *Militantes*, 237–239.

11. V. I. Lenin, "Draft Theses on National and Colonial Questions for the Second Congress of The Communist International" (1920), in Lenin, *Collected Works*, vol. 31 (Progress Publishers, 1966), 149.

12. In the late 1920s, the use of this term as applied to Latin America was the subject of intense debates, which I describe in chapter 4.

13. "Las garras del imperialismo internacional en China," *El Machete*, no. 17, 16–23 October 1924.

14. "Gompers, agente del imperialismo yanqui," *El Machete*, no. 19, 30 October–6 November 1924 and no. 20, 6–13 November 1924; "Los servicios de Gompers a los trabajadores de la América Latina," *El Machete*, no. 21, 13–20 November 1924; "La oposición comunista en la próxima convención de la Federación Americana del Trabajo," *El Machete*, no. 19, 30 October–6 November 1924; "Manifiesto a los delegados al congreso de la Federación Panamericana del Trabajo," *El Machete*, no. 23, 27 November–4 December 1924.

15. "Llamamiento a los Trabajadores de Chile y el Perú" and "Samuel Gompers, agente de la Casa Blanca," *El Machete*, no. 24, 4–11 December 1924.

16. Kersffeld, *Contra el imperio*, 49.

17. Kersffeld, *Contra el imperio*, 59; "Manuel Gómez" report on III PCM Congress, 23 April 1925, RGASPI, F. 495, op. 108, d. 48: 23

18. Stirner, "The Question of the Location of the Headquarters of the Liga Anti-Imperialista," n.d., RGASPI, F. 542, op. 1, d. 19: 88–89.

19. Kersffeld, *Contra el imperio*, 61; Morales to Stirner, 6 November 1926, RGASPI, f. 542, op. 1, d. 1: 16.

20. Stirner, "Question of the Location," 88.

21. See the report on the "Gran Mitín en el Teatro Fábregas," *El Libertador*, no. 17, April 1928, 12–13.

22. A list of branches appears in *El Libertador*, no. 16, March 1928, 10.

23. "Copy of letter sent to the American Party," 14 January 1925, RGASPI, F. 495, op. 108, d. 54: 1.

24. See "La Deportación de Bertram D. Wolfe," *El Libertador*, no. 4, July 1925, 2.

25. Federico Bach to Willi Münzenberg, Mexico City, 25 August 1927, RGASPI, F. 542, op. 1, d. 18: 47.

26. "Cuerpo internacional de colaboradores," *El Libertador*, no. 12, June 1927.

27. "El Peligro; Las Posibilidades; El Propósito," *El Libertador*, no. 1, March 1925, 2.

28. Jolibois to Victor Cauvin, March 1928, cited in Rivera Mir, *Militantes*, 238.

29. *El Libertador*, no. 9–10, September–October 1926, 2.

30. *El Libertador*, no. 1, March 1925, inside front.

31. Haya de la Torre to Eudocio Ravines, London, 17 October 1926, cited in Rivera Mir, *Militantes*, 224–25.

32. "El Peligro; Las Posibilidades," 2.

33. "El Congreso Bolivariano de Panamá," *El Libertador*, no. 8, April 1926, 1–2.

34. Untitled item, *El Libertador*, no. 3, June 1925, 1; "La Desgracia de Haití," *El Libertador*, no. 7, February 1926, 10; "La ocupación de Haití," *El Libertador*, no. 15, February 1928, 12; "Aniversario de la Ocupación de Haity [*sic*]," *El Libertador*, no. 17, April 1928, 16.

35. *Excélsior*, 15 January 1928, 1; *El Machete*, no. 109, 7 April 1928, 4.

36. On Gómez, see for example "Venezuela y Cuba," *El Libertador*, no. 4, July 1925, 7; "Una Amnistía para Ocultar un crimen," *El Libertador*, no. 6, October 1926, 2; "Venezuela Bajo el Terror Yanqui," *El Libertador*, no. 11, December 1926, 14–15; on Leguía, see "Leguía Instrumento Imperialista," *El Libertador*, no. 7, February 1926, 7.

37. J. A. Mella, "Machado: Mussolini tropical," *Juventud*, March 1925, in *Mella: Documentos y artículos*, 169–170.

38. "La obra de Machado," *El Libertador*, no. 9–10, October 1926, 13.

39. J. A. Mella, "Cuba, un pueblo que jamás ha sido libre," in *Mella: Documentos y artículos*, 181–182. An incomplete version of this text was reprinted in *El Libertador*, no. 3, June 1925, 7.

40. Mella, "Cuba, un pueblo," 181.

41. J. Rodríguez García, "México y los Estados Unidos," *El Libertador*, no. 1, April 1925, 5–6.

42. "Primero los Yanquis," *El Libertador*, no. 1, April 1925, 15.

43. Mella, "Cuba, un pueblo," 178.

44. See Scott Nearing, "Los Bancos Norteamericanos Mandan en el Mar Caribe," and Samuel Inman, "El Tío Sam como Rey Financiero," *El Libertador*, no. 3, June 1925, 11, 12.

45. J. A. Mella, "Hacia la Internacional americana," 2 December 1925, in *Mella: Documentos y artículos*, 211–214. The article was reprinted in *El Libertador*, no. 7, February 1926, 5–6.

46. "El Peligro; Las Posibilidades," 2.

47. "Como la esclavitud del trabajador argentino se transforma en libras esterlinas," *El Libertador*, no. 6, October 1925, 6; Rafael Carrillo, "La Mexicanización de Chile," *El Libertador*, no. 1, April 1925, 13–14.

48. José López, "El Balance Anti-Imperialista de 1925," *El Libertador*, no. 7, February 1926, 1–4, 8–9.

49. Mella, "Hacia la Internacional americana," 5.

50. Mella, "Hacia la Internacional americana," 5.

51. "El imperialismo sobre todo el mundo," *El Libertador*, no. 6, October 1925, 10.

52. Untitled items, *El Libertador*, no. 3, 1925, 8 and 14; "Lucha por la independencia filipina," *El Libertador*, nos. 9–10, September–October 1926, 11, 15.

53. Haya de la Torre, "El asesinato de un pueblo," *El Libertador*, no. 7, February 1926; Rafael Carrillo, "La próxima ofensiva en Marruecos," *El Libertador*, no. 8, April 1926.

54. "Imperialismo de Clase, no de Raza," *El Libertador*, no. 3, June 1925.

55. Editorial, "El imperialismo en China," *El Libertador*, no. 4, July 1925; José Carlos Mariátegui, "El imperialismo en China," *El Libertador*, no. 6, October 1925, 8, 10; "La masacre imperialista en China," *El Libertador*, no. 7, February 1926; J. A. Mella, "El Kuo Min Tang y la revolución china," *El Libertador*, no. 8, April 1926; Jacobo Hurwitz, "La esperanza amarilla," *El Libertador*, no. 12, June 1927; and "Ante una nueva fase de la revolución china," *El Libertador*, no. 13, August 1927.

56. Mella, "El Kuo Min Tang y la revolución china," 11–12.

57. Planas, *Los orígenes del APRA*, 60–62.

58. For a range of reflections on the Brussels Congress and its aftereffects, see Michele Louro et al., eds., *The League Against Imperialism: Lives and Afterlives* (Leiden University Press 2020).

59. Fredrik Petersson, "'We Are Neither Visionaries Nor Utopian Dreamers': Willi Münzenberg, the League against Imperialism, and the Comintern, 1925–1933" (PhD thesis, Abo Akademi, 2013), 53, 90.

60. Kersffeld, *Contra el imperio*, 97. De Negri's presence helped burnish the anti-imperialist credentials of the Calles administration, which at the time was locked in disputes with the United States over oil companies' prerogatives.

61. See for example *El Libertador*, nos. 9–10, September–October 1926, 1, 10; and *El Machete*, nos. 51, 30 September 1926; 52, 15 October 1926; and 55, mid-November 1926.

62. The breakdown in this paragraph is based on "List of Organizations and Delegates Attending the Congress against Colonial Oppression and Imperialism," 10 February 1927, International Institute for Social History, League against Imperialism Archives, ARCH00804 inventory #2.

63. "List of Organizations and Delegates."

64. "Déclaration sur la situation et les nécessités de lutte contre l'imperialisme dans les Amériques," postscript, 13 February 1927, RGASPI, F. 542, op. 1, d. 19: 26.

65. "Manifiesto del Congreso Antimperialista de Bruselas," *El Libertador*, no. 12, June 1927, 6.

66. "Manifiesto del Congreso," 6.

67. "Las resoluciones sobre la América Latina," *El Libertador*, no. 12, June 1927, 10–11.

68. "Resolución sobre la raza negra," *El Libertador*, no. 12, June 1927, 13–14.

69. "Resolución sobre la raza negra," 14.

70. "Resolución sobre la raza negra," 14.

71. "Resolución sobre la raza negra," 14.

72. "Audifaz," "Basta de 'Razas,'" *El Libertador*, no. 1, March 1925, 9–10. According to Ricardo Melgar Bao, "Audifaz" was most likely Bertram Wolfe. The pseudonym itself is a variant spelling of Audifax, a minor Catholic saint martyred in Rome in 270 CE. Melgar Bao, "Anti-Imperialist League of the Americas," 16.

73. "Audifaz," "Apreciaciones falsas y correctas del problema indígena," *El Libertador*, no. 5, August 1925, 3–4.

74. "Audifaz," "Basta de 'Razas,'" 9.

75. "Audifaz," "El Indio Como Base de la Lucha Anti-Imperialista," *El Libertador*, no. 4, July 1925, 3–4.

76. Haya de la Torre, "El problema del indio," in *Obras completas*, vol. 1, 188.

77. Greg Grandin, *Empire's Workshop: Latin America, the United States, and the Making of an Imperial Republic*, rev. ed. (Picador, 2021), 29. On the occupation of Nicaragua see Alan McPherson, *The Invaded: How Latin Americans and Their Allies Fought and Ended U.S. Occupations* (Oxford University Press, 2014), ch. 7.

78. On Nicaragua solidarity as a whole, see Barry Carr, "Pioneering Transnational Solidarity in the Americas: The Movement in Support of Augusto C. Sandino 1927–1934," *Journal of Iberian and Latin American Research* 20, no. 2 (2014): 141–152.

79. Lorenzo Meyer, *México y el mundo: Historia de sus relaciones exteriores*, tomo VI, *La marca del nacionalismo* (El Colegio de México, 2010), 61–63.

80. For example, "El Heróico Sandino Derrota a las Tropas Americanas," *El Machete*, no. 96, 7 January 1928.

81. "Los cantos del pueblo: Nicaragua," *El Machete*, no. 99, 28 January 1928.

82. "'Gringolandia y anexos': La sucursal en Nicaragua," *El Libertador*, no. 3, June 1925; John Kenneth Turner, "Nicaragua, víctima del imperialismo norteamericano," *El Libertador*, no. 5, August 1925.

83. "Desde el campamento de Sandino" and "Carleton Beals con Sandino," *El Libertador*, no. 17, April 1928; Gustavo Machado, "El terror yanqui en Nicaragua," *El Libertador*, no. 18, June 1928; Gustavo Machado, "Con Sandino en las montañas de Nicaragua," *El Libertador*, no. 19, August 1928; Gustavo Machado, "Con Sandino en las montañas de Nicaragua" (continued); and "Desde el campamento de Sandino," *El Libertador*, no. 20, November 1928; "Carta del General Sandino a Barbusse," *El Libertador*, no. 21, May 1929.

84. "El Mitin contra los buitres imperialistas," *El Machete*, no. 40, 16 July 1925.

85. *El Machete*, no. 45, 8 April 1926; and no. 56, early December 1926.

86. Enclosure with letter from James Sheffield to Secretary of State, Mexico City, 8 December 1926, National Archives and Records Administration, Record Group 59 (hereafter NARA RG 59), microfilm publication M274.

87. *El Machete*, no. 100, 4 February 1928, 1; see also Daniel Kersffeld, "El Comité Manos Fuera de Nicaragua: Primera experiencia del sandinismo," *Pacarina del Sur* 4, no. 13 (2012): 547–581.

88. On Bach, see Jeifets and Jeifets, *Diccionario biográfico*, 66.

89. Bach to Münzenberg, Mexico City, 10 January 1928, RGASPI, F. 542, op. 1, d. 28, 1.

90. See for example the front pages of *Excélsior* on 4, 5, 6 January 1928, and on 9 January for an item about an anti-imperialist meeting in the Teatro Hidalgo.

91. "Garantías para los pueblos de habla española," *Excélsior*, 15 January 1928, 1.

92. *Excélsior*, 14 February 1928, 9; *El Machete*, no. 104, 3 March 1928, 1, 4; see also Kersffeld, "El Comité Manos Fuera de Nicaragua."

93. NARA, RG 59, 810.43 Anti-Imperialistic [*sic*] League.

94. *El Machete*, no. 109, 7 April 1928, 1, 4; Kersffeld, "El Comité Manos Fuera de Nicaragua."

95. "Report on the Meeting Held by the Anti-Imperialistic [*sic*] League of the Americas at the Salon Alambra [*sic*], Mexico City, July 4, 1928," NARA, RG 59, 810.43 Anti-Imperialistic [*sic*] League.

96. *El Machete*, no. 122, 7 July 1928, 1, 4.

97. *El Machete*, no. 123, 14 July 1928, 1.

98. *El Machete*, no. 123, 14 July 1928, 4.

99. *El Informador*, 4 September 1928, 4.

100. Laborde would be general secretary of the PCM from 1929–1939. See Jeifets and Jeifets, *Diccionario biográfico*, 336–337.

101. "Mandó Sandino una bandera de Estados Unidos," *Excélsior*, 11 October 1928, sec. II, 9.

102. *El Machete*, no. 141, 1 December 1928, 1, 4; the paper had carried a photograph of this same flag on its front page a few weeks earlier: no. 136, 20 October 1928, 1.

103. While Carr notes that the scale of financial support Mafuenic gave Sandino was "very modest," the contributions would have been a significant sacrifice for the Mexican workers and peasants giving the donations: Carr, "Pioneering Transnational Solidarity," 148.

104. Pavletich, "Alianza Popular Revolucionaria Americana", reproduced in Magda Portal, *El nuevo poema i su orientación hacia una estética económica* (Ediciones APRA, 1928), 22–23.

105. Raúl Roa, *El fuego de la semilla en el surco* (Editorial Letras Cubanas, 1982), 131–145, 205–210.

CHAPTER 3. ANTI-IMPERIAL RIFTS

1. "Iniciativa del C. Senador y General Higinio Álvarez, para que llegue a crearse la ciudadanía Latino-Americana," 16 September 1927, Archivo Histórico del Senado, XXXII Congreso, libro 9, tomo 1, exp. 158, 84–86.

2. Press coverage: "México dará derechos de ciudadanía a los latinoamericanos si otros países los dan," *Excélsior*, 24 December 1927; "Una ciudadanía latinoamericana," *El Informador*, 31 December 1927; "La Ciudadanía Continental," *Atuei*, no. 3, January 1928, 13; *Amauta*, no. 15, May–June 1928, 18–21. Telegram: "Iniciativa del C. Senador y General Higinio Álvarez," 92–94.

3. For this argument see Greg Grandin, "The Liberal Traditions in the Americas: Rights, Sovereignty, and the Origins of Liberal Multilateralism," *American Historical Review* 117, no. 1 (2012): 75–76.

4. See *Excélsior*, 12, 16, and 20 December 1927, items in each case in section II, 3.

5. "Iniciativa del C. Senador y General Higinio Álvarez," 88.

6. Broué, *Histoire de l'Internationale communiste*, 499–506.

7. Spenser, *Impossible Triangle*, 170–190.

8. For an account of the Haya–Mella disputes as marking the "original division" between Communism and populism, see Rafael Rojas, *El árbol de las revoluciones: El poder y las ideas en América Latina* (Turner Publicaciones, 2021), ch. 2.

9. "Déclaration sur la situation et les nécessités de lutte contre l'imperialisme dans les Amériques" and postscript, both 13 February 1927, RGASPI, F. 542, op. 1, d. 19: 23–25 and 26.

10. Haya's account appeared eight years later, in *El Antimperialismo y el APRA* (Ediciones Ercilla, 1936), ch. 2. On the Brussels Latin America debates, see Daniel Kersffeld, "Latinoamericanos en el Congreso Antiimperialista de 1927: Afinidades, disensos y rupturas," *Journal of Iberian and Latin American Research* 16, no. 2 (2010): 151–163.

11. Ravines was an early member of APRA but left to join the Peruvian Socialist Party in 1928, becoming its general secretary upon Mariátegui's death in 1930 and renaming it the Peruvian Communist Party. During the Cold War he became a staunch anti-Communist.

12. Haya to *Mañana*, Oxford, 9 February 1927, reprinted as "La realidad de América Latina no es la realidad de Europa," in *Obras completas*, vol. 1, 138.

13. Haya, "La realidad de América Latina," 137, 139.

14. *El Machete*, no. 62, early April 1927, 1.

15. Estimates of the death toll of the "April 12 incident" range between five and ten thousand; see Jonathan Fenby, *Modern China: The Fall and Rise of a Great Power, 1850–2009* (Ecco, 2008), 180.

16. Rebecca Karl, *Mao Zedong and China in the Twentieth-Century World* (Duke University Press, 2010), 32–33.

17. See for example *El Machete*, no. 64, early May 1927, 2; Jacobo Hurwitz, "La esperanza amarilla," *El Libertador*, no. 12, June 1927; and "Ante una nueva fase de la revolución china," *El Libertador*, no. 13, August 1927.

18. Victor Raúl Haya de la Torre, "El APRA y el Kuo Min Tang," *Atuei*, no. 3, January 1928, 9.

19. Meyer, *México y el mundo*, 61–71.

20. Kathleen Weaver, *Peruvian Rebel: The World of Magda Portal, with a Selection of Her Poems* (Pennsylvania State University Press, 2009), 39–42. For more on Portal's trajectory, see chapter 6.

21. Jesús Silva Herzog sponsored his entry, according to the Servicio de Migración's Registro de Extranjeros, Archivo General de la Nación (hereafter AGN), Migración F209/6/1/33, caja 1, exp. 69, ficha 17348.

22. Moisés Sáenz to Haya, 4 October 1927, cited in Melgar Bao, *Haya de la Torre y Julio Antonio Mella en México*, 66.

23. The series was announced in "Las Conferencias de Raúl Haya Delatorre [sic] en México," *Excélsior*, 4 December 1927, section II, 3.

24. The only surviving record of these lectures was reconstructed from notes made by Carlos Manuel Cox and published as "El problema histórico de Nuestra América," *Amauta*, no. 12, February 1928, 21–23.

25. Haya, "El problema histórico de Nuestra América," 21.

26. Haya, "El problema histórico de Nuestra América," 23.

27. Mariátegui's *Seven Essays of Interpretation of Peruvian Reality* was published in early 1928, but sections of the book appeared in article form starting in 1925. José Carlos Mariátegui, *Siete ensayos de interpretación de la realidad peruana*, vol. 2 of *Obras completas de José Carlos Mariátegui* (Biblioteca "Amauta," 1959).

28. Haya, "El problema histórico de Nuestra América," 23.

29. Karl Marx and Friedrich Engels, *The Communist Manifesto* (1848; Penguin Books, 2002), 221.

30. Haya, "El problema histórico de Nuestra América," 23.

31. Haya to Lozovsky, 14 April 1927, in Ricardo Melgar Bao and Osmar Gonzales, eds., *Víctor Raúl Haya de la Torre: Giros discursivos y contiendas políticas (Textos inéditos)* (Ediciones del CCC, 2014), 147. On Lozovsky, see Jeifets and Jeifets, *Diccionario biográfico*, 363–364.

32. Manuel Díaz Ramírez to Edgar [Stirner], Mexico, 17 September 1923, RGASPI, F. 495, op. 108, d. 33: 44.

33. LCAEV, *El agrarismo en México*, 27, 28, 29, 31.

34. See for example items in *El Machete*, no. 42, 3 September 1925; no. 61, early March 1927; no. 79, 10 September 1927; no. 80, 17 September 1927; no. 81, 24 September 1927; no. 94, 24 December 1927; no. 101, 11 February 1928; no. 118, 9 June 1928; no. 125, 4 August 1928; no. 129, 1 September 1928; no. 130, 8 September 1928; no. 135, 13 October 1928; no. 145, 29 December 1928; no. 149, 26 January 1929; no. 154, 2 March 1929.

35. On Tapia, see Reynoso, *El agrarismo radical en México*, 72–95.

36. "Informe de la Liga Nacional Campesina, del sept. 1927 a la Internacional Campesina," RGASPI, F. 495, op. 108, d. 76: 24.

37. "Informe de la Liga Nacional Campesina," 24–25.

38. Protocols of Krestintern Presidium meetings, 7 January 1926 and 7 September 1926, RGASPI, F. 535, op. 1, d. 23: 2, 75–76, and Protocols of Krestintern Commission meeting, 30 August 1926, RGASPI, F. 535, op. 1, d. 82: 39.

39. Reports by "Banderas" [Pestkovsky], November 1927, RGASPI, F. 535, op. 1, d. 142: 66–67 and 85. On other Latin American communists invited to the festivities, see Jeifets and Jeifets, *Diccionario biográfico*, 28–29.

40. Stenographic record of meeting of International Peasant Congress, 15 November 1927, RGASPI, F. 535, op. 1, d. 15: 60–63. Only a Russian-language summary of Rodríguez Favela's remarks remains.

41. Carr, *Marxism and Communism*, 41.

42. Carr, *Marxism and Communism*, 39.

43. Secretaría de Relaciones Exteriores, Archivo Histórico Genaro Estrada (hereafter AHGE), 36-2-17, 116–117. Vadillo's speech was reprinted in the Soviet daily *Izvestiia*; see "Vruchenie veritel'nykh gramot meksikanskim poslannikom," *Izvestiia*, no. 265, 20 November 1924.

44. Spenser, *Impossible Triangle*, 76.

45. Spenser, *Impossible Triangle*, 102.

46. On Kollontai's trajectory, see Cathy Porter, *Alexandra Kollontai: The Lonely Struggle of the Woman Who Defied Lenin* (Dial Press, 1980).

47. A. M. Kollontai, *Diplomaticheskie dnevniki*, tom 1 (Academia, 2001), 251.

48. Kollontai, *Diplomaticheskie dnevniki*, 260, 271–272.

49. Kollontai, *Diplomaticheskie dnevniki*, 268.

50. Kollontai, *Diplomaticheskie dnevniki*, 267. The following months would bring the final defeat of Trotsky's Left Opposition and his expulsion from the party, even as debates raged over economic policy that would ultimately result in the country's rapid industrialization. See E. H. Carr, *Foundations of a Planned Economy*, vol. 2 (Macmillan, 1971), 3–53.

51. Kollontai, *Diplomaticheskie dnevniki*, 272.

52. Kollontai, *Diplomaticheskie dnevniki*, 322.

53. Spenser, *Impossible Triangle*, 89.

54. Kollontai, *Diplomaticheskie dnevniki*, 273.

55. Kollontai, *Diplomaticheskie dnevniki*, 276.

56. Kollontai, *Diplomaticheskie dnevniki*, 288; see also Spenser, *Impossible Triangle*, 105.

57. Kollontai, *Diplomaticheskie dnevniki*, 290–291, 287.

58. "Orientirovochnye zametki," 30 May 1927, RGASPI, F. 535, op. 1, d. 158: 162.

59. "Orientirovochnye zametki," 165, 163, 169.

60. "Commission mexicaine," sessions of 29 and 30 December 1927, RGASPI, F. 495, op. 60, d. 219: 4–135.

61. "Commission mexicaine," session of 29 December 1927, 9, 20.

62. "Haya de la Torre va a figurar como candidato," *Excélsior*, 18 January 1928, 2.

63. "Plan de México," 22 January 1928, reproduced in Sánchez, *Apuntes para una biografía del APRA*, 76–80.

64. On the rift between Haya and Mariátegui, see Flores Galindo, *La agonía de Mariátegui*, 80–86.

65. Mariátegui to Pavletich, 25 September 1929, in Mariátegui, *Correspondencia (1915–1930)*, vol. 2 (Biblioteca "Amauta," 1984), 633–634.

66. Jacobo Hurwitz, "Por Qué No Estoy con el A.P.R.A.," *El Libertador*, no. 18, June 1928, 7, 13–14.

67. "Una traición a Nicaragua," *El Libertador*, no. 14, January 1928, 6.

68. "El 'APRA' enviará una legión a Nicaragua," *Excélsior*, 5 March 1928; and see Pavletich's report from Sandino's camp, "La leyenda de Sandino," *Boletín Titikaka*, no. 24, July 1928.

69. Later reprinted in two parts in *Amauta* as "La lucha revolucionaria contra el imperialismo: ¿Qué es el ARPA?," no. 31, June–July 1930, 41–49; and "¿Qué es el ARPA?," no. 32, August–September 1930, 24–37. Subsequent citations are to these two articles.

70. Mella, "¿Qué es el ARPA?," 36.

71. Mella, "La lucha revolucionaria," 44.

72. Mella, "¿Qué es el ARPA?," 34.

73. Mella, "La lucha revolucionaria," 47.

74. Mella, "La lucha revolucionaria," 48.

75. Mella, "¿Qué es el ARPA?," 27–28.

76. Mella, "¿Qué es el ARPA?," 24.

77. Mella, "La lucha revolucionaria," 46.

78. Mella, "¿Qué es el ARPA?," 26.

79. Mella, "¿Qué es el ARPA?," 24.

80. Late in life, Marx himself was receptive to the arguments of the *narodniks*, corresponding with Vera Zasulich and others and conceding the possibility of alternative paths to socialism. Mella would likely not have known of these writings, since they were not published until the mid 1920s. See Teodor Shanin, ed., *Late Marx and the Russian Road: Marx and the Peripheries of Capitalism* (Monthly Review Press, 1983).

81. Mella, "¿Qué es el ARPA?," 24.

82. See García-Bryce, *Haya de la Torre*, 35; Goebel, *Anti-Imperial Metropolis*, 209; and Rojas, *El árbol de las revoluciones*, ch. 2.

83. Haya, *El Antimperialismo y el APRA*, 82, 84.

84. See Aaron Navarro, *Political Intelligence and the Creation of Modern Mexico, 1938–1954* (Penn State Press, 2010), 152.

85. See reports by Agent 8 about *El Machete*, 20 May–17 June 1925, in AGN, Dirección General de Investigaciones Políticas y Sociales (hereafter DGIPS), caja 34, exp. 3, 3–8; on LADLA, see Oficina Confidencial memo to Agent 9, 29 December 1926, AGN–DGIPS, caja 8, exp. 14, 1; see also file on the Liga from February 1927, AGN–DGIPS, caja 286, exp. 2.

86. See the sequence of telegrams and correspondence in AGN–DGIPS, caja 58, exp. 25, 1–5.

87. See Rivera Mir, *Militantes*, ch. 2.

88. AGN–DGIPS, caja 260, exp. 6, 19–106.

89. For accounts of this turn in Comintern policy, see Broué, *Histoire de l'Internationale Communiste*, ch. XXIV; and Claudín, *Communist Movement*, 152–159.

90. "¡¡Arriba el Bloque Obrero y Campesino!!," *El Machete*, no. 149, 26 January 1929, 1. See also Arnaldo Córdova, *La clase obrera en la historia de México: En una época de crisis (1928–1934)* (Siglo XXI, 1980), 69–70.

91. "El periodista cubano Antonio Mella fue herido anoche de suma gravedad," *Excélsior*, 11 January 1929, 1, 6.

92. "Candentes discursos pronunciaron los comunistas," *Excélsior*, 13 January 1929, 1, 3; see also "Todos los elementos radicales de México unidos en la protesta y fraternizados en el homenaje al desparecido," *El Universal Gráfico*, 12 January 1929; "Cómo fue el sepelio del jóven Mella," *El Universal*, 13 January 1929; "Conmovedores funerals de J. A. Mella," *La Prensa*, 13 January 1929.

93. Magda Portal recalls forming part of the guard of honor alongside Mella's coffin: "La vida que yo viví," n.d., Benson Latin American Collection, Magda Portal Papers (hereafter MPP), box 2, folder 7, 35.

94. "Manifiesto del Partido Comunista a todos los obreros y campesinos de México," 5 March 1929, published in *El Machete*, no. 155, 9 March 1929.

95. "¿Gobierno fascista, o gobierno obrero y campesino?," *El Machete*, no. 151, 9 February 1929, 2.

96. E. Martin, "Dos caminos," *El Machete*, no. 158, 30 March 1929, 2.

97. *El Machete* special supplement, 27 May 1929; for a volley of anti-Galván arguments under the title "Contestando a un traidor," see *El Machete*, no. 170, 22 June 1929.

98. Haya to Cuadros Caldas, 23 August [1929], AGN–DGIPS, caja 326, exp. 1, pages not numbered.

99. Carr, *Marxism and Communism*, 44–45.

100. *El Machete*, no. 163, 4 May 1929, 1; no. 164, 11 May 1929, 1.

101. "El Camarada José Guadalupe Rodríguez asesinado en Durango por orden del General P. Elías Calles," *El Machete*, no. 165, 18 May 1929, 1. See also Reynoso, *El agrarismo radical*, 68.

102. "Acta de plática con los delegados mexicanos durante la primera conferencia comunista latinoamericana," Buenos Aires, 28 May 1929, RGASPI, F. 495, op. 108, d. 99: 14. See also Reynoso, *El agrarismo radical*, 62.

103. *El Machete*, no. 165, 18 May 1929, 1; no. 167, 1 June 1929, 4; no. 168, 8 June 1929, 4.

104. Spenser, *Impossible Triangle*, 165.

105. "Las oficinas del Partido Comunista y de 'El Machete' cerrados por el gobierno," *El Machete*, no. 168, 8 June 1929, 1.

106. "La experiencia pagada con la sangre de José Guadalupe Rodríguez," *El Machete*, no. 167, 1 June 1929, 3.

107. "Acta de plática con los delegados mexicanos" 15.

108. "ECCI Manifesto on Mexico," *Inprecor* 9, no. 34, 19 July 1929, 732; Spanish translation published in *El Machete*, no. 176, 5 August 1929.

109. "Programa del Bloque Obrero y Campesino Nacional. Reivindicaciones inmediatas," Mexico City, October 1929, Centro de Estudios del Movimiento Obrero y Socialista (CEMOS), Fondo PCM, caja 4 exp 16.

110. Jesús Silva Herzog, *Una vida en la vida de México* (Siglo XXI, 1975), 113.

111. Quoted in Spenser, *Impossible Triangle*, 130.

112. Spenser, *Impossible Triangle*, 160–165; Silva Herzog, *Una vida*, 117.

113. Memo to Agent 25 from Jefe del Departamento Confidencial, 7 November 1929, AGN–DGIPS, caja 62, exp. 8, 16; telegram from Delegado de Migración to Gobernación, 2 January 1930, AGN–DGIPS, caja 259, exp. 34, 4.

114. Jefe de Policía, Mexico City to Secretario de Estado y del Despacho de Gobernación, 12 February 1930, AGN–DGIPS, caja 259, exp. 34, 189; telegram from Delegado de Migración, Veracruz to Secretaría de Gobernación, 24 February 1930, AGN–DGIPS, caja 259, exp. 34, 212.

115. Vidali had arrived in Mexico in 1927 and joined the PCM; in the 1930s he worked for the Comintern in Moscow and Spain alongside Modotti. He is rumored to have been involved in the assassinations of both Mella and Trotsky, though hard evidence is lacking. See Jeifets and Jeifets, *Diccionario biográfico*, 634–636, and Letizia Argentieri, *Tina Modotti: Between Art and Revolution* (Yale University Press, 2003), ch. 10.

116. Agents 8 and 14 to Jefe del Departamento Confidencial, 13 June 1930, AGN–DGIPS, caja 62, exp. 27, 6. Martí, who had been in Mexico as Augusto Sandino's representative, returned to El Salvador and played a leading role in preparing a failed Communist uprising in 1932; he was executed in its wake.

117. See Jeifets and Jeifets, *Diccionario biográfico*, 305–306, and Javier Mac-Gregor Campuzano, "Comunistas en las Islas Marías, julio-diciembre de 1932," *Signos históricos* 8 (2002): 139–150.

118. "Resolución sobre el Comité Continental de la Liga Antimperialista de las Américas," [November] 1929, RGASPI, F. 495, op. 108, d. 102: 154.

119. "Resolución sobre el Comité Continental," 154.

120. "Resolución sobre el Comité Continental," 154.

121. "Resolución sobre el Comité Continental," 155.

122. Kersffeld, *Contra el imperio*, 242.

123. See for example Carr, *Marxism and Communism*, 43–46; and Spenser, *Impossible Triangle*, ch. 8.

124. Pavletich to Mariátegui, 30 July 1929, in Ricardo Melgar Bao and Perla Jaimes Navarro, *Esteban Pavletich: Estaciones del exilio y Revolución Mexicana, 1915–1930* (Instituto Nacional de Antropología e Historia, 2019), 372–374.

125. As "El Estado antimperialista," in *El Antimperialismo y el APRA*, 89–99. The reasons for the delayed publication remain obscure; Haya claimed financial constraints, but Nelson Manrique argues that the positions Haya took in 1928 were inexpedient until several years later. See Nelson Manrique, *"¡Usted fue aprista!" Bases para una historia crítica del APRA* (Fondo Editorial de la Pontificia Universidad Católica del Perú, 2009), 56.

126. Haya, *El Antimperialismo y el APRA*, 94.

127. Pavletich, "Una nueva concepción del Estado," *Boletín Titikaka*, no. 32, July 1929.

128. Pavletich, "Una nueva concepción del Estado."

CHAPTER 4. BLACK RADICALS, BOLSHEVIKS, AND SELF-DETERMINATION

1. On this phase in the Comintern's history, see Broué, *Histoire de l'Internationale Communiste*, 492–521.

2. "Programme of the Communist International Adopted at Its Sixth Congress", in Jane Degras, ed., *The Communist International, 1919–1943: Documents*, vol. II (Royal Institute of International Affairs, 1959), 497.

3. The landmark study is Robin D. G. Kelley, *Hammer and Hoe: Alabama Communists During the Great Depression* (University of North Carolina Press, 1990); see also Mark Solomon, *The Cry Was Unity: Communists and African Americans, 1917–1936* (University Press of Mississippi, 1998), 86–89.

4. See, for example, Caballero, *Latin America and the Comintern*, 57–58; Flores Galindo, *La agonía de Mariátegui*, ch. 1; and Rodolfo Cerdas Cruz, *La hoz y el*

machete: La Internacional Comunista, América Latina y la revolución en Centro-américa (Editorial Universidad Estatal a Distancia, 1986), ch. 7.

5. Mark Naison, *Communists in Harlem During the Depression* (University of Illinois Press, 1983), 18. The literature on US Communism is vast, but among many works addressing the self-determination policy in similar terms are Theodore Draper, *American Communism and Soviet Russia: The Formative Period* (1960; Octagon Books, 1977), 315–356; Harold Cruse, *The Crisis of the Negro Intellectual* (1967; New York Review Classics, 2005), 141–142; and Harvey Klehr and William Thompson, "Self-Determination in the Black Belt. Origins of a Communist Policy," *Labor History* 30 (1989): 354–366. For more nuanced perspectives, see Solomon, *Cry Was Unity*, 86–89; Susan Campbell, "'Black Bolsheviks' and Recognition of African-America's Right to Self-Determination by the Communist Party USA," *Science & Society* 58, no. 4 (1994): 440–470; and Oscar Berland, "The Emergence of the Communist Perspective on the 'Negro Question' in America: 1919–1931, Part Two," *Science & Society* 64, no. 2 (2000): 194–217.

6. See Weinstein, "Erecting and Erasing Boundaries."

7. Harry Haywood, *Black Bolshevik: Autobiography of an Afro-American Communist* (Liberator Press, 1978), 118.

8. Biographical details in this paragraph are drawn from Haywood, *Black Bolshevik*, 5–36.

9. Haywood, *Black Bolshevik*, 83.

10. As noted in previous chapters, the party went through various names in its early years, only becoming the Communist Party of the USA (CPUSA) in 1929. Here as elsewhere I refer to it as the US Communist Party.

11. "Theses on the National and Colonial Question Adopted by the Second Comintern Congress," 28 July 1920, in Jane Degras, ed., *The Communist International, 1919–1943: Documents*, vol. I (Royal Institute of International Affairs, 1956), 142.

12. Haywood, *Black Bolshevik*, 119.

13. Domingo, "Did Bolshevism Stop Race Riots in Russia?" *The Messenger*, September 1919, cited in Winston James, *Holding Aloft the Banner of Ethiopia: Caribbean Radicalism in Early Twentieth-Century America* (Verso, 1998), 165.

14. "Programme of the Social-Democratic Workers' Party," in *1903: Second Ordinary Congress of the Russian Social-Democratic Labour Party* (New Park Books, 1978), 6.

15. "Critical Remarks on the National Question" (1913) and "The Right of Nations to Self-Determination" (1914), in Lenin, *Collected Works*, vol. 20 (Progress Publishers, 1972), 17–51 and 393–454.

16. Otto Bauer, *The Question of Nationalities and Social Democracy* (1907; University of Minnesota Press, 2000).

17. Rosa Luxemburg, "The National Question and Autonomy" (1908–9), in Luxemburg, *The National Question: Selected Writings by Rosa Luxemburg* (Monthly Review Press, 1976), 135.

18. Lenin, "Critical Remarks on the National Question," 33–40.

19. Lenin, "Right of Nations to Self-Determination," 409–414.

20. "Resolutions of the Summer, 1913, Joint Conference of the Central Committee of the R.S.D.L.P. and Party Officials," in Lenin, *Collected Works*, vol. 19 (Progress Publishers, 1977), 417–431.

21. First published in the journal *Prosveshchenie*, nos. 3–5, March–May 1913, Stalin's article came out as a pamphlet the following year under the title "Marxism and the National Question." J. V. Stalin, *Collected Works*, vol. 2 (Foreign Language Publishing House, 1953), 307.

22. Richard Pipes, *The Formation of the Soviet Union: Communism and Nationalism 1917–1923* (Harvard University Press, 1954).

23. "Ko vsem trudiashchimsia musul'manam Rossii i Vostoka," *Izvestiia*, no. 232, 22 November 1917 [3 December New Style], 1–2. The discrepancy in dates is because the Bolsheviks switched from the Julian to the Gregorian calendar in 1918.

24. John Riddell, ed., *Workers of the World and Oppressed Peoples, Unite! Proceedings and Documents of the Second Congress of the Communist International, 1920*, vol. 1 (Pathfinder, 1991), 211–290.

25. "Manifesto of the Congress to the Peoples of the East," September 1920, in John Riddell, ed., *To See the Dawn! Baku, 1920: First Congress of the Peoples of the East* (Pathfinder, 1993), 230–231.

26. Haywood, *Black Bolshevik*, 118.

27. Haywood, *Black Bolshevik*, 132, 138.

28. On the ABB, see Jacob Zumoff, "The African Blood Brotherhood: From Caribbean Nationalism to Communism," *Journal of Caribbean History* 41, nos. 1–2 (2007): 200–206. On McKay, Huiswoud, and Fort-Whiteman, see Solomon, *Cry Was Unity*, chs. 1–2, and Glenda Elizabeth Gilmore, *Defying Dixie: The Radical Roots of Civil Rights, 1919–1950* (W. W. Norton, 2008), 33, 38.

29. Briggs to T. Draper, 17 March 1958, quoted in Adi, *Pan-Africanism and Communism*, 15.

30. Briggs quoted in Haywood, *Black Bolshevik*, 124.

31. Briggs quoted in Adi, *Pan-Africanism and Communism*, 19.

32. Haywood, *Black Bolshevik*, 124.

33. Hakim Adi, *Pan-Africanism: A History* (Bloomsbury, 2018), ch. 3.

34. Tony Martin, *Race First: The Ideological and Organizational Struggles of Marcus Garvey and the Universal Negro Improvement Association* (The Majority Press, 1986), 11, 15–16. On Garveyism's links to transnational flows of people and ideas in the interwar period, see Putnam, *Radical Moves*, 36–37, 191–193, 221–224.

35. James, *Holding Aloft the Banner of Ethiopia*, 270; Stevens, *Red International and Black Caribbean*, 67–68.

36. Briggs cited in Haywood, *Black Bolshevik*, 124–125. Briggs seemingly did not think Liberia, founded as a colony by freed African American slaves in 1820 and independent since 1847, fit the bill.

37. Haywood, *Black Bolshevik*, 106–107.

38. On McKay's visit to Moscow, see Kate Baldwin, *Beyond the Color Line and the Iron Curtain: Reading Encounters between Black and Red, 1922–1963* (Duke

University Press, 2002), 25–85; see also Adi, *Pan-Africanism and Communism*, 22–26. McKay wrote his own account at the time, published as two articles in W. E. B. Du Bois's *The Crisis*: McKay, "Soviet Russia and the Negro," *The Crisis*, December 1923, 61–65, and January 1924, 114–18.

39. "Report on the Black Question," 25 November 1922, in John Riddell, ed., *Toward the United Front: Proceedings of the Fourth Congress of the Communist International, 1922* (Brill, 2012), 800–807.

40. McKay, "For a Negro Congress," RGASPI, F. 495, op. 155, d. 43: 156–162.

41. McKay, "For a Negro Congress," 159.

42. McKay, "For a Negro Congress," 156.

43. Haywood, *Black Bolshevik*, 148.

44. On this period see Timothy Colton, *Moscow: Governing the Socialist Metropolis* (Harvard University Press, 1995), ch. 3.

45. Walter Benjamin, *One-Way Street and Other Writings* (Verso Books, 1997), 85.

46. Haywood, *Black Bolshevik*, 152.

47. On the International Lenin School, see Kirschenbaum, *International Communism and the Spanish Civil War*, ch. 1; on the schools overall, see Studer, *Transnational World*, 90–107.

48. Haywood, *Black Bolshevik*, 155–156.

49. On the African and Black US presence in KUTV and other Comintern schools, see Woodford McClellan, "Africans and Black Americans in the Comintern Schools, 1925–1934," *International Journal of African Historical Studies* 26, no. 2 (1993): 371–390; and Irina Filatova, "Indoctrination or Scholarship? Education of Africans at the Communist University of Toilers of the East in the Soviet Union, 1923–1927," *Paedagogica Historica* 35, no. 1 (1999): 41–66.

50. On the KUTV and its concept of "the East," see Masha Kirasirova, *The Eastern International: Arabs, Central Asians, and Jews in the Soviet Union's Anti-Colonial Empire* (Oxford University Press, 2024), esp. 60–91.

51. "Common Resolution on the Negro Question," 13 February 1927, RGASPI, F. 542, op. 1, d. 67: 47.

52. "Common Resolution on the Negro Question," 46–47.

53. Haywood, *Black Bolshevik*, 219.

54. Terry Martin, *The Affirmative Action Empire: Nations and Nationalism in the Soviet Union, 1923–1939* (Cornell University Press, 2001).

55. See Francine Hirsch, *Empire of Nations: Ethnographic Knowledge and the Making of the Soviet Union* (Cornell University Press, 2005), appendices 1 and 2, 327–333.

56. Yuri Slezkine, "The USSR as a Communal Apartment, or How a Socialist State Promoted Ethnic Particularism," *Slavic Review* 53, no. 2 (1994): 414.

57. Haywood, *Black Bolshevik*, 155–156.

58. Hirsch, *Empire of Nations*, 43–45.

59. Haywood, *Black Bolshevik*, 158, 159.

60. Haywood, *Black Bolshevik*, 205–206.

61. In this he echoed Briggs, who had also been greatly interested in the Irish national struggle; apparently Briggs partly modeled the ABB on Sinn Fein: Zumoff, "African Blood Brotherhood," 203.

62. Haywood, *Black Bolshevik*, 206.

63. For the few available pieces of biographical data on Nasanov, see Oscar Berland, "Nasanov and the Comintern's American Negro Program," *Science & Society* 65, no. 2 (2001): 226–228; and Solomon, *Cry Was Unity*, 332n3.

64. Haywood, *Black Bolshevik*, 219–221.

65. Haywood, *Black Bolshevik*, 221.

66. Haywood, *Black Bolshevik*, 221–222.

67. Haywood, *Black Bolshevik*, 112.

68. Haywood, *Black Bolshevik*, 230.

69. Haywood, *Black Bolshevik*, 227–228.

70. Haywood, "The Basis for Nationalist Movements Among Negroes in the United States, and What Should Be the Attitude of Our Party Towards Them," 10 June 1928, quoted in Jacob Zumoff, *The Communist International and U.S. Communism, 1919–1929* (Brill, 2014), 346.

71. "Is There a Basis for a Nationalist or Separatist Movement in the United States?," RGASPI, F. 495, op. 155, d. 56: 37–38. Hall is identified here under his alias, "Comrade Jones."

72. "The Tasks of the American Communist Party Regarding Negro Work," 2 August 1928, RGASPI, F. 495, op. 155, d. 56: 59.

73. "Tasks of the American Communist Party," 58–59.

74. "Meeting of the Negro Commission," 2 August 1928, RGASPI, F. 495, op. 155, d. 56: 47.

75. "Discussion at Negro Commission Meeting," 3 August 1928, RGASPI, F. 495, op. 155, d. 56: 52–53.

76. "Meeting of the Negro Commission," 49. On Bittelman, see Tony Michels, ed., *Jewish Radicals: A Documentary Reader* (New York University Press, 2012), 49; and Zumoff, *Communist International and U.S. Communism*, 327.

77. "Meeting of the Negro Commission," 49–50.

78. "Minutes of Meeting of Negro Commission of August 4, 1928," RGASPI, F. 495, op. 155, d. 56: 83, 95.

79. Haywood, *Black Bolshevik*, 259; and "Negro Commission, 7.8.28," RGASPI, F. 495, op. 155, d. 56: 97.

80. "Negro Commission, 7.8.28," 97. On Petrovsky (1886–1937), see Jeifets and Jeifets, *Diccionario biográfico*, 488–489.

81. "Minutes of Negro Commission of August 11, 1928," 112.

82. "To the Commission on Work Among Negroes" [9 August 1928], RGASPI, F. 495, op. 155, d. 56: 108–109. Little is known about Cárdenas (b. 1894), except that he was a journalist and attended both the 1928 Profintern Congress in Moscow and the Comintern's Sixth Congress. See Jeifets and Jeifets, *Diccionario biográfico*, 130.

83. "Sitzung des Presidiums des IKKI vom 16 Maerz 1927," RGASPI, F. 495, op. 2, d. 94: 128–129.

84. "Minutes of Negro Commission of August 11, 1928," 112.

85. "Negro Commission. 7.8.28," 101.

86. "Discussion on the Report of Comrade Bukharin" [25 July 1928], *Inprecor*, 8:46, 8 August 1928, 812.

87. "*die nationale Frage, oder anders gesprochen die Rassenfrage*": "Sitzung des Presidiums des IKKI," 128. For Bolshevik intellectuals such as Bukharin, the language of Marx and Hegel was their preferred lingua franca, and Comintern proceedings were sometimes conducted in German, though French was more commonly used.

88. "Sitzung des Presidiums des IKKI," 128–129.

89. "Minutes of Negro Commission of August 11, 1928," RGASPI, F. 495, op. 155, d. 56: 116.

90. "Comrade Bukharin's Opening Speech" [17 July], *Inprecor*, 8:39, 25 July 1928, 706.

91. See for example "Comrade Bukharin's Speech in Reply to the Discussion on the International Situation" [30 July], *Inprecor*, 8:49, 13 August 1928, 871.

92. "Discussion on the Report of Comrade Bukharin on the Draft Programme of the Comintern" [9 August], *Inprecor*, 8:66, 25 September 1928, 1177. On Paredes (1898–1979), see Jeifets and Jeifets, *Diccionario biográfico*, 468.

93. "Questions of the Latin-American Countries: Co-Report of Comrade Humbert-Droz" [16 August], *Inprecor*, 8:72, 17 October 1928, 1299–1305.

94. On Humbert-Droz (1891–1971), see Jeifets and Jeifets, *Diccionario biográfico*, 302–304.

95. Studer, *Transnational World*, 43.

96. "Questions of the Latin-American Countries," 1302, 1304.

97. "Questions of the Latin-American Countries," 1304–1305.

98. "Questions of the Latin-American Countries," 1305.

99. "Continuation of the Discussion on the Questions of the Revolutionary Movement in the Colonies" [18 August], *Inprecor*, 8:74, 25 October 1928, 1407, 1406.

100. "Continuation of the Discussion on the Questions of the Revolutionary Movement in the Colonies" [17 and 18 August], *Inprecor*, 8:74, 25 October 1928, 1356; and *Inprecor*, 8:76, 30 October 1928, 1395. Vidali appears as "Comrade Contreras."

101. "Discussion on the Report of Comrade Bukharin" [9 August], 1177.

102. The term *native* appears in the English translation published in *Inprecor*. Vidali likely spoke in French, and in the French version of the proceedings he refers to "*le problème indigene*." "VIe Congrès Mondial de l'International communiste: Trente-sixième séance, 18 août (matin)," *La Correspondance Internationale*, no. 130, 30 October 1928, 1419.

103. "Continuation of the Discussion" [18 August], 1394.

104. "Continuation of the Discussion" [18 August], 1394.

105. "Continuation of the Discussion" [18 August], 1407.

106. Martin, *Affirmative Action Empire*, 10–12.

107. "Continuation of the Discussion" [18 August], 1394.

108. "Discussion on the Report of Comrade Bukharin" [23 July 1928], *Inprecor*, 8:44, 3 August 1928, 772; "Discussion on the Report of Comrade Bukharin" [25 July 1928], *Inprecor*, 8:46, 8 August 1928, 812; "Continuation of the Discussion on the Report of Comrade Bukharin" [26 July 1928], *Inprecor*, 8:48, 11 August 1928, 856.

109. "Discussion on the Questions of the Revolutionary Movement in the Colonies" [16 August], *Inprecor*, 8:72, 17 October 1928, 1313.

110. "Discussion on the Questions of the Revolutionary Movement" [16 August], 1322. Petrovsky appears as "Bennet."

111. "Discussion on the Questions of the Revolutionary Movement" [16 August], 1320. Phillips appears under his alias "Manuel Gómez." Phillips had spent time in Mexico City during and after the First World War and was a key link between the US Communist Party and the PCM in the 1920s. See Jeifets and Jeifets, *Diccionario biográfico*, 489–490, and also Phillips's memoir, published under the name Charles Shipman, *It Had to Be Revolution* (Cornell University Press, 1993).

112. "Continuation of the Discussion" [17 and 18 August], 1346 and 1393.

113. "Continuation of the Discussion" [18 August], 1393.

114. "Continuation of the Discussion" [17 August], 1347.

115. "Continuation of the Discussion on the Report of Comrade Bukharin on the Draft Programme of the Comintern" [13 August], *Inprecor*, 8:66, 25 September 1928, 1198.

116. "Social Democracy and the Colonial Question: Co-Report of Comrade Ercoli (Italy)" [15 August], *Inprecor*, 8:68, 4 October 1928, 1239, 1241.

117. "Programme of the Communist International," 497.

CHAPTER 5. RACE, CLASS, AND
THE MAKING OF THE PRESENT

1. On the significance of the Buenos Aires conference, see Victor Jeifets and Lazar Jeifets, "Introduction: The Outcomes of Ten Years of Latin American Communism," in Marc Becker, ed., *The Latin American Revolutionary Movement: Proceedings of the First Latin American Communist Conference, June 1929* (Brill, 2023), 1–25.

2. Known as *shchelkovki*, from the Russian for silk, several of these credentials remain in the Comintern's personal files; for examples see Rafael Carrillo, RGASPI, F. 495, op. 241, d. 109: 32, 36; Sandalio Junco, RGASPI, F. 495, op. 241, d. 27: 25; and Julio Antonio Mella, RGASPI, F. 495, op. 241, d. 78: 11.

3. On the major disagreements at the Buenos Aires conference, see Caballero, *Latin America and the Comintern*, 54–58, and Flores Galindo, *La agonía de Mariátegui*, ch 1. The Montevideo proceedings were published as *Bajo la bandera de la C.S.L.A. Resoluciones y documentos varios del Congreso constituyente de la Confederación sindical latino-americana efectuado en Montevideo en mayo de 1929* (Imprenta La Linotipo, 1929); and a transcript of the Buenos Aires discussions appears

in *El Movimiento revolucionario latinoamericano: Versiones de la primera conferencia comunista Latino Americana* (La Correspondencia Sudamericana, 1929). For an English translation of the proceedings, see Marc Becker, ed., *The Latin American Revolutionary Movement: Proceedings of the First Latin American Communist Conference, June 1929* (Brill, 2023).

4. Among the few works on the Buenos Aires discussions of race, see Becker, "Mariátegui, Comintern, and Indigenous Question," and Melgar Bao, "La IC frente al dilema raza y nación."

5. See Caballero, *Latin America and the Comintern*, 57–58; and Cerdas Cruz, *La hoz y el machete*, 167–169.

6. Mariátegui's report to the Montevideo congress appears as "El problema indígena," in *Bajo la bandera de la C.S.L.A.*, 147–159, and the Peruvian delegation's Buenos Aires report appears under the pseudonym "Saco," in *El Movimiento revolucionario latinoamericano*, 263–291. The theses were subsequently republished under their original author's name as "El problema de las razas en América Latina," in *Ideología y política*, vol. 13 of *Obras completas de José Carlos Mariátegui* (Biblioteca "Amauta," 1969), 22–86.

7. Sandalio Junco, "El problema de la raza negra y el movimiento proletario," in *Bajo la bandera de la C.S.L.A.*, 172. Junco's remarks at Buenos Aires appear under the pseudonym "Juárez" in *El Movimiento revolucionario latinoamericano*, 291–294. Throughout this chapter, I have either used the term *Black* or the descriptor "of African descent," rather than using later terms such as *Afro-Cuban* or *Afro-Latino*. While often preferred today, they had a different valence at the time, and none of the actors in the debates discussed in this chapter would have used them.

8. "6ème séance de la Conf. Latin. Americaine, 10 avril 1928 (soir)," RGASPI, F. 495, op. 79, d. 46: 73.

9. The following paragraphs are indebted to Flores Galindo's *La agonía de Mariátegui*, ch. 1, though I diverge from his interpretation in one key respect: I believe he depicts the views of the Comintern representatives as being more monolithic and doctrinaire than they were. Further biographical information is drawn from Robert Paris, *La formación ideológica de José Carlos Mariátegui* (Ediciones Pasado y Presente, 1981); Jesús Chavarría, *José Carlos Mariátegui and the Rise of Modern Peru, 1890–1930* (University of New Mexico Press, 1979); Guillermo Rouillon, *La creación heroica de José Carlos Mariátegui*, tomo I, *La Edad de Piedra (1894–1919)* (Editorial Arica, 1975); and Estuardo Núñez, *La experiencia europea de José Carlos Mariátegui y otros ensayos* (Editora Amauta, 1978).

10. "Maximalismo peruano," *El Tiempo*, 30 December 1917, cited in Rouillon, *La creación heroica*, 202.

11. "El problema primario del Perú," *Mundial*, 9 December 1924, cited in Mariátegui, *Peruanicemos al Perú*, vol. 11 of *Obras completas de José Carlos Mariátegui* (Biblioteca "Amauta," 1970), 30–34.

12. Mariátegui, *Siete ensayos*. On the genesis of the essays, see César Falcon, *Anatomía de los 7 ensayos de Mariátegui* (Editora Amauta, 1978).

13. Mariátegui, *Siete ensayos*, 51.

14. Mariátegui, "Intermezzo polémico" (1927), in *Ideología y política*, 217.

15. Mariátegui, "Principios de política agraria nacional" (1927), in *Peruanicemos al Perú*, 109–110.

16. Flores Galindo, *La agonía de Mariátegui*, 24.

17. *El Movimiento revolucionario latinoamericano*, 263–65.

18. *El Movimiento revolucionario latinoamericano*, 265–266. Throughout this section, I use the terms *indigenous* and *Indian* to reflect, respectively, Mariátegui's usage of the terms *indígena* and *indio*.

19. *El Movimiento revolucionario latinoamericano*, 265.

20. *El Movimiento revolucionario latinoamericano*, 267–270.

21. *El Movimiento revolucionario latinoamericano*, 269.

22. *El Movimiento revolucionario latinoamericano*, 270.

23. *El Movimiento revolucionario latinoamericano*, 279, 290.

24. *El Movimiento revolucionario latinoamericano*, 288.

25. *El Movimiento revolucionario latinoamericano*, 286, 288.

26. *El Movimiento revolucionario latinoamericano*, 288.

27. *El Movimiento revolucionario latinoamericano*, 291.

28. *El Movimiento revolucionario latinoamericano*, 282, 283.

29. On the long history and profound effects of racial ideologies in Guatemala, see Greg Grandin, *The Blood of Guatemala: A History of Race and Nation* (Duke University Press, 2000).

30. *El Movimiento revolucionario latinoamericano*, 284, 287.

31. Biographical details in this paragraph are drawn from Junco's Comintern personnal file, RGASPI, F. 495, op. 241, d. 27: 1, 8–14, 39–40; and from Jeifets and Jeifets, *Diccionario biográfico*, 317–318. Among the few scholars to have focused on Junco, see Sergio Méndez Moissen, "El trotskismo cubano en la revolución de 1933," *Pacarina del Sur* 6, no. 23 (2015): 62–109; and Mahler, "Red and the Black in Latin America."

32. Hilda Tísoc Lindley, "De los orígenes del APRA en Cuba: El testimonio de Enrique de la Osa," *Cuadernos Americanos* 37 (1993): 204–205.

33. "Antecedentes de los individuos radicados en México, que vienen haciendo propaganda insidiosa contra Cuba," 25 July 1928, IHC–FJAM, 1/2:Pe2.5/12/96, 2–3; Kersffeld, *Contra el imperio*, 165.

34. Questionnaire for the International Lenin School, Moscow, February 1931, RGASPI, F. 495, op. 241, d. 27: 11.

35. Kersffeld, *Contra el imperio*, 302.

36. "Conmovedores funerales de J. A. Mella," *La Prensa*, 13 January 1929.

37. "Stenogramma zasedaniia 5 sessii TsS Profinterna," 1 April 1928, RGASPI, F. 534, op. 2, d. 43: 1.

38. "6ème séance de la Conf. Latin. Américaine," 59, 68; and "Protokol latinoamerikanskoi komissii Ispolbiuro Profinterna," 8 May 1928, RGASPI, F. 534, op. 3, d. 355: 25–26.

39. "Mezhdunarodnyi profkomitet rabochikh-negrov pri Profinterne," 31 July 1928, RGASPI, F. 534, op. 3, d. 359: 1. On the ITUCNW, see Adi, *Pan-Africanism and Communism*, chs 1, 5, 8, and 10.

40. "Resolution of the Executive Bureau of the RILU on the Organization of the International Trade Union Committee of Negro Workers," 31 July 1928, RGASPI, F. 534, op. 3, d. 359: 2–6.

41. Elías Barrios, *El escuadrón de hierro* (Ediciones de Cultura Popular, 1978), ch. 13.

42. Barrios, *El escuadrón de hierro*, 153.

43. Tísoc, "De los orígenes del APRA en Cuba," 204.

44. Barrios, *El escuadrón de hierro*, 156.

45. Junco, "El problema de la raza negra," 160.

46. Junco, "El problema de la raza negra," 161.

47. Junco, "El problema de la raza negra," 162–164.

48. Junco, "El problema de la raza negra," 164–65.

49. Junco, "El problema de la raza negra," 169; C. L. R. James, *The Black Jacobins: Toussaint L'Ouverture and the San Domingo Revolution*, 2nd ed. (1938; Vintage Books, 1963).

50. Junco, "El problema de la raza negra," 170.

51. Junco, "El problema de la raza negra," 170–172. On Palmares and its afterlives, see the essays in João José Reis and Flavio dos Santos Gomes, eds., *Freedom by a Thread: The History of Quilombos in Brazil* (Diasporic Africa Press, 2016).

52. Junco, "El problema de la raza negra," 172–173.

53. Junco, "El problema de la raza negra," 173.

54. Junco, "El problema de la raza negra," 176.

55. "Resolución sobre el problema de los trabajadores negros," in *Bajo la bandera de la C.S.L.A.*, 179.

56. Junco, "El problema de la raza negra," 160.

57. *El Movimiento revolucionario latinoamericano*, 291.

58. *El Movimiento revolucionario latinoamericano*, 284.

59. *El Movimiento revolucionario latinoamericano*, 291.

60. *El Movimiento revolucionario latinoamericano*, 291.

61. *El Movimiento revolucionario latinoamericano*, 292, 294.

62. On Basbaum (1907–1969), see Jeifets and Jeifets, *Diccionario biográfico*, 79–80. See also Basbaum's memoir, *Uma vida em seis tempos. Memorias* (Editora Alfa-Omega, 1976).

63. *El Movimiento revolucionario latinoamericano*, 295.

64. *El Movimiento revolucionario latinoamericano*, 297.

65. *El Movimiento revolucionario latinoamericano*, 309–310.

66. *El Movimiento revolucionario latinoamericano*, 302–303. Barreiro was using the pseudonym "Braceras."

67. *El Movimiento revolucionario latinoamericano*, 303, 308–309, 306–308.

68. Rabinovich died on the Eastern Front early in the Second World War, in 1941: see Jeifets and Jeifets, *Diccionario biográfico*, 511–512.

69. *El Movimiento revolucionario latinoamericano*, 297–298; emphasis in original. Rabinovich used the pseudonym "Peters."

70. *El Movimiento revolucionario latinoamericano*, 298–299.

71. *El Movimiento revolucionario latinoamericano*, 299; emphasis in original.

72. *El Movimiento revolucionario latinoamericano*, 301–302.

73. *El Movimiento revolucionario latinoamericano*, 304. Siquieros used the pseudonym "Suárez."

74. *El Movimiento revolucionario latinoamericano*, 305–306. Portocarrero used the pseudonym "Zamora."

75. *El Movimiento revolucionario latinoamericano*, 313.

76. *El Movimiento revolucionario latinoamericano*, 313.

77. *El Movimiento revolucionario latinoamericano*, 310. Humbert-Droz used the pseudonym "Luis."

78. Untitled notes, n.d. [1929], RGASPI, F. 495, op. 79, d. 117: 105–107.

79. *El Movimiento revolucionario latinoamericano*, 312.

80. Protocol of Latin American Secretariat meeting, 1 January 1930, RGASPI, F. 495, op. 79, d. 95: 11.

81. On Grieco (1893–1955) and Guralsky (1890–1960), see Jeifets and Jeifets, *Diccionario biográfico*, 276–277, 287–288.

82. On Yakobson (1897–1936), see Jeifets and Jeifets, *Diccionario biográfico*, 657–658.

83. "Le problème des races en Amérique latine," 1 January 1930, RGASPI, F. 495, op. 79, d. 95: 12.

84. "Le problème des races en Amérique latine," 25.

85. "Le problème des races en Amérique latine," 31.

86. "Le problème des races," 19 December 1929, RGASPI, F. 495, op. 79, d. 95: 8, 10.

87. "Le problème des races en Amérique latine," 20.

88. Untitled notes, n.d. [1929], 107.

89. "Le problème des races en Amérique latine," 25–26. Humbert-Droz did sound a note of caution, however, against endorsing separatist projects set in motion by imperialist powers; he cited the examples of Panama and the movement for autonomy in the Venezuelan state of Zulia.

90. "Question des races en Amérique latine," RGASPI, F. 495, op. 79, d. 95: 44, 47.

91. "Question des races en Amérique latine," 50.

92. "Question des races en Amérique latine," 33.

93. "Question des races en Amérique latine," 42.

94. "Question des races en Amérique latine," 57.

95. Protocol of Latin American Secretariat meeting, 11.

96. "Las tareas actuales de los P.C. de la América Latina," *La Correspondencia Sudamericana*, Segunda Epoca, June 1930, 11–12.

CHAPTER 6. CONTINENTAL NATIONALISM

1. "La Conferencia de Magda Portal," *El Mundo* (Santo Domingo), 10 July 1929, MPP, box 10, folder 11, Clippings, n.p.

2. "Con Magda Portal," *Libertad* (Lima), 26 October 1930, in Clippings, n.p.

3. *La Correspondencia de Puerto Rico*, 31 July 1929, in Clippings, n.p.

4. *La Correspondencia de Puerto Rico*, 1 August 1929, in Clippings, n.p.

5. See for example the classic studies by Peter Klarén, *Modernization, Disloca-tion, and Aprismo: Origins of the Peruvian Aprista Party, 1870–1932* (University of Texas Press, 1973), and Steve Stein, *Populism in Peru: The Emergence of the Masses and the Politics of Social Control* (University of Wisconsin Press, 1980).

6. Notable examples include Dorais, *Journey to Indo-América*; Manrique, *"¡Usted fue aprista!"*; García-Bryce, *Haya de la Torre and the Pursuit of Power*; and Martín Bergel, *La desmesura revolucionaria: Cultura y política en los orígenes del APRA* (La Siniestra Ensayos, 2021).

7. For the most fully developed version of this argument, see Dorais, *Journey to Indo-América*, chs. 5 and 6.

8. See for example Haya de la Torre, *Construyendo el aprismo: Artículos y cartas desde el exilio (1924–1931)* (Editorial Claridad, 1933), 199; Pedro Múñiz, *Lo que es el aprismo* (Editorial Cromos, 1932), 218; and the subtitle of the pamphlet *Programa de gobierno del Partido Aprista Peruano: Aprismo no es Comunismo* (n.p., n.d.), MPP, box 13, folder 14. Though this pamphlet is often dated to 1933, its use of the term "fifth column," which originated in the Spanish Civil War, suggests it was written no earlier than 1936.

9. "El APRA y la Liga Patriotica Haitiana," and "Mensaje que el General A. C. Sandino envía por intermedio del A.P.R.A. al Senador Higinio Alvarez," *Indoamé-rica*, no. 1, July 1928, 3, 4.

10. For full biographical portraits of Portal, see Weaver, *Peruvian Rebel*, and Myrna Ivonne Wallace Fuentes, *Most Scandalous Woman: Magda Portal and the Dream of Revolution in Peru* (University of Oklahoma Press, 2017). See also Iñigo García-Bryce, "Transnational Activist: Magda Portal and the American Popu-lar Revolutionary Alliance (APRA), 1926–1950," *The Americas* 70, no. 4 (2014): 677–705.

11. Magda Portal, *América Latina frente al imperialismo* (Cahuide, 1931), 49.

12. Weaver, *Peruvian Rebel*, 1–2.

13. Portal, "La vida que yo viví," n.d., MPP, box 2, folder 7, 15.

14. Weaver, *Peruvian Rebel*, 28–30; see also Wallace Fuentes, *Most Scandalous Woman*, 94–100.

15. Mariátegui, *Siete ensayos*, 322–327.

16. Weaver, *Peruvian Rebel*, 39; Portal, "La vida que yo viví," 27–28.

17. Portal, "La vida que yo viví," 29.

18. Portal, "La vida que yo viví," 33–34.

19. Magda Portal, "El imperativo de la hora indoamericana," *Indoamérica*, no. 1, July 1928, 5.

20. Portal, "El imperativo de la hora indoamericana," 5, 9.

21. Portal, "El imperativo de la hora indoamericana," 9.

22. "Mensaje que el General A. C. Sandino envía...," 4.

23. "La revolución rusa," *Indoamérica*, no. 5, November 1928, 2.

24. Portal, *El nuevo poema*, 7.

25. Dorais, *Journey to Indo-América*, 94.

26. Portal, "La vida que yo viví," 34; Wallace Fuentes, *Most Scandalous Woman*, 112.

27. Portal, *El nuevo poema*, 23.

28. Portal, *El nuevo poema*, 29, 5.

29. "Datos biográficos de M.P.," n.d., MPP digitized files, carpeta 74, 9.

30. The exact chronology of Portal's travels is difficult to establish, but she had clearly arrived in San Juan by June 1, in Santo Domingo by July 9, was back in Puerto Rico by the end of the month, and was in Barranquilla no later than August 11. See *El Tiempo* (San Juan), 1 June 1929; *El Mundo* (Santo Domingo), 9 July 1929; *La Correspondencia de Puerto Rico*, 30 July 1929; *El Porvenir* (Barranquilla), 12 August 1929, all in Clippings, n.p. See also Weaver, *Peruvian Rebel*, 72–80.

31. See *El Imparcial* (San Juan), 5 June 1929; *La Correspondencia de Puerto Rico*, 26 June 1929; *Listín Diario* (Santo Domingo), 15 July 1929; *La Correspondencia de Puerto Rico*, 19 July 1929; and *La Nación* (Barranquilla), 17 August 1929, all in Clippings, n.p.

32. *La Correspondencia de Puerto Rico*, [n.d.] 1929, Clippings, MPP, box 10, folder 11, n.p.

33. "La dama del mar," *El Mundo* (San Juan), 8 July 1929, Clippings, MPP, box 10, folder 11, n.p.

34. "Entrevista con Magda Portal," July 1–2, 1981, MPP digitized files, carpeta 57, Bio-2.

35. "La situación real de la América Latina ante el avance del imperialismo," *Listín Diario*, 15 July 1929; and "América Latina frente al Imperialismo," *La Correspondencia de Puerto Rico*, 4 August 1929, both in Clippings, n.p.

36. It was republished two days later in Puerto Rico with details of its original appearance: Portal, "Capitalismo y colonización," *La Correspondencia de Puerto Rico*, 30 May 1929, in Clippings, n.p.

37. Portal, "Capitalismo y colonización."

38. Portal, *América Latina frente al imperialismo*, 9–10.

39. Portal, *América Latina frente al imperialismo*, 15–16.

40. Weaver, *Peruvian Rebel*, 73.

41. Portal, *América Latina frente al imperialismo*, 45, 72.

42. Portal, *América Latina frente al imperialismo*, 47.

43. Portal, *América Latina frente al imperialismo*, 50–51.

44. Portal, *América Latina frente al imperialismo*, 78.

45. Portal, *América Latina frente al imperialismo*, 82–83.

46. Portal, *América Latina frente al imperialismo*, 45, 47–48, 50.

47. Portal, *América Latina frente al imperialismo*, 49, 84.

48. Weaver, *Peruvian Rebel*, 73.

49. Portal, "La vida que yo viví," 38–39; see also Weaver, *Peruvian Rebel*, 77.

50. On the links between Peruvian and Costa Rican political and intellectual worlds in the 1920s, see Jussi Pakkasvirta, *¿Un continente, una nación? Intelectuales*

latinoamericanos, comunidad política y las revistas culturales en Costa Rica y el Perú (1919–1930) (Editorial de la Universidad de Costa Rica, 2005).

51. Portal, "La vida que yo viví," 47.

52. Portal, "La vida que yo viví," 43, 48–49.

53. Portal, "La vida que yo viví," 52.

54. Portal, "La vida que yo viví," 58, 65, 61; "Entrevista con Magda Portal," A28.

55. Weaver, *Peruvian Rebel*, 100.

56. "Entrevista con Magda Portal," C8.

57. "Entrevista con Magda Portal," A26.

58. "Entrevista con Magda Portal," C1.

59. Portal, "La vida que yo viví," 54.

60. Portal, "El momento peruano," *APRA*, no. 1, 12 October 1930; the text is dated Santiago de Chile, September 1930.

61. "Manifiesto de Haya de la Torre," February 1932, in *Aprismo: Transcripción de los artículos y discursos de los líderes, oradores y parlamentarios; y de Haya de la Torre; el manifiesto del jefe del aprismo a la nación peruana* (Ediciones Corrientes, 1933), 42, 70–73.

62. "Manifiesto de Haya de la Torre," 46–48.

63. See Dorais, *Journey to Indo-América*, Ch. 5.

64. *Programa de gobierno del Partido Aprista Peruano*, 16.

65. Quoted in Weaver, *Peruvian Rebel*, 143.

66. Magda Portal, *¿Quiénes traicionaron al pueblo?* (Impr. Editora Salas e Hijos, 1950), 8.

67. Portal, *¿Quiénes traicionaron al pueblo?*, 22–23.

68. Portal, *¿Quiénes traicionaron al pueblo?*, 11.

69. Portal, *¿Quiénes traicionaron al pueblo?*, 8–9.

70. Weaver, *Peruvian Rebel*, 177. She remained affiliated with the Communists into the 1980s and ran unsuccessfully for office in 1978 and 1985 as a radical left candidate. She died in 1989.

71. Julio Cuadros Caldas, "Por la unión contra el imperialismo," *Indoamérica*, no. 4, October 1928, 10.

72. Julio Cuadros Caldas, *El Comunismo criollo* (Santiago Loyo, 1930), 7–9, 146.

73. Manuel Seoane, "Los dos grandes problemas del Perú," *APRA*, no. 1, 12 October 1930. On Seoane, see Bergel, *La desmesura revolucionaria*, 193–222.

74. Pavletich to Mariátegui, 30 July 1929, in Melgar Bao and Navarro, eds., *Esteban Pavletich*, 373–374.

75. Esteban Pavletich, *El mensaje de México* (n.p., 1934), 7–10, 205–206.

76. For a seminal later work making a similar argument, see Adolfo Gilly, *La revolución interrumpida* (Ediciones El Caballito, 1971).

77. Pavletich, *El mensaje de México*, 238–239.

78. Seoane, "Los dos grandes problemas del Perú."

79. Octavio Salamanca, "Obreros e indios de Bolivia: Escuchad la palabra de la Confederación Sindical Latino Americana" (1931), in Pilar Mendieta Parada and

Evgenia Bridikhina, eds., *Amanecer en rojo. Marxismo, comunismo y socialismo en Bolivia (1880–1932)* (Vicepresidencia del Estado Plurinacional de Bolivia, 2018), 473; emphasis in original.

80. Ulianova, "Levantamiento campesino de Lonquimay," 199.

81. "Resolución sobre la cuestión indígena," RGASPI, F. 495, op. 108, d. 150: 174.

CHAPTER 7. ANOTHER COUNTRY

1. "Los negros en Cuba como nacionalidad oprimida," 26 September 1932, RGASPI, F. 495, op. 105, d. 64: 5–26.

2. "Las elecciones en Cuba y el Partido Comunista," 15 December 1932, RGASPI, F. 495, op. 105, d. 55: 20; emphasis in original.

3. Melina Pappademos, *Black Political Activism and the Cuban Republic* (University of North Carolina Press, 2014), 180. In the period covered by this chapter, two different racialized vocabularies coexisted in Cuba. One assumed a binary racial structure, comprising "white" and "Black" people. The other, inherited from the Spanish colonial era, categorized people of African descent in multiple ways (*negro, mulato, mestizo, trigueño*). When historical documents use the Spanish word *negro*, it is not always apparent which schema they are following. I use the term *Black* to translate *negro*, keeping the lowercase form in direct quotations from the sources; I also note occurrences of other Spanish terminology when it appears. Although the term *Afro-Cuban* has become widely used in recent years, I have not used it here because in this period it was hotly contested by Cubans of African descent themselves. Complex slippages in racial terminology continue into the present; see Benson, *Antiracism*, 25–28.

4. Alejandro De la Fuente, *A Nation for All: Race, Inequality, and Politics in Twentieth-Century Cuba* (University of North Carolina Press, 2001), 191–192, 220; Alejandra Bronfman, *Measures of Equality: Social Science, Citizenship, and Race in Cuba, 1902–1940* (University of North Carolina Press, 2004), 172–179.

5. On the US Communist Party's adoption of the policy, see chapter 4.

6. Pablo Serviat, *El problema negro en Cuba y su solución definitiva* (Política, 1986), 122.

7. For a retrospective version of this argument by a direct participant, see Fabio Grobart, "The Cuban Working Class Movement from 1925 to 1933," *Science & Society* 39, no. 1 (1975): 73–103. See also Caridad Massón, "Comunismo y nacionalismo: Una relación conflictiva durante la revolución del 30," in Massón, ed., *Comunismo, socialismo y nacionalismo en Cuba (1920–1958)* (Instituto Cubano de Investigación Cultural Juan Marinello, 2013), 123–135; and Angelina Rojas Blaquier, *El primer Partido Comunista de Cuba: Pensamiento político y experiencia práctica. 1935–1952*, tomo 2 (Editorial Oriente, 2006), 169–170.

8. Ada Ferrer, *Insurgent Cuba: Race, Nation, and Revolution, 1868–1898* (University of North Carolina Press, 1998), 9.

9. Aline Helg, *Our Rightful Share: The Afro-Cuban Struggle for Equality, 1886–1912* (University of North Carolina Press, 1995), 16.

10. De la Fuente, *Nation for All*, 72–73; and Helg, *Our Rightful Share*, 165. Official Cuban sources put the toll at two thousand; other estimates range as high as six thousand. Ada Ferrer, *Cuba: An American History* (Scribner, 2021), 209, 213.

11. PCC program, 1 August 1929, RGASPI, F. 495, op. 105, d. 25: 17–25.

12. Mariátegui, "El problema de las razas en América Latina," in *Ideología y política*, 73.

13. Political Secretariat to PCC CC, 25 August 1929, RGASPI, F. 495, op. 105, d. 16: 21–24; Latin American Secretariat to PCC CC, 23 November 1930, RGASPI, F. 495, op. 105, d. 28: 56–57.

14. Report by Departamento de Organización, [early 1932], RGASPI, F. 495, op. 105, d. 58: 3–4.

15. "Report on the Work in Cuba and Mexico Given to L.A.B. July 19th, 1932," RGASPI, F. 495, op. 105, d. 61: 9–10.

16. "Report on the Work in Cuba and Mexico," 9–10.

17. "Al CD de Camagüey," 20 May 1933, IHC–FPPC, 1/2:1/14.2: 50.

18. "Report on the Work in Cuba and Mexico," 9–10.

19. Buró del Caribe, "Resolución sobre la cuestión cubana," 2 December 1931, and Buró del Caribe to PCC Central Committee, 13 May 1932, 25 May 1932, and 29 July 1932, RGASPI, F. 495. op. 105, d. 49: 1–10, 32–36, 37–40, 44–47.

20. Buró del Caribe to PCC Central Committee, 31 August 1932, RGASPI, F. 495, op. 105, d. 49: 56–58.

21. "Plataforma electoral del P.C. de Cuba para las elecciones de 1932" [September 1932], RGAPSI, F. 495, op. 105, d. 55: 30–45.

22. Details from Nicolau's personal file, RGASPI, F. 495, op. 230, d. 15; Suárez's personal file, RGASPI, F. 495, op. 230, d. 25; Jeifets and Jeifets, *Diccionario biográfico*, 451–452 and 593.

23. On the Lenin School curriculum, see Kirschenbaum, *International Communism*, ch. 1; on Soviet nationalities policy in the late 1920s, see chapter 4 of this book.

24. "Los negros en Cuba como nacionalidad oprimida," 14–15.

25. On the PIC, see Helg, *Our Rightful Share*, especially chs. 6 and 7.

26. "Los negros en Cuba como nacionalidad oprimida," 15–19.

27. "Los negros en Cuba como nacionalidad oprimida," 21–23; Stalin, "Marxism and the National Question."

28. "Los negros en Cuba como nacionalidad oprimida," 23, 25.

29. "Los negros en Cuba como nacionalidad oprimida," 25.

30. "Los negros en Cuba como nacionalidad oprimida," 21, 26.

31. "Las elecciones en Cuba," 20–21.

32. Loló de la Torriente, *Testimonio desde dentro* (Editorial Letras Cubanas, 1985), 218.

33. Fernando Martínez Heredia, *La revolución cubana del 30* (Editorial de Ciencias Sociales, 2007), 3–5; Robert Whitney, *State and Revolution in Cuba: Mass*

Mobilization and Political Change, 1920–1940 (University of North Carolina Press, 2001), 81–100.

34. De la Torriente, *Testimonio desde dentro*, 249.

35. Louis Pérez, *Cuba Under the Platt Amendment, 1902–1934* (University of Pittsburgh Press, 1986), 319–324.

36. Decreto Ley 2232, *Gaceta Oficial*, 19 October 1933, 5031–5032.

37. Decreto Ley 2583, *Gaceta Oficial*, 8 November 1933, 6145–6146.

38. Jorge Giovannetti-Torres, *Black British Migrants in Cuba: Race, Labor, and Empire in the Twentieth-Century Caribbean, 1898–1948* (Cambridge University Press, 2018), 197–213; and Matthew Casey, *Empire's Guest Workers: Haitian Migrants in Cuba During the Age of US Occupation* (Cambridge University Press, 2017), 139–142, 236.

39. See Barry Carr, "Identity, Class, and Nation: Black Immigrant Workers, Cuban Communism, and the Sugar Insurgency, 1925–1934," *Hispanic American Historical Review* 78, no. 1 (1998): 83–116; Gillian McGillivray, *Blazing Cane: Sugar Communities, Class, and State Formation in Cuba, 1868–1959* (Duke University Press, 2009), ch. 7; and Angel García and Piotr Mironchuk, *Los soviets obreros y campesinos en Cuba* (Editorial de Ciencias Sociales, 1987).

40. PCC flyer, "Obreros, campesinos, soldados y marinos: La salida revolucionaria de la crisis está en vuestras manos!," 10 November 1933, IHC–FPPC, 1/2:1/14.2, 164.

41. "A todos los Comités Distritales, Regionales y Seccionales: A todas las organizaciones y miembros del Partido," October 1933, IHC–FPPC, 1/2:1/14.2: 151.

42. "A todos los Comités Distritales, Regionales y Seccionales: A todas las organizaciones miembras del P.," 19 October 1933, IHC–FPPC, 1/2:1/14.2: 138.

43. "A todos los Comités Distritales, Regionales y Seccionales," 19 October 1933, 137–138.

44. "¡Declarad huelgas y demostrad en las calles, el 7 de noviembre, XVI aniversario de la Revolución Rusa!," 20 October 1933, IHC–FPPC, 1/2:1/14.2: 139; "A todos los Comités Distritales, Regionales y Seccionales," 19 October 1933, 137.

45. "¡Declarad huelgas y demostrad!," 139.

46. "Informe de la situación del movimiento revolucionario en las provincias de Oriente y Camagüey," 18 September 1933, RGASPI, F. 495, op. 105, d. 82: 29–35.

47. Central Tacajó to PCC CC, 10 October 1933, Archivo Histórico Provincial de Holguín, Colección Movimiento Comunista–Documentos (hereafter AHPH–MCD) 6: 1–2.

48. Arrested in the USSR in 1937 on suspicion of Trotskyism, Lovsky was executed in 1938. Jeifets and Jeifets, *Diccionario biográfico*, 365–366.

49. "Johnny" to Latin American Secretariat, 4 September 1933, RGASPI, F. 495, op. 105, d. 68: 3.

50. Letter from "Johnny," 14 September 1933, RGASPI, F. 495, op. 105, d. 68: 9.

51. "Juan" to "Alberto," 8 November 1933, RGASPI, F. 495, op. 105, d. 68: 15–19; and 29 November 1933, RGASPI, F. 495, op. 105, d. 68: 26–29.

52. Letter from "Juan," 2 December 1933, RGASPI, F. 495, op. 105, d. 68: 30–31.

53. Letter from "Juan," 2 December 1933, 31–32.

54. Letter from "Juan," 2 December 1933, 32.

55. Letter from "Juan," 2 December 1933, 38.

56. Letter from "Juan," 2 December 1933, 33–34.

57. All citations in this paragraph are from letter from "Juan," 2 December 1933, 35–36.

58. All citations in this paragraph are from letter from "Juan," 2 December 1933, 35–36.

59. Emphasis in original.

60. Biographical details from a note dated 13 July 1937 in Castellanos's Comintern file, RGASPI, F. 495, op. 230, d. 75: 1; and Jeifets and Jeifets, *Diccionario biográfico*, 138–139.

61. On Cuban Scottsboro solidarity efforts, see Frances Peace Sullivan, "'For the Liberty of the Nine Boys in Scottsboro and Against Yankee Imperialist Domination in Latin America,'" *Canadian Journal of Latin American and Caribbean Studies* 38, no. 2 (2013): 282–292.

62. According to Castellanos's own recollections: "Declaración al Buró Político sobre la conversación con el Dr Plasencia," 14 September 1934, RGASPI, F. 495, op. 105, d. 107: 40.

63. See Tomás Fernández Robaina, *El negro en Cuba: Colonia, República, Revolución* (Ediciones Cubanas/Artex, 2012), 47–52; Pappademos, *Black Political Activism*, ch. 6; and Bronfman, *Measures of Equality*, ch. 7.

64. Martín Castellanos, "Algo sobre la cuestión negra," *Masas*, no. 1, May 1934, 7.

65. "Resolución de la 1ra Conferencia Nacional" [7 December 1933], RGASPI, F. 495, op. 105, d. 70: 129–130. Emphasis in original.

66. "Acta de la conferencia celebrada en la Habana a los 7 días del mes de diciembre de 1933," RGASPI, F. 495, op. 105, d. 70: 89.

67. "Proyecto resolución negra," n.d., RGASPI, F. 495, op. 105, d. 107: 47–73.

68. "Proyecto resolución negra," 52, 53–54.

69. "Proyecto resolución negra," 61. The term *federal autonomous region* derives from Soviet nationalities policy, which Castellanos cites as a model. From 1918 onward, a string of "autonomous soviet republics" was established across the former tsarist empire. Some went on to become nominally sovereign republics of the USSR, but the majority became "autonomous regions" within the Russian component of the Soviet Union.

70. "Proyecto resolución negra," 65.

71. "Proyecto resolución negra," 62, 67.

72. "Proyecto resolución negra," 54–57, 59.

73. Details from Junco's personal file, RGASPI, F. 495, op. 241, d. 27.

74. "Reunión del Comité Central," 20 September 1932, and "Sesión ampliada del Comité Central del Partido Comunista de Cuba (S. de la I.C.) celebrada el 24 de septiembre de 1932," RGASPI, F. 495, op. 105, d. 50: 1–9 and 10–21.

75. On the early history of Trotskyism in Cuba, see Rafael Soler Martínez, "Los orígenes del trotskismo en Cuba," *Temas* 24–25 (January–June 2001): 45–55.

76. "Programa del Partido Bolchevique Leninista," January 1934, ARNAC, Fondo Especial, leg. 15, exp. 67 [2835]. Junco was assassinated in Sancti Spíritus by unknown assailants in 1942; many suspected the Communist Party was involved. See "Tres muertos y varios heridos en un acto que tenía lugar en memoria de Antonio Guiteras en Sancti Spíritus," *Diario de la Marina*, 9 May 1942.

77. "Proyecto resolución negra," 61–62, 69.

78. "Proyecto resolución negra," 54, 60, 69–71.

79. Alianza Nacional Feminista (National Feminist Alliance) manifesto of 1928, cited in Takkara Brunson, *Black Women, Citizenship, and the Making of Modern Cuba* (University of Florida Press, 2021), 123–126.

80. "La actitud del Partido Comunista de Cuba ante los acontecimientos de Trinidad," n.d. [January–February 1934], IHC–FPPC, 1/2:1/14.3: 28–29. See also See Frank André Guridy, "'War on the Negro': Race and the Revolution of 1933," *Cuban Studies* 40 (2010): 49–73.

81. "¡Trabajadores todos de la provincia de Oriente!," 25 May 1934, ARNAC, Fondo Especial, leg. 1, exp. 12; "Hacia las luchas decisivas por el poder soviético," n.d. [1934], ARNAC, Fondo Especial, leg. 15, exp. 75.

82. "Resolución del II Congreso del PCC sobre la situación actual, perspectivas y tareas," n.d. [April 1934], RGASPI, F. 495, op. 105, d. 98: 64.

83. "La Cuestión Nacional en Cuba," n.d., RGASPI, F. 495, op. 105, d. 95: 89–90. The ban had been enforced until 1933 by the mayor of Santiago, Desiderio Arnaz; ironically, his son, who became famous as Desi Arnaz, would help to popularize that very same musical style in the United States. See Robin Moore, *Nationalizing Blackness: Afrocubanismo and Artistic Revolution in Havana, 1920–1940* (University of Pittsburgh Press, 1997), 72.

84. Resolution from PCC CC III Plenum, n.d. [early 1934], RGASPI, F. 495, op. 105, d. 100: 58–59; "Proyecto de Resolución de Organización para el II Congreso del Partido Comunista de Cuba," IHC–FPPC, 1/2:1/3, 37.

85. Minutes of PCC Buró Político meeting, 17 October 1934, RGASPI, F. 495, op. 105, d. 101: 77.

86. Calculations based on PCC Departamento de Organización, n.d. [1932], RGASPI, F. 495, op. 105, d. 58: 3–4.

87. Calculations based on material from PCC V plenum, 30 August 1933, IHC–FPPC, 1/2:1/5, 1–13, 16.

88. For example, fifteen out of sixty-one members in Encrucijada, eleven out of twenty-five in Camajuaní, twelve out of thirty-five in Ciego de Ávila, five out of fourteen in Matanzas.

89. "Acuerdos tomados en reunión del CC del PC de Cuba en diciembre 14 de 1933," IHC–FPPC, 1/2:1/14.2, 248–250.

90. See Antolín Dickinson Abreu personal file, RGASPI, F. 495, op. 230, d. 27: 2–3, 29–32; and Jeifets and Jeifets, *Diccionario biográfico*, 182–183.

91. Portuondo would later write one of the few histories of the PIC published on the island; biographical information is from Fernando Martínez Heredia's prologue to it: "Prólogo a la presente edición," in Serafín Portuondo Linares, *Los*

independientes de color. Historia del Partido Independiente de Color (1950; Editorial Caminos, 2002), viii.

92. See Lucinda Miranda Fernández, *Lázaro Peña: Capitán de la clase obrera cubana* (Editorial de Ciencias Sociales, 1984), 5–24; Jeifets and Jeifets, *Diccionario biográfico*, 122–123; and "Murió el compañero Rubén Calderío," *Granma*, 23 March 1987.

93. See Jeifets and Jeifets, *Diccionario biográfico*, 535–537.

94. PCC membership data from 25 March 1934, IHC–FPPC, 1/2:1/1.4, 78–79.

95. "Resolución del II Congreso del Partido Comunista de Cuba sobre las tareas de organización," n.d. [April 1934], RGASPI, F. 495, op. 105, d. 98: 89–90.

96. "Informe de Bell sobre el II Congreso del Partido Comunista de Cuba," 5 May 1934, RGASPI, F. 495, op. 105, d. 98: 113.

97. Blas Roca, "Por la Unidad de Acción de Todo el Pueblo de Cuba: Contra el Ataque Imperialista; Contra la Reacción y Machadismo; Por la Libertad y Democracia," 22 October 1935, ARNAC, Fondo Especial, leg. 15, exp. 82, 15, 23.

98. Blas Roca, "Por la Unidad de Acción," 20.

99. Caridad Massón, "La cuestión racial en la política del Partido Comunista de Cuba (1925–1940)," *Perfiles de la Cultura Cubana*, No. 20 (2016).

100. Minutes of IV PCC CC Plenum, 10 February 1935, RGASPI, F. 495, op. 105, d. 123: 4–5.

101. Minutes of IV PCC CC Plenum, 12. Perhaps not coincidentally, around this time Castellanos felt compelled to write a newspaper article insisting "Yes, there is a black problem in Cuba." "Sí hay problema negro en Cuba," *La Palabra*, 17 February 1935.

102. Minutes of IV PCC CC Plenum, 13.

103. Blas Roca speech, 9 September 1935, RGASPI, F. 495, op. 105, d. 120: 2.

104. Minutes of PCC CC meeting, 8 February 1936, RGASPI, F. 495, op. 105, d. 142: 14. On Vivó's trajectory, see chapter 8.

105. Minutes of PCC CC meeting, 8 February 1936, 16.

106. "Conclusiones del 20 Pacto de México y Contraproposiciones del PC, de la reunión del C.C. celebrada el 8 de febrero de 1936," IHC–FPPC, 1/2:1/14.5, 39.

107. "Conclusiones del 20 Pacto de México," 40.

108. Letter to "Alberto" and "Napoleón," 16 February 1936, IHC–FPPC, 1/2.1/1.6, 29–31.

109. PCC CC, "Al País. El Partido Comunista ante los últimos atentados a los negros," 6 April 1936, IHC–FPPC, 1/2:1/14.5: 71.

110. PCC CC VII Plenum, 14 June 1936, IHC–FPPC, 1/2:1/9: 42–43.

111. "A los CD, CS y células y simpatizantes del Partido," Havana, 29 July 1936, IHC–FPPC, 1/2.1/1.6: 151–152.

112. PCC delegation to VII Comintern Congress to PCC CC, 9 January 1936 [but written in late 1935], RGASPI, F. 495, op. 105, d. 120: 39.

113. Alberto Arredondo, "El negro y la nacionalidad," *Adelante*, no. 10 (March 1936), 6; emphasis in original. Arredondo (1912–1968) went on to become a prominent economist in the 1940s and 1950s and a regular contributor to *Bohemia*. Exiled in Miami after the Cuban Revolution, he became an ardent critic of the new regime.

114. Arredondo, "El negro, factor más explotado," *Adelante*, no. 11 (April 1936), 9, 16; Agustín Alarcón, "¿Nación Negra? ¡No!," *Adelante*, no. 18 (November 1936), 12; Arredondo, "Dos palabras más sobre el negro y la nación," *Adelante*, no. (January 1937), 7–8.

115. Arredondo, *El negro en Cuba: Ensayo* (Editorial "Alfa," 1939), 80–98.

116. Blas Roca, "Por la Unidad de Acción," 21.

117. PCC CD Havana, "¡Fuera las manos del imperialismo italiano de Abisinia!," September 1935, ARNAC, Fondo Especial, leg. 1, exp. 42; PCC CC, "Defendamos al pueblo abisinio: A la lucha contra la guerra imperialista," 7 October 1935, IHC–FPPC, 1/2:1/14.4: 109–113.

118. PCC Buró Político, "A todas las organizaciones del partido," n.d. [8 October 1935], IHC–FPPC, 1/2:1/21:13: 71.

119. In what follows I still refer to the party as the PCC, though the situation is more complex. Formally proscribed, in 1937 the PCC created the Partido Unión Revolucionaria (PUR; Revolutionary Union Party) as its legal expression. When the ban on the PCC was lifted in 1938, the two parties existed in parallel, only to merge in 1939 as the Partido Unión Revolucionaria Comunista (PURC; Revolutionary Communist Union Party). This was then renamed the Partido Socialista Popular (PSP; Popular Socialist Party) in 1944.

120. Pappademos, *Black Political Activism*, 180.

121. See for example the interviews with Ana Pérez Santana, Eugenio Gutiérrez, Ramón Rondán Acosta, Lorenzo Noris, Adelaida Vidal, Gabriel Milord, Alfredo Sanches Basulto, and Humberto Dorrego Leyva: AHPH–MOE, 28, 149, 152, 172, 176, 207, 259, 267.

122. XII Plenum del Comité Nacional del PCC, [July] 1939, IHC–FPPC, 1/2:1/1/13, 56.

123. Martínez Heredia, "Prólogo a la presente edición," viii.

124. The PCC published a pamphlet detailing the reasons for Castellanos's expulsion: PCC, "*Cuidemos la unidad . . .*": *El caso del Dr Martín Castellanos* (Impr. Alfa, 1938). Castellanos gave his own account to a Santiago newspaper: "El sometimiento a la línea gobernante ha desorientado a las grandes masas populares," *Diario de Cuba*, 18 October 1938.

125. See Marcelino Hernández Ferrer personal file, RGASPI, F. 495, op. 230, d. 32: 7–16; and Jeifets and Jeifets, *Diccionario biográfico*, 296–297, 195–196.

126. On García Agüero's role, see Bronfman, *Measures of Equality*, 175.

127. Figures from Rojas Blaquier, *El primer Partido Comunista de Cuba*, 27, 43.

128. Cited in Kaitlyn Henderson, "Race, Discrimination, and the Cuban Constitution of 1940," *Hispanic American Historical Review* 100, no. 2 (2020): 258.

129. "A los CD, CS y células y simpatizantes del Partido," 151.

130. *Los partidos políticos y la asamblea constituyente: Inmigración, economía, trabajo, educación, discriminación; Conferencias de Orientación Ciudadana, Club Atenas, Feb. 13–Mayo 15, 1939* (Club Atenas, 1939), 142.

131. The other two nonwhite delegates were José Maceo González of the National Revolutionary Party and Antonio Bravo Acosta of the Democratic Republican

Party. See de la Fuente, *Nation for All*, 216, 228. On Sánchez, see Manuel Ramírez Chicharro and Michelle Chase, "Black Left Feminism in Pre-revolutionary Cuba: The Life and Work of Esperanza Sánchez Mastrapa (1901–1958)," *Women's History Review* 31, no. 5 (2022): 784–805.

132. On these debates, see Henderson, "Race, Discrimination, and the Cuban Constitution," 275–282.

133. Bronfman, *Measures of Equality*, 176–177.

134. *Constitución de la República de Cuba: Publicada en la Gaceta Oficial de Julio 8 de 1940* (Compañía Editora de Libros y Folletos, 1940), 7.

135. Whitney, *State and Revolution in Cuba*, 3.

136. De la Fuente, *Nation for All*, 215.

137. De la Fuente, *Nation for All*, 192.

138. Moore, *Nationalizing Blackness*, 37.

139. Solomon, *Cry Was Unity*, 86, 89.

CHAPTER 8. A PLURAL NATION

1. "El Primer Congreso Indigenista Interamericano que se efectúa en la ciudad de Pátzcuaro," *El Nacional*, 18 April 1940, 4.

2. "Primer Congreso Indigenista Interamericano, Acta Final," 9 May 1940, Archivo General de la Nación, Ramo Presidentes, Lázaro Cárdenas del Río (hereafter AGN–LCR), 533.4/1, 344–351.

3. The speech was reprinted in many places; here I cite "Discurso de inauguración pronunciado por el Presidente de la República Mexicana, Gral. de División Lázaro Cárdenas," in Confederación de Trabajadores de América Latina, *Primer Congreso Indigenista Interamericano* ([n.p.], 1940), 5–8, at 7.

4. On Gamio, see Claudio Lomnitz, *Deep Mexico, Silent Mexico: An Anthropology of Nationalism* (University of Minnesota Press, 2001), 250–253, and Rosemblatt, *Science and Politics of Race*, ch. 1.

5. The literature on the Mexican postrevolutionary state and education is extensive, but see notably Mary Kay Vaughan, *Cultural Politics in Revolution: Teachers, Peasants, and Schools in Mexico, 1930–1940* (University of Arizona Press, 1997). On Mexican anthropology and *indigenismo* in this period, see Alan Knight, "Racism, Revolution and Indigenismo: Mexico, 1910–1940," in Richard Graham, ed., *The Idea of race in Latin America, 1870–1940* (University of Texas Press, 1990), 71–113; Cynthia Hewitt de Alcántara, *Anthropological Perspectives on Rural Mexico* (Routledge and Kegan Paul, 1984), ch. 1; Lomnitz, *Deep Mexico, Silent Mexico*, ch. 11; and Jaime Noyola Rocha, "La visión de la sociedad nacional (1920–1934)," and Arturo España Caballero, "La práctica social y el populismo nacionalista (1935–1940)," both in Carlos García Mora, ed., *La antropología en México: Panorama histórico*, vol. 2 (SEP/INAH, 1987), 133–220 and 223–287.

6. See for example Andrés Fábregas Puig, *Historia mínima del indigenismo en América Latina* (El Colegio de México, 2021), ch. 2.

7. See Stephen Lewis, *Rethinking Mexican Indigenismo: The INI's Coordinating Center in Highland Chiapas and the Fate of a Utopian Project* (University of New Mexico Press, 2018), 3–6.

8. See Alexander Dawson, *Indian and Nation in Revolutionary Mexico* (University of Arizona Press, 2004), 83–86; "Primer Congreso Indigenista Interamericano, Acta Final," 344–351.

9. The outstanding contribution here is Rosemblatt, *Science and Politics of Race*; see also Guillermo de la Peña, "Nacionales y extranjeros en la historia de la antropología mexicana," in Mechthild Rutsch, ed., *La historia de la antropología en México. Fuentes y trasmisión* (Instituto Nacional Indigenista, 1996), 41–83.

10. *El Machete*, no. 172, 6 July 129; Programa del Bloque Obrero y Campesino Nacional, "Reivindicaciones inmediatas," October 1929, CEMOS, Fondo PCM, caja 4, exp. 16.

11. *El Machete*, no. 192, late February 1931.

12. *El Mauser*, no. 4, January 1932, in RGASPI, F. 533, op. 10, d. 2080: 4–7.

13. "Resolución sobre la cuestión indígena," RGASPI, F. 495, op. 108, d. 150: 173–178.

14. "Resolución sobre la cuestión indígena," 173–174.

15. "Resolución sobre la cuestión indígena," 174.

16. "Resolución sobre la cuestión indígena," 175.

17. Martin, *Affirmative Action Empire*, ch. 1.

18. Francisco Balderrama and Raymond Rodríguez, *Decade of Betrayal: Mexican Repatriation in the 1930s* (University of New Mexico Press, 2006), 195.

19. "El PCM en la senda de la bolchevización," July 1929, cited in Gerardo Peláez, "Los años de clandestinidad," in Arnoldo Martínez Verdugo, ed., *Historia del comunismo en México* (Grijalbo, 1983), 131.

20. Carr, *Marxism and Communism*, 10, table 1.

21. *El Machete*, no. 226, 20 May 1932.

22. *El Machete*, no. 230, 30 June 1932.

23. *El Machete*, no. 234, 10 August 1932; no. 258, 1 May 1933; no. 259, 10 May 1933; and no. 261, 30 May 1933.

24. "Proyecto de resolución para el pleno del CC" [n.d.], RGASPI, F. 495, op. 108, d. 171, 40.

25. "La cuestión nacional en México," 15 October 1934, RGASPI, F. 495, op. 108, d. 170, 20.

26. *La nueva política del Partido Comunista de México* (Ediciones del Frente Cultural, 1936), CEMOS, Fondo PCM Folletos, serie 2, 54: 6.

27. *La nueva política del P.C. de México*, 13.

28. Stephan Scheuzger, "La izquierda mexicana y la cuestión indígena: ¿Caminos al desencuentro?," in Yael Bitrán, ed., *México: Historia y alteridad* (Universidad Iberoamericana, 2001), 299–324.

29. See, respectively, Verdugo's *Historia del comunismo en México*; David Alfaro Siqueiros, *Me llamaban el coronelazo: Memorias* (Biografías Gandesa, 1977); and Valentín Campa, *Mi testimonio: Experiencias de un comunista mexicano* (Ediciones de Cultura Popular, 1978).

30. Among those to apply the term *pluralist* are Hewitt, *Anthropological Perspectives on Rural Mexico*, 14–19; Rosemblatt, *Science and Politics of Race*, ch. 4; and Dawson, *Indian and Nation*, 41.

31. See for example Consuelo Sánchez, *Los pueblos indígenas: Del indigenismo a la autonomía* (Siglo XXI, 1999), 32–38; Guillermo de la Peña, "The End of Revolutionary Anthropology? Notes on *Indigenismo*," in Paul Gillingham and Benjamin Smith, eds., *Dictablanda: Politics, Work, and Culture in Mexico, 1938–1968* (Duke University Press, 2014), 281; Dawson, *Indian and Nation*, 79–80; and Rosemblatt, *Science and Politics of Race*, 93.

32. "Entrevista del licenciado Vicente Lombardo Toledano con los representantes de la prensa de México, respecto de su viaje a la Unión Soviética," October 1935, Universidad Obrera de México (UOM), Fondo Histórico Vicente Lombardo Toledano (hereafter FHVLT), 15576, leg. 268.

33. For a comprehensive recent biography, see Daniela Spenser, *In Combat: The Life of Lombardo Toledano* (Brill, 2019).

34. See for example *El Machete*, no. 178, 7 November 1929; no. 208, 10 September 1931; no. 255, 20 March 1933; no. 267, 10 August 1933; no. 281, 10 January 1934; no. 290, 30 April 1934.

35. Daniela Spenser, "El viaje de Vicente Lombardo Toledano al mundo del porvenir," *Desacatos* 34 (2010): 85.

36. For a detailed account of his itinerary, see Spenser, "El viaje de Vicente Lombardo Toledano," 86–89.

37. Lombardo, "Moscú," August 1935, FHVLT, 15623, leg 266: 1, 2.

38. Lombardo, "El VII Congreso de la Internacional Comunista," August 1935, FHVLT, 15620, leg. 266: 4–5.

39. Vicente Lombardo Toledano and Víctor Manuel Villaseñor, *Un viaje al mundo del porvenir: Seis conferencias sobre la U.R.S.S.* (Universidad Obrera de México, 1936).

40. Lombardo, "Geografía de las lenguas de la Sierra de Puebla," in *Escritos acerca de la situación de los indígenas* (Centro de Estudios Filosóficos, Políticos y Sociales Vicente Lombardo Toledano, 2006), 67–115.

41. Lombardo, "El problema de la educación en México," in *Escritos acerca de la situación de los indígenas*, 45.

42. Lombardo, "Geografía de las lenguas de la Sierra de Puebla," 68.

43. Lombardo, "Cómo resolvió el régimen soviético el problema de las nacionalidades oprimidas," in *Un viaje al mundo del porvenir*, 97–120. The text also appears in *Escritos acerca de la situación de los indígenas*, 141–161, under the more modest title "El régimen soviético y el problema de las nacionalidades oprimidas"; since this is the most widely available version, I cite it in the remainder of this section.

44. Lombardo, "El régimen soviético," 148–149.

45. Lombardo, "El régimen soviético," 150–153.

46. Martin, *Affirmative Action Empire*, chs. 9 and 10. For a discussion of developments in the North Caucasus, see Tony Wood, *Chechnya: The Case for Independence* (Verso, 2007), 32–34.

47. R. W. Davies and Stephen Wheatcroft, *The Years of Hunger: Soviet Agriculture, 1931–33* (Palgrave Macmillan, 2003), 415.

48. Lombardo, "El régimen soviético," 160.

49. Lombardo, "El régimen soviético," 160–61.

50. Miguel Othón de Mendizábal, "El Departamento Autónomo Indígena de México: Sus fines, su táctica y su organización," in *Obras completas*, vol. 4 (Talleres Gráficas de la Nación, 1946), 331.

51. Mendizábal, "El Departamento Autónomo Indígena de México," 332–334.

52. Biographical information in this paragraph is from España Caballero, "La práctica social y el populismo nacionalista," 248–252; Tomás Bernal Alanís, "El camino de un antropólogo. La obra de Miguel Othón de Mendizábal: La época de reconstrucción nacional, 1920–1945" (PhD thesis, INAH, 2014), 125–162; and Gonzalo Aguirre Beltrán, *Obra antropológica*, vol. IX, *Obra polémica* (Fondo de Cultura Económica, 1992), 190–192.

53. Miguel Othón de Mendizábal, *La influencia de la sal en la distribución geográfica de los grupos indígenas de México* (Museo Nacional de Arqueología, Historia y Etnografía, 1928). On Mendizábal's role at the museum, see Museo Nacional de Antropología (henceforth MNA), vol. 423, exp. 53, vol. 424, exp. 3, vol. 424, exp. 10, and vol. 424, exp. 16.

54. See entries for 4 and 11 August 1927 in "Anlage 3. Tagesordnung der Sektion Mexiko D.F.," RGASPI, F. 542, op. 1, d. 19: 76.

55. Aguirre Beltrán, citing personal communication from Rafael Carrillo, in *Obra polémica*, 190n178.

56. Mendizábal, "El Departamento Autónomo Indígena de México," 336.

57. See Miguel Othón de Mendizábal, "El problema social de las lenguas indígenas," in Departamento de Asuntos Indígenas, *Memoria de la Primera Asamblea de Filólogos y Lingüistas* (Departamento Autónomo de Asuntos Indígenas, 1940), 33–45.

58. Mendizábal, "El problema de las nacionalidades oprimidas y su resolución en la U.R.S.S.," in *Obras completas*, vol. 4, 389–399. The text is undated, but the inclusion of a reference to Henry Wallace's "Century of the Common Man" speech suggests it was written no earlier than 1942.

59. Andrés Medina Hernández, "Un capítulo en la olvidada historia de la antropología en México (1906–1940): Miguel Othón de Mendizábal, el constructor," in *Bérose: Encyclopédie internationale des histoires de l'anthropologie* (Ministère de la Culture/IIAC-CNRS-EHESS, 2019), 12.

60. Miguel Othón de Mendizábal, *La evolución del noroeste de México* (Departamento de la Estadística Nacional, 1930), 63–64.

61. Miguel Othón de Mendizábal, *Historia económica y social de México, 5a Conferencia* (Secretaría de Educación Pública, 1935), 13.

62. "Ley de Secretarías y Departamentos de Estado," *Diario Oficial*, 31 December 1935, 1550.

63. Despite its significance, relatively little has been written about the DAI to date. The most substantive treatments are in Dawson, *Indian and Nation*, and Patricia

Legarreta Haynes, "Ingeniería social en Mesoamérica. Revolución, intervención, desarrollo y cooperación internacional" (PhD thesis, UAM-Iztapalapa, 2016). See also Haydée López Hernández, "De la gloria prehispánica al socialismo. Las políticas indigenistas del Cardenismo," *Cuicuilco*, no. 57 (May–August 2013): 47–74.

64. Dawson, *Indian and Nation*, 97–98.

65. *El Nacional*, 26 September 1936.

66. For Ixmiquilpan coverage, see *El Nacional*, 6 September, 21 September, 25 September, 26 September, 28 September, and 30 September 1936. The DAI republished the proceedings as *Memoria del Primer Congreso Regional Indígena celebrado en Ixmiquilpan, Hgo., 25–26 Sept 1936* (Departamento Autónomo de Prensa y Publicidad, 1938).

67. Dawson, *Indian and Nation*, 105.

68. Vivó, "México y el Indio," *El Nacional*, 9 May 1937; the series continued on 10 May, 13 May, and 14 May 1937.

69. Dawson, *Indian and Nation*, 83.

70. Vivó, *Geografía de México* (Fondo de Cultura Económica, 1948).

71. Details in this paragraph are drawn from an autobiographical text Vivó wrote during his stay in Moscow in 1934–35, kept in his personal file: [Vivó autobiography], RGASPI, F. 495, op. 230, d. 134: 36–47; and Jeifets and Jeifets, *Diccionario biográfico*, 640–643; see also Jeifets and Jeifets, "La odisea roja: Varias líneas al retrato político de Jorge Vivó d'Escoto," *Revista CS* (Calí), no. 14 (2014): 167–200.

72. "Simón" to "Paco," 20 March 1937, IHC–FPPC, 1/2:1/1.6, 210.

73. [Vivó autobiography], 43.

74. Vivó, "La Unión Soviética y el problema nacional," *El Nacional*, 23 August, 29 August, 10 September, 3 October, 24 October, 31 October, 7 November, and 14 November 1938. Retyped versions consulted in the Archivo Histórico de la Escuela Nacional de Antropología e Historia (hereafter AH–ENAH), Fondo ENA, caja 16, exp. 72, and Fondo ENA, caja 6, exp. 73.

75. Abkhazia had been a Soviet Republic in its own right from 1921 to 1931, before being incorporated into Georgia with autonomous status.

76. *El Nacional*, 10 September 1938.

77. *El Nacional*, 3 October 1938.

78. *El Nacional*, 24 October, 31 October, 7 November, and 14 November 1938.

79. *El Nacional*, 10 May, 13 May, and 14 May 1937.

80. See Vivó, "Tamazunchale," *El Nacional*, 15 May 1938.

81. Alfonso Fabila, *Las tribus Yaquis de Sonora: Su cultura y anhelada autodeterminación* (Departamento de Asuntos Indígenas, 1940).

82. Biographical details in this paragraph are drawn from María del Rosario Casco Montoya and René Avilés Fabila, "El indigenismo, el indígena y Alfonso Fabila (Breve estudio y bibliografía)," *B.B.A.A. Boletín Bibliográfico de Antropología Americana* 26/28, no. 1 (1963–1965): 89–95; and Luis Vázquez León, "Alfonso Fabila," in García Mora, ed., *La antropología en México*, 10:56–59.

83. Alfonso Fabila, *El problema de la emigración de obreros y campesinos mexicanos* (Secretaría de Gobernación, 1929).

84. On Fabila and the Committee, see Balderrama and Rodríguez, *Decade of Betrayal*, 164, 175.

85. Early works include *El en Sí* (1922), *Sangre de mi sangre* (1924), and *Los brazos en cruz* (1929). More followed over the rest of Fabila's life, including short stories in *Hoz* (1934) and *Aurora campesina* (1941), the novels *Norte* (1943) and *Entre la tormenta* (1946), and a collection of poems, *Sur* (1952).

86. Fabila, *Las tribus Yaquis de Sonora*, vii. In Stalin's definition, "A nation is a historically constituted, stable community of people, formed on the basis of a common language, territory, economic life, and psychological make-up manifested in a common culture." Stalin, "Marxism and the National Question," 300–381.

87. Fabila, *Las tribus Yaquis de Sonora*, viii, ix, xv.

88. For scholarly overviews, see Evelyn Hu-DeHart, "Peasant Rebellion in the Northwest: The Yaqui Indians of Sonora, 1740–1976," in Friedrich Katz, ed., *Riot, Rebellion, and Revolution: Rural Social Conflict in Mexico* (Princeton University Press, 1988), 141–175; and Cynthia Radding, "Peasant Resistance on the Yaqui Delta," *Journal of the Southwest* 31, no. 3 (1989): 330–361.

89. Fabila, *Las tribus Yaquis de Sonora*, 70–111.

90. Fabila, *Las tribus Yaquis de Sonora*, ix.

91. See Radding, "Peasant Resistance," 341, 348–349.

92. Juventino Espinosa Sánchez to Cárdenas, 25 July and 9 September 1936, AGN–LCR, 533.11/1, 812–813 and 809–811.

93. The agreement is reproduced in Fabila, *Las tribus Yaquis de Sonora*, 301–303.

94. On interactions between local conceptions of the land and the Mexican state's view, see Daniel Nugent and Ana María Alonso, "Multiple Selective Traditions in Agrarian Reform and Agrarian Struggle: Popular Culture and State Formation in the Ejido of Namiquipa, Chihuahua," in Joseph and Nugent, eds., *Everyday Forms of State Formation*, 209–248.

95. Cárdenas to Román Yocupicio, 4 May 1937, AGN–LCR, 533.11/1, 602.

96. Fabila, *Las tribus Yaquis de Sonora*, 136.

97. Fabila to Cárdenas, 3 August 1938, AGN–LCR, 533.11/1, 515.

98. Fabila, *Las tribus Yaquis de Sonora*, ix.

99. Fabila, *Las tribus Yaquis de Sonora*, ix, xiv.

100. Fabila, *Las tribus Yaquis de Sonora*, xv.

101. "A los C.C. Gobernadores de los 8 Pueblos de la Tribu Yaqui," 10 June 1939, AGN–LCR, 533.11/1, 556–560.

102. Chávez Orozco to Cárdenas, 10 July 1939, AGN–LCR, 533.11/1, 453; emphasis in original.

103. "A los C.C. Gobernadores," 557–558.

104. DAI, *Memoria de la Primera Asamblea*, 10.

105. Roderic Ai Camp, *Mexican Political Biographies, 1935–1993* (University of Texas Press, 1995), 152.

106. Luis Chávez Orozco, *La civilización maya-quiché* (Talleres Gráficos Nacionales, 1932); *La civilización nahoa* (SEP, 1933); *Historia de México*, 2 vols. (Editorial Patria, 1934).

107. See his pamphlet in support of it: Chávez Orozco, *La educación socialista* (SEP, 1937).

108. Kirchhoff (1900–1972) is best known for coining the term *Mesoamerica*; a member of the Communist Workers' Party of Germany (KAPD), he arrived in Mexico in 1936. See Adriana Zapett Tapia, "Paul Kirchhoff," in García Mora, ed., *La antropología en México*, 10:352–360.

109. *El Nacional*, 29 May, 30 May, 8 June 1939; retyped versions consulted at AH–ENAH, Fondo ENA, caja 16, exp. 73.

110. DAI, *Memoria de la Primera Asamblea*, 16. Most Indigenous delegates were from Oaxaca; only three were women.

111. "Entrevista de historia oral con Luis Chávez Orozco," in James W. Wilkie and Edna Monzón de Wilkie, *Frente a la Revolución Mexicana: 17 protagonistas de la etapa constructivista. Entrevistas de historia oral* (Universidad Nacional Autónoma Metropolitana, 1995), 1:87.

112. "Entrevista de historia oral con Luis Chávez Orozco," 87.

113. DAI, *Memoria de la Primera Asamblea*, 43–44.

114. DAI, *Memoria de la Primera Asamblea*, 23–32.

115. See Shirley Brice Heath, *Telling Tongues: Language Policy in Mexico, Colony to Nation* (Teachers College Press, 1972), 118–119, 128, 144–147.

116. Andrés Lemos Pastrana, *La Escuela Nacional de Ciencias Biológicas IPN: Una visión histórica* (Instituto Politécnico Nacional, 2009), 60.

117. "Labores y conclusiones del 20 Congreso de Higiene Rural celebrado en San Luis Potosí del 21 al 26 de noviembre de 1938 y la agitación provocada al derredor de dicho congreso," AGN–LCR, 433/332, [n.p.]. See also Lemos Pastrana, *La Escuela Nacional de Ciencias Biológicas*, 59–60.

118. Laura Giraudo, "Un campo indigenista transnacional y 'casi profesional': La apertura en Pátzcuaro (1940) de un espacio por y para los indigenistas," in Giraudo and Juan Martín-Sánchez, eds., *La ambivalente historia del indigenismo: Campo interamericano y trayectorias nacionales, 1940–1970* (Instituto de Estudios Peruanos, 2011), 25–26.

119. Cárdenas to Agustín Leñero, 5 October 1939, AGN–LCR, 533.4/1, 459.

120. Sáenz to Cárdenas, 5 January 1939, AGN–LCR, 533.4/1, 487–489.

121. Sáenz, "Sobre la creación de un Departamento de Población Indígena," September 1935, AGN–LCR, 533.4/1, 562–584.

122. Sáenz, "Sobre la creación," 564–565.

123. Moisés Sáenz, *México Íntegro* (1939; Consejo Nacional para la Cultura y las Artes, 2006), 40.

124. Sáenz, *México Íntegro*, 143–144.

125. Cárdenas to Sáenz, 22 March 1939, AGN–LCR, 533.4/1, 481.

126. Chávez Orozco to Cárdenas, 22 April 1939, AGN–LCR, 533.4/1, 471–472.

127. Lombardo, "El problema fundamental del indio," in *Escritos acerca de la situación de los indígenas*, 196.

128. Lombardo, "En el seno de la patria mexicana deben convivir, libre y fraternalmente, todos los núcleos raciales," in *Escritos acerca de la situación de los indígenas*, 183.

129. Lombardo, "Nueva división político-territorial en las zonas habitadas por indígenas," in *Escritos acerca de la situación de los indígenas*, 203–204.

130. "Primer Congreso Indigenista Interamericano, Acta Final," 377.

131. Azcárate, "Ponencia del Comité Nacional de Ayuda al Niño Indígena ante el Primer Congreso Indigenista Interamericano," Universidad Nacional Autónoma de México (UNAM), Programa Universitario de Estudios de la Diversidad Cultural y la Interculturalidad, Biblioteca Manuel Gamio, Fondo Instituto Indigenista Interamericano (hereafter PUIC–UNAM, Fondo III), caja 1, Congresos indigenistas, tomo 3, 319–322.

132. Vivó, "Aspectos económicos fundamentales del problema indígena," PUIC–UNAM, Fondo III, caja 1, Congresos indigenistas, tomo 6, 388–394.

133. Vivó, "Rasgos tribales y nacionales del problema indígena," PUIC–UNAM, Fondo III, caja 1, Congresos indigenistas, tomo 6, 395–404.

134. Vivó, "Rasgos tribales y nacionales," 396–397.

135. Vivó, "Rasgos tribales y nacionales," 399–403.

136. Vivó, "Rasgos tribales y nacionales," 403.

137. Vivó, "Rasgos tribales y nacionales," 404.

138. Luis Chávez Orozco, "El Primer Congreso Indigenista Interamericano," *Educación* (June 1940): 19–22.

139. "Discurso de inauguración," 5–7.

140. See for example the account by Guatemalan writer David Vela, *Orientación y recomendaciones del Primer Congreso Indigenista Interamericano* (Comité Organizador del IV Congreso Indigenista Interamericano, 1959).

141. Ángel Corzo to Ávila Camacho, 14 February 1941, cited in Dawson, *Indian and Nation*, 135.

142. Dawson, *Indian and Nation*, 137–138.

143. DAI, *Memoria del Departamento de Asuntos Indígenas, 1941–42* (Talleres Gráficos Nacionales, 1942), 17–55, 85.

144. Ai Camp, *Mexican Political Biographies*, 152. Chávez Orozco also produced many more historical works before his death in 1966.

145. "Anuarios de la ENA, 1943–1948," in AH–ENAH, Fondo ENA, caja 17, exp. 7. On Vivó's later years, see Jeifets and Jeifets, "La odisea roja," 194–195.

146. Casco Montoya and Avilés Fabila, "El indigenismo, el indígena y Alfonso Fabila," 91–92. On Fabila's work in Guerrero in the 1950s, see Rebecca Overmyer-Velázquez, *Folkloric Poverty: Neoliberal Multiculturalism in Mexico* (Pennsylvania State University Press, 2010), ch. 2.

147. Fabila, "Misión Cultural 17 (Hueyapan)," [n.d.], Instituto Nacional de los Pueblos Indígenas, Biblioteca Juan Rulfo, Fondo Documental, 52/0167, 20.

148. Alfonso Fabila, *El problema indígena de México: Contribución para resolverlo* (Imprenta de la Escuela Rafael Dondé, 1941), 16.

149. Fabila, *El problema indígena*, 16.

EPILOGUE

1. Lewis, *Rethinking Mexican Indigenismo*, 1–2.

2. Alfonso Caso, "Alfonso Fabila," *Acción Indigenista*, no. 85, July 1960, 1.

3. See A. S. Dillingham, *Oaxaca Resurgent: Indigeneity, Inequality, and Development in Twentieth-Century Mexico* (Stanford University Press, 2021), 93–118; and Karin Rosemblatt, "Modernization, Dependency, and the Global in Mexican Critiques of Anthropology," *Journal of Global History* 9 (2014): 94–121.

4. Guillermo Bonfil Batalla, "Del indigenismo de la Revolución a la antropología crítica" (1970), in *Obra escogida*, tomo 1, *Obra publicada* (INI/INAH, 1985), 296.

5. See Maria L. O. Muñoz, *Stand Up and Fight: Participatory Indigenismo, Populism, and Mobilization in Mexico, 1970–1984* (University of Arizona Press, 2016), esp. chs. 4 and 5.

6. "Carta de las comunidades indígenas, Pátzcuaro" (1975), reproduced in María Consuelo Mejía Piñeros and Sergio Sarmiento Silva, *La lucha indígena: Un reto a la ortodoxia* (Siglo XXI, 1987), 259.

7. "Carta de las comunidades indígenas," 260.

8. David Recondo, *La política del gatopardo: Multiculturalismo y democracia en Oaxaca* (CIESAS, 2007), ch. 2.

9. Jeffrey Rubin, *Decentering the Regime: Ethnicity, Radicalism, and Democracy in Juchitán, Mexico* (Duke University Press, 1997).

10. *Diario Oficial*, 28 January 1992, 5.

11. *Diario Oficial*, 14 August 2001, 2–4.

12. Consuelo Sánchez's *Los pueblos indígenas* makes clear that it was inspired by this conjuncture.

13. Yásnaya Elena Aguilar Gil, "Nosotros sin México: Naciones indígenas y autonomía," *Nexos*, May 18, 2018.

14. The partial exceptions are Sánchez, *Los pueblos indígenas*, and Scheuzger, "La izquierda mexicana y la cuestión indígena."

15. Pablo González Casanova, "Sociedad plural, colonialismo interno y desarrollo," *América Latina* 6, no. 3 (1963): 15–32.

16. Amid the polemics unleashed by post-1968 critiques of *indigenismo*, Aguirre Beltrán was frustrated that the current generation of Marxists knew so little of their predecessors, including Lombardo's and Mendizábal's endorsement of the Soviet nationalities model. *Obra polémica*, 157–158, 190–195.

17. Héctor Díaz-Polanco, *Autonomía regional: La autodeterminación de los pueblos indígenas* (Siglo XXI, 1991), 200.

18. International Labor Organization, "Indigenous and Tribal Peoples Convention, 1989 (No. 169)," accessed February 28, 2025, https://www.ilo.org/dyn/normlex /en/f?p=1000:12000:0::NO:::.

19. On indigenous movements in Ecuador and Bolivia, see Marc Becker, *Pachakutik: Indigenous Movements and Electoral Politics in Ecuador* (Rowman and Littlefield, 2011), and Forrest Hylton and Sinclair Thomson, *Revolutionary Horizons: Past and Present in Bolivian Politics* (Verso, 2007).

20. Rodolfo Disi Pavlic, "Indigenous Voices and Votes: Assessing the Dynamics of Indigenous Politics in Chile's Constitutional Referendum of 2022," *PS: Political Science & Politics* 57, no. 2 (April 2024): 267–273.

21. For the case of Peru, see Anthony Bebbington, ed., *Minería, movimientos sociales y respuestas campesinas: Una ecología política de transformaciones territoriales* (IEP/CEPES, 2011); and Fabiana Li, *Unearthing Conflict: Corporate Mining, Activism, and Expertise in Peru* (Duke University Press, 2015).

22. See David Covin, *The Unified Black Movement in Brazil, 1978–2002* (McFarland & Company, 2006), esp. ch. 4.

23. David Lehmann, *The Prism of Race: The Politics and Ideology of Affirmative Action in Brazil* (University of Michigan Press, 2018).

24. Andrew Francis-Tan and Maria Tannuri-Pianto, "Affirmative Action in Brazil: Global Lessons on Racial Justice and the Fight to Reduce Social Inequality," *Oxford Review of Economic Policy* 40, no. 3 (Autumn 2024): 645–646.

25. On race and the literacy campaign, see Benson, *Antiracism in Cuba*, ch. 5.

26. Benson, *Antiracism in Cuba*, 2.

27. "Discurso pronunciado por el Comandante Fidel Castro Ruz, Primer Secretario de la Dirección Nacional de las ORI y Primer Ministro del Gobierno Revolucionario, en la Segunda Asamblea Nacional del Pueblo de Cuba, celebrada en la Plaza de la Revolución, el 4 de febrero de 1962," accessed February 28, 2025, http:// www.cuba.cu/gobierno/discursos//1962/esp/f040262e.html.

28. On the emergence of this persistent trope, see Ferrer, *Insurgent Cuba*, 7–10.

29. For accounts that take this split as foundational, see Jorge Castañeda, *Utopia Unarmed: The Latin American Left after the Cold War* (Alfred A. Knopf, 1993), ch. 2, and Rojas, *El árbol de las revoluciones*, ch. 2.

30. See Grandin, "Liberal Traditions in the Americas."

BIBLIOGRAPHY

PRIMARY SOURCES

Archival Collections and Libraries

Mexico

Archivo General de la Nación (AGN), Mexico City
    Dirección General de Investigaciones Políticas y Sociales (DGIPS)
    Ramo Presidentes
        Lázaro Cárdenas del Río (LCR)
    Servicio de Migración
        Registro de Extranjeros
Archivo Histórico de la Escuela Nacional de Antropología e Historia (AH–ENAH),
        Mexico City
    Fondo ENA
Archivo Histórico del Senado, Mexico City
Biblioteca Miguel Lerdo de Tejada, Mexico City
    Hemeroteca
Biblioteca Nacional de México, Mexico City
    Hemeroteca Nacional de México
Centro de Estudios del Movimiento Obrero y Socialista (CEMOS), Mexico City
    Fondo PCM
    Fondo PCM Folletos
Centro de Estudios Filosóficos; Políticos y Sociales Vicente Lombardo Toledano,
        Mexico City
    Biblioteca del Centro Lombardo
        Acervo histórico
        Acervo hemerográfico
Instituto Nacional de los Pueblos Indígenas, Mexico City
    Biblioteca Juan Rulfo (BJR)
        Fondo Documental

Museo Nacional de Antropología (MNA), Mexico City
    Archivo Histórico
Secretaría de Relaciones Exteriores, Mexico City
    Archivo Histórico Genaro Estrada (AHGE)
Universidad Nacional Autónoma de México (UNAM), Mexico City
    Programa Universitario de Estudios de la Diversidad Cultural y la
        Interculturalidad (PUIC)
        Biblioteca Manuel Gamio
            Fondo Instituto Indigenista Interamericano
Universidad Obrera de México (UOM), Mexico City
    Fondo Histórico Vicente Lombardo Toledano (FHVLT)

Cuba

Archivo Nacional de Cuba (ARNAC), Havana
    Fondo Especial
Archivo Histórico de la Provincia de Holguín (AHPH), Holguín
    Colección Movimiento Comunista–Documentos (MCD)
    Movimiento Obrero–Entrevistas (MOE)
Biblioteca Nacional de Cuba José Martí, Havana
Biblioteca Pública Provincial Elvira Cape, Santiago de Cuba
Instituto de Historia de Cuba (IHC), Havana
    Fondo Julio Antonio Mella (FJAM)
    Fondo Primer Partido Comunista (FPPC)
    Hemeroteca

Russia

Russian State Archive of Social and Political History (RGASPI), Moscow
    Fond 495
    Fond 534
    Fond 535
    Fond 542

Netherlands

International Institute for Social History, Amsterdam
    League against Imperialism Archives

Peru

Biblioteca Nacional del Perú, Lima
    Fondo Antiguo
    Hemeroteca
Pontificia Universidad Católica del Perú, Lima
    Colecciones Especiales de Ciencias Sociales
        Colección Arturo Sabroso Montoya
    Hemeroteca

United States

Benson Latin American Collection, Austin, TX
  Magda Portal Papers (MPP)
National Archives and Records Administration (NARA), College Park, MD
  Record Group 59 (RG) (State Department)
New York Public Library, New York City, NY

Newspapers and Periodicals

Acción Indigenista
Adelante
Amauta
APRA
Atuei
Boletín Titikaka
La Correspondance Internationale
La Correspondencia Sudamericana
The Crisis
Diario de Cuba (Santiago)
Diario de la Marina (Havana)
Diario Oficial (Mexico)
Excélsior
Gaceta Oficial (Cuba)
Granma
Indoamérica
El Informador
Inprecor
Izvestiia
Juventud (Havana)
El Libertador
El Machete
Masas (Havana)
El Nacional (Mexico City)
La Palabra (Havana)
La Prensa (Mexico City)
El Productor
El Universal (Mexico City)
La Voz del Campesino

Published Primary Sources

Aprismo: Transcripción de los artículos y discursos de los líderes, oradores y parlamentarios; y de Haya de la Torre; el manifiesto del jefe del aprismo a la nación peruana. Ediciones Corrientes, 1933.

Arredondo, Alberto. *El negro en Cuba: Ensayo*. Editorial "Alfa," 1939.

Bajo la bandera de la C.S.L.A. Resoluciones y documentos varios del Congreso constituyente de la Confederación sindical latino-americana efectuado en Montevideo en mayo de 1929. Imprenta La Linotipo, 1929.

Barrios, Elías. *El escuadrón de hierro*. Ediciones de Cultura Popular, 1978.

Basbaum, Leôncio. *Uma vida em seis tempos: Memorias*. Editora Alfa-Omega, 1976.

Bauer, Otto. *The Question of Nationalities and Social Democracy*. University of Minnesota Press, 2000. Originally published in 1907.

Becker, Marc, ed. *The Latin American Revolutionary Movement: Proceedings of the First Latin American Communist Conference, June 1929*. Brill, 2023.

Benjamin, Walter. *One-Way Street and Other Writings*. Verso Books, 1997.

Campa, Valentín. *Mi testimonio: Experiencias de un comunista mexicano*. Ediciones de Cultura Popular, 1978.

"Carta de las comunidades indígenas, Pátzcuaro" (1975). In María Consuelo Mejía Piñeros and Sergio Sarmiento Silva, *La lucha indígena: Un reto a la ortodoxia*, 257–264. Siglo XXI, 1987.

Chávez Orozco, Luis. "El Primer Congreso Indigenista Interamericano." *Educación* (June 1940): 19–22.

Chávez Orozco, Luis. *Historia de México*. 2 vols. Editorial Patria, 1934.

Chávez Orozco, Luis. *La civilización maya-quiché*. Talleres Gráficos Nacionales, 1932.

Chávez Orozco, Luis. *La civilización nahoa*. Secretaría de Educación Pública, 1933.

Chávez Orozco, Luis. *La educación socialista*. Secretaría de Educación Pública, 1937.

Constitución de la República de Cuba: Publicada en la Gaceta Oficial de Julio 8 de 1940. Compañía Editora de Libros y Folletos, 1940.

Cuadros Caldas, Julio. *El Comunismo criollo*. Santiago Loyo, 1930.

De la Torriente, Loló. *Testimonio desde dentro*. Editorial Letras Cubanas, 1985.

De la Torriente Brau, Pablo. "Realengo 18." *Ahora*, November 16, 1934.

Degras, Jane, ed. *The Communist International, 1919–1943: Documents*. Vols. I and II. Royal Institute of International Affairs, 1956–65.

Dekrety Sovetskoi vlasti, t. 1, 25 oktiabria 1917 g.–16 marta 1918 g. Politizdat, 1957.

Departamento de Asuntos Indígenas (DAI). *Memoria de la Primera Asamblea de Filólogos y Lingüistas*. Departamento Autónomo de Asuntos Indígenas, 1940.

Departamento de Asuntos Indígenas (DAI). *Memoria del Departamento de Asuntos Indígenas, 1941–42*. Talleres Gráficos Nacionales, 1942.

Departamento de Asuntos Indígenas (DAI). *Memoria del Primer Congreso Regional Indígena celebrado en Ixmiquilpan, Hgo., 25–26 Sept 1936*. Departamento Autónomo de Prensa y Publicidad, 1938.

"Discurso de inauguración pronunciado por el President de la República Mexicana, Gral. de División Lázaro Cárdenas." In Confederación de Trabajadores de América Latina, *Primer Congreso Indigenista Interamericano*. N.p., 1940.

"Discurso pronunciado por el comandante Fidel Castro Ruz, Primer Secretario de la Dirección Nacional de las ORI y Primer Ministro del Gobierno Revolucionario, en la Segunda Asamblea Nacional del Pueblo de Cuba, celebrada en la Plaza de la

Revolución, el 4 de febrero de 1962." Accessed March 10, 2025. http://www.cuba
.cu/gobierno/discursos//1962/esp/f040262e.html.

*El Movimiento revolucionario latinoamericano: Versiones de la primera conferencia
comunista Latino Americana*. La Correspondencia Sudamericana, 1929.

Fabila, Alfonso. *El problema de la emigración de obreros y campesinos mexicanos*. Secretaría de Gobernación, 1929.

Fabila, Alfonso. *El problema indígena de México: Contribución para resolverlo*. Imprenta de la Escuela Rafael Dondé, 1941.

Fabila, Alfonso. *Las tribus Yaquis de Sonora: Su cultura y anhelada autodeterminación*. Departamento de Asuntos Indígenas, 1940.

Grobart, Fabio. "The Cuban Working Class Movement from 1925 to 1933." *Science &
Society* 39, no. 1 (1975): 73–103.

Haya de la Torre, Víctor Raúl. *Construyendo el aprismo: Artículos y cartas desde el
exilio (1924–1931)*. Editorial Claridad, 1933.

Haya de la Torre, Víctor Raúl. *El Antimperialismo y el APRA*. Ediciones Ercilla, 1936.

Haya de la Torre, Víctor Raúl. *Obras completas*. Vol. 1. Librería-Editorial Juan Mejía
Baca, 1977.

Haya de la Torre, Víctor Raúl. "What Is the A.P.R.A.?" *Labour Monthly* 8, no. 12
(1926): 756–759.

Haywood, Harry. *Black Bolshevik: Autobiography of an Afro-American Communist*.
Liberator Press, 1978.

Ho Chi Minh. "Report on the National and Colonial Questions at the Fifth Congress of the Communist International" [July 8, 1924]. In *Selected Works of Ho Chi
Minh*, vol. 1. Foreign Languages Publishing House, 1960.

International Labor Organization. "Indigenous and Tribal Peoples Convention, 1989
(No. 169)." Accessed 10 March 2025. https://www.ilo.org/dyn/normlex/en/f?p
=1000:12000:0::NO:::.

Jeifets, Victor, and Andrey Schelchkov, eds. *La Internacional Comunista en América
Latina: En documentos del archivo de Moscú*. Aquilo-Press/Ariadna ediciones,
2018.

Kollontai, A. M. *Diplomaticheskie dnevniki*. Tom 1. Academia, 2001.

Lenin, V. I. "Critical Remarks on the National Question" (1913). In Lenin, *Collected
Works*, 20:17–51. Progress Publishers, 1972.

Lenin, V. I. "Draft Theses on National and Colonial Questions for the Second Congress of the Communist International" (1920). In Lenin, *Collected Works*, 31:144–151. Progress Publishers, 1966.

Lenin, V. I. "Resolutions of the Summer, 1913, Joint Conference of the Central Committee of the R.S.D.L.P. and Party Officials." In Lenin, *Collected Works*, 19:417–431. Progress Publishers, 1977.

Lenin, V. I. "The Right of Nations to Self-Determination" (1913). In Lenin, *Collected
Works*, 20:393–454. Progress Publishers, 1977.

Liga de Comunidades Agrarias del Estado de Veracruz (LCAEV). *El agrarismo en
México: La cuestión agraria y el problema campesino*. N.p., 1924.

Liga Nacional Campesina (LNC). *Primer congreso de unificación de las organizaciones campesinas de la República*. Santiago Loyo, 1927.

Lombardo Toledano, Vicente. *Escritos acerca de la situación de los indígenas*. Centro de Estudios Filosóficos, Políticos y Sociales Vicente Lombardo Toledano, 2006.

Lombardo Toledano, Vicente, and Víctor Manuel Villaseñor. *Un viaje al mundo del porvenir: Seis conferencias sobre la U.R.S.S.* Universidad Obrera de México, 1936.

Los partidos políticos y la asamblea constituyente: Inmigración, economía, trabajo, educación, discriminación; Conferencias de Orientación Ciudadana, Club Atenas, Feb. 13–Mayo 15, 1939. Club Atenas, 1939.

Luxemburg, Rosa. *The National Question: Selected Writings by Rosa Luxemburg*. Monthly Review Press, 1976.

Mariátegui, José Carlos. *Correspondencia (1915–1930)*. Vols. 1 and 2. Biblioteca "Amauta," 1984.

Mariátegui, José Carlos. *Ideología y política*. Vol. 13 of *Obras completas de José Carlos Mariátegui*. Biblioteca "Amauta," 1969.

Mariátegui, José Carlos. *Peruanicemos al Perú*. Vol. 11 of *Obras completas de José Carlos Mariátegui*. Biblioteca "Amauta," 1970.

Mariátegui, José Carlos. *Siete ensayos de interpretación de la realidad peruana* (1928). Vol. 2 of *Obras completas de José Carlos Mariátegui*. Biblioteca "Amauta," 1959.

Marx, Karl, and Friedrich Engels. *The Communist Manifesto*. Penguin Books, 2002. Originally published in 1848.

Melgar Bao, Ricardo, and Osmar Gonzales, eds. *Víctor Raúl Haya de la Torre: Giros discursivos y contiendas políticas (Textos inéditos)*. Ediciones del CCC, 2014.

Melgar Bao, Ricardo, and Perla Jaimes Navarro. *Esteban Pavletich: Estaciones del exilio y Revolución Mexicana, 1915–1930*. Instituto Nacional de Antropología e Historia, 2019.

Mella, Julio Antonio. *J. A. Mella: Documentos y artículos*. Editorial de Ciencias Sociales, 1975.

Mendizábal, Miguel Othón de. *Historia económica y social de México, 5a Conferencia*. Secretaría de Educación Pública, 1935.

Mendizábal, Miguel Othón de. *La evolución del noroeste de México*. Publicaciones del Departamento de la Estadística Nacional, 1930.

Mendizábal, Miguel Othón de. *La influencia de la sal en la distribución geográfica de los grupos indígenas de México*. Museo Nacional de Arqueología, Historia y Etnografía, 1928.

Mendizábal, Miguel Othón de. *Obras completas*. Vol. 4. Talleres Gráficos de la Nación, 1946.

Múñiz, Pedro. *Lo que es el aprismo*. Editorial Cromos, 1932.

1903: Second Ordinary Congress of the Russian Social-Democratic Labour Party. New Park Books, 1978.

Partido Comunista de Cuba (PCC). *"Cuidemos la unidad . . .": El caso del Dr Martín Castellanos*. Impr. Alfa, 1938.

Pavletich, Esteban. *El mensaje de México*. N.p., 1934.

Portal, Magda. *América Latina frente al imperialismo*. Cahuide, 1931.

Portal, Magda. *El nuevo poema i su orientación hacia una estética económica*. Ediciones APRA, 1928.

Portal, Magda. *¿Quiénes traicionaron al pueblo?* Impr. Editora Salas e Hijos, 1950.

Riddell, John, ed. *To See the Dawn! Baku, 1920: First Congress of the Peoples of the East*. Pathfinder, 1993.

Riddell, John. *Toward the United Front: Proceedings of the Fourth Congress of the Communist International, 1922*. Brill, 2012.

Riddell, John. *Workers of the World and Oppressed Peoples, Unite! Proceedings and Documents of the Second Congress of the Communist International, 1920*. Pathfinder, 1991.

Roa, Raúl. *El fuego de la semilla en el surco*. Editorial Letras Cubanas, 1982.

Sáenz, Moisés. *México Íntegro*. Consejo Nacional para la Cultura y las Artes, 2006. Originally published in 1939.

Salamanca, Octavio. "Obreros e indios de Bolivia: Escuchad la palabra de la Confederación Sindical Latino Americana" (1931). In Pilar Mendieta Parada and Evgenia Bridikhina, eds., *Amanecer en rojo. Marxismo, comunismo y socialismo en Bolivia (1880–1932)*, 467–480. Vicepresidencia del Estado Plurinacional de Bolivia, 2018.

Sawhney, Savitri. *I Shall Never Ask for Pardon: A Memoir of Pandurang Khankhoje*. Penguin Books, 2008.

Serviat, Pablo. *El problema negro en Cuba y su solución definitiva*. Política, 1986.

Shipman, Charles. *It Had to Be Revolution*. Cornell University Press, 1993.

Silva Herzog, Jesús. *Una vida en la vida de México*. Siglo XXI, 1975.

Siqueiros, David Alfaro. *Me llamaban el coronelazo: Memorias*. Biografías Gandesa, 1977.

Stalin, J. V. "Marxism and the National Question." In Stalin, *Collected Works*, 2:300–381. Foreign Language Publishing House, 1953.

Tísoc Lindley, Hilda. "De los orígenes del APRA en Cuba: El testimonio de Enrique de la Osa." *Cuadernos Americanos* 37 (1993): 198–207.

Vela, David. *Orientación y recomendaciones del Primer Congreso Indigenista Interamericano*. Publicaciones del Comité Organizador del IV Congreso Indigenista Interamericano, 1959.

Vivó, Jorge. *Geografía de México*. Fondo de Cultura Económica, 1948.

Wilkie, James W., and Edna Monzón de Wilkie. *Frente a la Revolución Mexicana: 17 protagonistas de la etapa constructivista. Entrevistas de historia oral*, vol. 1. Universidad Nacional Autónoma Metropolitana, 1995.

SECONDARY SOURCES

Adi, Hakim. *Pan-Africanism: A History*. Bloomsbury, 2018.

Adi, Hakim. *Pan-Africanism and Communism: The Communist International, Africa and the Diaspora, 1919–1939*. Africa World Press, 2013.

Aguilar Gil, Yásnaya Elena. "Nosotros sin México: Naciones indígenas y autonomía." *Nexos*, May 18, 2018.

Aguirre Beltrán, Gonzalo. *Obra antropológica*. Vol. IX, *Obra polémica*. Fondo de Cultura Económica, 1992.

AHR Editors. "Introduction to AHR Forum: Transnational Lives in the Twentieth Century." *American Historical Review* 118, no. 1 (2013): 45.

Ai Camp, Roderic. *Mexican Political Biographies, 1935–1993*. University of Texas Press, 1995.

Anderson, Benedict. *Under Three Flags: Anarchism and the Anti-Colonial Imagination*. Verso, 2005.

Appelbaum, Nancy, Anne S. Macpherson, and Karin Alejandra Rosemblatt, eds. *Race and Nation in Modern Latin America*. University of North Carolina Press, 2003.

Argentieri, Letizia. *Tina Modotti: Between Art and Revolution*. Yale University Press, 2003.

Balderrama, Francisco, and Raymond Rodríguez. *Decade of Betrayal: Mexican Repatriation in the 1930s*. University of New Mexico Press, 2006.

Baldwin, Kate. *Beyond the Color Line and the Iron Curtain: Reading Encounters Between Black and Red, 1922–1963*. Duke University Press, 2002.

Bartra, Armando. *Los herederos de Zapata: Movimientos campesinos posrevolucionarios en México 1920–1980*. Ediciones Era, 1985.

Bayly, C. A., et al. "AHR Conversation: On Transnational History." *American Historical Review* 111, no. 5 (2006): 1441–1464.

Bebbington, Anthony, ed. *Minería, movimientos sociales y respuestas campesinas: Una ecología política de transformaciones territoriales*. Instituto de Estudios Peruanos/CEPES, 2011.

Becker, Marc. *Indians and Leftists in the Making of Ecuador's Modern Indigenous Movements*. Duke University Press, 2008.

Becker, Marc. "Mariátegui, the Comintern, and the Indigenous Question in Latin America," *Science and Society* 70, no. 4 (2006): 450–479.

Becker, Marc. *Pachakutik: Indigenous Movements and Electoral Politics in Ecuador*. Rowman and Littlefield, 2011.

Becker, Marc, Margaret Power, Tony Wood, and Jacob Zumoff, eds. *Transnational Communism Across the Americas*. University of Illinois Press, 2023.

Behrens, Benedikt. "El movimiento inquilinario de Veracruz, México, 1922–1927: Una rebelión de mujeres." *Journal of Iberian and Latin American Research* 6, no. 1 (2000): 57–92.

Benson, Devyn Spence. *Antiracism in Cuba: The Unfinished Revolution*. University of North Carolina Press, 2016.

Bergel, Martín. *La desmesura revolucionaria: Cultura y política en los orígenes del APRA*. La Siniestra Ensayos, 2021.

Berland, Oscar. "The Emergence of the Communist Perspective on the 'Negro Question' in America: 1919–1931, Part Two." *Science & Society* 64, no. 2 (2000): 194–217.

Berland, Oscar. "Nasanov and the Comintern's American Negro Program." *Science & Society* 65, no. 2 (2001): 226–228.

Bernal Alanís, Tomás. "El camino de un antropólogo: La obra de Miguel Othón de Mendizábal: La época de reconstrucción nacional, 1920–1945." PhD thesis, INAH, 2014.

Boittin, Jennifer. *Colonial Metropolis: The Urban Grounds of Anti-Imperialism and Feminism in Interwar Paris.* University of Nebraska Press, 2010.

Bonfil Batalla, Guillermo. "Del indigenismo de la Revolución a la antropología crítica" (1970). In *Obra escogida*, tomo 1, *Obra publicada*, 293–316. INI/INAH, 1985.

Bronfman, Alejandra. *Measures of Equality: Social Science, Citizenship, and Race in Cuba, 1902–1940.* University of North Carolina Press, 2004.

Broué, Pierre. *Histoire de l'Internationale communiste, 1919–1943.* Fayard, 1997.

Brunson, Takkara. *Black Women, Citizenship, and the Making of Modern Cuba.* University of Florida Press, 2021.

Caballero, Manuel. *Latin America and the Comintern, 1919–1943.* Cambridge University Press, 1986.

Campbell, Susan. "'Black Bolsheviks' and Recognition of African-America's Right to Self-Determination by the Communist Party USA." *Science & Society* 58, no. 4 (1994): 440–470.

Cappelletti, Angel. *Anarchism in Latin America.* AK Press, 2017.

Carr, Barry. "Identity, Class, and Nation: Black Immigrant Workers, Cuban Communism, and the Sugar Insurgency, 1925–1934." *Hispanic American Historical Review* 78, no. 1 (1998): 83–116.

Carr, Barry. *Marxism and Communism in Twentieth-Century Mexico.* University of Nebraska Press, 1992.

Carr, Barry. "Pioneering Transnational Solidarity in the Americas: The Movement in Support of Augusto C. Sandino 1927–1934." *Journal of Iberian and Latin American Research* 20, no. 2 (2014): 141–152.

Carr, E. H. *Foundations of a Planned Economy.* Vol. 2. Macmillan, 1971.

Casco Montoya, María del Rosario, and René Avilés Fabila. "El indigenismo, el indígena y Alfonso Fabila (Breve estudio y bibliografía)." *B.B.A.A. Boletín Bibliográfico de Antropología Americana* 26/28, no. 1 (1963–65): 89–95.

Casey, Matthew. *Empire's Guest Workers: Haitian Migrants in Cuba During the Age of U.S. Occupation.* Cambridge University Press, 2017.

Castañeda, Jorge. *Utopia Unarmed: The Latin American Left After the Cold War.* Alfred A. Knopf, 1993.

Cerdas Cruz, Rodolfo. *La hoz y el machete: La Internacional Comunista, América Latina y la revolución en Centroamérica.* Editorial Universidad Estatal a Distancia, 1986.

Chavarría, Jesús. *José Carlos Mariátegui and the Rise of Modern Peru, 1890–1930.* University of New Mexico Press, 1979.

Claudín, Fernando. *The Communist Movement: The Crisis of the Communist International.* Monthly Review Press, 1975.

Colton, Timothy. *Moscow: Governing the Socialist Metropolis.* Harvard University Press, 1995.

Córdova, Arnaldo. *La clase obrera en la historia de México: En una época de crisis (1928–1934)*. Siglo XXI, 1980.

Covin, David. *The Unified Black Movement in Brazil, 1978–2002*. McFarland & Company, 2006.

Cruse, Harold. *The Crisis of the Negro Intellectual*. New York Review Classics, 2005. Originally published in 1967.

Davies, R. W., and Stephen Wheatcroft. *The Years of Hunger: Soviet Agriculture, 1931–33*. Palgrave Macmillan, 2003.

Dawson, Alexander. *Indian and Nation in Revolutionary Mexico*. University of Arizona Press, 2004.

De la Fuente, Alejandro. *A Nation for All: Race, Inequality, and Politics in Twentieth-Century Cuba*. University of North Carolina Press, 2001.

De la Peña, Guillermo. "The End of Revolutionary Anthropology? Notes on *Indigenismo*." In Paul Gillingham and Benjamin Smith, eds., *Dictablanda: Politics, Work, and Culture in Mexico, 1938–1968*, 279–298. Duke University Press, 2014.

De la Peña, Guillermo. "Nacionales y extranjeros en la historia de la antropología mexicana." In Mechthild Rutsch, ed., *La historia de la antropología en México: Fuentes y trasmisión*, 41–83. INI, 1996.

Díaz-Polanco, Héctor. *Autonomía regional: La autodeterminación de los pueblos indígenas*. Siglo XXI, 1991.

Dillingham, A. S. *Oaxaca Resurgent: Indigeneity, Inequality, and Development in Twentieth-Century Mexico*. Stanford University Press, 2021.

Disi Pavlic, Rodolfo. "Indigenous Voices and Votes: Assessing the Dynamics of Indigenous Politics in Chile's Constitutional Referendum of 2022." *PS: Political Science & Politics* 57, no. 2 (April 2024): 267–273.

Dorais, Geneviève. *Journey to Indo-América: APRA and the Transnational Politics of Exile, Persecution, and Solidarity, 1918–1945*. Cambridge University Press, 2021.

Drachewych, Oleksa. "The Communist Transnational? Transnational Studies and the History of the Comintern." *History Compass* 17, no. 2 (2019).

Draper, Theodore. *American Communism and Soviet Russia: The Formative Period*. Octagon Books, 1977. Originally published in 1960.

Fábregas Puig, Andrés. *Historia mínima del indigenismo en América Latina*. El Colegio de México, 2021.

Falcón, César. *Anatomía de los 7 ensayos de Mariátegui*. Editora Amauta, 1978.

Fenby, Jonathan. *Modern China: The Fall and Rise of a Great Power, 1850–2009*. Ecco, 2008.

Fernández Robaina, Tomás. *El negro en Cuba: Colonia, República, Revolución*. Ediciones Cubanas/Artex, 2012.

Ferrer, Ada. *Cuba: An American History*. Scribner, 2021.

Ferrer, Ada. *Insurgent Cuba: Race, Nation, and Revolution, 1868–1898*. University of North Carolina Press, 1998.

Filatova, Irina. "Indoctrination or Scholarship? Education of Africans at the Communist University of Toilers of the East in the Soviet Union, 1923–1927." *Paedagogica Historica* 35, no. 1 (1999): 41–66.

Fisch, Jörg. *The Right of Self-Determination of Peoples: The Domestication of an Illusion.* Cambridge University Press, 2015.

Flores Galindo, Alberto. *La agonía de Mariátegui.* Editorial Revolución, 1991.

Fowler-Salamini, Heather. *Agrarian Radicalism in Veracruz, 1920–38.* University of Nebraska Press, 1978.

Francis-Tan, Andrew, and Maria Tannuri-Pianto. "Affirmative Action in Brazil: Global Lessons on Racial Justice and the Fight to Reduce Social Inequality." *Oxford Review of Economic Policy* 40, no. 3 (Autumn 2024): 642–655.

García, Angel, and Piotr Mironchuk. *Los soviets obreros y campesinos en Cuba.* Editorial de Ciencias Sociales, 1987.

García Mora, Carlos, ed. *La antropología en México: Panorama histórico.* 15 vols. SEP/INAH, 1987–88.

García-Bryce, Iñigo. *Haya de la Torre and the Pursuit of Power in Twentieth-Century Peru and Latin America.* University of North Carolina Press, 2018.

García-Bryce, Iñigo. "Transnational Activist: Magda Portal and the American Popular Revolutionary Alliance (APRA), 1926–1950." *Americas* 70, no. 4 (2014): 677–705.

Getachew, Adom. *Worldmaking After Empire: The Rise and Fall of Self-Determination.* Princeton University Press, 2019.

Gilly, Adolfo. *La revolución interrumpida.* Editorial El Caballito, 1971.

Gilmore, Glenda Elizabeth. *Defying Dixie: The Radical Roots of Civil Rights, 1919–1950.* W. W. Norton, 2008.

Giovannetti-Torres, Jorge. *Black British Migrants in Cuba: Race, Labor, and Empire in the Twentieth-Century Caribbean, 1898–1948.* Cambridge University Press, 2018.

Giraudo, Laura. "Un campo indigenista transnacional y 'casi profesional': La apertura en Pátzcuaro (1940) de un espacio por y para los indigenistas." In Laura Giraudo and Juan Martín-Sánchez, eds., *La ambivalente historia del indigenismo: Campo interamericano y trayectorias nacionales, 1940–1970,* 21–98. Instituto de Estudios Peruanos, 2011.

Gobat, Michel. "The Invention of Latin America: A Transnational History of Anti-Imperialism, Democracy, and Race." *American Historical Review* 118, no. 5 (December 2013): 1345–1375.

Goebel, Michael. *Anti-Imperial Metropolis: Interwar Paris and the Seeds of Third World Nationalism.* Cambridge University Press, 2015.

González Casanova, Pablo. "Sociedad plural, colonialismo interno y desarrollo." *América Latina* 6, no. 3 (1963): 15–32.

Gould, Jeffrey, and Aldo Lauria-Santiago. *To Rise in Darkness: Revolution, Repression, and Memory in El Salvador, 1920–1932.* Duke University Press, 2008.

Graham, Jessica. "A virada antirracista do Partido Comunista do Brasil, a Frente Negra Brasileira e a Ação Integralista Brasileira na década de 1930." In Flávio Gomes and Petrônio Domingues, eds., *Políticas da raça: Experiências e legados da abolição e da pós-emancipação no Brasil,* 353–375. Selo Negro Edições, 2014.

Graham, Jessica. *Shifting the Meaning of Democracy: Race, Politics, and Culture in the United States and Brazil.* University of California Press, 2019.

Grandin, Greg. *The Blood of Guatemala: A History of Race and Nation*. Duke University Press, 2000.

Grandin, Greg. *Empire's Workshop: Latin America, the United States, and the Making of an Imperial Republic*. Rev. ed. Picador, 2021.

Grandin, Greg. "The Liberal Traditions in the Americas: Rights, Sovereignty, and the Origins of Liberal Multilateralism." *American Historical Review* 117, no. 1 (2012): 68–91.

Guridy, Frank André. *Forging Diaspora: Afro-Cubans and African Americans in a World of Empire and Jim Crow*. University of North Carolina Press, 2010.

Guridy, Frank André. "'War on the Negro': Race and the Revolution of 1933." *Cuban Studies* 40 (2010): 49–73.

Harper, Tim. *Underground Asia: Global Revolutionaries and the Assault on Empire*. Belknap Press, 2021.

Hart, John Mason. *Revolutionary Mexico: The Coming and Process of the Mexican Revolution*. University of California Press, 1987.

Hatzky, Christine. *Julio Antonio Mella (1903–1929): eine Biographie*. Vervuert, 2004.

Hatzky, Christine, and Rina Ortiz. "Julio Antonio Mella: Huelga de hambre y expulsión del Partido Comunista de Cuba. Una laguna en su biografía." *Historias* (Mexico) 49 (2001): 107–145.

Heath, Shirley Brice. *Telling Tongues: Language Policy in Mexico, Colony to Nation*. Teachers College Press, 1972.

Heatherton, Christina. *Arise! Global Radicalism in the Era of the Mexican Revolution*. University of California Press, 2022.

Helg, Aline. *Our Rightful Share: The Afro-Cuban Struggle for Equality, 1886–1912*. University of North Carolina Press, 1995.

Henderson, Kaitlyn. "Race, Discrimination, and the Cuban Constitution of 1940." *Hispanic American Historical Review* 100, no. 2 (2020): 257–284.

Hewitt de Alcántara, Cynthia. *Anthropological Perspectives on Rural Mexico*. Routledge and Kegan Paul, 1984.

Hirsch, Francine. *Empire of Nations: Ethnographic Knowledge and the Making of the Soviet Union*. Cornell University Press, 2005.

Hooker, Juliet. "Indigenous Inclusion/Black Exclusion: Race, Ethnicity and Multicultural Citizenship in Latin America." *Journal of Latin American Studies* 37, no. 2 (2005): 285–310.

Hooker, Juliet. *Theorizing Race in the Americas: Douglass, Sarmiento, Du Bois, Vasconcelos*. Oxford University Press, 2017.

Hu-DeHart, Evelyn. "Peasant Rebellion in the Northwest: The Yaqui Indians of Sonora, 1740–1976." In Friedrich Katz, ed., *Riot, Rebellion, and Revolution: Rural Social Conflict in Mexico*, 141–175. Princeton University Press, 1988.

Hylton, Forrest, and Sinclair Thomson. *Revolutionary Horizons: Past and Present in Bolivian Politics*. Verso, 2007.

Illades, Carlos. *Las otras ideas: Estudio sobre el primer socialismo en México, 1850–1935*. Ediciones Era, 2008.

James, C. L. R. *The Black Jacobins: Toussaint L'Ouverture and the San Domingo Revolution.* 2nd ed. Vintage Books, 1963.

James, Winston. *Holding Aloft the Banner of Ethiopia: Caribbean Radicalism in Early Twentieth-Century America.* Verso, 1998.

Jansen, Jan C., and Jürgen Osterhammel. *Decolonization: A Short History.* Princeton University Press, 2017.

Jeifets, Victor, and Lazar Jeifets. *América Latina en la Internacional Comunista, 1919–1943: Diccionario biográfico.* Santiago de Chile: Ariadna Ediciones, 2015.

Jeifets, Victor, and Lazar Jeifets. "Haya de la Torre, la Comintern y el Perú: Acercamientos y desencuentros." *Pacarina del Sur* 4, no. 16 (2013): 332–374.

Jeifets, Victor, and Lazar Jeifets. "Introduction: The Outcomes of Ten Years of Latin American Communism." In Marc Becker, ed., *The Latin American Revolutionary Movement: Proceedings of the First Latin American Communist Conference, June 1929,* 1–25. Brill, 2023.

Jeifets, Victor, and Lazar Jeifets. "La odisea roja: Varias líneas al retrato político de Jorge Vivó d'Escoto." *Revista CS* (Cali), no. 14 (2014): 167–200.

Jeifets, Victor, and Irving Reynoso Jaime. "Del Frente Único a clase contra clase: Comunistas y agraristas en el México posrevolucionario, 1919–1930." *Izquierdas* 19 (2014): 15–40.

Joseph, Gilbert, and Daniel Nugent, eds. *Everyday Forms of State Formation: Revolution and the Negotiation of Rule in Modern Mexico.* Duke University Press, 1994.

Karl, Rebecca. *Mao Zedong and China in the Twentieth-Century World.* Duke University Press, 2010.

Kelley, Robin D. G. *Hammer and Hoe: Alabama Communists During the Great Depression.* University of North Carolina Press, 1990.

Kent Carrasco, Daniel. "Breath of Revolution: Ghadar Anti-Colonial Radicalism in North America and the Mexican Revolution." *South Asia: Journal of South Asian Studies* 43, no. 6 (2020): 1077–1092.

Kent Carrasco, Daniel. "M. N. Roy en México: Cosmopolitismo intelectual y contingencia política en la creación del PCM." In Carlos Illades, ed., *Camaradas: Nueva historia del comunismo en México,* 37–71. Fondo de Cultura Económica, 2017.

Kersffeld, Daniel. *Contra el imperio: Historia de la Liga Antimperialista de las Américas.* Siglo XXI, 2012.

Kersffeld, Daniel. "El Comité Manos Fuera de Nicaragua: Primera experiencia del sandinismo." *Pacarina del Sur* 4, no. 13 (2012): 547–581.

Kersffeld, Daniel. "Latinoamericanos en el Congreso Antiimperialista de 1927: Afinidades, disensos y rupturas." *Journal of Iberian and Latin American Research* 16, no. 2 (2010): 151–163.

Khuri-Makdisi, Ilham. *The Eastern Mediterranean and the Making of Global Radicalism, 1860–1914.* University of California Press, 2010.

Kirasirova, Masha. *The Eastern International: Arabs, Central Asians, and Jews in the Soviet Union's Anti-Colonial Empire.* Oxford University Press, 2024.

Kirschenbaum, Lisa. *International Communism and the Spanish Civil War: Solidarity and Suspicion.* Cambridge University Press, 2015.

Klaiber, Jeffrey L. "The Popular Universities and the Origins of Aprismo, 1921–1924." *Hispanic American Historical Review* 55, no. 4 (1975): 693–715.

Klarén, Peter. *Modernization, Dislocation, and Aprismo: Origins of the Peruvian Aprista Party, 1870–1932.* University of Texas Press, 1973.

Klehr, Harvey, and William Tompson. "Self-Determination in the Black Belt: Origins of a Communist Policy." *Labor History* 30 (1989): 354–366.

Knight, Alan. *The Mexican Revolution.* 2 vols. University of Nebraska Press, 1986.

Knight, Alan. "Racism, Revolution and Indigenismo: Mexico, 1910–1940." In Richard Graham, ed., *The Idea of Race in Latin America, 1870–1940,* 71–113. University of Texas Press, 1990.

La Botz, Dan. "American 'Slackers' in the Mexican Revolution: International Proletarian Politics in the Midst of a National Revolution." *Americas* 62, no. 4 (2006): 563–590.

Laforcade, Geoffroy de, and Kirwin Shaffer, eds. *In Defiance of Boundaries: Anarchism in Latin American History.* University Press of Florida, 2015.

Legarreta Haynes, Patricia. "Ingeniería social en Mesoamérica: Revolución, intervención, desarrollo y cooperación internacional." PhD thesis, UAM-Iztapalapa, 2016.

Lehmann, David. *The Prism of Race: The Politics and Ideology of Affirmative Action in Brazil.* University of Michigan Press, 2018.

Lemos Pastrana, Andrés. *La Escuela Nacional de Ciencias Biológicas IPN: Una visión histórica.* IPN, 2009.

Lewis, Stephen. *Rethinking Mexican Indigenismo: The INI's Coordinating Center in Highland Chiapas and the Fate of a Utopian Project.* University of New Mexico Press, 2018.

Li, Fabiana. *Unearthing Conflict: Corporate Mining, Activism, and Expertise in Peru.* Duke University Press, 2015.

Lindner, Thomas. *A City Against Empire: Transnational Anti-Imperialism in Mexico City, 1920–1930.* University of Liverpool Press, 2023.

Lomnitz, Claudio. *Deep Mexico, Silent Mexico: An Anthropology of Nationalism.* University of Minnesota Press, 2001.

Lomnitz, Claudio. *The Return of Comrade Ricardo Flores Magón.* Zone Books, 2015.

López, Kathleen. *Chinese Cubans: A Transnational History.* University of North Carolina Press, 2013.

López Hernández, Haydée. "De la gloria prehispánica al socialismo: Las políticas indigenistas del Cardenismo." *Cuicuilco,* no. 57 (May–August 2013): 47–74.

Louro, Michele, Carolien Stolte, Heather Streets-Salter, and Sana Tannoury-Kharam, eds. *The League Against Imperialism: Lives and Afterlives.* Leiden University Press, 2020.

MacGregor Campuzano, Javier. "Comunistas en las Islas Marías, julio-diciembre de 1932." *Signos históricos* 8 (2002): 139–150.

Mahler, Anne Garland. "The Red and the Black in Latin America: Sandalio Junco and the 'Negro Question' from an Afro-Latin American Perspective." *American Communist History* 17, no. 1 (2018): 16–32.

Makalani, Minkah. *In the Cause of Freedom: Radical Black Internationalism from Harlem to London, 1917–1939*. University of North Carolina Press, 2011.

Manela, Erez, and Heather Streets-Salter, eds. *The Anticolonial Transnational: Imaginaries, Mobilities, and Networks in the Struggle Against Empire*. Cambridge University Press, 2023.

Manjapra, Kris. *Age of Entanglement: German and Indian Intellectuals Across Empire*. Harvard University Press, 2010.

Manrique, Nelson. *"¡Usted fue aprista!" Bases para una historia crítica del APRA*. Fondo Editorial de la Pontificia Universidad Católica del Perú, 2009.

Marentes, Luis. *José Vasconcelos and the Writing of the Mexican Revolution*. Twayne Publishers, 2000.

Martin, Terry. *The Affirmative Action Empire: Nations and Nationalism in the Soviet Union, 1923–1939*. Cornell University Press, 2001.

Martin, Tony. *Race First: The Ideological and Organizational Struggles of Marcus Garvey and the Universal Negro Improvement Association*. The Majority Press, 1986.

Martínez Heredia, Fernando. *La revolución cubana del 30*. Editorial de Ciencias Sociales, 2007.

Martínez Heredia, Fernando. "Prólogo a la presente edición." In Serafín Portuondo Linares, *Los independientes de color: Historia del Partido Independiente de Color*, vi–xxiii. Editorial Caminos, 2002. Originally published in 1950.

Martínez Verdugo, Arnoldo, ed. *Historia del comunismo en México*. Grijalbo, 1983.

Massón, Caridad. "Comunismo y nacionalismo: Una relación conflictiva durante la revolución del 30." In Caridad Massón, ed., *Comunismo, socialismo y nacionalismo en Cuba (1920–1958)*, 123–135. Instituto Cubano de Investigación Cultural Juan Marinello, 2013.

Massón, Caridad. "La cuestión racial en la política del Partido Comunista de Cuba (1925–1940)." *Perfiles de la Cultura Cubana*, no. 20 (2016).

McClellan, Woodford. "Africans and Black Americans in the Comintern Schools, 1925–1934." *International Journal of African Historical Studies* 26, no. 2 (1993): 371–390.

McGillivray, Gillian. *Blazing Cane: Sugar Communities, Class, and State Formation in Cuba, 1868–1959*. Duke University Press, 2009.

McGuire, Elizabeth. *Red at Heart: How Chinese Communists Fell in Love with the Russian Revolution*. Oxford University Press, 2018.

McPherson, Alan. *The Invaded: How Latin Americans and Their Allies Fought and Ended U.S. Occupations*. Oxford University Press, 2014.

Medina Hernández, Andrés. "Un capítulo en la olvidada historia de la antropología en México (1906–1940): Miguel Othón de Mendizábal, el constructor." In *Bérose: Encyclopédie internationale des histoires de l'anthropologie*. Ministère de la Culture/IIAC-CNRS-EHESS, 2019.

Mejía Piñeros, María Consuelo, and Sergio Sarmiento Silva. *La lucha indígena: Un reto a la ortodoxia*. Siglo XXI, 1987.

Melgar Bao, Ricardo. "The Anti-Imperialist League of the Americas Between the East and Latin America." *Latin American Perspectives* 35, no. 2 (2008): 9–24.

Melgar Bao, Ricardo. *Haya de la Torre y Julio Antonio Mella en México: El exilio y sus querellas, 1928.* Ediciones del CCC, 2013.

Melgar Bao, Ricardo. "La IC frente al dilema raza y nación en América Latina." *Memoria* 27 (1989): 337–342.

Melgar Bao, Ricardo. "Redes y espacio público transfronterizo: Haya de la Torre en México (1923–24)." In Marta Elena Casaús Arzú and Manuel Pérez Ledesma, eds., *Redes intelectuales y formación de naciones en España y América Latina (1890–1940),* 65–105. Ediciones de la Universidad Autónoma de Madrid, 2004.

Melgar Bao, Ricardo. "Un neobolivarianismo antimperialista: La Unión Centro Sud Americana y de las Antillas." *Políticas de la memoria* 6/7 (2006–7): 149–163.

Méndez Moissen, Sergio. "El trotskismo cubano en la revolución de 1933." *Pacarina del Sur* 6, no. 23 (2015): 62–109.

Meyer, Lorenzo. *México y el mundo: Historia de sus relaciones exteriores.* Tomo VI, *La marca del nacionalismo.* El Colegio de México, 2010.

Michels, Tony, ed. *Jewish Radicals: A Documentary Reader.* New York University Press, 2012.

Miranda Fernández, Lucinda. *Lázaro Peña: Capitán de la clase obrera cubana.* Editorial de Ciencias Sociales, 1984.

Moore, Robin. *Nationalizing Blackness: Afrocubanismo and Artistic Revolution in Havana, 1920–1940.* University of Pittsburgh Press, 1997.

Muller, Dalia. *Cuban Émigrés and Independence in the Nineteenth-Century Gulf World.* University of North Carolina Press, 2017.

Muñoz, Maria L. O. *Stand Up and Fight: Participatory Indigenismo, Populism, and Mobilization in Mexico, 1970–1984.* University of Arizona Press, 2016.

Naison, Mark. *Communists in Harlem During the Depression.* University of Illinois Press, 1983.

Navarro, Aaron. *Political Intelligence and the Creation of Modern Mexico, 1938–1954.* Pennsylvania State University Press, 2010.

Nugent, Daniel, and Ana María Alonso. "Multiple Selective Traditions in Agrarian Reform and Agrarian Struggle: Popular Culture and State Formation in the Ejido of Namiquipa, Chihuahua." In Gilbert Joseph and Daniel Nugent, eds., *Everyday Forms of State Formation: Revolution and the Negotiation of Rule in Modern Mexico,* 209–248. Duke University Press, 1994.

Núñez, Estuardo. *La experiencia europea de José Carlos Mariátegui y otros ensayos.* Editora Amauta, 1978.

Overmyer-Velázquez, Rebecca. *Folkloric Poverty: Neoliberal Multiculturalism in Mexico.* Pennsylvania State University Press, 2010.

Pakkasvirta, Jussi. *¿Un continente, una nación? Intelectuales latinoamericanos, comunidad política y las revistas culturales en Costa Rica y el Perú (1919–1930).* Editorial de la Universidad de Costa Rica, 2005.

Palacios, Guillermo. "Julio Cuadros Caldas: Un agrarista colombiano en la revolución mexicana." *Historia mexicana* 49, no. 3 (2000): 431–476.

Pappademos, Melina. *Black Political Activism and the Cuban Republic.* University of North Carolina Press, 2014.

Paris, Robert. *La formación ideológica de José Carlos Mariátegui.* Ediciones Pasado y Presente, 1981.

Pennybacker, Susan. *From Scottsboro to Munich: Race and Political Culture in 1930s Britain.* Princeton University Press, 2009.

Pérez, Louis. *Cuba Under the Platt Amendment, 1902–1934.* University of Pittsburgh Press, 1986.

Petersson, Fredrik. "'We Are Neither Visionaries Nor Utopian Dreamers': Willi Münzenberg, the League Against Imperialism, and the Comintern, 1925–1933." PhD thesis, Abo Akademi, 2013.

Pipes, Richard. *The Formation of the Soviet Union: Communism and Nationalism 1917–1923.* Harvard University Press, 1954.

Planas, Pedro. *Los orígenes del APRA: El joven Haya.* Okura Editores, 1986.

Porter, Cathy. *Alexandra Kollontai: The Lonely Struggle of the Woman Who Defied Lenin.* Dial Press, 1980.

Pujals, Sandra. "A 'Soviet Caribbean': The Comintern, New York's Immigrant Community, and the Forging of Caribbean Visions, 1931–1936." *Russian History* 41 (2014): 255–268.

Putnam, Lara. *Radical Moves: Caribbean Migrants and the Politics of Race in the Jazz Age.* University of North Carolina Press, 2013.

Quinn-Judge, Sophie. *Ho Chi Minh: The Missing Years, 1919–1941.* University of California Press, 2003.

Radding, Cynthia. "Peasant Resistance on the Yaqui Delta." *Journal of the Southwest* 31, no. 3 (1989): 330–361.

Ramírez Chicharro, Manuel, and Michelle Chase. "Black Left Feminism in Prerevolutionary Cuba: The Life and Work of Esperanza Sánchez Mastrapa (1901–1958)." *Women's History Review* 31, no. 5 (2022): 784–805.

Recondo, David. *La política del gatopardo: Multiculturalismo y democracia en Oaxaca.* CIESAS, 2007.

Reina, Leticia. *Indio, campesino y nación en el siglo XX mexicano: Historia e historiografía de los movimientos rurales.* Siglo XXI, 2011.

Reis, João José, and Flavio dos Santos Gomes. *Freedom by a Thread: The History of Quilombos in Brazil.* Diasporic Africa Press, 2016.

Reynoso Jaime, Irving. *El agrarismo radical en México en la década de 1920: Úrsulo Galván, Primo Tapia y José Guadalupe Rodríguez (una biografía política).* Instituto Nacional de Estudios Históricos de las Revoluciones de México, 2009.

Rivera Mir, Sebastián. *Militantes de la izquierda latinoamericana en México, 1920–1934: Prácticas políticas, redes y conspiraciones.* El Colegio de México, 2018.

Rojas, Rafael. *El árbol de las revoluciones: El poder y las ideas en América Latina.* Turner Publicaciones, 2021.

Rojas Blaquier, Angelina. *El primer Partido Comunista de Cuba: Pensamiento político y experiencia práctica. 1935–1952.* Tomo 2. Editorial Oriente, 2006.

Rosemblatt, Karin. "Modernization, Dependency, and the Global in Mexican Critiques of Anthropology." *Journal of Global History* 9 (2014): 94–121.

Rosemblatt, Karin. *The Science and Politics of Race in Mexico and the United States, 1910–1950*. University of North Carolina Press, 2018.

Rouillon, Guillermo. *La creación heroica de José Carlos Mariátegui*. Tomo I, *La Edad de Piedra (1894–1919)*. Editorial Arica, 1975.

Rubin, Jeffrey. *Decentering the Regime: Ethnicity, Radicalism, and Democracy in Juchitán, Mexico*. Duke University Press, 1997.

Sánchez, Consuelo. *Los pueblos indígenas: Del indigenismo a la autonomía*. Siglo XXI, 1999.

Sánchez, Luis Alberto. *Apuntes para una biografía del APRA*. [Volume] I, *Los primeros pasos 1923–1931*. Mosca Azul Editores, 1978.

Scheuzger, Stephan. "La izquierda mexicana y la cuestión indígena: ¿Caminos al desencuentro?" In Yael Bitrán, ed., *México: historia y alteridad*, 299–324. Universidad Iberoamericana, 2001.

Seigel, Micol. *Uneven Encounters: Making Race and Nation in Brazil and the United States*. Duke University Press, 2009.

Shaffer, Kirwin. *Anarchists of the Caribbean: Countercultural Politics and Transnational Networks in the Age of US Expansion*. Cambridge University Press, 2020.

Shanin, Teodor, ed. *Late Marx and the Russian Road: Marx and the Peripheries of Capitalism*. Monthly Review Press, 1983.

Slezkine, Yuri. "The USSR as a Communal Apartment, or How a Socialist State Promoted Ethnic Particularism." *Slavic Review* 53, no. 2 (1994): 414–452.

Soler Martínez, Rafael. "Los orígenes del trotskismo en Cuba." *Temas* 24–25 (2001): 45–55.

Solomon, Mark. *The Cry Was Unity: Communists and African Americans, 1917–1936*. University Press of Mississippi, 1998.

Spenser, Daniela. "El viaje de Vicente Lombardo Toledano al mundo del porvenir." *Desacatos* 34 (2010): 77–96.

Spenser, Daniela. *The Impossible Triangle: Mexico, Soviet Russia, and the United States in the 1920s*. Duke University Press, 1999.

Spenser, Daniela. *In Combat: The Life of Lombardo Toledano*. Brill, 2019.

Spenser, Daniela. *Stumbling Its Way Through Mexico: The Early Years of the Communist International*. University of Alabama Press, 2011.

Spenser, Daniela. "Stanislav Pestkovsky: A Soldier of the World Revolution in Mexico." *Journal of Iberian and Latin American Research* 8, no. 1 (2002): 35–56.

Stavans, Ilan. *José Vasconcelos: The Prophet of Race*. Rutgers University Press, 2011.

Stein, Steve. *Populism in Peru: The Emergence of the Masses and the Politics of Social Control*. University of Wisconsin Press, 1980.

Stepan, Nancy Leys. *"The Hour of Eugenics": Race, Gender, and Nation in Latin America*. Cornell University Press, 1996.

Stevens, Margaret. *Red International and Black Caribbean: Communists in New York City, Mexico and the West Indies, 1919–1939*. Pluto Books, 2017.

Studer, Brigitte. *The Transnational World of the Cominternians*. Palgrave, 2015.

Studer, Brigitte. *Travellers of the World Revolution: A Global History of the Communist International*. Verso, 2023.

Sullivan, Frances Peace. "'For the Liberty of the Nine Boys in Scottsboro and Against Yankee Imperialist Domination in Latin America.'" *Canadian Journal of Latin American and Caribbean Studies* 38, no. 2 (2013): 282–292.

Thornton, Christy. *Revolution in Development: Mexico and the Governance of the Global Economy*. University of California Press, 2021.

Trivellato, Francesca. "Is There a Future for Italian Microhistory in the Age of Global History?" *California Italian Studies* 2, no. 1 (2011).

Ulianova, Olga. "Levantamiento campesino de Lonquimay y la Internacional Comunista." *Estudios públicos* 89 (2003): 173–223.

Vaughan, Mary Kay. *Cultural Politics in Revolution: Teachers, Peasants, and Schools in Mexico, 1930–1940*. University of Arizona Press, 1997.

Wade, Peter. *Race and Ethnicity in Latin America*. Pluto Press, 1997.

Wallace Fuentes, Myrna Ivonne. *Most Scandalous Woman: Magda Portal and the Dream of Revolution in Peru*. University of Oklahoma Press, 2017.

Weaver, Kathleen. *Peruvian Rebel: The World of Magda Portal, with a Selection of Her Poems*. Pennsylvania State University Press, 2009.

Weinstein, Barbara. "Erecting and Erasing Boundaries: Can We Combine the 'Indo' and the 'Afro' in Latin American Studies?" *Estudios Interdisciplinarios de América Latina y el Caribe* 19, no. 1 (2008): 129–144.

Weitz, Eric. "Self-Determination: How a German Enlightenment Idea Became the Slogan of National Liberation and a Human Right." *American Historical Review* 120, no. 2 (2015): 462–496.

Whitney, Robert. *State and Revolution in Cuba: Mass Mobilization and Political Change, 1920–1940*. University of North Carolina Press, 2001.

Wood, Tony. *Chechnya: The Case for Independence*. Verso, 2007.

Yashar, Deborah. "The Left and Citizenship Rights." In Steven Levitsky and Kenneth Roberts, eds., *The Resurgence of the Latin American Left*, 184–210. Johns Hopkins University Press, 2011.

Young, Kevin, ed. *Making the Revolution: Histories of the Latin American Left*. Cambridge University Press, 2019.

Zumoff, Jacob. "The African Blood Brotherhood: From Caribbean Nationalism to Communism." *Journal of Caribbean History* 41, nos. 1–2 (2007): 200–206.

Zumoff, Jacob. *The Communist International and U.S. Communism, 1919–1929*. Brill, 2014.

INDEX

Abad Ramos, José, 160

Abash, Shaavan, 223

ABB (African Blood Brotherhood), 105

Abkhazia, 222–23

Abyssinia, 200

Adelante (Forward), 188, 199–200

Africa: Black sovereignty and, 200; Brussels Congress "Common Resolution on the Negro Question" (1927), 107–8; Congress against Colonial Oppression and Imperialism (1927), 59–60; UNIA (Universal Negro Improvement Association) in, 105. *See also* specific country names

African Blood Brotherhood (ABB), 105

African National Congress (ANC), 77

agrarian reform: DAI (Department of Indigenous Affairs; Departamento de Asuntos Indígenas) role of, 219–20; in Mexican Constitution (1917), 18, 21–22, 39; in 1920s Mexico, slow pace of, 81, 92; PAP (Partido Aprista Peruano) demand for in Peru, 167. *See also* land

agrarismo: defined, 17, 22; *El agrarismo en México* (Agrarianism in Mexico), 24

agraristas, 17

Agrupación Comunista, 36

Aguascalientes Convention (1914), 39

Aguilar Gil, Yásnaya Elena, 244

Albizu Campos, Pedro, 51

Alianza Nacional de Profesionistas Bilingües Indígenas (National Alliance of Indigenous Bilingual Professionals), 243

Alianza Popular Revolucionaria Americana. *See* APRA

Almazán, Juan Andreu, 58

Álvarez, Higinio, 68

Álvarez, Simón. *See* Suárez Pérez, Aggeo (Simón Álvarez)

Amador, Graciela, 34

Amauta, 44, 156

América Latina frente al imperialismo (Latin America against imperialism) (Portal), 155, 161

América Libre, 44

American Federation of Labor (AFL), 47

American Popular Revolutionary Alliance. *See* APRA

Amsterdam News, 104

anarchists: Partido Liberal Mexicano (PLM; Mexican Liberal Party), 20; in Peru, González Prada, Manuel, 27; in Peru, *La Protesta,* 52; radical left and, 2, 3

ANERC (Association of New Revolutionary Cuban Emigres; Asociación de Nuevos Emigrados Revolucionarios Cubanos), 37, 49, 221

anti-capitalism: Black and Indigenous peoples and the struggle against capitalism, 105–6, 110–11, 126, 137; "Capitalism and Colonization" (Portal), 161; Junco and, 139–41; PCM, view of Mexican Revolution, 77. *See also* capitalism

anti-colonialism: "Appeal to the Toiling Masses of the World" (1917) (Bolsheviks), 18–19; Black radicals and, 99–100, 104,

Calles, Plutarco Elías (*continued*)
government, 75; peasant leagues and, 76–77; United States relations and, 78–79

Campa, Valentín, 212

campesinos: ambiguity of the category, 22; BOC (Workers' and Peasants' Bloc; Bloque Obrero y Campesino), 87, 209, 210–11; *campesino* internationalism, 38–40; CGOCM (General Confederation of Workers and Peasants of Mexico), 214; divergence of peasant leagues from Communists, 70, 89–94; as engine of insurgency in Mexican Revolution, 21–22; *La Voz del Campesino* (The voice of the peasant), 51. *See also* LCAEV (League of Agrarian Communities of the State of Veracruz, Liga de Comunidades Agrarias del Estado de Veracruz); LNC (National Peasant League; Liga Nacional Campesina)

capitalism: Black and Indigenous peoples and the struggle against capitalism, 105–6, 110–11, 126, 137, 215–16; Bolshevik continuum of national development and, 108–9, 144, 148; "Capitalism and Colonization" (Portal), 161; class against class strategy, Comintern, 4–5, 69–73, 87, 92–94; dependency theory, 117; Latin America's evolution toward, Haya on, 74–75; Lombardo on Soviet model as alternative to, 215–16; Mella's analysis of, 54–56; US hemispheric dominance and, 29, 43, 54–56, 66, 117, 152

Cárdenas, Lázaro, 207, 211, 214, 217, 240; Indigenous policies, 219–20, 231; Mexican *indigenismo* and, 205–8, 207*fig*, 237; Yaquis, state policy toward, 225–28

Caribbean: Brussels Congress "Common Resolution on the Negro Question" (1927), 107–8; Garveyism, 105; Portal lecture tour, 160–65; Portal's analysis of US influence in Latin America, 161–62; UNIA (Universal Negro Improvement Association) in, 105. *See also* Portal, Magda; specific country names

Carr, Barry, 77, 89, 210

Carranza, Venustiano, 86

Carrillo, Rafael, 27, 29, 88, 221; *El Libertador* articles by, 56; LADLA and, 47–48; at LNC founding congress, 38

castellanización, 229

Castellanos, Martín, 176, 201, 221; "Black Resolution" *(Resolución negra)*, 190; formulation of PCC's self-determination policy, 187–93; on PCC's support for Black equality, 196–204

Castro, Fidel, 247

Castro Pozo, Hildebrando, 127

Catholics: assassination of Obregón, 86–87; in Mexico, insurgency of the Cristeros, 69

Central America: Congress against Colonial Oppression and Imperialism (1927), representation at, 58; Portal's analysis of US influence in Latin America, 152, 161–62, 166; UNIA (Universal Negro Improvement Association) in, 105. *See also* specific country names

Central South American and Antillean Union (Unión Centro Sud Americana y de las Antillas; UCSAYA), 45

Centro Obrero de Habla Española (Spanish-Speaking Workers' Center), 221

CGOCM (General Confederation of Workers and Peasants of Mexico; Confederación General de Obreros y Campesinos de México), 214

Chávez Orozco, Luis, 206, 207; historical scholarship, 229, 304n144; on Indigenous self-determination, 228–31, 236–37; at Inter-American Indigenista Congress (1940), 233

Chiang Kai-shek, 72–73

Chiapas, Mexico, 50

Chicherin, Georgii, 78

Chihuahua, Mexico, 50

Chile: APRA in, 31; disputed territories, Tacna and Arica, 47; draft constitution (2022), 246; Pan-American Federation of Labor and, 47; Portal in, 165; Portal's analysis of US influence on Latin America, 161–62

Chilean Communist Party, 172

China, 35; Congress against Colonial Oppression and Imperialism (1927), representation at, 57–58; *El Libertador* articles on, 56–57; KMT (Nationalists) and Communists, rupture between, 72–73; Mexican radicals in solidarity with, 72–73; United Front strategy in, 31. *See also* Chinese Communist Party; KMT (Chinese Nationalist Party, Kuomintang)

Chinese Communist Party: KMT's purge of communists, 72–73; United Front strategy, 46

Chinese Nationalist Party. *See* KMT

Chontal Maya (people), 220

Ciudad Victoria, Mexico, 64

Claridad, 44

class: Bolshevik policy on the national question and, 101–3; Comintern's Third Period, class against class strategy, 4–5, 69–73, 92–94; cross-class alliances, debates about, 70, 71–72, 81, 83–84, 93–94, 97–98, 101–2, 118, 120; Cuba, Morúa Law, banning of race- or class-based parties, 178; debates on anti-imperialist strategy, 85–86, 93–94; Junco's proletarian view of Black liberation, 139–41; Mella on racial categories being replaced by class categories, 84–85; Pavletich on lesson of Mexican Revolution, 170–71; Portal on need for cross-class united front, 163–64; Rabinovich on race and class, 143; race, nationality, and self-determination, debates at Buenos Aires conference (1929), 129–30, 139–51. *See also* bourgeoisie; proletariat

CNOC (Confederación Nacional Obrera de Cuba; National Workers' Confederation of Cuba), 133

CNPI (National Council of Indigenous Peoples; Consejo Nacional de Pueblos Indígenas), 243

COCEI (Coalition of Workers, Peasants, and Students of the Isthmus; Coalición Obrera, Campesina, Estudiantil del Istmo), 243–44

Collier, John, 207

Colombia: Congress against Colonial Oppression and Imperialism (1927),

representation at, 58; exiles in Mexico, 20; LADLA and, 48; Portal in, 160; Portal's analysis of US influence in Latin America, 161–62

colonialism. *See* anti-colonialism; anti-imperialism

Comercio, El, 156

Comité Manos Fuera de Nicaragua (Hands Off Nicaragua Committee). *See* Mafuenic

Communism: debates on anti-imperialist strategy, 85–86, 93–94; debates on race and racism, 97–98; growth of in 1920s, 19; notion of Communism as alien to Latin America, 170–72

Communist International (Comintern), 2–3; APRA, strategy differences with, 29–32, 154, 162–65, 167–72; Black Belt thesis, 98–100, 116, 122, 124, 176, 204; Buenos Aires conference of Latin American parties (1929), 123–26, 128–33, 140–46; China, policy in, 72–73; class against class strategy (Third Period), 4–5, 69–70, 72–73, 92–94, 97–98; creation of, 18–19; Cuba, encouraged to support Black liberation, 179–82; debates on anti-imperialist strategy, 85–86, 93–94; dissolution of, 5; encouragement of national liberation movements, 103; endorsement of black and Indigenous self-determination, 1, 145–48, 208–9; Fourth Congress (1922), 105; Haywood-Nasanov thesis (1928), 111–13, 120–22, 148, 149, 150; Krestintern (Peasant International), 22–23; LADLA and, 46, 47, 48; language barriers, 23; Latin America as "colonial and semicolonial," 116–18; "Manifesto on Mexico" (1929), 90–91; Mexican Commission, 80–81; Mexican delegates to, 22–23; Mexican government anti-Communist campaign, 90–94; Mexican peasant leagues and, 76–77; Negro Commission, 111–16; Pan-Africanism, impact on race policy, 105–6; PCM and, 33–35, 34*fig*, 78–81; policy shifts by, 4–5; Popular Front strategy, 4–5, 177, 196–98, 211–12, 214, 250; Portal's differences

Inter-American Indigenista Congress
(1940), 205–8, 207*fig*
internal colonialism, 245
internationalism: APRA and, 167–68, 170;
Black internationalism, 7, 9, 99–100,
103, 104; *campesino* internationalism,
38–40; Comintern's class against class
strategy, 70; Haya's views on, 167–68;
LADLA and, 44, 48–49, 67; LCAEV,
23–25; Mella's view of, 37; PCC and,
200; PCM and, 43; Portal's criticism of,
155, 164; proletarian internationalism,
146; Stirner's views on, 48–49; transnational connections and, 8, 18–20,
39–40, 43, 248; United States anti-
imperialist movement and, 48–49
International Labor Organization: "Indigenous and Tribal Peoples' Convention"
(1989), 245–46
International Lenin School (Mezhdun-
arodnaia Leninskaia Shkola; MLSh),
109, 147, 175, 180–81, 191
International Red Aid (Socorro Rojo
International, SRI), 62–63
International Trade Union Committee of
Negro Workers (ITUCNW), 134–35
IPN (National Polytechnic Institute;
Instituto Politécnico Nacional), 230–31
IPS (Political and Social Investigations;
Investigaciones Políticas y Sociales),
86–87
Ireland, radicals from, 109
Italy, 35, 57–58, 127, 200
ITUCNW (International Trade Union
Committee of Negro Workers), 134–35
IWW (Industrial Workers of the World), 20

Jalisco, Mexico, 64
Jamaica, 101, 104–5, 137, 179, 183–84, 187
James, C. L. R., 138
Jeifets, Lazar, 5
Jeifets, Victor, 5
Jolibois, Joseph (fils), 45, 52–53, 65
Junco, Sandalio, 1, 9, 88, 133–136, 135*fig*,
137fig, 142, 143–44, 210; arrest and
deportation, 91; on Black and Indig-
enous self-determination, 125–26,
136–41; founding of PBL and, 191;

interpretation of race in the Americas,
125–26
Juventud, 44–45

Katayama, Sen, 120
Kellogg, Frank, 79
Kersffeld, Daniel, 5
Khaikis, Lev, 79, 80, 147, 148
Khankhoje, Pandurang, 45
KIM (Communist Youth International;
Kommunisticheskii Internatsional
Molodezhi), 143, 179
Kirchhoff, Paul, 229
KMT (Chinese Nationalist Party;
Kuomintang), 31; *El Libertador* articles
on, 57; in Havana, Cuba, 36; Mexican
radical solidarity with, 72–73; United
Front strategy, 46; White Terror, 72
Kollontai, Aleksandra, 1, 78–80
Kommunisticheskii Internatsional Molo-
dezhi. *See* KIM
Kommunisticheskii Universitet Trudiash-
chikhsia Vostoka. *See* KUTV
Korea, 57–58
Krestintern (Peasant International), 22–23,
29, 76–77
Kuomintang. *See* KMT
KUTV (Communist University for the
Toilers of the East; Kommunisticheskii
Universitet Trudiashchikhsia Vostoka),
107–9
Kuusinen, Otto, 113

Laborde, Hernán, 65, 88
labor / labor movement: anarchism and, 3;
BOC (Workers' and Peasants' Bloc;
Bloque Obrero y Campesino), 87;
campesinos and proletarians, overlap of,
22; Cuba, Machado's suppression of,
53–54, 134; Cuba, Spanish migrants and
whitening of employment, 183–84;
Cuba's Grau San Martín government
and, 183–84, 187; Cuba's nationalization
of labor, 183–84, 195, 199; Garveyism as
hostile to, 105; Humbert-Droz's views
on race and the labor movement, 147;
Junco and Cuban labor movement,
133–36; LADLA and, 46, 47, 49–50;

México Íntegro (Integral Mexico) (Sáenz), 232

Mezhdunarodnaia Leninskaia Shkola. *See* International Lenin School

Michel, Concha, 65

Michoacán, Mexico: LADLA and, 50; PCM in, 33

Middle East, Congress against Colonial Oppression and Imperialism (1927), 57–58

Mikhrovsky, Mendel, 185

miscegenation, racist fears of, 184–85, 187

Mistral, Gabriela, 25

Mixtecs, 220, 229, 244

MLSh. *See* International Lenin School

Modotti, Tina, 21, 91

Moncada, Guillermo, 198

Monterrey, Mexico, 64

Montevideo, Uruguay: CSLA meeting in (1929), 123–26, 128, 136–40, 150–51

Morocco, 31, 35

Morpeau, Charles, 45

Morpeau, Pierre Moravia, 45

Movimiento Nacional Indígena (National Indigenous Movement), 243

mulato/a, use of term, 13

Mundo, El (Santo Domingo), 152, 160

Muñoz, María, 242

Münzenberg, Willi, 57

Nacional, El (Mexico), 51, 220, 222, 229

Nahuas, 220, 223, 229

narodniks, 85

Nasanov, Nikolai: Comintern discussions of race and nation, 113–16; on Black self-determination, 109–10; Haywood-Nasanov thesis, 111–13, 120–22, 148, 149, 150

National Alliance of Indigenous Bilingual Professionals (Alianza Nacional de Profesionistas Bilingües Indígenas), 243

National Congress of Indigenous Peoples (1975), 242–43, 244

National Council of Indigenous Peoples. *See* CNPI

national cultural autonomy, 101–2, 132, 213

National Federation of Black Societies, Cuba, 201

National Indigenista Institute. *See* INI

National Indigenous Movement (Movimiento Nacional Indígena), 243

nationalism, 7; Bolshevik policy on the national question, 1, 99, 101–3, 108–9; Comintern's rift with bourgeois nationalists, 97–98; continental nationalism, 154–55, 157–59, 164–65; debates on anti-imperialist strategy, 85–86, 93–94; in Cuba, 184, 198–200; Garveyism as Black nationalism, 110–11; Haya's "Plan de México," 81–83; Haya's view of *aprismo* as nationalism, 166–69; Latin American anti-imperialist movement and, 48–49; plurinationalism, 246; progressive nationalists, Popular Front strategy and, 4–5; United Front strategy, Comintern, 31

Nationalist Liberation Party of Peru. *See* PNL

National Miners' Union, 137

National Peasant League. *See* LNC

National Polytechnic Institute (Instituto Politécnico Nacional; IPN), 230–31

national question: Bolshevik policy and, 1, 99, 101–3, 108–9; Bukharin's views on blurring distinction between race and nation, 115, 120–21; Haywood and Black self-determination, 108–9, 110; Latin American debates on concepts of race and nation, 124; Luxemburg's views on, 131; Nicolau and Suárez Pérez, the "Black problem" in Cuba as national question, 180–82; PCM and, 208–12; Portal's views on continental nationalism, 164; Rabinovich's views on questions of race and class, 143; Stalin on, 102–3; Vivó's views on, 222–24. *See also* Black self-determination; Indigenous self-determination; nations/nationalities

National School of Agriculture, 45

National Workers' Confederation of Cuba. *See* CNOC

nations/nationalities, 98, 99, 108–9, 148, 302n86; autonomous Soviet republics, 293n69; Chávez Orozco's views on Indigenous self-determination, 228–31; Comintern and Latin American

Communists' disagreements on, 124–26; Cuba and Black self-determination, 175–204; Fabila's views on Yaquis self-determination, 224–28; Haywood-Nasanov thesis (1928) and, 111–13, 120–22, 148, 149, 150; Indigenous peoples, self-determination for, 118–22; internal colonialism, 245; Lombardo's views on, 216–17; Mendizábal's views on, 217–19; Mexico, radical pluralists and Indigenous self-determination, 213–31; Pátzcuaro, Inter-American Indigenista Congress (1940), 232–38; race, nationality, and self-determination, debates at Buenos Aires conference (1929), 129–30, 139–51; in South Africa, 115; Vivó's views on Indigenous self-determination, 222–24, 235. See also *indigenismo*

The Nation, 53

Nearing, Scott, 51, 159

negro/a, use of term, 13

negro en Cuba, El (Arredondo), 200

Negro World, 105

Nehru, Jawaharlal, 57–58

Nevis, 104

The New Poem and Its Orientation Towards an Economic Aesthetic (Portal), 157–59

newspapers: *Amsterdam News,* 104; *Bandera Roja,* 155, 194; *El Comercio,* 156; *El Demócrata,* 51; *El Diario de Cuba,* 161; *El Machete,* 34–35, 209; *El Mundo,* 152, 160; *El Nacional,* 51, 220; *El Productor,* 133; *Excélsior,* 49, 51, 63; *La Protesta,* 52; *La Voz del Campesino,* 51, 77; *Mañana,* 72; *Negro World,* 105; radical publishing scene, 44–45, 51–52

New York City, NY, 31

New York Times, 61

Nicaragua: LADLA on the danger of US imperialism, 53; LADLA and *El Libertador,* solidarity events and, 61–66; Mafuenic and, 62–66, 63*fig,* 64*fig;* Mexican solidarity with, 44; United States bombing of, 61, 64, 64*fig;* United States occupation of, 61–66; William Walker and, 52

Nicolau, Ramón (Justo Ríos), 175, 176, 180–82

North Africa, 56, 57–58

North American Free Trade Agreement (NAFTA), 241

Nuestra comunidad indígena (Our indigenous community) (Castro Pozo), 127

Nuestros indios (Our Indians) (González Prada), 27

Nuevo León, Mexico, 50

Oaxaca, Mexico, 50, 64, 211, 225, 243–44

Obregón, Álvaro, 69; assassination of, 86–87; foreign policy stance, 73; PCM's support for, 81; peasant leagues and, 76–77

October Revolution. *See* Bolshevik Revolution (1917)

Oriente, Cuba: Castellanos and the self-determination policy, 187–93; labor tensions in, 184–85; Lovsky's assessment of, 185–87; organizing efforts among Black workers, 179–80; PCC membership data, 193–94; PCC outreach in, 192–93; PCC policy of "black predominance" in, 199–200; self-determination for, 175, 176, 181–82, 198; sugar and tobacco industry in, 180; uprising in (1912), 178

Orozco, José Clemente, 34, 34*fig,* 51

Ortiz, Fernando, 188

Otomí (people), 219–20, 229

Pachuca, Mexico, 64

Palacios, Alfredo, 44, 51

Palmares, Brazil, 138–39

Pan-Africanism, 6–7, 9, 99, 103–6; Comintern debates on racial oppression, 107–9

Panama, 53, 69, 221; continental citizenship proposal and, 69; Haya and, 25; LADLA on the danger of US imperialism, 53; racial discrimination in, 85, 137–38, 140, 142; tenants' strike in, 85, 137–38; US and, 36, 53, 59

Panama Canal, 32, 36

Pan-American Anti-Imperialist League, 47; name change, 48

Pan-American Conference (1928), 63–64

Pan-American Conference (1938), 232

Pan-American Federation of Labor, 47

38–40; Mafuenic and, 62–63, 65–66; Nicaragua, solidarity with, 62–66; Partido Liberal Mexicano (PLM; Mexican Liberal Party), 20; relationship to Mexican state, 75–77

peasants: *campesinos*, 22; Mariátegui's emphasis on revolutionary potential of, 127–29; semifeudal structures in Latin America, 127–29. See also *campesinos*

Pedroso, Regino, 201

Peña, Lázaro, 194, 201

Peru: APRA in, 31, 152–53; Congress against Colonial Oppression and Imperialism (1927), representation at, 58; continental citizenship proposal and, 68; disputed territories, Tacna and Arica, 47; elections in, 153; exiles from, 3, 20, 21, 35–36, 73–74; Haya's run for presidency, 81–82; LADLA and, 48; at LNC founding congress, 38; overthrow of Leguía government, 165–66; Pan-American Federation of Labor and, 47; Portal in, 155–56; Portal's imprisonment, 166; Portal's analysis of US influence in Latin America, 161–62; Rumi Maki (Stone Hand) uprising, 27; semifeudal structures in, 127–29. *See also* APRA; Haya de la Torre, Víctor Raúl; Mariátegui, José Carlos; Portal, Magda

Peruvian Aprista Party. *See* PAP

Peruvian Communist Party, 165, 169

Peruvian Socialist Party, 82, 93, 128, 165

Pesce, Hugo, 140, 142, 143, 145

Pestkovsky Stanislav, 33–34, 34*fig*, 37, 47, 78

Petrovsky, David, 113, 114, 115, 120

Philippines, 35, 36, 56

Phillips, Charles, 48, 120

PIC (Independent Party of Color, Partido Independiente de Color), 178, 180–81, 190

Platt Amendment, 52

PLM (Mexican Liberal Party; Partido Liberal Mexicano), 20

plurinationalism, 246

PNL (Nationalist Liberation Party of Peru, Partido Nacionalista Libertador del Perú), 81–82

Political and Social Investigations (Investigaciones Políticas y Sociales, IPS), 86–87

Popular Front strategy, 4–5, 177, 211–12, 214, 250

Portal, Magda, 1, 10, 73, 152–55; *América Latina frente al imperialismo* (Latin America against imperialism), 155; analysis of US influence in Latin America, 161–62; break with APRA, 169; "Capitalism and Colonization," 161; Caribbean lecture tour, 160–65; detention in Cuba, 156; differences in strategy from Communists, 162–65; economics, study of, 159; Haya, tensions with, 166–69; imprisonment in Peru, 166; on Indoamerica and anti-imperialist politics, 156–59; in Mexico, 156–59; on need for cross-class united front, 163–64; *The New Poem and Its Orientation Towards an Economic Aesthetic*, 157–59; PAP, role in, 165–69

Portocarrero, Julio, 142, 145

Portuondo, Serafín, 194, 201

Prebisch, Raúl, 117

PRI (Institutional Revolutionary Party; Partido Revolucionario Institucional), 242

Productor, El, 133

Profintern, 123, 126, 134

Pro-Indigenous Association, 27

proletariat: *campesinos* and, 22–25; class conflict and, 93–94; global struggles of, 39, 55–56; Haya's views of Indoamérica, 27–28; Humbert-Droz's views of Indigenous and Black self-determination, 146; Junco's proletarian view of Black liberation, 139–41; Mariátegui's views on Indigenous and Black struggles, 131–33; peasant problem and, 24–25; proletarian revolution, 4, 86, 127–28. *See also* class; workers

Protesta, La, 53

Proveyer, José, 192

PRV (Partido Revolucionario Venezolano, Venezuelan Revolutionary Party), 49

Puebla, Mexico, 64, 211, 214, 215

Puerto Rican Nationalist Party, 58

Russian Social Democratic Labor Party (RSDLP), 101, 102

SACP (South African Communist Party), 114–15
Saénz, Aarón, 79
Sáenz, Moisés, 218, 231–33
Sánchez Cerro, Luis Miguel, 165–66
Sánchez Mastrapa, Esperanza, 202
Sandino, Augusto, 61, 63–66, 82, 157
Sandino, Sócrates, 65
Santiago, Cuba, 179
Santo Domingo, 53
Scottsboro Boys, 188
Secretaría de Educación Pública. *See* SEP
self-determination, 7; Afro-Latino/a movements (2000s), 246–48; APRA and Communists' disagreements about, 171–72; Bolshevik policy, defining of, 101–3; Chávez Orozco's views on, 228–31; Comintern and Latin American Communists' disagreements on, 124–26; Comintern's endorsement of Black and Indigenous self-determination, 145–48; Comintern's Sixth Congress (1928), Black Belt thesis and, 98–100, 116, 122, 124, 204; Fabila's views on Yaqui self-determination, 224–28; Haywood-Nasanov thesis (1928), 111–13, 120–22, 148, 149, 150; "Indigenous and Tribal Peoples' Convention" (1989), 245–46; Indigenous movements (late twentieth century), 246–48; Inter-American Indigenista Congress at Pátzcuaro (1940), 231–38; Junco's view of Black and Indigenous self-determination, 125–26, 136–41; Lombardo's views on, 215–17, 233–34; Mariátegui's view of Black and Indigenous self-determination, 125–33; Mendizábal's views on, 217–19; Mexico, return of Indigenous *autodeterminación* (1970s–present), 243–45; PCC and Black self-determination in Cuba, 10, 175–82, 184, 187–93, 196–98; race, nationality, and self-determination, debates at Buenos Aires conference (1929), 129–30, 139–51; Vivó's views on, 219–24, 234–35. *See also* indigenismo

Semard, Pierre, 120–21
semi-colonial world, 46–47, 48–49; Latin America and Comintern categories, 116–18
Seoane, Manuel, 170, 171
SEP (Secretariat of Public Education, Secretaría de Educación Pública), 25, 74, 218, 223, 224, 229, 231, 232, 238, 239; Department of Education and Culture for the Indigenous Race, 206
Serrano, Francisco, 76
Serviat, Pedro, 176
Shanghai, China, 72–73
Siete ensayos de interpretación de la realidad peruana (Seven Interpretive Essays on Peruvian Reality) (Mariátegui), 127, 130–31
Silva Herzog, Jesús, 51, 91
Sinclair, Upton, 51
Singer, Hans, 117
Siqueiros, David Alfaro, 34, 35, 46, 62, 90, 142, 144, 212
slavery: Cuba, history of, 175, 178, 180–81; Junco's account of, 141; League Against Imperialism and Colonial Oppression, manifesto of (1927), 58, 108; Portal's views on Spanish colonialism, 158–59; Seoane's views on Peru's Indigenous people, 171
Slezkine, Yuri, 108
SNTE (National Union of Education Workers, Sindicato Nacional de Trabajadores de la Educación), 238
social-democrats: Popular Front strategy, 4–5, 177; rift with Communists, 87, 97–98, 121
socialism, 2; ABB (African Blood Brotherhood) and, 104; Comintern's class against class strategy, 4; cross-racial unity and the struggle for socialism, 110; Indigenous communities as basis for socialist society, 85; Mariátegui's views on Peru's socialist future, 127–28, 130–31; Mexico, Cárdenas's socialist education policy, 229; Pavletich's views on unfinished Mexican Revolution, 171; Peruvian Socialist Party, 82, 93, 128, 165; Russian *narodniks*, 85. *See also* Union of

socialism (*continued*)
Soviet Socialist Republics (USSR); specific individuals and organizations
Socialist Party (Mexico), 32–33
sociedades de color, Cuba, 176, 192, 198–99, 201–2
Socorro Rojo International (International Red Aid, SRI), 62–63
Solomon, Mark, 204
Sonora, Mexico, 50, 209, 224–26
Soustelle, Jacque, 229
South Africa: Congress against Colonial Oppression and Imperialism (1927), representation at, 57–58; *El Libertador* articles on, 56; UNIA (Universal Negro Improvement Association) in, 105
South African Communist Party (SACP), 114–15
Soviet Union. *See* Union of Soviet Socialist Republics (USSR)
Spanish-American War (1898), 36
Spanish Morocco, 31
Spanish-Speaking Workers' Center (Centro Obrero de Habla Española), 221
SRI (International Red Aid, Socorro Rojo International), 62–63
Stalin, Joseph, 4–5, 78–79, 302n86; definition of a nation, 102; tainted legacy of Stalinism, 245; "The National Question and Social Democracy," 102
Stirner (Edgar Woog), 29–30, 48, 81, 147, 148
Suárez Pérez, Aggeo (Simón Álvarez), 175, 176, 180–82
Sugar Workers' Bureau (Buró Azucarero), PCC, 194
Sulzbachner, Fritz (Federico Bach), 62.
Suriname, 104
Swadesh, Morris, 229

Tacna, 47
Tamaulipas, Mexico, 50
Tampico, Mexico, 22, 33, 64
Tarahumaras, 209
Tarascans, 219–20, 238
Tejeda, Adalberto, 45, 76, 80, 90

Terreros, Nicolás, 49, 51, 62, 73, 82–83, 156
Third International. *See* Communist International (Comintern)
Third Period (class against class strategy), Comintern, 4–5, 69–73, 92–94
Tito, Josip Broz, 107
Togliatti, Palmiro, 121
Townsend, William Cameron, 229, 230
trade unions: CSUM (Unitary Trade Union Confederation of Mexico: Confederación Sindical Unitaria de México), 87; ITUCNW (International Trade Union Committee of Negro Workers), 134–35; Latin American Trade Union Confederation, 172. *See also* CSLA (Latin American Trade Union Confederation, Confederación Sindical Latino Americana); labor / labor movement
transnational radical networks, 6; APRA, origins in, 28–32; at Krestintern (Peasant International) congress, 22–23; LADLA and, 46, 47–48, 66–67; debates on anti-imperialist strategy, 85–86, 93–94; LNC founding congress and, 38–40; local and national contexts, connections with wider world, 19–20; in Mexico, 20–21; in Mexico City, 41–42; PCM and, 32–35, 34*fig*
Trinidad (Cuba), 192
Tzotzil (people), 220

UCSAYA (Central South American and Antillean Union, Unión Centro Sud Americana y de las Antillas), 45, 49, 63
UNIA (Universal Negro Improvement Association), 104–6
Unión Latinoamericana, 44
Union of Soviet Socialist Republics (USSR), 215–16; as "affirmative-action empire," 108; autonomous Soviet republics, 293n69; formation of, 2–3, 103; Haywood's time in, 106–11; Lombardo's view of, 214–17; Mexican delegates to Comintern congresses, 22–23; Mexico, break in diplomatic ties with, 69–70, 90–91; Mexico, relations with, 19, 78–81
Union Patriotique d'Haiti. *See* UPH

unions. *See* labor / labor movement; trade unions

Unitary Trade Union Confederation of Mexico. *See* CSUM

United Front strategy, Comintern, 4–5, 31, 46

United Fruit, 53

United States: African Blood Brotherhood (ABB) in, 104–5; Black Belt thesis for Black self-determination, 98–100, 116, 122, 124, 204; Briggs' call for a colored autonomous state, 104; Bureau of Indian Affairs, 207, 217; Brussels Congress "Common Resolution on the Negro Question" (1927), 107–8; dollar dominance and US imperialism, 54–55; exiles from, 21, 27; Garveyism, 105, 110–11; Guantánamo Bay and, 185; Haiti, occupation of, 53, 117; as imperial power, 25, 27–28, 29–30, 31–32, 36, 52–56, 65, 116, 117, 139, 152, 161–62, 164; lynchings in, 35; McKay's movement for Black liberation, 105–6; Nicaragua, occupation of, 61–66, 63*fig*, 64*fig*; Portal's analysis of US influence in Latin America, 161–62; tensions over Mexico's relationship with Soviet Union, 78–80

United States Communist Party: ABB (African Blood Brotherhood) and, 104; Black Belt thesis, 98–100, 116, 122, 124, 204; Black self-determination, Comintern's support for, 120–22; Black self-determination, Haywood's views on, 110–12; Haywood and, 103; Haywood-Nasanov thesis (1928), 111–13, 120–22, 148, 149, 150; LADLA and, 47–48; PCM and, 33

Universal Negro Improvement Association (UNIA), 104–5

Universidades Populares González Prada, 44

Universidad Popular José Martí, 44

UPH (Haitian Patriotic Union; Union Patriotique d'Haiti), 45, 49, 53, 63

Urrutia, Gustavo, 188

Uruguay, 48, 116, 137, 143, 162

USSR. *See* Union of Soviet Socialist Republics (USSR)

Vadillo, Basilio, 78

Valle, Rafael Heliodoro, 49

Vasconcelos, José, 25–26, 51, 58, 73, 158–59, 205–6

Vasiliev, Boris, 81

Venezuela: Congress against Colonial Oppression and Imperialism (1927), representation at, 58; exiles from, 20, 35–36; LADLA and, 48; Portal's analysis of US influence in Latin America, 161–62

Venezuelan Revolutionary Party. *See* PRV

Veracruz: Mafuenic and, 64, 65; PCM in, 33; tenants' strike of 1922 in, 22

Veracruz Peasant League. *See* LCAEV

Vidali, Vittorio, 91, 118, 119, 121, 275n115

Vietnam, 1, 57–58

Villaseñor, Víctor Manuel, 214

Vivó, Jorge, 197, 206, 207–8, 220–22, 229, 245; on Indigenous self-determination, 219–24; at Inter-American Indigenista Congress (1940), 233, 234–35; "Mexico and the Indian," 220

Voz del Campesino, La, 51, 77

Walker, William, 52

Wall Street: crash of 1929, 161, 182, 210; US hemispheric dominance and, 54–55, 66, 117, 162

Weaver, Kathleen, 162

West Africa, 57–58, 105

white chauvinism, 111, 113, 120, 143–44, 179, 181–82, 192–93

Whitney, Robert, 202

Wolfe, Bertram, 21, 27, 33, 47, 50, 118, 119, 121

Wolfe, Ella, 47, 50

Woog, Edgar (Stirner), 29–30, 48, 81, 147, 148

workers: BOC (Workers' and Peasants' Bloc; Bloque Obrero y Campesino), 87; *campesinos* and, 22; CSUM (Unitary Trade Union Confederation of Mexico, Confederación Sindical Unitaria de

workers (*continued*)
    México), 87; LADLA and, 46, 47,
    49–50; Soviet support for Mexican
    railway worker strike, 80. *See also* class;
    labor / labor movement; proletariat
Workers' and Peasants' Bloc. *See* BOC
Workers International Defense (DOI,
    Defensa Obrera Internacional), 188
World War I, 19, 20–21

Yakobson, Genrikh, 147, 148
Yaqui (people), 209, 224–28, 229

Zapata, Emiliano, 17–18, 35, 82
Zapatista Army of National Liberation.
    See EZLN
Zapatistas, rebellion of (1994), 241, 244
Zapotecs, 209, 229, 243–44
Zionism, 131, 139

Founded in 1893,
UNIVERSITY OF CALIFORNIA PRESS
publishes bold, progressive books and journals
on topics in the arts, humanities, social sciences,
and natural sciences—with a focus on social
justice issues—that inspire thought and action
among readers worldwide.

The UC PRESS FOUNDATION
raises funds to uphold the press's vital role
as an independent, nonprofit publisher, and
receives philanthropic support from a wide
range of individuals and institutions—and from
committed readers like you. To learn more, visit
ucpress.edu/supportus.